Dhows to Deltas

RENATO 'Sonny' LEVI

Dhows to Deltas

Erroll Bruce
Richard Creagh-Osborne
Peter Johnson

Hon. President:
Adlard Coles

Nautical House
Lymington, Hampshire

Nautical Publishing Company

in association with George G. Harrap & Co. Ltd.,
London, Toronto, Sydney, Wellington

First published in Great Britain by
NAUTICAL PUBLISHING COMPANY
Nautical House, Lymington, Hampshire

ISBN 0 245 59956 8

Photoset and printed in Great Britain
by BAS Printers Limited, Wallop, Hampshire

To My Father who believed in me and started the ball rolling

Contents

Part III

Plates

Drawings & Diagrams

Acknowledgements

I am most grateful to the *Daily Express*, the Temple Press, Keith Beken and many others for the splendid photographs, drawings and diagrams which appear in these pages; they contribute so much to a book of this kind.

I also received generous help from numerous other people, all of whom it is not possible to mention by name.

My special thanks though are due to Klaus Suhrbier and Peter Du Cane for their excellent contribution on "Propellers" and to Peter for his generous preface; to Anne Ricotti who typed out most of the manuscript and tied up my thoughts in an orderly fashion; to Lucio Isabella who did the major part of the drawings which appear in this book; to Erroll Bruce, without whose encouragement, help and patience I would not have had the perseverance to finish; lastly to my wife Ann who gave me many ideas and did a considerable amount of typing for me.

I had not realized when I started this book what I had taken on but the task has been made much lighter for me by the enormous interest and help I have received from everyone I approached and I am most grateful.

Introduction Commander Peter Du Cane

Any book coming from the brain and pen of Sonny Levi is bound to be well worth reading. I consider Sonny to be the most inventive designer to work in this field up to date.

This book shows the range of his accomplishments which are far wider than I realized and include a number of sailing craft as well as racing power craft and aircraft.

Sonny has of course been extremely lucky with some of his owners who have in many cases been superb engineers and test pilots as well. These qualities count for a lot; probably more than most designers realize.

Only one example of this is *Surfury*, which won the *Daily Express* Cowes-Torquay Race in 1967, was second in 1968, and when six years old came a good third in the 1970 event. Specially was this creditable when one realizes the tremendous help to designers offered by advanced equipment such as the power trim which is now fitted to all the winners, but was not available when *Surfury* was designed.

Sonny is now saying it requires more than a pair of outdrives to win.

If you want to know how this is to be done I recommend anyone interested to read this book.

Explanation

For some time now I have been wanting to write a book about my experiences in connection with designing and building fast craft—what has in fact been a life-long interest for me and, indeed, my profession. Two reasons in particular have prompted me to start this venture: first, the wish to record my experiences to date in some sort of chronological order for my own pleasure and, perhaps, for that of those who are interested in this subject; secondly, the hope that the recording of these past events may help in some measure to reach possible new solutions for the many complex problems which are encountered constantly in the designing of power-boats. I felt that it might have the same clarifying effect that jotting down sketches often does when one is following up a new idea.

I have called this book "Dhows to Deltas" since it starts in Bombay, where in early days I used to be fascinated by the numerous types of dhow which plied along the west coast of India, and culminates in my originating the Delta line for fast powerboats. In a lot of ways the Deltas (perhaps rather unexpectedly) recall to my mind those original dhows, with their very heavily raked stems, wide sterns, and fine bows. I do not know to what extent this analogy actually influenced me in developing the Delta line, but it certainly shows the evolution in my thinking from the slow, leisurely movement of the dhow to the swift, intense pace of the Delta.

"Dhows to Deltas" deals mainly with the work I have been doing for very nearly twenty years and discusses a variety of fast powerboats of all types, with the emphasis perhaps on racing. Although my association with pure racing craft has been relatively recent, it has done a great deal to mould a number of original ideas and, I am convinced, has enabled me to design boats which have had a measure of success in fields other than racing.

This book is not intended to be either a historical record of what has been done in the past in the field of fast planning hulls, or a text-book covering the various and manifold technical aspects of these fascinating craft.

The opinions expressed in these pages are based naturally on
my own personal experiences and on those of people with
whom I have had close working relationships. These opinions
may not, of course, be popular with everyone who has occasion
to read them, but to those who may disagree I can only say
that it would indeed be a dull subject if we were all of one
opinion and that disagreement is a healthy sign of vitality.

I hope that those who have the patience to read through these
pages will find some of my comments of value; if this should
be the case it will add yet a third reason to my list, as well as
a justification for having put these thoughts down on paper.
Since a number of the events recorded took place a good many
years ago, it is possible that my memory may at times be at
fault. However, I have made every effort to check facts
wherever possible and hope that as a result there are not any
noteworthy discrepancies.

Renato Levi

Lavinio,
December, 1969

Part One

CHAPTER I

The Beginning

A very good ocean-racing friend of mine once said to me during a rather wet and uncomfortable race: "You don't have to be crazy to do this, but it helps".

In some ways I feel the same applies to the work I have been connected with in designing offshore and circuit racing powerboats. The designer of any kind of racing craft is rather sticking his neck out, since his reputation depends on his creating winners. So many factors can contribute to the success or failure of a boat in a race (not the least being the capricious element of luck) that even the finest of designs can come to grief. Common sense should convince one to leave this particular field to others, but the gamble is irresistible and rouses immense enthusiasm—at any rate in myself. Financially a designer can gain more from the normal pleasure craft or work boat than from racing craft, but if the latter are successful they can certainly bring him a far higher degree of publicity.

To go back to the beginning: I was born in Karachi during the floods of 1926, which apparently at the time were said to be the worst in living memory. Perhaps this is why boats have loomed large in my life from early years, though I suppose my interest in pure speed as such started when I designed a demonstration planing cruiser for my father some fifteen years ago. Up till then my designing activities had been mainly confined to work boats and some smallish yachts, although I had already designed a number of relatively fast planing patrol boats for various government departments in India and other Far Eastern countries.

Unlike my father I had always been an ardent admirer of sailing boats, a passion which went back to the days when, as a child, I used to spend many hours in our Bombay shipyard day-dreaming as I sat astride a teak-log and watched the sails of the traditional dhows slipping silently past up and down the coast.

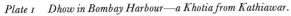
Plate 1   Dhow in Bombay Harbour—a Khotia from Kathiawar.

15

When I was older I used to go on board these intriguing boats, reeking of oil, fish and salt, and watch the sailors at work, hard sinewy men often with beards and moustaches and with enigmatic eyes under their ancient, picturesque turbans. Their skins were blackened and had the texture of parchment through constant exposure to salt spray and tropical sun. The sea was their life: they spent their days trafficking in wood, oil, or indeed any merchandise which needed transporting, at times even contraband. The skippers were taciturn, inscrutable men who sailed the seas without maps, trusting in their Gods and occasionally consulting an old compass.

The boats were Patiamars from Ratnagiri, with woven straw cabins on top of which the cordage lay coiled with meticulous neatness, or Buglas from Mangalore, with transoms painted in brilliant colours—orange, red, and yellow—or Khotias from Kathiawar, with high imposing sterns, or—last but not least—Arab dhows from the Red Sea and the Persian Gulf, true works of art, with their wooden planks steeped in fish oil and small, elegant windows in their transoms like old men-of-war.

These silent barks with their heavily raked stems and lofty lateen sails stealing the wind from the sea, both fascinated and inspired me; later on they also provided a means of relaxation and escape from my usual work of designing and building the heavy, noisy work boats (cargo boats, patrol boats, lifeboats, survey craft, tugs, etc.) which were our yard's normal bread-and-butter production.

I used to spend a great deal of my spare time designing sailing boats, and this hobby not only gave me an enormous amount of pleasure but also brought a certain success; in nearly all the international competitions I entered (*Yachting World, Glasgow Herald, Svenska Kryssar Klubben Arsskrift*, etc.) my designs were either classified in the first three or mentioned as interesting.

Even now, when the bulk of my work consists in designing fast powerboats, I occasionally return to my old love for sailing craft. A few years ago I designed a 22·25-metre (73 ft) RORC Class I yacht for a client here in Italy, a sailing enthusiast who followed my work throughout all the various stages of planning and building. This craft, *Hermitage*, had a displacement of approximately 50 tons and a sail area of 240 square metres; the sail plan was by John Illingworth and Angus Primrose, famous specialists in this line as well as two very good friends of mine. Angus, in fact, navigated for me most

efficiently on several occasions in the Cowes-Torquay Offshore Powerboat Race. I remember with amusement Angus turning to me after *Hermitage* was launched and asking rather anxiously: "Is this going to be a dry boat, Sonny?" One of the Italian guests present, thinking that something was wrong with the boat, repeated the remark to the owner who had to be reassured that "dry" on this occasion only meant that no-one had as yet had a drink on board her.

I found this return to sailboat designing very agreeable, not only for the work itself but also for the people I met. In fact I repeated the experience very willingly recently, designing a One Ton Cup (RORC 22' rating), *Dany*, which has quite a few rather interesting innovations built into her (*see* Chapter X).

My father, however, did not share this enthusiasm for sailing. He was a dynamic personality, full of energy and constantly on the move, and his particular predilection was speed.

His own yachting activities dated back to 1937, when he and a very firm friend, Billie Rooksby, bought in partnership a second-hand motorboat which they called *Enchantress*. This was not only the first craft my father owned, but the first time he ever actually set foot on a small boat.

Enchantress was an open boat, around 25 feet overall, and powered with the latest German outboard engine which, judging by its size, must have been of some 15 or 20 H.P. She was a round bilge carvel built hull, entirely of teak, and was long and narrow with the seating accommodation consisting of thwarts and a U-shaped bench aft. Certain "improvements" were carried out on her in those pre-yard days at the furniture factory which my father owned at that time. Among other things, a streamlined wooden awning was built over the entire length of the boat, which in consequence must have been extremely heavy. In fact, she needed 32 coolies to launch her, 16 "non-swimming" in town clothes for the shallower water and 16 "swimming" in loincloths for the deeper water—a valuable distinction worth 2 or 3 annas per head.

My parents and the Rooksbys had a great deal of fun in *Enchantress* and carried out some very ambitious journeys, such as the circumnavigation of Bombay Island which included perforce quite a long stretch of open water cruising from Bassein to Bombay. They always travelled with an immense amount of luggage, stowed away on top of the famous awning so as not to cramp movement on board, but this habit

Plate 2   Dany, *a 1 Ton Cup yacht I designed early in 1969. Unusual features include a very large overlap on the genoa.*

17

only lasted for the first few trips since the result of all this top hamper, round bilge and narrow hull was a continuous rolling motion, which at times was most alarming. It took them some time to realize why the boat was so tender; when they did, not only was the luggage swiftly removed but also the awning.

A year or so later my father was talking over some of his adventures in *Enchantress* with another friend, Douglas Nielson, an extremely keen and knowledgeable yachtsman, and was easily convinced that he needed something a little more ambitious. It so happened that Nielson too wanted a new boat, a fast commuter to get to his weekend shack on Manori Island, and my father suddenly made the bold suggestion that both boats should be built in his furniture factory.

Once the decision was taken, he immediately hired an Indian shipwright and seconded to him some of his finest carpenters. Work began first on Nielson's boat, *Manori*, which was built to the designs of a Scandinavian naval architect. She was 29′11″ overall —the eleven inches had something to do with concession on permits which I never really understood. She was powered with a pair of Gray Fireball engines and was designed for a speed of 27 knots, which was considerable for those days. The accommodation was extremely spartan as speed was the object.

My father's boat, *Lucci* (named after my mother), was 37′ overall and unlike *Manori* had considerable accommodation built into her. As far as I can remember, the plans were drawn up by himself and Moschetti, one of his furniture designers, who was versatile when it came to pencil and paper and could turn his hand to anything, from chairs and tables to marble decorations for Indian palaces (yet another of my father's activities at that time). The same Gray Fireball engines powered this boat too, but in her case they were fitted on V-drives in a small engine-room under the aft deck, thus leaving more space available for accommodation. I do not think that anyone ever knew what *Lucci*'s maximum speed was, nor do I think that my parents were particularly interested in this aspect at that time. It was later that speed became something of a mania.

It should be said in all fairness that both boats were beautifully built. This was really a most remarkable achievement, considering that they were my father's first attempt. The one criticism which might perhaps be levelled was that, while *Lucci* was a very pretty-looking boat, she was extremely heavy with exaggerated scantlings and, as a result, was slow for a planing craft considering that there was over 200 h.p. installed.

Both Douglas Nielson and my father enjoyed themselves immensely with their respective *Manori* and *Lucci* right up to the beginning of the war, when both these boats were handed over to the then Royal Indian Navy for patrol duties. *Lucci* unfortunately caught fire and burned out completely during one of her harbour patrols, but as far as I know *Manori* is still in active use in the hands of the Bombay police.

The outbreak of war proved to be the turning point in transforming into a commercial enterprize what had begun as a hobby. Craft built to very detailed specifications were required by various allied navies in the Far East and my father was asked whether he would undertake this work. A small shipyard was therefore set up which soon expanded and built many hundreds of small craft during the war years, varying from whalers to motor launches, from landing-craft to ammunition barges. I think I am right in saying that the yard was responsible for almost half the total production in India at that time.

I was still at school during the early part of the war, first at St. Paul's in Darjeeling and then at Bishop Cotton's in Simla. I used to return to Bombay for the longer holidays and spent most of my time nosing round the yard or else fishing, swimming and sailing. I also remember making several models of sailing yachts to my own design.

My interests at that time seem to have been connected almost entirely with the sea and with boats, but there was one important exception which later prompted me, on leaving school, to go to England and join the R.A.F. This exception was a passion for aeroplanes dating back to my pre-India school days in France, at a college where not only were there model aeroplane classes but also expeditions to various air shows, air displays, and so on. In those days I knew the names of all the famous French pilots by heart. Later on, my secret ambitions were to be a test pilot and to design aircraft. I did not succeed in becoming a test pilot, but perhaps this early interest in aeroplanes (coupled with the fact that I studied aircraft design after demobilization) has played an important part in influencing my way of thinking on the subject of boat structures.

When the war ended the Bombay yard continued its boat-building activity, although on a reduced scale. The main work was still the construction of all

Plate 3   An early police patrol boat with a constant section deadrise. Surya.

Plate 4   Self and Dias, our chief mechanic at the launching of my first design in Bombay 1951, a patrol boat for the Bombay Police. Mahalaxmi II.

types of motor craft, which plied on government service on rivers and in harbours all over India, but several types of sailing yacht were added for extra interest. These included the Royal Bombay Yacht Club one-design "Seabird", as well as some Merlin Rocket Class dinghies.

The next boat my father acquired for his own amusement was *Valdora*, a 72 foot HDML which he purchased after the war and converted into a yacht. He had already done some fairly lengthy cruises in *Lucci*, but I think his passion for long passages really started with *Valdora*. He cruised up and down the west coast of India in her many times. One of his most popular party stories still is the famous storm weathered in the Gulf of Manaar between India and Ceylon when even a sizeable cargo ship advised them to turn back.

He also tells another tale of the time he was nearly arrested as a smuggler when, on the way back to Bombay, he put in to Goa, then Portuguese territory and a duty-free port, and loaded up with every conceivable brand of liquor only to be met at the Bombay quayside by the forewarned Customs officials. After rather a heated argument a compromise was reached: the precious cargo was bonded on board *Valdora* and could only be consumed outside the three-mile limit. Long cruises became the order of the day after that, and *Valdora* was certainly a very popular boat!

I myself never sailed on *Valdora* as she had been sold by the time I eventually returned to the yard in 1950, this time to the drawing office where I soon became Chief Designer.

The drawing office work at that time consisted of workboat designs of all types, a large number of which were planing craft. When I first started designing these craft I was in a particularly fortunate position, since we had been awarded a number of contracts by the Indian Government for patrol boats. These contracts were always for several boats at a time, and on some occasions were even for a considerable number. In this way I was able to make minor modifications when a contract for several boats was awarded, and often quite substantial changes from one contract to another. I was able to try out a wide range of deadrise hull forms in the warped plane and constant section categories, from extremely deep vee in the bows with completely flat transoms to relatively shallow vees in the bows and fairly heavily vee-ed sections at the transom.

I obtained the best results on boats where there was the minimum amount of variation in the dead-

rise coupled with a fairly good degree of vee in the stern. These boats not only assumed a tolerably level trim at cruising speed, but were also extremely steady on their course in following sea conditions. They were reasonably soft at speed going into head seas providing the angle of deadrise was sufficient in the region of the point of impact.

The very heavily warped plane hulls, on the other hand, some of which we see being produced even today (viz. the type of hull which is very heavily vee-ed in the bows with a completely flat transom), were anything but fast and were also extremely wet and a handful in following seas.

Against this background my father one day asked me to draw up the plans for a new boat which he wanted as a show-window, a practical demonstration of what his yard was capable of producing. She was also to serve as a test bed for new ideas and, in addition, had to be comfortably fitted out, have a crisp and pleasing appearance and, last but not least, have an outstanding performance. He proposed to call her *Speranza*, but later had to change to *Speranza Mia* in order to distinguish her from the countless other boats named *Speranza* which we discovered were plying in waters all over the world.

I started the design of this cabin cruiser in 1954, following innumerable and lengthy discussions with my father as to what she should look like, what she should be capable of doing, type of construction, and so on. After completing several preliminary sketches we settled for an overall length of 38′6″, 35′ on the waterline, and a maximum beam of 12′. The boat was to be powered with two of the famous S6 Perkins marine diesel engines, to be fitted aft driving through V-drives so as to leave the rest of the boat free for accommodation, reduce the noise level, and at the same time enable us to have a separate engine-room.

Speed was to be an important factor this time. We were aiming at over 20 knots and the structure therefore had to be very light; a particularly close study was made of every weight-saving refinement that could be thought of. I think I am right in saying that, for her day, *Speranza Mia* had a lot of novel ideas and that, from a performance point of view, the boat was equal to anything of the same size and power in the world. The boat attained a maximum mean speed of over 21 knots at 2000 r.p.m. on our first trials in Bombay Harbour soon after her launching in December 1956, and she had a range of 800 sea miles with normal fitted tanks.

As far as I know, *Speranza Mia* was the first boat of

Plate 5   Speranza Mia *anchored in front of Karachi Yacht Club after our 550 Mile cruise from Bombay.*

that size to be built in India employing such timbers as red cedar for all the joinery work, and laminated chir, which is a variety of Cashmere spruce for the frames. Teak was, in fact, only used for the hull shell, external deck and longitudinals. The generous use of epoxy resins and glass mat was also a novelty in those days. I was particularly proud of the ventilated cabin top, as in this way we at last found a system for keeping the cabin temperature really cool even on the hottest tropical day.

I think it is also worth mentioning that *Speranza Mia* was very well publicized by various nautical papers throughout the world and that, as a result, we sold drawings to clients in countries as far apart as South Africa, New Zealand and Sweden. Many fine examples of this boat have been built since, and I believe that a Sports Fisherman version built in Cape Town by the Hare brothers still holds the record for the highest number of tunny caught in one day. A more detailed description of this boat can be found in Chapter VIII.

A great deal was being written at that time in yachting magazines and books on the pros and cons of the warped plane versus the constant section planing hull. Some of these articles were highly controversial; much was said about suction loads being generated aft in warped plane hulls, and about the extremely fine sea-keeping qualities of constant section deadrise hulls.

My own findings on the best types of warped plane and constant section or monohedron hull forms were, now that I come to think about it, unconsciously leading to what we know today as the deep vee or deep deadrise hull. After all, what is a deep vee hull? It can be a warped plane hull, admittedly with a small degree of warpage and a high angle of deadrise throughout, or it can be a monohedron hull with a very deep deadrise.

Today practically any boat which has a certain degree of vee at the transom and some longitudinal risers on the bottom is termed a deep vee hull. This is clearly quite wrong. In my opinion one should not define a hull as having a deep vee unless the aft planing sections have a deadrise angle of near 20°. There were, after all, monohedron planing hulls designed during the war which had a noteworthy degree of deadrise in their aft sections and, as far as I know, no reference was made in those days to their being classified as "deep vees".

These early constant or near constant section boats of mine were, of course, a marked improvement on anything which I had designed and built before; they were reasonably fast in calm weather, given the necessary power, and were without doubt very much better in rough going. Owing to rather full-bodied sections forward, however, most of these boats were prone to land with a bump after taking off the crest of a wave, although they were nevertheless extremely good in following seas.

Generally speaking, the size of these boats ranged

from 20 to 45 feet. It should be borne in mind that in those days we did not have engines with the sort of power-to-weight ratio which we have today for such sizes of boat, and that consequently the speeds we were achieving were in the 20 knot range. Another point, too, is that we were building very largely in teak and other heavy tropical timbers.

It is I feel worth mentioning here that in 1958 our yard was approached by the Food and Agriculture Organization of the United Nations (acting as advisers to the Indian Government Fisheries Department) and asked to design and produce an inexpensive surf boat for use off the many hundreds of miles of the Indian coast.

This boat had to be capable of being launched and beached through surf. In order to meet these conditions I prepared a design which, for those days,

had quite a deep deadrise in its aft section. The deadrise was in fact 18° and was constant section from amidship to transom. The boat was comparatively slow under her own power ($V = 2\sqrt{L}$), but she was capable of planing when running before the surf.

Incidentally, two longitudinal stringers were also placed on each side under the hull, rather reminiscent of the spray strakes used on deep vee hulls today. The object of these longitudinals was to provide framing to the bottom and to protect the hull planking when beached, but I think they also contributed in some measure to directional stability when surfing.

A photograph and description of this boat can be found in the FAO publication *Fishing Boats of the World, Vol. 2*.

CHAPTER II

Move to Italy

I left India in 1960 with mixed feelings. On the one hand, business in our Bombay yard was becoming increasingly difficult and I felt that the political climate was anything but healthy. On the other hand, I had spent quite a number of my younger years in the yard, where I had a great many friends among my fellow-workers, and understandably felt a certain regret and nostalgia when the moment came to say goodbye in the late autumn of 1960.

In my farewell speech to the staff I congratulated them on the many outstanding achievements they had been responsible for and expressed my hopes that the future would bring them even greater success. During the ten years I was with the yard we had built, I suppose, close on a thousand craft of all types, ranging from light skiffs to heavy work boats and tugs, in a variety of materials such as timber, steel and light alloy. We even produced what was, as far as I know, the first glass reinforced plastic hull in the Far East.

We pioneered laminated structures in India and also patented a form of construction which we called "ply-glass", this consisted of joining plywood panels with fillets of glass mat impregnated with epoxy resins. This cut down labour costs a great deal and proved very profitable for the yard.

We had also created an aeronautical section where we built quite a number of gliders for the Indian Government, as well as a prototype two-seater light aircraft which I had designed and christened "Monsoon". Chapter X gives a description of this aircraft. This newly formed department made impellers for cooling towers, too, which was quite a specialized business.

In fact we were well known all over India as people who would tackle practically anything and, as a result, we received at times the most extraordinary inquiries.

I shall never forget one which came to us from a dam project. The officer in charge of navigation issued a tender stating that his department wished to buy fast patrol boats with rubber bottoms—in order to bounce off the crocodiles' heads without damaging the hulls. We had, I may say, a small section in the yard headed by a genial chemist which dealt with various forms of rubber and plastic material, and the problem was duly handed over to them. I cannot remember exactly how the story finished, but I seem to recall that we settled for a generous layer of fibreglass over the wood on the bottoms of these boats in the hopes that this might crack the crocodiles' skulls, or at least induce them to get out of the way.

Another time we got mixed up with a hydrofoil project, put forward by the indenting officer of a particular government department which needed craft capable of plying up and down rivers during the dry season, when they had only a few inches of water in their beds. A hovercraft would no doubt have been the solution, but I do not think that these had been thought up at that time.

Although I did not actually move to Italy till 1961, I had already been designing boats from Bombay for a yard at Anzio for a couple of years. This contact had been made through an old friend of my fathers, Commander Attilio Petroni, who was then owner of the yard in question. The boats I designed included a Government Customs launch, a relatively fast twin screw powered fishing trawler, and two small runabouts. The yard had hoped to produce the latter in reasonable quantities, but as things turned out the popularity of the runabout was already on the wane, there was an enormous amount of competition in this category, and only a few of these craft were actually built. This was a pity as they were rather nice little boats, and the bigger of the two, with a 200 H.P. petrol engine, was

Plate 6   The Monsoon *on her test flight.*

capable of something around 40 knots.

During the hiatus between India and Italy I seized the opportunity to travel around Europe and see what was going on in the boat-building world. I also visited some yards in the United States as well as the Experimental Aircraft Association, of which I had been a member for some years, who had been so helpful over the design of my prototype aeroplane "Monsoon". While I was there I was presented with the Barber-Colman Company Award for 1960 for my efforts in designing and building this small two-seater aircraft.

This interim period was invaluable in that it gave me time to reorientate myself and get adjusted to the new atmosphere and to what were going to be the new design requirements. In Europe the emphasis was clearly on elegant, highly finished, luxurious pleasure craft for private customers rather than on the more Spartan, strictly functional work boats for government departments to which I was accustomed. Government contracts were naturally also to be hoped for, but they would obviously be a very minor percentage of the overall work.

In January 1961 I visited the London Boat Show, as had always been my habit whenever possible even when I was in India. While I was there, an old colleague of mine from student days, who was in the Show's Advisory Bureau, handed me a form saying: "Why not have a crack at this?". "This" was the first *Daily Express* Cowes-Torquay Offshore Powerboat Race. The idea captured my imagination at once. Here was a challenge I could not resist, the chance to see if I could produce a boat capable of winning what promised to be a very exciting event.

The immediate problem was a financial one: what would such a boat cost, and would it make too much of a hole in my Indian savings?

About this time *Speranza Mia* was being shipped from India to Italy, for my father had decided to retire and sell the yard. I went to Naples to collect her shortly after my arrival in Anzio, and had a very pleasant 100-mile cruise in her up the coast—a cruise which in fact turned out to be my last on board her as she was sold within ten days of being slipped at Anzio. I designed and built *'A Speranziella* with the proceeds. I might add that Navaltecnica (the Anzio yard for which I had been designing while I was still in India and where I had now started working) built this craft in record time: three and a half months from drawing-board to launching.

'*A Speranziella* was intended not only to take part in the first Cowes-Torquay Offshore Powerboat Race but also as the prototype for the cabin cruiser Navaltecnica planned to produce as a standard model (with less powerful engines than the original craft). Cabin cruisers were becoming the order of the day, and a number of yards were starting to build them in the hopes that they would later go into large-scale production.

'*A Speranziella* was the first deep-vee hull to be built in Italy, she was 30′ overall and was powered with a pair of American Crusader engines with low compression heads, rated at 300 HP. The boat seemed to be very lively and fast on our first trials and in fact her speed was close to 40 knots; she also seemed to be a fairly comfortable boat through moderate waves. I remember feeling quite exhilarated and wondering whether after all we might not stand a good chance in the race. '*A Speranziella*'s technical points are dealt with in more detail in Chapter VII.

An unexpected complication, which had its amusing side, arose over '*A Speranziella*'s official race number. The number allotted by the *Daily Express* was "17"; when I dashed with this news into the shed where the boat was being given the final touches prior to being sent off to Calais by rail, I at once noticed a general consternation. Indeed, the boat builders utterly refused to paint this number on the craft and I was told vehemently and at length that "diciassette porta iella": in fact this number is considered extremely unlucky in Italy, rather like thirteen in England. No boat, according to them, could possibly race under such a number with any chance of success. I of course had known nothing of this, but we were all very relieved when after a frantic exchange of telegrams with the *Daily Express* '*A Speranziella* was allotted "16" instead—a number which she carried all through her racing days.

The 1961 edition of the Cowes-Torquay Offshore Powerboat Race was, for me, the most unforgettable race I have ever taken part in. It was my first off-shore powerboat race, and I had absolutely no idea of what we were in for. Of course I knew that the competition would be pretty stiff. I had only to look at the race card to realize that. Among others, Dick Bertram and Sam Griffith had brought over

from America *Glass Moppie* — a particularly impressive piece of machinery—and Dick and Sam were veterans at the game who had already won countless Miami-Nassau races.

The night before the race I met both Sam and Dick for the first time at the cocktail party which has since become traditional. Even without the background of their racing skill these two were imposing figures. Dick radiated complete self-confidence, although he always expressed himself in a very quiet and modest way, while Sam's rugged and weatherbeaten look was enough to give any "green" competitor cold feet. I remember most vividly, however, that in his conversation he never traded on being the experienced driver he was and in no way made the new boy feel too small. I got to know him better before he died and I must say that he was an exceptional person who gave me a lot of valuable advice and left a lasting impression on me. His death was a sad loss to all of us in powerboat racing.

That 19th August dawned cold, windy and drizzly, and as I sat down to my pre-race breakfast and saw Sam and Dick all dressed up in their overalls emblazoned with numerous badges announcing various victories, I suddenly thought: "What the hell am I doing here?". My appetite was none too good either, but once on board with the engines ticking over as we slowly motored to the starting area I had thoughts only for the race ahead.

I opened the throttles to their maximum on that first leg east towards Southsea, but in spite of this *Glass Moppie* and the two *Christina*'s built by Bruce Campbell, one of them driven by himself, the other by Tommy Sopwith, shot into the lead. These three boats were designed by the American Raymond Hunt and were also of the deep-vee category.

The going was comparatively smooth in the sheltered waters of the Solent, but once we got out into the Channel I had a good idea of what was to come for the fresh wind had caused quite a chop as we headed out to the Nab Tower. It was on the leg immediately after rounding the Nab that *Glass Moppie* had to retire with a broken gear-box. She was a good way ahead of the next boat and I remember thinking how well she had been behaving before she ran into trouble. Bruce also had to stop owing to some electrical problem. Only Tommy Sopwith was now ahead.

It was a great thrill when we passed him off St. Catherine's Race, and in fact we held this lead until just before Portland Bill when he passed us again,

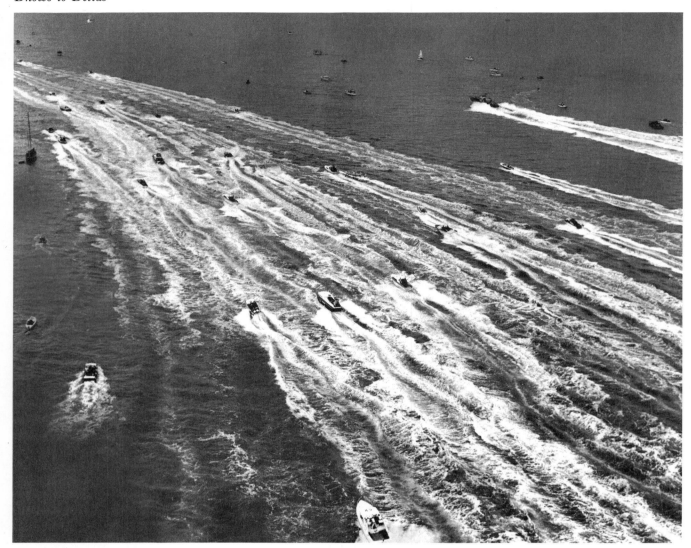

Plate 7   The start of the Cowes-Torquay race. (Photo Daily Express)

and went on to win the race. We ran into trouble ourselves early in Lyme Bay, splitting a tank as well as having a fuel pump out of order; later on a small electrical fire broke out, which fortunately was controlled pretty rapidly by wrenching out all the wiring from the boat and throwing it over the side. Our mechanic, Pierino, did a wonderful repair job and we managed to limp into Torquay in sixth position. Only nine boats finished out of a total of twenty-seven, and quite a number of these showed signs of rough treatment. Jim Wynne, the bearded American champion, came second in his *Yo-yo*, which was powered by two Volvos. This was a remarkable performance since he had about a third

of the power of the winner.

Although this race had not been particularly fortunate for us I nevertheless felt extremely satisfied with the behaviour of *'A Speranziella*. I learned an enormous amount from this first race too, since not only did we have quite a lot of mechanical failures but the structure of the boat had also been subjected to a severe test which had revealed weaknesses in a number of places. There certainly was a lot of work to be done if we were to do better in future events.

We had no transverse framing in this boat, but longitudinal members of spruce running along the planking inside the hull; some of these had fractured two feet or so from the transom, indicating that this

Plate 8 'A Speranziella *takes the lead off St. Catherines in the first Cowes-Torquay Power Boat race in 1961.*
(*Photo Daily Express*)

was one of the areas which received rather high impact loads although the actual pounding seemed to be more violent amidships. I imagine that the reason why this damage occurred aft rather than amidships was because the deadrise aft was a good deal less, being just over 20° at the transom.

Some of the main bulkheads had also come adrift; these were of sandwich construction, consisting of two external one eighth-of-an-inch thick layers of plywood and an internal core of polystyrene foam —no doubt a medium density polyurethane would have been better.

The cabin top, which was very lightly made, had also fractured at the corner bars. Strangely enough the deck, which was only quarter-of-an-inch ply, was in perfect condition.

Internally, the joinery work had been pushed around a lot, and the head was smashed to smithereens. We had five fuel tanks made of copper, two of which had been rather badly concertina-ed and, as a consequence, had developed leaks in several places. The water tank, a tiny affair situated under one of the bunks in the main cabin, had cracked the vertical support of the bunk. The engines had suffered considerable damage and both units had to be completely opened up and put right.

In view of new work which Navaltechnica had taken on, we decided to repair the damage as best we could for the 1962 season (which included two races, Viareggio-Bastia for the first time, and Cowes-Torquay) and to postpone any radical modifications

to a later date. I might mention, however, that we did re-position the risers on the bottom of the boat and, as a result, were able to increase the pitch of the propellers an inch and still obtain the same r.p.m. as before. The reason this particular job was done was because we had experienced very rapid corrosion on the propellers which was thought to be due to a disturbed flow of water in their vicinity. Changing the position of the risers not only increased the speed, but also eliminated any further occurrence of this phenomenon of erosion.

Commander Petroni raced *'A Speranziella* in the 1962 Viareggio-Bastia, which he won quite easily. The boat also took part in the 1962 Cowes-Torquay race, just managing to finish despite continuous engine trouble. This was the end of her racing career with the Crusader engines as we then installed, first, a pair of 5 litre fuel injection Maseratis and, later, a pair of 427 cu. in. (7 litre) Ford Interceptors, with which she won the 1963 Cowes-Torquay.

Before she took part in that race, however, we had had to take more drastic measures to counteract renewed signs of weakness in the old patched-up structural damage of 1961. New bulkheads, a new cabin top, and some fairly stout longitudinal girders were installed, and the boat was also given a thorough overhaul. After this we never again experienced any sort of structural damage, even though *'A Speranziella* cruised for many hundreds of miles through all sorts of mixed weather conditions and was pushed particularly hard in her victorious run at Cowes in 1963.

Plate 9 'A Speranziella *in the winning berth at Torquay after the race in 1963.*
(*Photo Daily Express*)

CHAPTER III

Early Racing Powerboats

'*A Speranziella* must have created an impression in that first race for later in the year Don Shead asked me to design a 23-foot outdrive racer for him. He called this boat *Trident* and it had a noteworthy measure of success in subsequent years, both in his hands and in those of its next owner, Don Robertson.

Trident, which was built by Bob and Wally Clark, appeared for the first time in the 1962 Cowes-Torquay event powered with three 110 HP Aquamatic Volvo engines (hence her name). That particular race was an unfortunate one for *Trident* as shortly after the start the bottom was holed and Don had to drive her back to Cowes at high speed and slip her before she sank. Bob and Wally made quite a few more *Tridents* in laminated timber, and further examples were moulded by the Tyler Boat Company in glass reinforced plastics.

Thinking back to the damage incurred by *Trident* in that first race, I cannot help feeling that possibly I had been a little too weight conscious. I remember going into the cabin during the pre-race trials and seeing the bottom pulsating quite appreciably, but I did not have sufficient experience at that time to judge with any certainty whether this flexing of the bottom was beyond the elastic limit. It is not known whether the holing was due in fact to her hitting something hard in the water, but I suspect that it could well have been caused by a series of hard punches received during that leg towards Nab Tower. *Trident* was, moreover, heavily trimmed by the stern owing to her three engines, a fact which aggravated her habit of lifting her bows in choppy water.

At almost the same time that *Trident* was being built in England, another 23 footer was being con-

Plate 10 Trident *wins her class in 1963 Cowes-Torquay race. (Photo Beken of Cowes).*

29

structed here in Anzio at Navaltecnica. This craft was somewhat similar to *Trident*, but had a good deal more deadrise—30° at the transom, far more than I had adopted in any of my previous designs. This prototype was called *Settimo Velo* (Seventh Veil), perhaps a rather unusual name but I felt the boat would be a lively dancer and it seemed too obvious to call her *Salome*. She was later produced by Navaltecnica as a cabin cruiser with reduced deadrise. A sizeable quantity of these cabin cruisers were built, including a batch of some eight boats for the Italian Customs authorities.

The first *Settimo Velo* was quite an interesting exercise, although she never really had very much success in racing owing to a series of mechanical failures which continued to plague her until her engines were changed. Eventually she proved quite an exciting boat with a pair of 225 HP MerCruisers, and in fact was second in the 1965 Viareggio-Bastia race when she was driven by the well-known Jacoby mother and daughter team.

Settimo Velo was the first boat I designed with a water ballasting arrangement. This consisted of a double bottom which was ventilated at the transom. When the boat was stationary the double bottom filled up with approximately three-quarters-of-a-ton of water, giving the craft a greater waterline beam and, therefore, extra stability which she needed since she was very tender on account of her pronounced deadrise and short waterline length.

The ballast tank could either be emptied by leaving the seacock on the transom aperture open, in which case the tank would empty when the boat started planing, or the water ballast could be retained by keeping the seacock closed. I found that with the latter system the boat was far more manageable in rough water. Owing to the shape of this double bottom, the centre of gravity of the water ballast was rather far aft and so was not quite as effective in keeping the bow down as the bow ballast tanks which we subsequently adopted.

The construction of this boat was also quite interesting. The hull was a laminated shell in one piece from sheer to sheer. There was no keel, but only a stem which started just before the turn of the forefoot. In order to laminate the shell in one piece, it was necessary to have quite a generous radius at the keel so as to enable the laminates to be bent round. I found that this radius of the keel produced rather an unusual swaying motion at high speed, when the boat was literally skimming on top of the water, and constant helm correction was necessary to keep her

upright. In fact, driving her gave one the sensation of being on ice skates. Filling in the radius and producing a sharp vee (a modification carried out when the engines were changed) did much to correct this somewhat nerve-racking motion.

I also felt that the freeboard was rather too high, so about a foot was chopped off the sheer during the early part of the 1965 season and the deck was lowered. The open (O.P.) class of offshore powerboats was permitted to race that year in Europe, and so the minimum height previously required under deck was no longer necessary. This pruning made the boat far more manageable and, being lighter, the windage was also reduced and her speed much improved.

Another unusual feature of the flush-decked *Settimo Velo* was the deck; this was a single laminated moulding heavily cambered for rigidity, dispensing completely with beams or any form of framing.

Navaltecnica received some inquiries for a fast cabin cruiser version of *'A Speranziella* and exhibited the prototype at the first Genoa Boat Show in 1962. It was at this Boat Show that I was approached by Pietro Baglietto, builder of an internationally renowned line of luxury cabin cruisers, and asked whether I would be interested in designing a boat for one of his clients—with the object of winning the 1962 Cowes-Torquay race. I did not know at the time who the prospective owner was, but I took up the challenge with enormous enthusiasm.

The boat was the *Ultima Dea* and the owner the well-known industrialist Giovanni Agnelli, now Chairman of the FIAT motor car company.

Ultima Dea was quite a power-house for those days, for we installed three 5·4 litre Maserati engines which developed 430 HP each at 6000 r.p.m. The craft was 36' long with a beam of 12'6", and looking back now on the design she was quite a monument. I put into this design all the experience I had gained with *'A Speranziella* and, even though *Ultima Dea* was heavy by today's standards, she was a very comfortable sea boat and never suffered from any kind of structural failure. When we had sorted out all the problems, and there were many (mostly on the mechanical side), we clocked something over 45 knots.

I think one of the most impressive things about *Ultima Dea* was her noise level, which was quite ear-splitting when all three engines were going at 6000 r.p.m. We had side exhausts and at night you could see flames shooting out of these even though they were water injected.

Plate 11 Ultima Dea *being driven by Gianni Agnelli in the 1962 Cowes-Torquay race. He finished 3rd but sportingly retired on hearing that he had taken a buoy on the wrong side. (Photo Beken).*

I learned a lot from building this boat, as well as having the pleasure of meeting some very highly qualified technicians connected with motor car racing. These included Giulio Alfieri (Maserati's Chief Engineer), Pollio (his right-hand man), and Guerino Bertocchi the test-driver, a most colourful personality who has been associated in his time with a great many of the world's most famous drivers.

Guerino Bertocchi came down to Anzio for the trials of *Ultima Dea*, and I thus had the opportunity not only to admire his skill with engines but also to appreciate his splendid sense of humour.

Our morale was low after two days of rather disappointing results with the new boat. The best we had managed to do was 3000 r.p.m. on all three engines, instead of 6000. Guerino had tried every trick in the book, and I might add that he is a wizard at discovering faults and tuning carburettors on these highly sensitive racing engines, so I was sure that nothing was wrong in that field. As nearly always happens when the maximum r.p.m. cannot be reached, the propellers were said to be at fault.

These particular propellers had been made in America of stainless steel, were 3-bladed, had cost a fortune, and had taken many months to prepare. I was therefore naturally rather reluctant to start tinkering around with them and did everything I could to suggest that the fault might lie elsewhere. On the night of the second day of trials we at last dis-

covered that although we had three pumps on each of the fuel lines (two electric and one mechanical) these were connected in parallel, and in this way were supplying the carburettors with insufficient fuel. In a very short time the piping was changed round so that all three pumps worked in series, and we were ready for the third set of trials.

We set out very early that August morning, full of hopes that "third time lucky" would prove true for us too. Time was running out since we were barely ten days away from shipping *Ultima Dea* to England for the 1962 Cowes-Torquay contest. There was a long swell in Anzio Bay, although the weather was good. The cockpit of *Ultima Dea* was aft and the engine room was entered through a hatch on the forward bulkhead of this cockpit. The steering position was to port, with all the engine controls adjacent to the wheel. On the instrument panel in front of the wheel there were only the three revolution counters, the engine instruments being on a separate panel on the starboard side of the cockpit.

Guerino sat on the cockpit floor with his legs dangling into the engine room so that he could see all three engines, and I was at the helm. As we opened the throttles and at last passed 3000 r.p.m. my spirits rocketed sky-high. "3,500", I shouted, leaning over to give Guerino a hearty thump on the back— "4,000 . . . 5,000 . . . 5,500 . . . 6,000!" There we were, storming through the water at what seemed a

31

Plate 12 Thunderfish III (*ex Merry-Go-Round*) *destroyed by fire during the 1967 Cowes-Torquay race.* (Photo Daily Express).

Plate 13 Merry-go-Round *driven by Sir Max Aitken during his diesel World Speed record-breaking run in March 1966.* (Photo Beken of Cowes).

very exhilarating speed. My eyes were fixed on the magic revolution counters, but out of the corner of one I could see Guerino's hands gripping the top of the cabin above the engine-room hatch each time we took off the crest of one of the long waves and went through the next in a cloud of spray. He never said a word but later, when we went ashore, he turned to me and said: "I have often driven with Nuvolari, Ascari, Villoresi, and Fangio—but with you, once is quite enough. Never again! All you seemed to think about were those revolution counters and getting your 6000 r.p.m. whatever the consequences!" I discovered later that Guerino was a non-swimmer.

A month or two afterwards it was his turn: he came to the yard with a 5 litre Maserati car and took me for a run. As we hurtled down a narrow road at what seemed to me to be at least 200 m.p.h., he changed down from fifth to fourth and, pointing at the revolution counters, said: "Look! 7,000 r.p.m.!".

It was certainly a scramble getting the boats ready for Cowes that year. There were four to ship: *Ultima Dea*, *'A Speranziella* (out for another try at the Trophy), *Settimo Velo*, and a diesel-powered boat similar to *'A Speranziella* called *Spumante* (ordered by an English client who wanted to use her as a fast pleasure craft and at the same time have a crack at the diesel prize).

After investigating various possible solutions Navaltecnica decided to charter a small cargo ship, the *Altair*, and send some of the yard's key men with her so that last-minute finishing touches could be added to the boats on the way. Three of the boats were lowered into the hold, while the *Ultima Dea*, owing to her size, was securely lashed down over the hatches on deck. The voyage to England was uneventful, but on the return trip the *Altair* was involved in a collision with another cargo boat in the Bay of Biscay and very nearly sank; the holds were awash and the craft actually afloat. This collision, with all its legal corollaries, etc., delayed the return of the boats to Anzio for many months.

1962 certainly was not our lucky year. Each boat encountered some sort of trouble in the race itself. Some of this was due no doubt to lack of time for final testing, but we were also I think dogged by sheer bad luck.

I was to have driven *Settimo Velo* (racing under our old bugbear, number "17", which this time could not be avoided), but only just managed to crawl to the start and then had to retire with, among other things, water in one of the engines. *Spumante* nearly sank because one of her shaft stern glands came adrift, and *'A Speranziella* limped into Torquay with both engines in very bad shape. Only *Ultima Dea*, driven by Gianni Agnelli himself, proved her worth and finished third—to be disqualified for leaving a buoy on the wrong side off Bournemouth. Gianni drove a splendid race and took his disqualification in a very sportsmanlike way.

The race was won most convincingly by Dick Wilkins's massive *Tramontana*, designed by Peter Du Cane and built by Vosper, she was powered by a pair of C.R.M. (Isotta-Fraschini) engines each delivering 1,150 HP at 2,000 r.p.m. *Tramontana* was driven by Jeffrey Quill, who was incidentally the original Spitfire test pilot. Dick Bertram's *Blue Moppie* was second, driven magnificently by

Plate 14 Altair, *which carried our 4 racing power boats to England in 1962, leaving Anzio Port. The* Ultima Dea *can be seen on the deck as she was too large to go in the hold.*

33

C

Plate 15 *Sir Max Aitken* (left) *presents Cmdr. Attilio Petroni* (centre) *and myself with awards for our unsuccessful efforts in 1962.* (*Photo Daily Express*).

Sam Griffith. I was able to follow the race very well as I had asked my navigator, Glen Bowker, to take *Settimo Velo* back to the *Altair* and had then scrambled on board the escort motor torpedo boat, *Brave Borderer*. From *Brave Borderer*'s bridge I was able to see Sam spending more time in the air than in the water as he tried desperately hard to get the better of *Tramontana* just ahead of him. It was the most magnificent display of driving I have ever seen and, sad to say, Sam's last Cowes-Torquay race.

Our luck fortunately changed for the better in 1963. Results in the Viareggio-Bastia race were encouraging, and even though *'A Speranziella* and *Speranziella Seconda* did not win the Golden Propeller Trophy on points, they each won one of the legs of the race. Later in the year, as I have already mentioned, I won the Cowes-Torquay in *'A Speranziella* with her new 427 cu. in. Interceptor engines.

Jim Wynne came over to Italy that summer to race a *Settimo Velo* in the Viareggio-Bastia and spent some time in Anzio giving me a helping hand in procuring the Interceptor engines and also in the trials we carried out before leaving for Cowes.

We had meant to race *Ultima Dea* in the Cowes-Torquay event as well that year, but unfortunately she broke a gear-box a few days before she was due to leave for the Channel. When Johnny Coote, one of the main organizers of the race, heard that *Ultima Dea* would not be competing after all, he very kindly sent me a telegram expressing his regret and adding that he thought *'A Speranziella* would stand a good

chance of winning the Visitors' Prize. I somewhat over-confidently cabled back asking whether he had by any chance withdrawn the main trophy.

I was rather sticking my neck out as getting the boat over to Cowes that year was quite a complicated business; she went up from Anzio to Genoa under her own power, then was loaded onto a Belgian freighter for Antwerp, and finally crossed the Channel to Cowes (again under her own power). Angus Primrose kindly navigated for me on the last lap, and I feel that it was largely due to his invaluable help that we arrived just in time for scrutineering after a somewhat lively crossing.

It is curious how fate takes a turn now and then. The year before we had admittedly left things to the last minute, but there were far fewer question-marks along our route and we had four boats competing; this year, we had all sorts of obstacles to overcome and only the one boat to gamble with. And yet this proved to be the successful occasion. Don Shead also won his class in 1963 with *Trident*.

This 1963 win of mine at Cowes brought me a whole load of new work. My design ideas were also beginning to change, and were in fact inclining towards what eventually crystallized as the Delta configuration.

Before going on to deal with the Delta hulls, however, I feel I should mention the second series of *Speranziella* which were also built at Navaltecnica. This boat was slightly longer, had more deadrise,

Plate 16 *'A Speranziella* displayed at the London Boat Show in 1964. (*Photo Daily Express*)

and was structurally somewhat modified in that the hull shell had no break at the chine. The engines were fitted well aft with V-drives.

Speranziella was a good deal faster than her predecessor, even though she had the same Ford Interceptor engines. The increased deadrise of the aft planing surfaces and the steering position further aft made her much more comfortable in rough going. I thought she was rather an attractive-looking boat. I raced her that same year at Viareggio and at Cowes (Race Number 1 according to tradition), but without much success on either occasion. The best we did was a second on the first leg from Viareggio to Bastia (in those days the race was conducted in two legs, staying overnight at Bastia).

During the years I was with Navaltecnica I was also designing for other yards, just as I had done when I was working for my father's yard in India. After this period I set up on my own as a free lance designer and consultant. Whilst working on one's own involves a certain element of insecurity. I must confess that there is a great satisfaction in being independent and able to do more or less the work that really interests one—in my case designing without being involved in the actual running of a yard.

Personally I feel that it is a great handicap for a designer to have to take part in the administration of a yard; designing is a full-time job and a yard has inevitably many routine problems which crop up and interfere with one's trend of thought. In my opinion, also, designers and organizers have (generally speaking) totally different mentalities. Running a yard requires an organizing mind and it is seldom that this quality is inherent in a creative mind.

There is yet another negative aspect to belonging to one particular yard: a designer may find that other yards are less likely to approach him for designs, since they feel that his best work is utilized by the yard he is attached to, even if this may not actually be the case. The yard, on the other hand, will probably profit from his presence as more private clients will be attracted, especially if he is well known.

I am not of course suggesting that a designer should have no contacts at all with a yard. His presence can, I am sure, contribute a great deal to the final product, while at the same time he himself will be made aware of the various difficulties which can arise in the realization of one of his creations. In this way he will be more likely to produce practical designs, but nonetheless he should never be in any way responsible for the administrative side of the business.

CHAPTER IV

The Design Trend

Offshore powerboat racing has certainly given me a better understanding of the problems involved in designing fast craft. It is also of course, a fascinating game and has been described as combining the thrills and hazards of steeplechasing and parachute jumping.

Someone else once said that perhaps the most perfect moment is when the race is over and the banging around finished. A rough race is without doubt quite a test of physical endurance, and I know that I have often felt in the middle of a race that it would be more than pleasant to slow down and relax. However, no sooner is one race over than one immediately starts planning for the next, and the hard going is forgotten in the interest of thinking up modifications to one's craft—or even of designing something entirely new.

The Cowes-Torquay Powerboat Race was the first of its kind in Europe, although in America the Miami-Nassau had been in existence for some years. The Americans had quite a start on us here. Their ace driver, Sam Griffith, had developed a very convincing driving technique, and its results proved beyond doubt that he had the knack of pushing a boat hard in rough water.

Sam always drove in the standing position and invariably well back in the craft, where the pounding is less. He used very long throttle levers and drove with one hand on these and the other on the wheel. The purpose of these long levers was to enable him to accelerate and decelerate smoothly when driving fast in choppy conditions. He was amongst the first, if not the first, to work the throttle in this way.

This technique lessens the strain on the engines, shafts, propellers, and so on by reducing the revolutions of the engines when the craft is about to take to the air and by increasing them again just as the boat is re-entering the water. It does much to save the structure of the boat, too, but undoubtedly needs an immense amount of skill on the part of the driver as the engine speeds have to be varied at the right moment so as to keep the boat moving as fast as possible without incurring too much punishment. It also demands a lot of stamina to keep up this technique hour after hour without a moment's relaxation. Those early races could last anything up to ten hours when the weather was rough.

I must confess that I never did work the throttles in this way in my earlier races, but merely selected an appropriate throttle setting for the sea conditions and held the wheel firmly with both hands. In these early races, I still thought it would be possible to adopt the sitting position for driving if the seats were sufficiently comfortable but, as I discovered subsequently, it was far easier to stand. Later on still we found that leaning into a back-rest was even better. Charles Gardner devised two very ingenious reclining seats for *Surfury* which worked extremely well. Since then I have adopted a variety of semi-circular back-rests which have proved effective. *'A Speranziella* was first fitted with heavily upholstered seats which were removed after the 1961 Cowes-Torquay race, never to be replaced.

It is interesting to note that, among other modifications, we lengthened the throttle levers of *'A Speranziella*. The steering position, which was just aft of amidship, was not altered since it required quite a lot of work to move further aft. We would certainly have had a more comfortable ride had we done so, for we used to get pushed around quite a bit situated where we were. To aggravate the situation, we did not have well-located or adequate hand-holds, with the result that we were often black and blue while I finished that first race with a broken rib.

Once in a while someone comes up with a new idea which either alters or, in a few cases, revolutionizes what has been done in the past—like, for

Plate 17   Sam Griffiths (right) and Dick Bertram in Blue Moppie.
This was one of Sam's last races. (Photo Morse Instrument Co.).

Plate 18   The start of the 1966 Miami-Nassau race (Photo Roland Rose).

example, the deep vee hull for fast planing craft. Such innovations do not occur very frequently, but when they do they change the face of things considerably. It is quite astonishing how much the design trend has altered in the offshore powerboat field during the past five or six years. If we were to compare the leading contenders in those early *Daily Express* Cowes-Torquay races with the leaders of today, we would see a tremendous difference in the lines of the craft. This is one of the reasons for the higher speeds achieved nowadays.

Before examining the evolution of my own designs over this period, I think it is of interest to quote an article which I wrote after winning the 1963 Cowes-Torquay contest and which was published in the following year's *Daily Express* Race Programme. *Racing as a Proving Ground* gives the reasons which I

believed then, and believe still, were responsible for many of these changes.

"The International *Daily Express* Offshore Powerboat Race, which was first started in 1961, has established itself in this short period of time as a true world classic.

"How has this come about? There are many reasons.

"This particular race is the best organized of its kind in the world. The publicity connected with the race has been excellent. The courses have been very interesting ones and well thought out. But I don't think all this could be enough to give this race the fame it enjoys today. I feel one of the most important reasons for its success is that it is really a tough test for both crews and

Plate 19   Speranzella Seconda No. 1 amongst the leaders soon after the start of the 1964 Cowes-Torquay race. The Gardner Bros. "Surfrider", No. 66 was the eventual winner. (Photo Daily Express).

boats. One has only to look at the number of starters and finishers to qualify in the previous races to realize this: in 1961—9 out of 27; in 1962—15 out of 42; in 1963—29 out of 50.

"It is therefore an achievement even to finish.

"I have been competing in this race since it was started and when I think back to the reasons which prompted me to take part in the first one, I think it would be honest if I said that apart from the sport, it was also the hope of winning and the resulting publicity which such a victory would give me in my profession as a designer.

"Now, after several years of offshore powerboat racing, I must admit that there is more to it for me than just the sport and publicity. It is also a means of testing and proving new ideas.

"I have learnt possibly more about the behaviour of fast powerboats by participating in these races than I think I learnt in all the years that I have been connected with the design and building of these craft.

"A moment's reflection will show that the very same thing applies to the motor car industry, for example, where motor racing has probably contributed more to improving cars than anything else.

"Why is it necessary to race in order to prove a particular product? Surely this could be done by severe testing? To some extent this is true, but no matter how severe a test programme may be, it is impossible to stimulate the conditions which exist in a race. Apart from the meter of comparison which the other competitors pro-

Plate 20 Delta Synthesis *leaps into the air during the Dauphin d'Or race in 1967. In spite of mechanical trouble and a navigational error came in 2nd and had the same placing later in the Cowes-Torquay. (Photo Ricard).*

39

vide and which enables one to judge one's own performance, there is the mental condition of the driver. Enthusiasm and the will to win result in harder driving than is otherwise normally possible.

"Fom a designer's point of view, there are two main aspects to test and prove.

"There is the basic hull design and the design of the structure. These two aspects are of course inter-related since a soft riding hull can have a lighter structure than a hull which makes heavy weather of it. It is therefore an advantage to have a soft riding hull not only from a structure point of view, but also for the comfort of the crew. These soft riding qualities in the basic design must be achieved with the least sacrifice to speed and performance, which is not very easy. Like all design work, this is full of compromise. Similarly the structure must be both light and strong at the same time, which has led to much experimenting in new hull shapes and methods of construction.

"Another interesting aspect of the basic design which is becoming more and more evident, is the necessity for a variable trim hull. That is a hull whose trim can be altered to suit the condition or direction of the sea which it has to travel through. This can be done either by changing the weight distribution with ballast tanks or by altering the shape of the bottom with flaps or by the use of both of these together.

"I have only mentioned so far the effect racing has on the design of the boats themselves, but it should be borne in mind that the constant call for higher speeds has necessitated much development work on engines, propellers, high speed compasses, radios and the many other items which go into a powerboat.

"Whilst all this may seem to suggest that the successful fast offshore racing powerboat will be a highly sophisticated machine, without question a lot of these new 'race proven' ideas will be incorporated in standard production cruisers so as to give the public a faster, safer and more comfortable ride."

Racing has, therefore, done a great deal to influence the design trend in the field of fast offshore craft. Broadly speaking, these improvements can be summed up as more efficient hull forms, more crew comfort, better structures, and more power.

The hull design of powerboats has undergone more changes during the last ten years than possibly in the preceding twenty, or even thirty. The speed of these craft in open water increased considerably with the advent of the deep vee hull, but although these first deep deadrise powerboats were very much more comfortable at sea than their warped plane predecessors they had, nevertheless, a number of undesirable characteristics which made really fast travel through rough water (for instance during a race) at times a nightmare. They were also hard riding in certain conditions of sea, and would often land at the most alarming angles when they took off from the crest of a wave.

They had other drawbacks as well. Some of these craft were inclined to be wet in quartering seas and, in these conditions, would at times assume a marked degree of windward list according to the relative wind speed. This windward list did not help matters either, for it offered flatter sections of the bottom to the oncoming waves and made the boat pound more than it would were it upright as well as slowing down the craft, since quite a lot of rudder correction was required to prevent the boat from yawing off course. Any correction of the rudder obviously results in drag, which in turn reduces speed.

Deep vee hulls, incidentally, have a more pronounced inboard bank characteristic than other types of planing hull forms owing to their being tender at the initial angles of heel. It is necessary to apply a certain amount of helm into the direction of the wind in order to maintain a steady course. This helm correction produces a degree of banking in the direction to which the helm is applied; this explains the phenomenon of windward list.

These early racing boats did not of course have trim correction devices, such as flaps and ballast tanks. When these eventually became the order of the day it was possible to correct to some extent a lot of the undesirable characteristics mentioned above. The riding qualities into head seas were, for instance, much improved by the use of positive flaps and by ballasting the bows; the awkward flying tendencies were also ameliorated by ballasting the bows and thus moving the centre of gravity forward; while the windward list phenomenon could be corrected by depressing the windward flap.

I could not help feeling, however, that the basic concept of the hull itself required changing, so that the minimum use of correction devices would be necessary. I therefore arrived, via a succession of gradual modifications on these racing craft, at what

I called the Delta Configuration on account of its geometrical form: an elongated triangle when seen both in plan view and in profile.

The principal differences between the Delta hull form and its predecessors were:

(1) Cutaway forefoot and high chine with raised and deep deadrise sections so as to improve the head sea riding qualities.

(2) Complete elimination of bow flare so as to counteract the awkward flying characteristics due to aerodynamic lift.

(3) Marked reverse sheer with very low bows, so as to move the aerodynamic centre further aft and thereby reduce the windward list phenomenon.

(4) A longer craft for the same volume, and therefore for the same weight, since sea-keeping qualities are directly related to length.

In addition to these main features, the Delta form offered other notable advantages for racing, or indeed for very fast travel through water. The long, over-hanging, narrow bow gave good aerodynamic penetration, produced an extremely dry craft without the use of bow flare, and also permitted a two-stage planing craft; that is to say, a hull which had the shortest possible waterline length in favourable conditions and a very long waterline length in rough

Plate 21   Surfury *wins 1967 Cowes-Torquay race.* (Photo Daily Express).

weather. Trim changing devices were obviously necessary to achieve this. Apart from the advantage already mentioned in point (3), the marked reverse sheer with low bows also made possible a very much cleaner and lower frontal area when the craft was running at the high angles of incidence necessary to reduce waterline length. In these conditions the visibility was also excellent.

All the sections were convex in shape without a noticeable chine; this was done so as to permit a continuous structure from keel to sheer without any break at the chine. The advantages were an extremely sturdy structure with an economy of weight, the actual chine being superimposed on the basic shell. The convex sections, of course, provided rigidity of form and here again permitted a reduction in weight for a given strength, rather like an egg.

Another unusual characteristic of the Delta configuration was that the topside sections were raked outward throughout the length of the hull. This was intended to increase the range of stability in the event of the boat assuming large angles of heel in adverse sea conditions. This question of stability clearly became less important as the dimensions of the craft were increased and it followed, therefore, that the degree of topside flare or rake could be varied to suit a particular dimension of craft.

Depending on the weight distribution, a certain amount of "rocker" could be incorporated in the aft planing surfaces below the chine, thus enabling the bows to be lifted in calm seas, reducing the wetted surface and obtaining optimum speed.

It was still necessary to incorporate flaps and ballast tanks for coping with varying sea conditions, but one seemed to lean less on these devices with this new Delta hull form than one did with the former type, which certainly suggested an increase in efficiency.

It is hard to be impartial about something which one has thought up, but I believe that this Delta form is a marked improvement in the design of fast racing powerboats, not only from the point of view of pure speed but also from the standpoint of sea-keeping qualities and comfort, even when running fast before the sea in rough weather.

A great deal has also been learned in recent years about structures. The object here has been to obtain the lightest possible hull, which at the same time could withstand the enormous strains imposed on it when travelling at high speed through waves. Various materials have been used for the construction of these craft, from light alloy and glassfibre to timber. Experiments have been carried out with these different materials, and while I think that they are all valid if properly designed and executed most of my own boats have been built utilizing a laminated wooden monocoque type of structure (at times adopting different densities of timber). This is hard to beat in my opinion, and has possibly the edge on other methods of construction, particularly for one-off craft.

It is interesting to note that if we compare two 36′ hulls, *Surfury* and *Ultima Dea*, the hull weight of *Surfury* (designed and built in 1965) is practically half that of *Ultima Dea* (designed and built in 1962). A boat of this size today could no doubt weigh even less. Of course, it must not be forgotten that the volume of *Surfury*'s hull is considerably less than that of *Ultima Dea*, owing to the Delta form (less volume), and that there is therefore less material in her. Nevertheless, the actual structure is much lighter if taken per unit area.

Turning for a moment to the subject of power, the most powerful engines we had in 1961 (qualifying within the 500 cu. in. capacity) were advertized at 325 HP, while today (still within the 500 cu. in. range) we have engines of more or less the same weight which can deliver up to 600 HP. Regretfully, it cannot be said that there has been a great deal of improvement in reliability; this may be due, of course, to the rapid rate of the increase in horsepower output which, for commercial reasons, has possibly left insufficient time for adequate trials.

The various changes in design have permitted immense increases in speed. Some five or six years ago the fastest of these powerboats were doing around 45 knots—today they are approching the 70 knot mark. This is a really remarkable increase when one considers that it has been achieved in a relatively short time, and I am convinced that it is very largely due to the competition produced by offshore powerboat racing.

CHAPTER V

Realization of the Deltas

Towards the end of 1963, therefore, I was mulling over in my mind the obvious need for a new and radical design not only for offshore racing power-boats but also for circuit racers, such as those used for the Paris Six Hour Race.

One day Don Shead, who had already raced in this French classic on several occasions, asked me if I had any ideas for a new boat capable of licking the competition. During the next few weeks I spent a lot of time sketching futuristic-looking, needle-nosed contraptions on every available tablecloth, envelope and cigarette packet, and was getting quite interested when I happened to run into Len Melly and John Merryfield at the 1964 Earl's Court Boat Show. They had won the Paris Six Hour Race a few months before and asked me whether I had anything in mind for the coming year's event. This circuit race had by this time roused considerable interest not only in Europe but also in the United States.

Len and John wanted an outboard boat, while Don asked for an inboard craft with outdrive propulsion. A few months later I came up with two designs: the *Levi 16* for the 1500 c.c. outboard category, and the *Levi 17·5* for the 2 litre inboard category. These two boats were my first attempts at what eventually came to be known as the Delta configuration. They had very deep deadrise aft, which was carried right through to the bows. The forefoot was practically non-existent and the widest part of the chine, seen in plan view, was aft. The topsides were raked heavily outward from the chine for the whole length of the boat.

The Deltas have been described in a number of ways: toothpicks, needles, and by an American nautical journalist as "boats whose bows start at the transom".

The *Levi 16* and *Levi 17·5* were quite a departure from anything which had been done before. Circuit racing craft till then had nearly all been flat-bottomed. There were a few examples of deep vees, but these greatly resembled the bigger offshore boats and in my opinion were in no way superior (as far as speed was concerned) to the flat-bottomed craft racing at that time, although they were certainly far more comfortable.

Later that year I was delighted when both Don with his 17·5 *Fifi* and Len and John with their 16 *Thunderbolt X* won a number of important races, including an overall win by the latter in the Paris Six Hour Race. This was their second consecutive Paris victory and, understandably, created quite a sensation.

After the undisputed successes of these two Delta-shaped circuit racers, I was approached by several yards in Europe for designs of similar craft. Copies of the 16 and 17·5 were also rapidly produced by various yards, and I do not think that there is a builder today wishing to turn out a front-line monohull boat who would deviate very much from the basic lines which they inaugurated. Of course there have been cases of unauthorized near-replicas being made as well, but this is something all designers experience at one time or another and, although it is a pity that there are people who pirate in this way, I suppose to some extent it can be said to be a back-handed compliment. It is understandable that everyone wants to jump on the bandwagon, but back-handed compliments unfortunately do nothing to help the bank balance! I wonder whether it is not time for something to be done to protect designers against these sort of eventualities?

Both the *Levi 16* and the *Levi 17·5* are being built under licence in various European countries as well as in South Africa, where I have been consultant designer for Thesen of Knysna for some years. The first 17·5 built there was for the South African driver Paul Winsley, who not only won several very important races, including the 1965 *Rand Daily Mail*

Plate 22   The start of a Paris 6 Hour.

Plate 23   The prototype Levi 16 *winning the 1964 Paris 6 Hour race driven by Len Melly. (Photo Temple Press).*

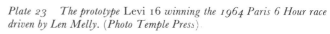

Plate 24   Levi 17.5, "*Fi-fi*" *executing a tight turn in a Paris 6 Hour.* (*Photo Revue Neptune*).

200 and the first South African Offshore powerboat race in False Bay in 1966, when he covered the 70 mile course at an average speed of 49·6 m.p.h.; but he also set up a new South African record in 1965 for the 2 litre class inboard runabouts at a speed of 56·56 m.p.h. He used a 1800 c.c. Volvo Penta engine with outdrive propulsion.

In England Melly and Merryfield have produced considerable numbers of 16s, and their clients have been responsible for winning the more important races fairly regularly. Bob and John May besides Dennis Burton have had an impressive series of wins in a great many European classics, including the Berlin Six Hour Race, the Duchess of York, and the Twenty-four Hours Marathon at Chasewater. It should not be forgotten, of course, that although many Melly and Merryfield clients are extremely skilled drivers, a tremendous amount of hard and detailed work has been put into the development of these two hulls by the builders themselves.

The successes of these circuit racers were certainly highly satisfactory, but perhaps even more important

to me was the indication they gave that this hull form could also be used to advantage in larger offshore powerboats.

Shortly after completing the drawings of these two boats I started on the design study of a 36′ hull which, after seeing the behaviour and results of the smaller craft, I hoped to propose to some prospective client as worth building in an attempt to meet and overcome the ever-increasing competition. It did not follow, of course, that the scaled-up version of the *Levi 16* and the *Levi 17·5* would have quite the same behaviour characteristics as its smaller predecessors, but nevertheless I felt that it would give me an indication as to whether longer Deltas were a feasible proposition, and in particular on the question as to whether they would tend to dig in in big following seas.

Soon after John and Len's victory in the 1964 Paris Six Hour Race, Peter Du Cane, the designer of some of the fastest patrol boats in existence as well as the two *Tramontanas*, came to spend a few days with me here in Lavinio.

45

I always find it both interesting and stimulating exchanging ideas with Peter on the subject of fast powerboats; he is unquestionably one of the world authorities in this field and is a very versatile and original thinker as well. Among the many things we talked about was naturally the Paris race, and I remember that we discussed at some length the reasons which might have caused the capsizing of his new 2 litre inboard *007*. It is always very difficult to pinpoint the origin of these mishaps—they happen so quickly, and often out of sight of spectators qualified to describe accurately what has occurred. I have had a number of my circuit boats capsize and the reasons have not always been the same. A combination of awkward waves, an obstruction in the water, pilot error, a tendency for the hull to be tricky in certain wind and surface conditions; all these are factors which can cause this sort of misadventure.

During our talks I also showed Peter the lines drawing of the 36 footer which I had prepared as a design study. He must have found this quite interesting for he offered to have a powered scale model built and tried out in the sheltered waters around Vosper's yard in Portsmouth.

The model was subsequently made by Sam Hutchins of Vosper, an expert in these matters who has built countless powered models for the company. I was present for one of the first trials in Gosport Bay. There was a fresh breeze blowing, which was equivalent to quite a sea for the model. We tried the boat out beating into the wind, running across it, and in following sea conditions. I was most encouraged since the model showed no tendency to dig in her nose at speed even in following seas, and altogether suggested considerable promise. I was also highly amused as yellow had been chosen as a conspicuous colour and someone had stuck a Fyffe's label appropriately on her bows. These Deltas do look a bit like bananas with their reverse sheer and somewhat long, thin, pointed hulls, and when painted yellow as well . . .

Early in January 1965 the opportunity came to put theory into practice when Charles and Jimmy Gardner entrusted me with the design of what was to be my first Delta offshore powerboat: *Surfury*.

Going back for a moment, Charles and Jimmy Gardner had won the 1964 Cowes-Torquay race in their 31′ Daytona-powered Bertram *Surfrider*. This was a most popular win, for both brothers are great sportsmen and charming personalities, although it was actually due to pilot error on the part of Dick Bertram's *Lucky Moppie* which was first in at Torquay, but unfortunately went on the wrong side of the mark boat on the finish line. As Jack Knights rather ruefully put it in his "Story of the Race", which appeared in the 1966 Cowes-Torquay Race Programme, Dick's "navigator who was, it has to be whispered, an Englishman took him the wrong side of the yacht marking the finishing line so they actually missed the line altogether. By the time the penny dropped and they were turned round to cross properly, Charles and Jimmy Gardner had swept by in *Surfrider*".

It may seem incredible that such things can happen, but after a longish race both drivers and navigators are fairly tired and the finish line at Torquay is usually densely crowded with boats of all kinds; it is quite possible that one of these yachts was mistaken for the mark boat. Dick Bertram, being the great sportsman he is, took this disappointment in his stride and came back next year with his diesel-powered *Brave Moppie* to prove he could do it again—and this time on the right side of the line.

Lucky Moppie was a very fast boat. Like *Surfrider* she was powered with a pair of Daytonas. I had raced against her in July that year in the Viareggio-Bastia, when I was driving the prototype of the second series of *Speranziella* powered with a pair of Interceptor engines. Dick ran into some minor engine trouble early in the race and I took the lead, but when we hit a fairly rough patch off the island of Gorgona I saw Dick coming up astern very fast indeed. We did not have flaps fitted in that race (these had not arrived in time from the manufacturers) and as a result we were spending more time in the air than in the water in the chop off Gorgona. This may have been one reason why Dick was able to catch up with us so quickly, but his speed in over-hauling me in the lee of Corsica was most impressive; I suspect that he was not running at full throttle either.

After the race Dick told me that *Lucky Moppie* was built for him earlier that year utilizing a hull shell which had been in his yard for some time. When I complimented him on the exceptional speed of his craft he laughed, and said that he thought it was due to the rather heavily rockered bottom which the hull had developed while lying around his yard in shell form. Dick, no doubt, was as usual being a master of under-statement, but I think there is no question that beautiful *Lucky Moppie* was the fastest boat in Europe that year.

I do not know to what extent Charles and Jimmy Gardner were influenced in their decision to build

Plate 25   The author driving Delta Synthesis *at the start of the 1967 Naples race. (Photo Partenocraft).*

Plate 26   The Author with Jim Wynn (centre) and Walt Walters (right) on Navaltecnica's quayside in Anzio just before leaving for the Viareggio—Bastia race in 1964.

a new boat by seeing *Lucky Moppie*'s performance at Cowes, but it must have been obvious to them, as it was to me after Viareggio-Bastia, that quite a lot of homework was necessary to produce a boat capable of beating Dick Bertram's. As it happened, *Lucky Moppie* never raced in Europe again.

I found the preparation of the drawings of *Surfury* a particularly interesting challenge. The design had many novel aspects, the engine installation was rather unusual, and I was in constant touch with one of the owners, Charles Gardner, who made several trips to Rome and closely followed every stage of the project. I found his enthusiasm extremely catching, with the result that the original design of *Surfury* went through countless changes from start to finish; the final version did not in fact much resemble the original conception. The actual lines of the bottom were, I think, the only thing which remained un-altered.

Every weight-saving refinement either Charles or I could think up was incorporated in the design. I remember that the door of the head, for instance, had to double up as the dining-room table (an extra which the rules called for), and the light aluminium boat-hook was also the mast.

Surfury was built by Souter's yard at Cowes. She was very well built in true Souter tradition and was launched in August 1965, less than a month before the Cowes-Torquay event. I am glad to say that we were all amply rewarded for the painstaking care which had been put into her design and building, since she showed up very well in that first race. I am convinced that had it not been for mechanical trouble (which was of a minor nature but quite sufficient to lose her a lot of valuable time), *Surfury* would have won. As it was, she finished third. Dick Bertram's *Brave Moppie* was first, while Merrick Lewis came second in his own *Thunderbird*.

I was driving *Speranzella Seconda* again that year, and still remember my feeling of disappointment when, on entering Torquay in fifth position, I saw *Surfury* lying in third place in the winners' enclosure. Later, when I had heard about the mechanical bother during the race I felt happier and full of hopes for next day's 'Bollinger Goblet'.

Charles asked me whether I would like to ac-company them during this race, an opportunity which of course I jumped at. It was only then that I got some idea of *Surfury*'s potentialities. We walked away from the fleet with the engines running very comfortably and nowhere near their maximum. Upon nearing Portland Bill there was not another boat in sight. I do not know how far ahead we actually were when we ran into trouble again, this time with the cooling water pipe which came adrift in the zip strut. This was irreparable, and to make matters worse there was no way of stopping the water from coming in. We only just made it into Weymouth. There we had quite a time plugging the water intake and preparing a jury cooling ar-rangement in the hopes of getting back to Cowes, but we had to put into Poole in the end as we were only able to run very slowly and it was getting dark.

1966 also proved a disappointing season for *Surfury*, owing to various setbacks, but in 1967 she at last won her first Cowes-Torquay, making the Gardner brothers the first to win this race twice. It was a very successful race from my point of view too as *Delta Synthesis*, another boat to my design, finished second.

Surfury also did well during the 1968 season, win-ning the Wills Trophy, the Deauville race, and the Bollinger Goblet, and placing second in the Cowes-Torquay. She could probably have won this last race too had Charles and Jimmy realized earlier on that Tommy Sopwith had slipped in front of them in Lyme Bay.

I was particularly pleased with Jack Knights' comment after this race: "For my money, four years after she was built, *Surfury* remains the world's best offshore racer".

Indeed, *Surfury* must have captured the imagina-tion of a considerable section of powerboat enthusiasts judging by the amount of requests I get from keen model makers for outline drawings, photographs, and so on of this first offshore Delta hull. I was once even approached by a toy manufacturer who wished to build radio-controlled scale models of this craft.

Planking had already been started on another Delta offshore powerboat at about the time *Surfury* was being launched. This was *Delta 28*, designed for Don Shead; Don wanted a Class II boat with the same tandem arrangement as *Surfury*. The object was to produce a boat which would be capable of achieving very high speeds when conditions per-mitted.

At that time the U.I.M. rules were such that, at least as far as we in Europe were concerned, all boats had to have cabins with certain minimum requirements. Class I boats over 28′, for example, had to have a minimum height of 6′ in the cabin, while the minimum height in Class II boats was 4′9″. *Delta 28* was thus able to do away with the cabin top as the required height was obtainable under a flush deck.

Plate 27 Delta 28 *with her air-rudder on; this did not cure her steering problem at high speed.* (*Photo Beken of Cowes*).

Delta 28 turned out in fact to be a faster boat than *Surfury*. Aerodynamically the lower profile, coupled with the fact that she was smaller and lighter, certainly meant more speed. Her limit of speed in those early days was governed not so much by lack of power as by steering problems which cropped up at the higher velocities. She was never, in fact, able to open her throttles to their fullest extent owing to these problems of directional instability. I will be discussing this in more detail in Part II, Chapter VII.

Delta 28 appeared for the first time in the 1966 Wills Trophy, which she won very convincingly. Later in the same year she won the Senior Service Race and the Royal Southern Yacht Club's International Powerboat Race. Cowes-Torquay proved her to be a very fast boat, but mechanical trouble prevented her from completing the course. The following year she won the Naples International and the Viareggio-Bastia in Italy, and was also the first in

the Swedish Oregrund-Mariehamm but was disqualified for having missed a buoy in the course. She had to retire once again from the Cowes-Torquay race after catching fire.

Soon after *Delta 28* was completed, another Delta was on the stocks. This was *Merry-go-round*, a diesel-powered craft for Sir Max Aitken. At that time the diesel record was held by Dick Bertram's *Brave Moppie*, with a speed of 57·66 m.p.h. Soon after *Merry-go-round* was launched, an attempt was made at the record, a successful attempt as she clocked an average speed of 60·21 m.p.h. (approx. 53 knots).

Merry-go-round's hull was actually moulded on the plug of *Surfury*, though the stern section was changed and her transom raked quite heavily forward (for further details see Part II, Chapter VII).

Another of my earlier Delta hulls was *Delta Synthesis*, already mentioned above as finishing second to *Surfury's* first in the 1967 Cowes-Torquay

D

race. I was commissioned to design this craft in 1966 by Italo Gargiulo, owner of Cantiere Partenocraft of Naples. He wanted a Delta shaped Class I off-shore powerboat with the latest ideas which I felt were worth trying. The boat was to be powered with a pair of 427 cu. in. turbo-charged Daytona engines, adopting the conventional system of a twin shaft arrangement driving propellers through V-drives.

I lengthened the boat out from the 36' of *Surfury* to 40', narrowed the chine width, and increased the deadrise aft to 28°.

Delta Synthesis started her racing career with a major set-back. The afternoon before the 1966 Viareggio Bastia race I was carrying out final pre-race trials in rather a long swell just off Viareggio. The boat was going beautifully into the head seas when suddenly there was a most expensive noise and within four minutes all that remained afloat was about four inches of the bows. Fortunately the bow ballast tank was partially empty so that the boat did not sink completely.

I had no idea at the time what had actually happened, but as I saw the water gushing into the cockpit I automatically switched off and put the keys in my pocket. I had a Neapolitan mechanic with me who could not swim, but luckily another competitor picked us up before we even got our feet wet. It was only when the boat was hauled out of the water that we could see the extent of the damage, which was considerable. One of the propeller blades had flown off and the resulting vibration from the unbalanced propeller had twisted the shaft into an S-shape, creating a hole about a foot square where the intermediate support had been fixed to the hull.

We worked furiously all that night in an attempt to patch up the damage and get *Delta Synthesis* in condition to race the following day. Fortunately for us Merrick Lewis had come over from the States that year to race in Europe, bringing with him a vast workshop in the form of a gigantic trailer-lorry with every conceivable replacement part for his boats loaded onto it—including two new Daytona engines, shafts, struts, propellers, and so on. He immediately put everything at our disposal, including his crew, and we were indeed grateful to him for this character-istically generous and sporting gesture. I might add that he himself stayed up all night lending a hand, despite the fact that he was racing the next day. No doubt a bit of sleep would have helped, but he managed to win all the same. We were naturally all delighted when his *Thunderbolt* came in first. Our all-night effort made it possible for us to

launch *Delta Synthesis* next morning, but the jury repairs did not prove satisfactory; the boat leaked rather badly and we had to retire. However, I do not think I have ever seen such a monumental task being done in a matter of twelve hours or so.

I had occasion to race *Delta Synthesis* a couple of times in 1967, but without success as she was constantly plagued with various troubles. She was, however, an extremely comfortable boat to drive in hard going and also, I may say, very fast. Her best result in all the races she took part in was her second place in the 1967 Cowes-Torquay.

While *Delta Synthesis* was being built at Naples two other Deltas were under construction in Italy at Anzio: *Ultima Volta*, Gianni Agnelli's diesel-powered 36 footer, and *Delta Blu*, Vincenzo Balestrieri's twin Daytona engined hull of the same length. Many other Deltas followed. I will be giving more detailed descriptions of these later (Part II, Chapter VII).

I feel that a new trend of thought was also introduced into Class III mini-offshore craft by the appearance in 1965 of *Mongaso*, a modified version of the original Delta configuration *Levi 16* produced by Len Melly and John Merryfield. The modifica-tions consisted in raising the freeboard to conform with the class requirement as far as the internal volume was concerned; the boat was also a foot longer and was generally beefed up.

Mongaso, driven by Mike Beard, had a very successful season winning three prominent races that year. The following year James Beard, Mike's brother, won a very impressive array of races in his 17' *Volare* (also built by Len and John and almost identical in form to *Mongaso*), culminating in the 1966 season's points for Class III.

Although *Volare* had proved superior to the competition in Class III, I could not help feeling that, with her 17' length, she was a bit short for fast off-shore work. I later produced a 20' design for Len and John, and they built the first boat to these lines for Keith Horseman. I was told that Keith drove *Vertigo*, as she was called, with great skill in the 1967 Class III championships but owing to bad luck only placed third overall position. However, I think the validity of the increased length was proved very satisfactorily.

Like a lot of prototypes, *Vertigo* needed modifying. This is nearly always the case. If you are lucky, the modifications are of a minor nature; if not, they can involve substantial changes. I myself have never seen *Vertigo* race, but judging from all accounts she proved extremely fast in calm weather—though I understand that she was a bit of a handful in following lumpy seas. This is quite understandable since the bows were possibly too drawn in; on the other hand, fineness forward is an advantage in certain conditions. Some modifications were made to the original lines, however, and the trials of the second of these craft, *Vertigo Too*, showed improvement.

Unfortunately the 1968 season was not a very lucky one for Keith and *Vertigo Too*, although he won the Putney-Calais. Since then he has had the added misfortune of losing the boat altogether, owing to fire which broke out on the trailer carrying *Vertigo Too* and destroyed her completely before it could be extinguished.

This particular hull was also adopted for several 18-foot models, and I was delighted to hear from New Zealand, where the boat is being built under licence, that in its first race at Wellington the boat was first in performance and economy as well as first single outboard home.

Many other versions of the basic hull form adopting the Delta configuration have been built all over the world, both for circuit and for offshore racing. On looking through the 1967 Cowes-Torquay Race Programme, for instance, it is very encouraging to see that ten boats to my design were entered that year, of which six were Delta hulls, while many other boats competed whose design was strongly influenced by the Delta geometry.

Plate 28   The start of the 1968 Wellington, N.Z. Epiglass 60 mile race. (Photo Evening Post).

Part Two

CHAPTER VI

Circuit Racers

The Union Internationale Motonautique in Belgium is the governing authority for the rules concerning the various classes of craft that constitute circuit racing. At the moment there are over forty countries in the world affiliated to the U.I.M. through their national authorities. The organization issues a booklet every year or so, when it becomes necessary to bring the rules up to date, for those who are interested in the regulations governing the design of these various classes of craft. This small booklet is of the utmost importance for a designer who must continually try to improve and better his designs. In it are laid down the various limits of size, weight, and engine power for each class, and it is always a challenge to try and produce something new within the limitations of these rules that looks good and works well.

From time to time changes are understandably incorporated in the U.I.M. rules. In the past few years some rather substantial alterations have been made; possibly the most important of these was the admission of a category of craft in the outboard classes with no restriction whatsoever on hull shape.

The result was an invasion of catamarans, constructed by a great many builders but all based on the same highly successful Molinari design. Today these boats have outclassed their monohulled predecessors, at least as far as circuit racing is concerned. There have been very few classics in recent years in which monohulled craft have had the better of a well-trimmed catamaran, and when they have their success this has generally been due to some misfortune befalling the twin-hulled craft.

Catamarans, however, are not at their best in gusty conditions. Since they rely to a great extent on aerodynamic lift their success is largely due to their being correctly trimmed, so as to give their tunnels the ideal angle of incidence, and in adverse conditions they are rather prone to taking off. The reason for this is that their centre of aerodynamic lift is well forward in relation to the centre of gravity.

In all fairness, I do not really know how this category of craft came to be accepted, since there is a very definite clause in the rules governing these boats which reads as follows:

401. Lifting devices

401.1. Any device which tends to lift the boat by aerodynamic effect is prohibited, as also is any extension in size or form with this object in mind.

However, clause or no clause, catamarans are accepted. In my opinion the whole situation is rather ambiguous, since any really fast craft, particularly with a multi-hull configuration, automatically brings aerodynamic lift effect into play. Without wishing to criticize the formulators of these rules, I feel that I must add that in this case the designer's ability seems to lie in his capacity to produce a design involving aerodynamic lift principles and get it accepted. Would it not be better to have a category which is completely free?

The brilliant young Italian driver, Renato Molinari, son of Angelo the original designer of these catamarans, has I think convinced us of the superiority of these craft for circuit racing. I myself have had occasion to design a few of these racers and will describe one of them in more detail later in this chapter.

In my opinion catamarans have also been influential in bringing about another change in the U.I.M. rules; as from 1st January 1970 there are no restrictions on hull design for both inboard and outboard classes in the Sport category, although the aerodynamic effect rule still remains. This may mean that monohulls will be on their way out unless monohulled craft with lifting aerodynamic fins are accepted. Incidentally, it baffles me what criteria will be used for judging these lifting devices; a monohulled craft with very heavily outward raked topsides does

Plate 29   *The L.20 during the successful record breaking run on Lake Iseo in May 1969. Speed 140.36 Kmh (87.22 mph).*

after all constitute a camouflaged lifting device. The absence of monohulls in racing certainly would be rather a pity, and I do feel that any rules for racing should be formulated around the basic concept of more speed for a given power.

Lifting the aerodynamic ban completely would open up a whole new era of design revolving to a great extent around aerodynamic principles. This might possibly turn the art of design into more of a science than it has been in the past. Such problems as aerodynamic stability, for instance, necessitate a knowledge of the phenomena involved and, in my

opinion, make the whole business much more interesting and exciting. Speeds will inevitably shoot up too, and my guess is that driving (or perhaps, more appropriately, flying) these future craft will be a far more specialized matter than it is today.

I have designed several different types of circuit racers for various classes since I started designing these craft in 1964. I will be describing a selection of these boats in the following pages, irrespective of whether they were successful or not; my choice has been based on the interesting problems these craft presented and on what I learned from them.

LEVI 16

(Qualifying for "Hors-bord Utilitaire" Classes IU, NU, ZU)

Length overall   — *16'3¾" (m. 4.90)*   Deadrise transom — *25°*
Beam maximum — *4'10½" (m. 1.50)*   Minimum weight — *220 kg*
Beam chine   — *4'0" (m. 1.22)*   Engine   — *100/140 HP Johnson, Evinrude, Mercury*

It all started at the 1964 London Boat Show, when first Don Shead and then Len Melly and John Merryfield asked me to design a couple of circuit racers, as I have already mentioned in Chapter V.

The first Levi 16, *Thunderbolt X*, which I designed for Len and John, had a deadrise at the transom of

25° which was kept constant for a short length and then subsequently increased progressively to the bows. The top sides were raked outward some 55° and this rake was retained for the whole length of the craft. I used the same convex sections throughout the hull while the sections of the bottom and top sides

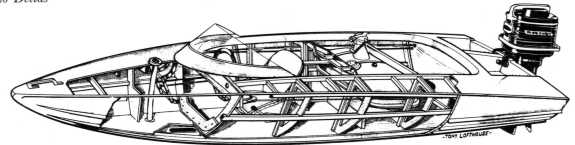

Fig. 1   LEVI 16

were radiused off at the chine to enable a continuous hull structure.

I wanted these boats to be of laminated construction with a continuous shell from keel to sheer without any break at the chine. This type of structure does not require any framing in the hull other than the main bulkheads, and also offers an excellent strength to weight ratio.

The convex sections gave the hull tremendous rigidity of form. I had worked in four risers per side (not including the chine) on the bottom of these hulls and these also acted as longitudinal stringers, thus contributing further to the overall strength of the bottom.

I incorporated a double bottom lined with fibreglass in the original design, which could be filled up when the boat was at rest and emptied when it was under way. I did this because I felt that the boats would be extremely tender when at rest, especially in view of the rather high centre of gravity of some of the outboard engines which would be fitted. In the end this double bottom was not necessary, which was a blessing for Len and John as it would have been quite a headache to build.

The letter I sent with the original drawing in February, 1964 gives some idea of my anxiety on this point:

"Enclosed herewith finally are drawings of the Melly Merryfield Racer. As you well know it is not easy to arrive first shot at something successful especially when dealing with a new approach to the problem.

"As you will see, I did not incorporate the flat triangular planing surface we spoke about because I felt that this would give too much lift right at the deepest part of the bottom and perhaps render the boat laterally unstable. I think as it is at the moment the boat should give a good comfortable ride and also should be fast as there won't be much of it in the water at speed.

"You will also note that I have not incorporated any fin as I feel that turning should be good without it. Should this not be so, a fin can easily be added later. The boat should bank inwards on turns and here it will need quite a bit of practice, I imagine, to know how tight to go and also coming out of a turn will have to be watched to avoid rolling over outward (because of the high C.G. and tender bottom).

"The problem here is the stability at rest, especially with the high C.G. of the engine. I have therefore decided to water-ballast the bottom with approx. 300 lbs. which will improve things considerably. Longitudinally the boat will be very far down by the stern when launched and it may be necessary to hold the boat till the double bottom fills up. Also to keep the bow down till the crew get in, full fuel tanks before launching would help.

"I am perhaps making all this sound worse than it actually will be, but I think it best that all concerned should know this, so that these points don't pop up as a surprise later.

"I have deliberately kept the hull free board to the very minimum allowed by the rules which you told me, i.e. $23\frac{1}{2}''$ amidship (on section 4 from top of hog to underside of deck at sheer), this is to keep the hull C.G. as low as possible. I am always presuming that the double bottom will not be considered as the top of the keel for it is nothing less than a floor board screwed down! Should this not be considered so for some reason or the other, then the ballasting should be done in another way.

"I would suggest two 6" diameter or so plastic or soft rubber pipes each 12' long, placed in the bilges well clamped and then floor boards over the top in the normal way. The inlet of water to these pipes will be as before through the transom and a couple of vents will be necessary forward. Since in this latter case the double bottom will

54

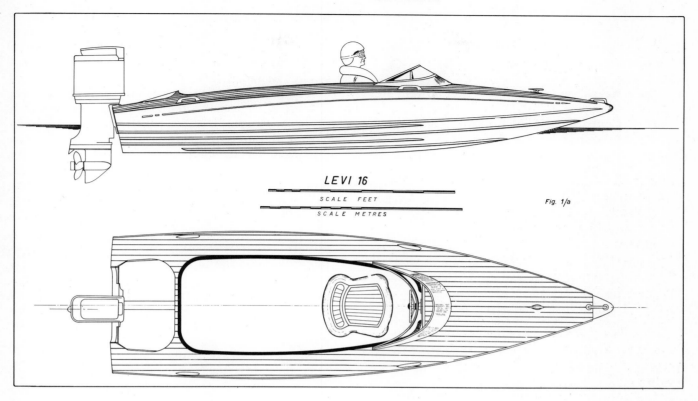

LEVI 16

SCALE FEET

SCALE METRES

Fig. 1/a

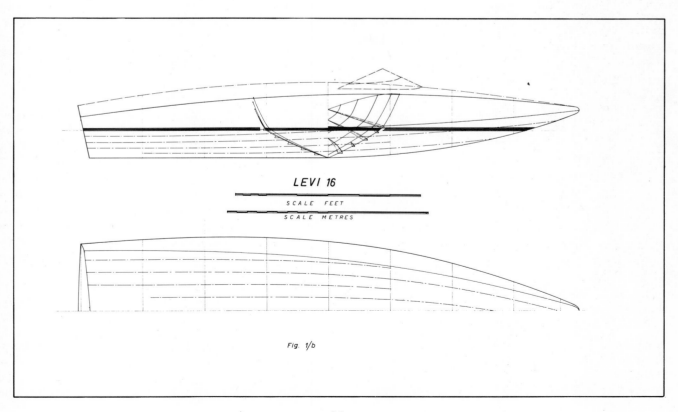

LEVI 16

SCALE FEET

SCALE METRES

Fig. 1/b

be done away with, the bulkheads should be carried down to the keel obviously.

"The double bottom solution to the ballasting problem is by far the best, though, for the following reasons:

(1) Keeps the water ballast C.G. lower.
(2) Occupies less space.
(3) Contributes to the hull strength.
(4) It is simpler to do, I feel.
(5) If properly done will be trouble free.
(6) Is altogether a cleaner job.
(7) Will weigh very little more.

"There is furthermore no problem with rot etc., as this will be lined with fibreglass.

"Obviously it would have been simpler to design something less radical but I felt that if we are to go in for something new it would be best to go the whole way rather than adopt half measures.

"I hope that you agree with my line of reasoning."

I also produced a set of drawings for Len and John of a 14 footer based on the lines of the *Levi 16*. Whilst in those days the *Levi 16* was intended for engines of up to 100 HP qualifying for Class XU, today (depending on the engines fitted) this boat can qualify for Classes IU, NU and ZU; the 14 footer, on the other hand, was for engines of up to 65 HP qualifying for Classes EU and FU.

After Len and John's victory in the 1964 Paris Six Hour Race the *Levi 16* became a very popular and successful boat, but the 14 footer never achieved the same popularity. Why this was so I do not exactly know, but certainly the shorter boat was far more lively and rather a handful in rough going, while trimming was trickier than on the 16. The 14s were also slower boats and I suspect that this contributed

to their lack of appeal. I am sure that Len and John were wise to concentrate on the 16, since the outright wins of the prototype that first season had created quite a stir in racing circles and they stood to gain far more from the publicity angle.

The deep V sections in the after planing surfaces of the *Levi 16* caused a reduction of waterline width at speed, and this in turn resulted in a torque problem. If an outboard engine with a right-hand rotation propeller was used, for instance, the boat would lie over to port, taking some fairly heavy whacks on that side, and constant helm correction was necessary to try and keep her upright. This inconvenience was overcome by setting the engine off-centre some $1\frac{1}{2}''$ on the starboard side, which not only gave a physical correction, since the engine weight was placed against the torque, but also contributed (at least in theory) to a dynamic correction. In fact, the thrust being on the starboard side did tend to push the bows to port; this had to be corrected by slight starboard helm, which straightened out the port list.

Many changes of a minor nature have been made since those first boats, principally to the structure. These alterations were mainly necessitated by the increased power of the big outboards. When the first *Levi 16* appeared the biggest of these engines was rated at around 100 HP, whereas today some engines even claim to produce around 140 HP.

A fair number of *Levi 16*s have been made, among them the following which can be said to have been particularly successful in those early days (apart from *Thunderbolt X*): *Uncle Den*, *Miss Chief*, *Kayotic*, *Mayvee*. Recently *Mister H* and *Voodoo* have also been giving a good account of themselves. The boat has also been produced in numerous other European and Far Eastern countries. See Figs. 1, 1/a, 1/b.

LEVI 17.5

(Qualifying for "Runabouts Europeens" Class 1)

Length overall	— *17′6¾″ (m. 5.33)*	*Deadrise transom* — *25°*	
Beam maximum	— *5′6½″ (m. 1.70)*	*Minimum weight* — *500 kg*	
Beam chine	— *4′0″ (m. 1.22)*	*Engine*	— *Volvo Aquamatic 1800 c.c., and others*

Don Shead's *Levi 17.5*, *Fi-Fi*, was similar in hull design to the *Levi 16*, as can be seen from the drawings. The only fundamental difference was that the sheer aft was considerably higher owing to the outdrive

engine installation. As mentioned earlier, the boat had a 1800 c.c. inboard Volvo engine fitted with a Volvo 100 outdrive.

This engine and outdrive were basically the

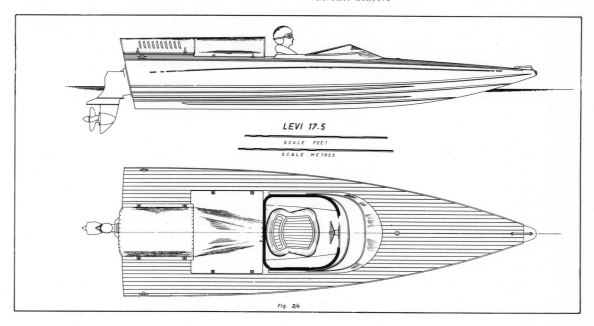

LEVI 17.5

SCALE FEET

SCALE METRES

Fig. 2/a

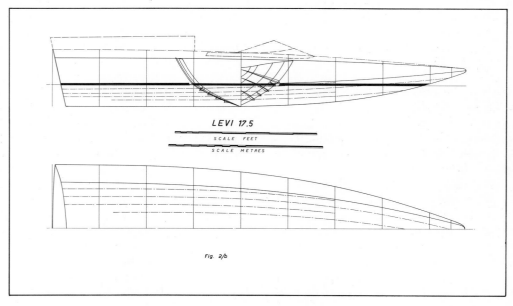

LEVI 17.5

SCALE FEET

SCALE METRES

Fig. 2/b

commercial unit with minor hotting-up for racing. The changes included higher compression, special cams and carburettors, tuned exhausts, and a racing underwater unit with a bronze propeller. This was the rig with which the original boat raced. Later, further modifications were carried out to the engine, including the fitting of Weber carburettors.

Many of these later modifications to Don's engine were done by Jim Whitehouse, who unquestionably showed notable skill with these Volvos; *Fi-Fi's* various successes bear witness to his thorough know-

ledge of the art of preparing racing engines as well as to Don's great enthusiasm and driving ability.

I rather liked the look of this boat, with its aluminium engine cowling reminding me of those early Auto Union racing cars with rear mounted engines. Souters of Cowes built the prototype, and many others afterwards. We had the same torque problem as we had had with the *Levi 16*, but in this case since the engine had left-hand rotation it was off-set to port.

An interesting point in my opinion was that the

fuel tank was built into the hull. It consisted of a U-shaped plywood box situated forward of the driving position, the bottom and sides of which were the hull shell itself. The box was entirely lined with glass reinforced plastics; it was U-shaped since the pilot's legs went into it in the normal driving position.

Performance-wise I was very happy with this boat since trials soon after she was built revealed a speed of over 50 knots.

Examples of the *Levi 17.5* have been made in Italy, France, Sweden, and South Africa. The original design was for construction in laminated wood, but craft have also been made in glassfibre. Perhaps one of the most impressive glassfibre examples was produced by Chantier Blanc, of Villevaudé in France, for the inboard 2-litre category. The deck, which was also in glassfibre, was beautifully moulded and incorporated a well-proportioned head-rest which faired into the engine cowling. The engineering work was also of the highest order. The power plant was a Gordini racing engine driving a propeller through a V-drive.

This French boat appeared at the 1965 Paris Six Hour Race, but unfortunately without success. This may have been due to the fact that she was heavier than she need have been; she also had a conventional shaft line. But I think that possibly insufficient time was spent preparing her for the race. Even so, she was a very attractive prototype. See Figs. 2/a, 2/b.

L. 22

(Qualifying for "Runabouts Europeens" Class 5)

Length overall	— 22′1½″	*(m. 6.75)*	*Weight*	— *1200 kg*
Beam maximum	— 7′0″	*(m. 2.14)*	*Engine*	— *8-litre BPM Vulcano 450*
Beam chine	— 5′0″	*(m. 1.53)*	*Speed*	— *70 knots*
Deadrise transom	— 20°			

In 1966 I was asked to design a racing craft to fall into the European inboard runabout Class 5 for a very enthusiastic Italian sportsman, Achille Roncoroni, who had already built numerous boats in this category for himself.

The big event in Italy for this class of boat is the "Cento Miglia del Lario", which takes place every year towards the end of September. This is possibly one of the most important circuit races on the Italian calendar, and the Mario Verga Trophy is much sought after and keenly contested.

At the time I was preparing the design, one of Eugenio Molinari's *Freccia Bianca* series captured the world speed record at 133·6 km per hour (over 70 knots), which is quite a speed for a runabout.

Freccia Bianca was a very purposeful-looking boat, although in some respects she was rather conventional. She was built of plywood and had a warped plane bottom with shallow deadrise at the transom. Some rather small spray rails were fitted to the bottom which did not extend right forward. The freeboard was very low and the stem heavily cut away. The 8-litre BPM Vulcano racing engine was fitted right aft, driving the propeller shaft through a V-drive. The pilot sat just forward of the engine.

I remember seeing this boat on several occasions when trials were being carried out and was very struck by her speed, considering that she trimmed out extremely flat. There was no porpoising whatsoever and the boat did not at any time leave the water, which was rather unusual for a fast monohull boat. The speed of this craft was all the more remarkable since it appeared to me that there was a lot of boat in the water and, consequently, a fairly large amount of wetted surface.

It was against this background of competition that I started on the design of the *L. 22*. The owner had very definite ideas as to what he wanted; the object was not a purely racing machine but a craft which could also be used as a fast pleasure runabout. The seating position had to be right aft, for three people, and Roncoroni also wanted the engine to be fitted forward of the steering cockpit with a straight through shaft in the interests of simplicity.

I would personally have preferred to have fitted the engine with a V-drive, giving me the possibility of having a flatter shaft angle, of using a multiplication gear in the V-drive, and of getting the centre of gravity further aft. As it was, I was tied down to the 4500 r.p.m. of the propeller which was the maximum

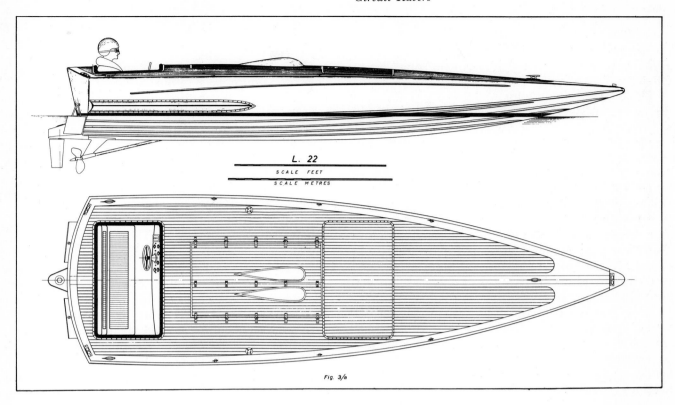

L. 22

SCALE FEET

SCALE METRES

Fig. 3/a

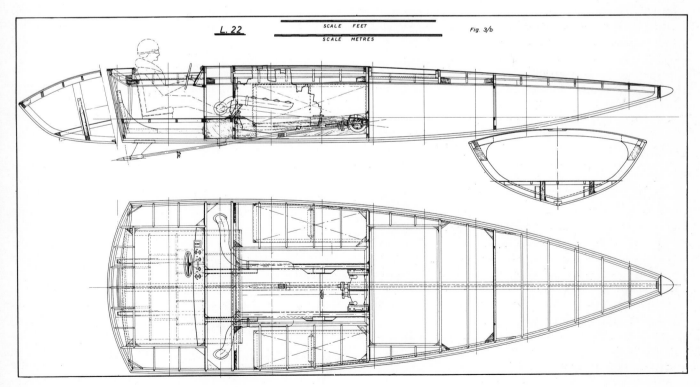

L. 22

SCALE FEET

SCALE METRES

Fig. 3/b

r.p.m. of the engine with a direct drive gear. This necessitated rather a high pitch/diameter ratio for the propeller; the shaft inclination was very high, and I felt that all this would result in some loss of efficiency.

The boat was fitted with an 8 litre BPM Vulcano racing engine developing 400 HP, and was built by the Riva Boat Service at Menaggio on Lake Como. Trials were not altogether satisfactory for although the boat achieved a speed of around 115 km per hour (just over 60 knots), we could not manage to better this even though we tried many different propellers and rudders. I did not really feel that we could get much more out of the boat as she stood, and it was therefore decided to go ahead with the V-drive arrangement which would make it possible to try out various gear ratios. We were eventually rewarded by obtaining a top speed of 128 km per hour (just under 70 knots).

L. 22 first raced in the 1967 "Cento Miglia del Lario" and finished 2nd in the monohull category (*Freccia Bianca* was 1st). We were considerably encouraged by this result and carried out further modifications, always retaining the V-drive. These modifications consisted in trying out different sets of gear ratios and different rudders and propellers, in moving the engine, and in reducing the "rocker" of the bottom. The "rocker" was originally quite high and produced an excessive amount of porpoising. Transom flaps had been fitted on this boat right from the start and these could damp out the porpoising completely when depressed, but with some sacrifice as far as speed was concerned. The drag of the flaps to keep the boat's bows down was under-

standably considerable. Incidentally, as far as I know, *L. 22* was the first boat in this category to be fitted with moveable transom flaps.

The modifications did not substantially increase her maximum speed, but her handling qualities were considerably improved—so much so that, when she raced again in 1968, *L. 22* was described by many experts as the best trimmed boat in the race. Unfortunately she threw a propeller blade when lying third. Her driver told me after the race that he had not been forcing the pace in any way and felt that he could have closed in on the leaders if the boat had remained in the running. I know such declarations are often made, but he seemed very sure of his judgment. Personally, I do not feel so sure that *L. 22* was in fact fast enough to have competed successfully with Renato and Eugenio Molinari's boats, which placed an easy 1st and 2nd. Shortly after this race, Renato Molinari's boat captured the Class 4 record at a speed of 135 km per hour (73 knots).

L. 22 was, of course, a bigger boat than the others, and also a heavier one; on the other hand, she appeared to be much more comfortable at speed in the water. I think she really did fulfil in good measure the original requirements laid down by Roncoroni—namely, a fast and stable boat which could also be used as a runabout.

Roncoroni's enthusiasm in no way waned with these not particularly brilliant race results; on the contrary, he decided to go ahead with a second boat, which this time was to be an out-and-out racer with no compromises at all. He also wished to have a crack at the existing world speed record.

This new craft was the *L. 20*. See Figs. 3/a, 3/b.

L. 20

(Qualifying for "Runabouts Europeens"
Classes 4 and 5)

Length overall	— 20'	(m. 6.10)	*Weight*	— 1000 kg
Beam maximum	— 6'	(m. 1.82)	*Engines*	— 427 cu. in. MerCruiser 450 HP, 7·5 litre BPM Super Vulcano 500 HP
Beam chine	— 4'11"	(m. 1.50)		
Deadrise transom	— 12°		*Speed*	— 75 knots

As can be seen from the drawings, the *L. 20* was quite a different kettle of fish. I designed this craft early in 1968, but before going on to describe her in detail I would first like to explain the line of reasoning

behind this new design.

As I have already mentioned, I was amazed at the speed of Molinari's *Freccia Bianca*. She was clearly a faster craft than my *L. 22* design. At that time I was convinced that a boat with heavy deadrise and well-placed spray strakes would be faster than a flatter bottomed craft. This had been amply demonstrated by my Paris boats, so why not here?

I had given *L. 22* a deep deadrise hull for two reasons:

(1) Lake Como can get quite rough when there is a fresh wind blowing and I felt that deep dead-

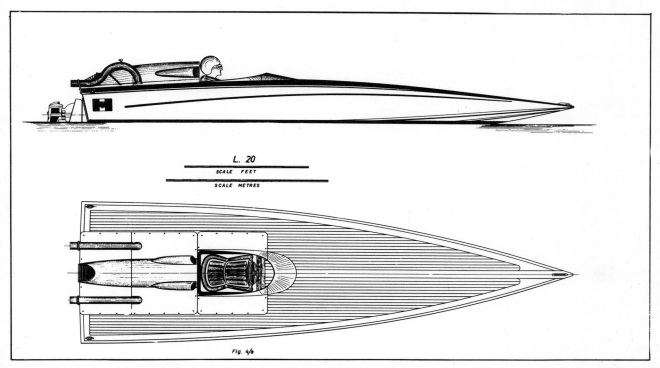

L. 20

SCALE FEET

SCALE METRES

Fig. 4/a

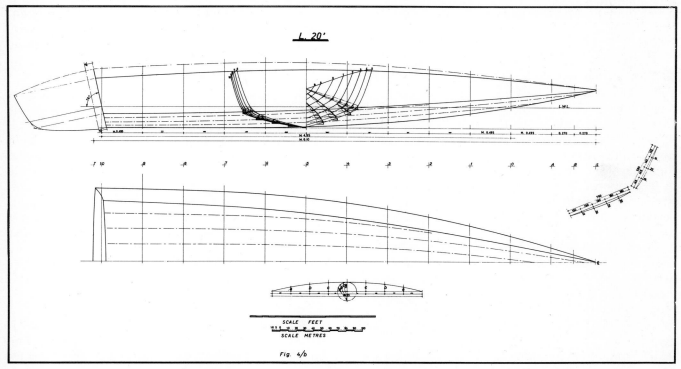

L. 20'

SCALE FEET

SCALE METRES

Fig. 4/b

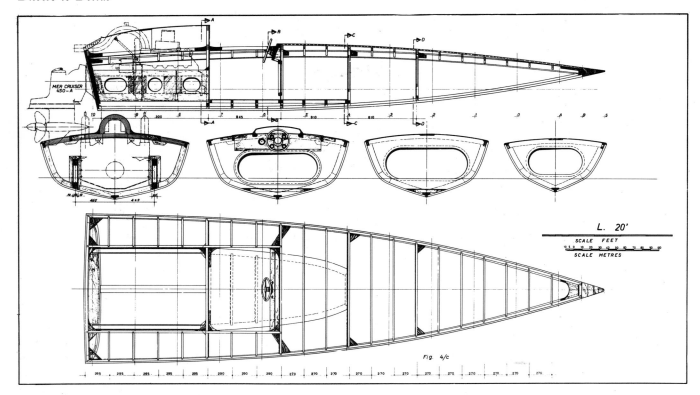

Fig. 4/c

rise would make the boat more comfortable and enable her to maintain high speeds in these conditions.

(2) I thought that, irrespective of the weather, such a hull might prove faster against the competition of flatter hulls.

The weather was in fact calm, and the water very flat indeed, on the occasion of both the 1967 and 1968 "Cento Miglia del Lario", but I do not think it would have made any difference had it been rough. Later on I saw both *Freccia Bianca* and *L. 22* on trials in what was considered lively conditions, and I noticed that although the waves were comparatively high they were short and their general level was more or less uniform. The ride in *Freccia Bianca* may have been more uncomfortable than in *L. 22*, but she certainly went through the waves flat out and without losing any speed.

I had not fully appreciated until that moment that conditions on Lake Como were so different to those in open water, where even on the calmest day there is a gentle swell. The effect of this long, gentle swell is to make a boat fly out of the water at speed, whereas in a level, short chop it seems to stay in the water and go through the crests of the waves. The analogy which comes to my mind is that of a motor-car running on a flat road full of potholes where it can nevertheless keep up a high speed, whereas on a road with a good surface but with long humps it tends to take off the crest of these unless speed is reduced.

On this score, therefore, deep deadrise did not appear to have much to recommend it other than the fact that it gave a more comfortable ride.

Why was the deep vee not faster? After considerable reflection I came to the conclusion that while low deadrise is clearly best for low speeds, and high deadrise gives the best results for medium to high speeds, for very high speeds a flattening again of the deadrise becomes more efficient. I suspect that the reason for this curious phenomenon is that an aerodynamic effect comes into play at very high speeds which reduces the wetted surface by creating a sort of ram cushion of air between the water surface and the bottom. I was also led to this conclusion by my findings on the sponson design of a 1300 c.c. racer which is described later in this chapter (see also Part III, Chapter XI for a further discussion on deadrise and speed length ratios).

For this reason, the deadrise aft on *L. 20* was much reduced, as can be seen from the lines drawing. The boat was also cut to the limit of the Class 5 rules

Plate 30   The L.22 racing in the "Cento Miglia del Lario" on Lake Como in 1968. (Photo Moro).

dimensionally and kept just within the minimum weight requirement.

This time Roncoroni wanted to try a 450 HP MerCruiser competition engine with stern drive propulsion and racing underwater unit, machinery which had certainly given a very good account of itself in Renato Molinari's 1968 "Cento Miglia del Lario" winner. The power to weight ratio of this engine is not quite up to that of the BPM 8 litre Vulcano or the 7·5 litre Super Vulcano, but it will be nevertheless extremely interesting to see how the stern drive propulsion compares in efficiency with the conventional propeller and shaft.

These MerCruiser stern drives are fitted with what is called "power tilt", which is really a mechanism enabling the thrust line to be varied by means of electrical switches at the driving position. Being able to vary the thrust line in this way is most useful for obtaining optimum trim; the boat can be made to run with literally just a portion of the propeller and underwater unit in the water, thus considerably reducing hull drag.

I have been criticized by some experts for having designed an "extreme" boat which, they feel, will prove a handful to drive at speed. But it is my firm conviction that as few compromises as possible must be brought into the design if one is going all out for a record breaker. In the case of the *L. 20*, the compromise seemed to lie between ease of handling and sheer speed. The two do not go very well together; as speed increases so does the driving technique demand extra skill. But I think it is fair to say that this is the case with any machine built for pure speed, whether it is a boat, an aircraft, or a racing car.

The owner once remarked: "If looks are any indication, *L. 20* should be a real flier". In the event, *L. 20* lived up to her looks. On May 20th, 1969 Giovanni Mondelli drove her over the official course at Sarnico on Lake Iseo at an average speed of 140·36 km per hour to gain the world speed record for the U.I.M. Class 4 Inboard Runabout. He actually did one run at 141·73. The previous record for this class was 135·08 km, established by Beppe Roda in a Molinari hull. Like her predecessor *L. 22*, *L. 20* was also built by Giacomo Colombo's Riva Boat Service at Menaggio on Lake Como.

I was particularly pleased at the way the boat behaved on this record run. A great deal of the credit must go, of course, to Mondelli's driving skill, but the "power tilt" mechanism incorporated in the MerCruiser engine also played its part; we were able to trim the boat out in such a way that most of the time she was right out of the water with only a portion of the hub and half the propeller immersed.

It is clearly difficult to see how hydrodynamic drag can be reduced any further, while aerodynamic drag is also obviously low since the boat has a very small frontal area with good penetration on account of its pronounced Delta shape.

A three-bladed aluminium-nickel-bronze propeller with a pitch of 500 mm was used on the record run. Experiments are now being made with steel propellers, which should produce an increase in speed owing to the thinner blade sections possible with this material of higher tensile strength.

See Figs. 4/a, 4/b, 4/c.

1300 C.C. RACER

(Qualifying for "Racers" Classes KA and LV)

Length overall	— 13'2" (m. 4.00)	Deadrise aft on	
Beam maximum	— 6'11" (m. 2.10)	sponsons	— 16°
Beam chine	— 5'5" (m. 1.65)	Weight	— Under 250 kg
		Engine	— Alfa Romeo 1300 c.c.

I am including the drawings of this particular boat not because it achieved anything spectacular in this highly competitive class of racing in Italy, but because I found it a most interesting and instructive craft to design.

When I was originally approached to produce the design of a three point suspension hydroplane for this class I made it quite clear that I had never designed a boat of this type and that, if I did so, I would like to try out some new ideas without, however, being able to give any assurance whatsoever of success. These conditions were accepted and I went ahead.

I approached the problem of this design with the following very definite points in mind:

(1) *Minimum frontal area.* In order to achieve this, the tunnel was shaped like a gull's wing so as to get the engine and pilot as low as possible and still have sufficient clearance between the bottom of the hull and the water. The deck was shaped like the roof of a pagoda, with inverted camber instead of the conventional convex shape.

(2) *A different sponson design*, for more speed and better turning (it is no secret that three point suspension hydroplanes are not top of the class when turning). The sponsons, therefore, were vee-shaped and had a deadrise of 16° with spray strakes like a circuit craft. I thought that this would prove more efficient as far as speed was concerned and that the pronounced vee would have a digging effect when cornering, thereby improving the turning qualities of the boat. I was right on the second supposition, but quite wrong on the first. I will go into this point in more detail later.

(3) *A new system of construction*, so as to keep the craft within the weight limits without any possible risk of structural failure. Here again, the conventional type of structure of plywood with longitudinal and transverse framing is somewhat prone to working itself loose. I am not, of course, suggesting that all boats built in this way are afflicted by this defect, but undoubtedly a great many are after racing for some time. The hull, then, was laminated with an external and an internal layer of aircraft birch plywood, $\frac{1}{16}''$ thick, with internal diagonal laminates of poplar. In this way we were able to dispense with the multitude of framing these boats usually have and just fit two longitudinal girders, which were the engine beds, and a few webbed frames —and that was all. This method also made it possible to have the engine set lower in the hull since there were no structures in the way of the sump, thus obtaining a low centre of gravity and a reduced shaft angle.

Structurally, the boat was a complete success. She was light and at the same time very sturdy. I might add that all joints, such as the keels of the sponsons and the sheer, were reinforced with glass cloth and epoxy resin, making the whole construction a very solid body. This sort of structure is undoubtedly more expensive than the conventional plywood, but I think it is well worth considering for a racing boat of this type when cost is not the governing factor. These boats, in fact, are not very expensive and the increase in cost is minor.

We did quite a few trials on this racer, but unfortunately not enough; if we had persevered I think we would have had better results.

The striking point about these first trials was that the pronounced vee sponsons produced most interesting results. The boat was not particularly fast— we never actually timed her but estimated that her speed was around 140 km per hour (well below the record at that time for this class). The centre of gravity of the craft in relation to the end of the sponsons was within acceptable limits for this type of boat, but the trim at speed was decidedly tail heavy.

We ballasted the bows with sandbags, getting the best results with something like 40 lbs. I was

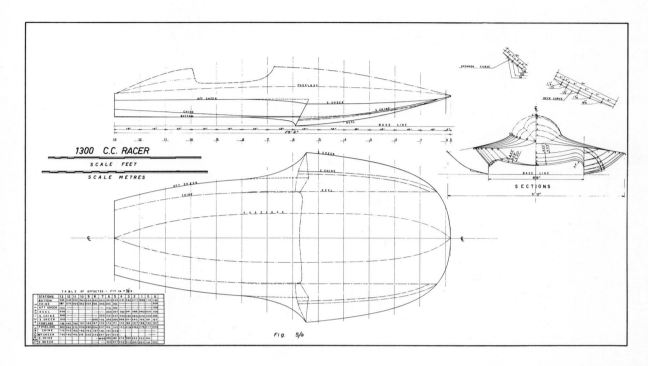

1300 C.C. RACER

SCALE FEET

SCALE METRES

TABLE OF OFFSETES

Fig. 5/a

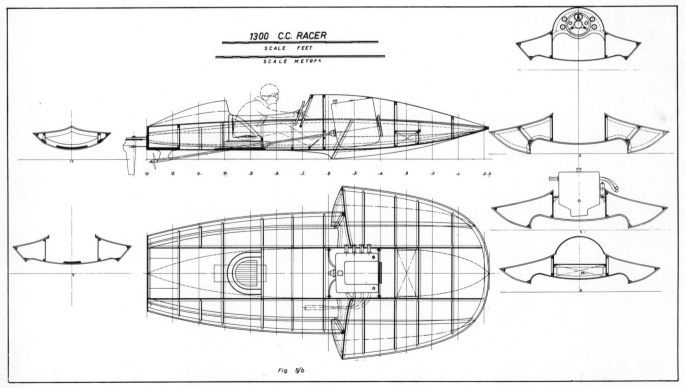

1300 C.C. RACER

SCALE FEET

SCALE METRES

Fig. 5/b

surprised at this and immediately considered the possibility of moving the engine forward, so as to do away with the extra ballast. Before actually doing so, however, I fortunately decided that it would be advisable to experiment first of all with different sponson shapes and leave the engine where it was. In fact, by superimposing a flat plane with a deadrise of 10° or so on each sponson, we managed to increase the speed and considerably reduce the tail heavy condition. A further modification, consisting of widening the flat plane on the sponson and reducing the deadrise of this to 5°, increased the speed further and eliminated the tail heavy effect altogether.

It was indeed fortunate that I had observed the golden rule of trials; that is, to tackle one thing at a time so as to be really sure of the effects of each separate modification. Owing to shortage of time, or perhaps over-enthusiasm, there is a temptation to carry out two or more modifications simultaneously—with the result that it is difficult to know which modification is actually responsible for the increase, or decrease, in performance. Sometimes it also happens that the improvement gained from one modification is cancelled out by the negative effect of another.

In this case, anyway, it was clear that the deep deadrise design of the sponsons required more incidence to obtain lift, and that it was this which had been causing the tail heavy effect.

At this point trials were suspended. This was a pity as I think that had we widened and flattened the planing surfaces still more we would have achieved even better results. However, the boat gave a good account of herself in the 1967 Pavia-Venezia race, competed on the river Po, being in the lead until fuel problems forced her to withdraw.

There are quite a few changes I would make were I to design another boat of this type. Lengthening the hull would add to stability and improve aerodynamic penetration; a reduction in the tunnel area forward would also, I believe, be an advantage in cutting down lift at the nose. There is, too, a tendency today to put the driver forward of the engine; many boats have now been tried with this layout and have proved successful. See Figs. 5/a, 5/b.

LEVI CAT 18.5

(Qualifying for "Hors-bord Course"
Classes OI, ON, OZ)

Length overall	— *18'5" (m. 5.60)*	*Deadrise at transom on floats*	— *10°*
Beam maximum	— *6'6" (m. 1.98)*		
Beam chine	— *4'10" (m. 1.48)*	*Engine*	— *100/140 HP Johnson, Evinrude, Mercury*
Tunnel width	— *3'6" (m. 1.07)*		

I based this design not only on the concept of the Molinari catamarans but also on that of many others which have recently been produced, all of which qualify under the present rules in the OI, ON and OZ categories. I had designed catamarans of this kind before, but none of them had ever been built.

As I saw them, the main problems to overcome here were:

(1) *Correct trim*, i.e. the optimum angle of incidence in the tunnel in order to obtain the required aerodynamic lift and thereby reduce the wetted surface, so that just the tip of the two sponsons aft would be skimming the water at speed, while still maintaining the good longitudinal and transverse stability of the craft.

(2) *Structure*, which had to be light and at the same time strong enough to withstand the buffeting to which these boats are prone. A lot of catamarans have suffered damage in races, from minor holing to actual tearing apart; I have even seen some craft neatly cracked in half.

Several factors influence the question of trim: centre of gravity, shape of aft sponsons, thrust line. This last, in particular, requires a lot of patient trial and error.

The height of the cavitation plate in relation to the bottom of the tunnel also has an important bearing on the speed of the craft. Obviously, the higher the cavitation plate can be positioned without preventing the propeller from biting efficiently into the

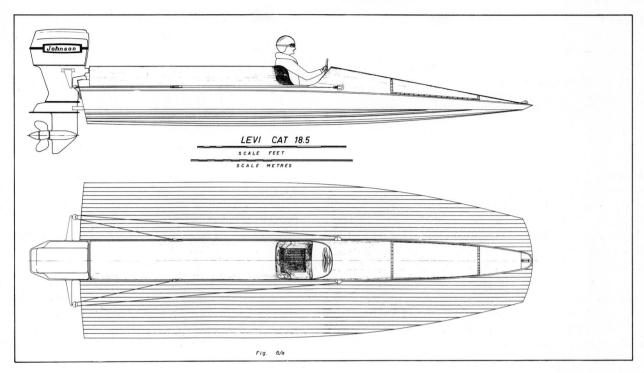

LEVI CAT 18.5

SCALE FEET

SCALE METRES

Fig. 6/a

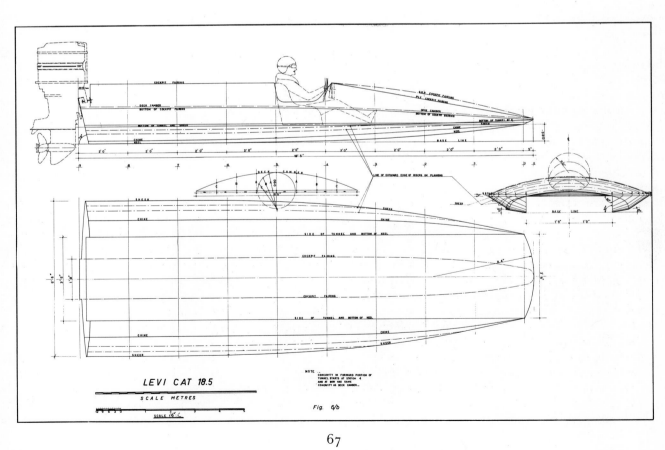

LEVI CAT 18.5

SCALE METRES

Fig. 6/b

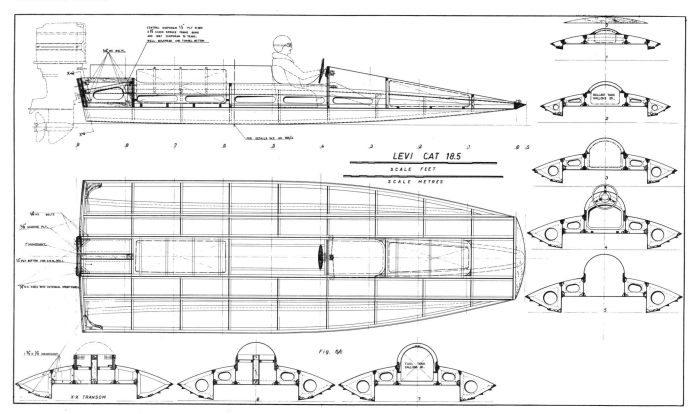

water, the more the speed will increase (owing to the reduction in appendage drag). Some catamarans at speed are trimmed out so that just a portion of the boss and half the propeller are in the water, somewhat similar to three point suspension hydroplanes.

With regard to the second problem, I wanted to keep the structure as simple as possible and therefore adopted a sturdy twin longitudinal diaphragm girder arrangement, upon which the centre section and sponsons were mounted with the minimum of transverse framing.

When it comes to racing I believe that driving technique and pilot weight are deciding factors as far as the success of one catamaran rather than another is concerned. I have often seen some thirty or forty of these boats, with more or less the same characteristics (and in one or two cases apparently identical models), racing against each other, and two or three invariably pull away and leave the others well behind. Almost always these winning craft have the same drivers.

See Figs. 6/a, 6/b, 6/c.

Plate 31   A fine display of cups won by Paul Winsley of South Africa in his RL 17 built by Thesens. (Photo Blackwell)

CHAPTER VII

Offshore Racing
Powerboats

(1) CLASS I & II

Offshore powerboat racing as we know it today started in 1956 with the first Miami-Nassau, which was won by the lengendary Sam Griffith driving a 30 foot Christ Craft called *Doodles II*. This boat was powered with a pair of 215 HP Interceptor engines. Sam took nine hours and twenty minutes to cover the 184 mile course. He won again the following year in *Doodles III*, a 35 foot Enterprise powered by two 275 HP Cadillac engines; this time he took ten hours forty-two minutes to complete the course.

Sam has been the only driver to date to win this classic four times; his other two wins were in 1960 and 1961, when his co-driver was Dick Bertram, both times in boats built by Dick. The first, *Moppie*, was a 30 foot Ray Hunt designed wooden craft, and the second was another Ray Hunt design, the glass reinforced plastic prototype of the highly popular 31 foot *Moppie* series, appropriately called *Glass Moppie*. This race was competed each year from 1956 except in 1959.

The next races on record also took place in America: the Miami-Havana (1958) and the Hennessy Long Island (1959). The first European classic was the Cowes-Torquay race, which started in 1961; the next was the Italian Viareggio-Bastia-Viareggio in 1962. Since then offshore powerboat races have been springing up all over the place like mushrooms, proving the growing popularity of this comparatively new sport.

In the early days of offshore racing the rules were not unified on both sides of the Atlantic. Open boats were permitted to race in the United States, while in Europe racing craft were required to be cabin cruisers with certain minimum accommodation requirements. As far as European boats were concerned, the initial object was to improve the breed of cabin cruisers and, as a result, the racing craft were really hotted up versions of these. But this trend did not last very long, as can be expected, since in their efforts to produce the fastest boats possible designers usually end by designing to the letter rather than to be spirit of the rule, taking every advantage of any loopholes they can find.

Unification of these rules was carried out happily a few years ago, satisfying both sides in that two basic categories of boats could be raced: the open (O.P.) and the cabin cruiser (C) versions. These two basic categories were further subdivided into Classes I and II, Class I being boats of 28–45 foot overall and Class II boats of 20–28 foot overall. The maximum engine capacity permitted in each case was 1000 cu. in. (16·4 litres) for petrol engines and 2000 cu. in. (32·8 litres) for diesel machinery*.

The question of turbine propulsion has often been discussed, but so far no satisfactory method of rating these engines has been found; for the moment the decision as to whether turbine engines are accepted or not in a particular race is left entirely to the discretion of the race organizers. I cannot help feeling, however, that general acceptance of turbines is inevitable; they are in my opinion the engines of the future.

Within this general framework of rules and various national race authorities can (and do) incorporate local class regulations, limiting engine capacity, price of propulsive equipment, and so on.

In recent years, a selection of these offshore powerboat races has been chosen to qualify for the U.I.M. Drivers Championship Points. The award is supposed to denote the world champion driver. My

---

* 1970 marks a milestone in powerboat racing history with all categories of racing having new rules. As far as offshore is concerned, Class I and Class II are differentiated by engine capacity and not by dimension—the boat length for both classes is identical, 20–45 feet. Maximum engine capacity is now 1000 cu. in. for petrol engines and 2000 cu. in. for diesel in the case of Class I, while Class II limits are 500 cu. in. for petrol engines and 1000 cu. in. for diesel.

overall impression is that it is not always the most qualified driver who achieves the World Championship. It is hard to know of course which one factor influences victory in a race more than another: a good hull, reliable engines, or clever driving. In the case of Sam Griffith there can be no question of doubt: it was his driving skill. After all, he won four Miami-Nassau races in four different boats with three different engines!

A private individual undoubtedly needs a fairly large and elastic bank account to meet the very considerable expenses involved in taking part in these races, particularly if he wishes to compete on both sides of the Atlantic. I do not think I would be far wrong in saying that a serious attempt at the Championship Points is possibly one of the most expensive hobbies one can choose. Not only is the initial cost of these boats in some cases very heavy, but transporting the craft from race to race is also no mean feat. Without for a moment wishing to minimize the relative merits of past drivers who have qualified for this award, it must be said that it certainly helps either to have the financial wherewithal to meet these expenses oneself or the good fortune to find a sponsor.

It is conceivable that powerboat racing will in time become a battle between big companies, in an effort to improve their products and gain the publicity which successful racing brings, rather than between individuals or small concerns. This has already happened with motor cars, and powerboats will undoubtedly follow suit the day boats become big business.

As I mentioned earlier, the first racing powerboats were almost always hotted up versions of production boats. Nowadays, on the contrary, they are generally specially designed and prepared craft—a precaution which is necessary if any real measure of success is wanted. I feel I cannot do better here than quote some comments by the American racing pilot and boat builder, Carl Moesly, who is also a foremost authority on offshore racing:

"Years ago, stock boats were used for ocean racing, eventually being modified above the water line and strengthened on the bottom. Competition no longer permits the use of boats designed for a cruising speed of 30 m.p.h. and a low planing speed. There can be no compromises in design for average use. This must be a 'Racing Machine', every pound of weight counts. Every design facet is judged by its contribution to winning. This is the sole governing factor. A high deadrise is required for high speed operation in rough water; forget the lateral stability requirements of the family boat. A fine entry is needed forward for wave shock absorbtion; forget manoeuvrability for the ski boat enthusiast. Get the props down deep so they will bite while the hull is air-borne; forget about the shallow water fisherman. Lower the freeboard to a minimum, lose the weight and air resistance; forget the size of the waves. You are supposed to be flying over them or through the tops. Just deck her over!"

It would not be far wrong to say that we have just turned the first page in offshore powerboat racing; we have passed those initial days, which could be compared with motorcar racing at the turn of the century when keen and often wealthy sportsmen, sitting bolt upright at the wheel in soft caps and goggles, achieved what for them no doubt were hairraising speeds in their monumental vehicles with wooden-spoked wheels and leather-strapped bonnets. Fatal accidents, too, were rare and the same fortunately still applies to offshore powerboat racing.

It is not, however, hard to predict that in the years to come we shall find ourselves in the same situation as motorcar racing today, when speeds will have increased considerably and the racing craft will be the product of a stable with highly-paid skilled drivers forming part of a professional team. There will then no longer be any doubt as to the need for intensively trained pilots with flash-point reflexes and a thorough understanding of the sea.

Tomorrow we will be facing the same problem with our powerboats as the racing car drivers do today, when the smallest error can result in fatal disaster. We may wish that we could avoid arriving at this point, but it will be an inevitable state of affairs if racing is to continue—the quest for speed will see to that.

The Class I and II boats which are described in the following pages are divided into two parts: A covers my early racing powerboats—pre-Delta, and B deals with those which came just afterwards—the Deltas.

A. *PRE DELTA* **'A SPERANZIELLA**

Length overall	— *30′ 0″ (m. 9.14)*	*Deadrise transom*	— *20°*
Length waterline	— *26′ 9″ (m. 8.16)*	*Weight*	— *5 tons*
Beam maximum	— *10′10″ (m. 3.30)*	*Engines*	— *Crusader, Maserati, Ford*
Beam chine	— *8′11″ (m. 2.72)*	*Speed*	— *43 knots*
Draught hull	— *2′ 2″ (m. 0.66)*		

I had been mulling over for some time the design of a really fast rough weather cabin cruiser, and had actually prepared the design of a boat around thirty feet. The hull of this craft had a pronounced dead-rise throughout. Later, when I heard of the first *Daily Express* Cowes-Torquay powerboat race, I thought that here was an excellent way of testing the validity of the design. *'A Speranziella* thus became the

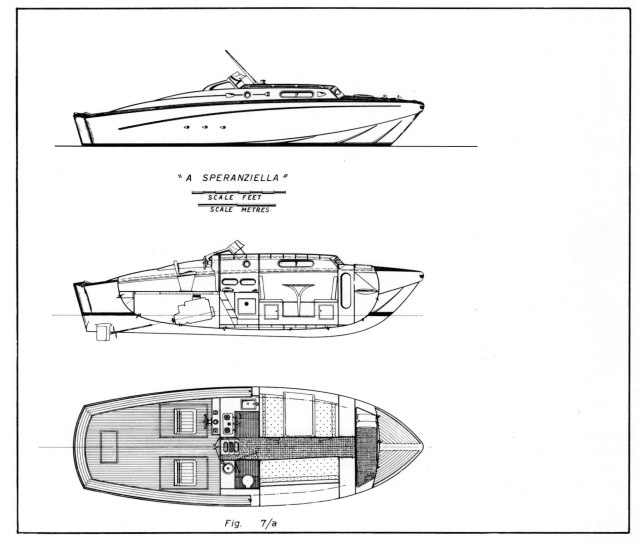

Fig. 7/a

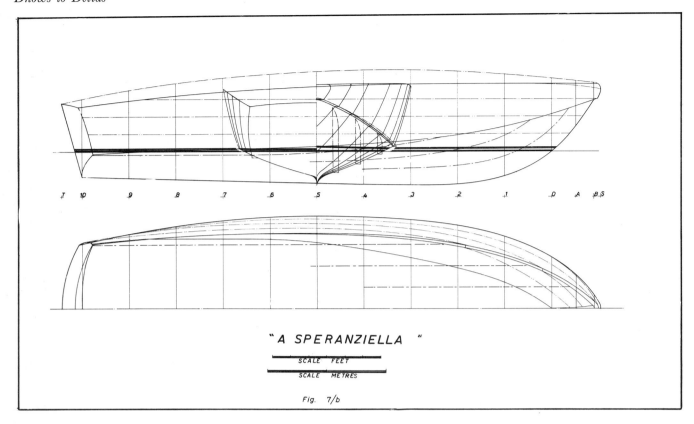

"'A SPERANZIELLA"

SCALE FEET

SCALE METRES

Fig. 7/b

first offshore racing powerboat I designed, although the original concept had been actually intended to serve as the prototype for a fast cabin cruiser which Navaltecnica intended to produce in a limited series for an exclusive type of customer.

'A Speranziella changed face many times between the original design and the craft which eventually won the *Daily Express* race in 1963. Many structural modifications were carried out during those intervening years in the light of experience gained in the numerous races in which she took part. Various engine installations were also tried: first, Crusaders (a marinized version of the Cadillac engine), then fuel-injection Maseratis, and finally Ford Interceptors. 'A Speranziella won races with all three engines, but her greatest victory (the 1963 Cowes-Torquay) was with the Interceptors.

I think I learned more about the problems of these fast offshore powerboats from 'A Speranziella than I did from any other boat. Apart from the fact that the boat was mine, I lived with her night and day; she was never far from my thoughts, and I can still remember all the technical details which had to be settled at every stage of her development. At that time we were all new to the game and what seems obvious now had to be learned the hard way.

I was striving after something new and different. I wished to produce a purposeful, good-looking boat which would be capable of negotiating rough seas at high speed with a reasonable degree of comfort. It is no secret that a fast boat must be light, but it must also be strong. I studied all sorts of ways, therefore, to lighten the structure while at the same time making it strong enough to cope with the stresses to which it would be subjected, and eventually came to the conclusion that a laminated-wood construction would be the best answer.

I had already built several boats with this method in our yard in India, and although Navaltecnica had no experience of this type of construction, they were builders of wooden craft using traditional methods. I simplified the design as much as possible, owing to shortage of time; all the sections for the bottom, in fact, were of constant shape, thus eliminating many man hours in producing the mould. This is a system which I have adopted ever since.

The bottom of the hull was laminated in four layers of mahogany, each 5 mm thick, producing a total of

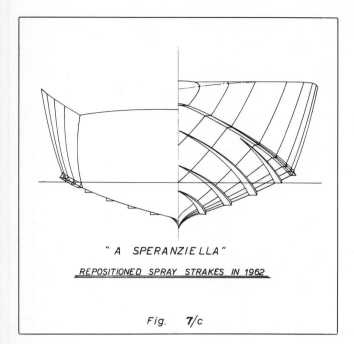

" A SPERANZIELLA "

REPOSITIONED SPRAY STRAKES IN 1962

Fig. 7/c

20 mm. There was a break at the chine with a flat chine member 3″ × 1″, also of mahogany. The topsides were laminated in three layers of mahogany, with a total thickness of 15 mm. The bottom and the topsides were framed longitudinally with $2\frac{1}{2}″ \times 1\frac{1}{4}″$ framing; three of these were placed on either side on the bottom, and two per side on the topsides. All these frames were of Sitka spruce.

I wanted to keep the deck and superstructure as light as possible and therefore used $\frac{1}{4}″$ marine plywood for both deck and cabin top, and $\frac{3}{8}″$ marine plywood for the cabin sides. The bulkheads were

made of two $\frac{1}{8}″$ marine plywood external layers with a foam inner core; this was a big error for the weight saved was not worth the risk incurred. No doubt even this would have worked out all right if the various plywood panels had been scarfed where joints were necessary and not just butted together.

In my opinion, an interesting point in the structure of '*A Speranziella* was the system I adopted for the keel and hog and for the chine forward. Details of this can be seen in the drawings of this craft.

I devoted particular attention to the question of the propellers. After lengthy calculations as to the best gear ratio to adopt and the most suitable propellers to install, I wrote for further advice to some of the leading propeller manufacturers in Europe and America. I asked them two questions: which gear ratio did they consider to be the best (we had a choice of 2:1, 1·5:1, or direct drive), and what propeller did they recommend for the gear ratio selected. The replies were very varied. Some suggested direct drive on the grounds that the smaller diameter would reduce appendage drag (smaller shafts, etc.) and would also lessen the stern's tendency to lift. This solution was the lightest. Others suggested the higher reduction gear, i.e. 2:1, since this would reduce the tendency to cavitation. There were all kinds of reasons given for adopting intermediate gear ratios, but eventually I settled on a 1·5:1 reduction gear as the various calculations and conclusions I had made seemed to favour this.

I had accompanied my propeller enquiries with a rough sketch of the lines of '*A Speranziella* and was more than somewhat crestfallen when one famous manufacturer commented in his reply: "I never saw any boat with the deep vee aft that worked efficiently

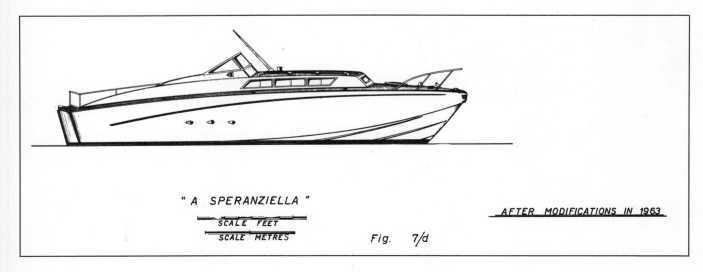

" A SPERANZIELLA "

SCALE FEET

SCALE METRES

Fig. 7/d

AFTER MODIFICATIONS IN 1963

or was any good for racing. Several have been much faster after the flattening at the transom. Also the bow is not very graceful or easy to drive in rough water. It looks like a 1920 model from stem to stern".

Looking at '*A Speranziella*'s lines now I am inclined to agree with him. Nevertheless, when she made her début at Cowes that summer of 1961 she attracted a lot of attention, and even though we did not win we made the front page of the *Sunday Express* next day with a photograph as large as life captioned: "Airborne! A boat starts to fly". Some of the finest photographs ever taken of '*A Speranziella* were taken that day off St. Catherine's when we took the lead in this her first race.

In all fairness to '*A Speranziella* it should be said that there had not been enough time to put her through her paces before the actual race. She had been launched by my wife, Ann, on her birthday, July 23rd, which left less than a month for trials as well as for the long train journey to Calais and the Channel crossing under her own power to Cowes.

When we joined the boat at Calais there was a gale blowing in the North Sea, and we had to hang around several days before being able to leave. As can be easily imagined, those days of suspense were nerve-racking, and most of the time we sat in the cockpit waiting for the weather to improve and not knowing what to do with ourselves. One afternoon a tall figure stopped on the quayside, looked down into the cockpit, and began to describe various details of the boat in English to a young man who appeared to be his son. At this point I joined the conversation and, on being asked if the craft were made of glass-fibre, replied rather generally that the hull was cold moulded before going on to describe in elementary language and in considerable detail the whole method of construction. My audience listened with great politeness and interest and it was only later, when I went on board their yacht for a drink, that I realized that I had been lecturing a "Maestro". In fact, the tall man was Peter Du Cane. After this perhaps rather inauspicious beginning (which I may say he never held against me) we have become good friends and colleagues over the years, and on countless

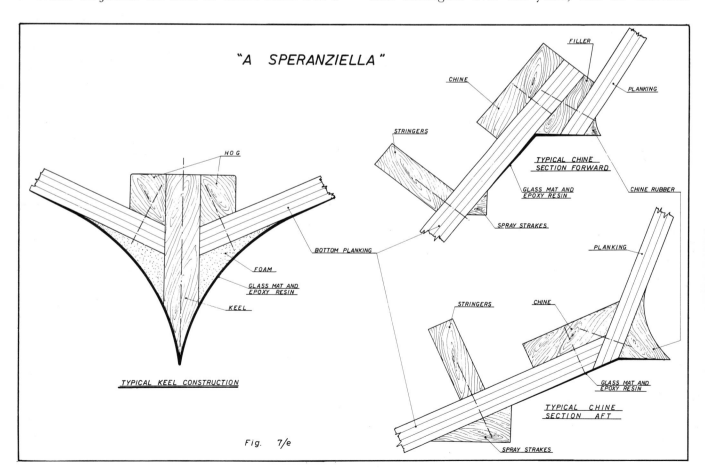

"A SPERANZIELLA"

HOG

FOAM

GLASS MAT AND EPOXY RESIN

KEEL

TYPICAL KEEL CONSTRUCTION

FILLER

CHINE

PLANKING

STRINGERS

TYPICAL CHINE SECTION FORWARD

GLASS MAT AND EPOXY RESIN

CHINE RUBBER

SPRAY STRAKES

BOTTOM PLANKING

PLANKING

STRINGERS

CHINE

GLASS MAT AND EPOXY RESIN

TYPICAL CHINE SECTION AFT

SPRAY STRAKES

Fig. 7/e

occasions I have been more than grateful to him for much invaluable advice.

I have already dealt with the many structural failures which '*A Speranziella* suffered in that first race (cf. Chap. II), but we also ran into an interesting problem with the propellers. We were using 17″ diameter × 18″ pitch cupped nickel bronze racing propellers and after only forty hours' service they were already completely useless, being pitted all over in the classic radial pattern both on the face and on the back of the blades. I wrote to the manufacturers asking them whether they had any explanation for this phenomenon; they replied that they were definitely cavitation burns, probably due either to the propellers being overloaded or to a common type of cavitation caused by a stream of bubbles reaching the propellers from some strut or obstruction ahead of them.

I had taken the *Daily Express* rules too literally when it came to the question of the underwater hull, where no longitudinal or transverse steps were permitted, and had chopped the risers very far forward. I learned later that this was not necessary and the risers were therefore replaced with new full-length ones extending right aft. Their position was also altered. The accompanying lines drawing shows how these strakes were placed both before and afterwards. The underwater hull was not modified in any other way.

Upon trials the new 17″ × 18″ propellers proved far too light, and we were able to increase the pitch 1″ with a gain in speed of some two knots; the phenomenon of cavitation burns disappeared completely and never recurred, even though the boat ran for many hundreds of miles in sometimes heavily loaded conditions, particularly when driven under her own power to various races.

This was the first clear indication I had that underwater risers needed careful positioning and that they played an appreciable part in the question of the speed of the boat.

'*A Speranziella* was never a fast boat, as can be seen from the following data of her three different engine installations:

1. *Crusader Engines* — 390 cu. in.
   - H.P. — 300 each
   - R.P.M. — 4400
   - Reduction gear — 1·52 : 1
   - Prop R.P.M. — 2900
   - Props original fitted — 17″ D × 18″ P
     - Speed — 36 knots
   - Props after changing strakes — 17″ D × 19″ P
     - Speed — 38 knots

2. *Maserati Engines* (fuel injection) — 5 litre
   - H.P. — 330 each
   - R.P.M. — 5500
   - Reduction gear (port) — 2·1 : 1
   - Reduction gear (starb.) — 1·9 : 1
   - Prop R.P.M. (port) — 2620
   - Prop R.P.M. (starb.) — 2900
   - Prop (port) — 17″ D × 22″ P
   - Prop (starb.) — 17″ D × 20″ P
   - Speed — 38 knots

3. *Ford Interceptor Engines* — 427 cu. in.
   - H.P. — 400 each
   - R.P.M. — 4800
   - Reduction gear — 1·52 : 1
   - Prop R.P.M. — 3150
   - Props — 17″ D × 22″ P
   - Speed — 43 knots

The fuel injection Maserati engines were specially prepared in their marinized version for '*A Speranziella*. The reason for the two different gear ratios was that both these engines had the same rotation and, since we wanted handed propellers, the rotation was changed in the reduction gear. I thought that the Maseratis deserved a better chance than they got in '*A Speranziella* but, as always, time was running out for further trials and the more powerful new Ford Interceptors were already in the yard waiting to be installed for the next race.

There were many reasons why '*A Speranziella* was not a particularly fast boat, although she was as comfortable at speed in a chop as any craft I tried at that time. I did not adopt any trim changing devices on her (no flaps or ballast tanks), and consequently her centre of gravity was far forward; it was in fact slightly aft of Section 5 in her original form with three aft and two forward fuel tanks. As a result, there was a lot of boat in the water even at high speed.

By today's standards she was a heavy boat for her length. I suspect that her stern gear also offered quite a lot of appendage drag, and the shaft angle of 12° could have been reduced. At that time I felt that propellers placed well under the hull would work more efficiently.

The cockpit was protected by a Venturi type deflector which was quite effective when the boat was going fast, but the high pressure air out of the Venturi was not sufficiently strong to deflect any heavy spray. We therefore fitted a normal windshield when we did the last face-lift on '*A Speranziella* with a new cabin. The accompanying drawings show these particulars.

See Figs. 7/a, 7/b, 7/c, 7/d, 7/e.

TRIDENT

Length overall	— *23′0″ (m. 7.01)*	*Deadrise transom*	— *25°*
Length waterline	— *19′0″ (m. 5.80)*	*Weight*	— *2.2 tons*
Beam maximum	— *8′11″ (m. 2.72)*	*Engines*	— *Twin Volvo Penta Aquamatic 240*
Beam chine	— *7′4″ (m. 2.24)*		*HP*
Draught hull	— *1′½″ (m. 0.47)*	*Speed*	— *35 knots*

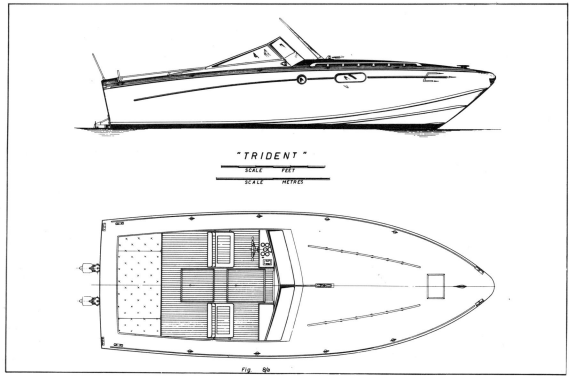

"TRIDENT"

SCALE   FEET

SCALE   METRES

Fig. 8/a

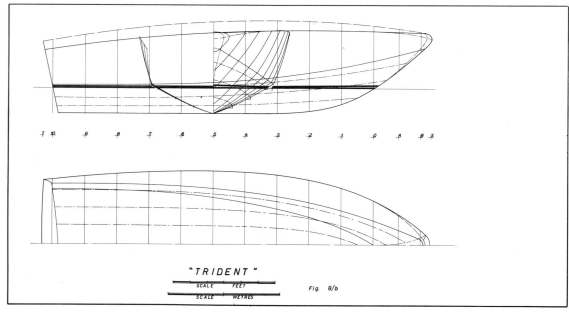

"TRIDENT"

SCALE   FEET

SCALE   METRES

Fig. 8/b

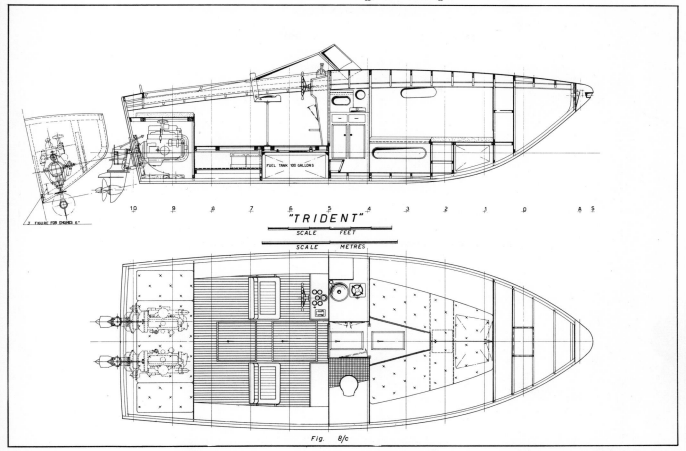

"TRIDENT"

SCALE   FEET

SCALE   METRES

Fig. 8/c

I prepared this design for Don Shead at the end of 1961. The prototype was built by R. & W. Clark of Cowes, and was subsequently followed by many other Tridents. Some were also moulded in glass reinforced plastics by Tyler of Tonbridge (supporting a small cabin top), but the boats built by Clark's were of laminated construction and flush-decked.

Briefly the scantlings were as follows:
Hull shell: three skins of $\frac{3}{16}''$ mahogany laid diagonally; decks: two layers of $\frac{1}{4}''$ marine plywood; gunnels: spruce, $2\frac{3}{4}''$ by $\frac{7}{8}''$; hull longitudinal stringers: afzalia, $2\frac{3}{4}''$ by $1\frac{1}{16}''$; upper stringers: afzalia, $2\frac{1}{2}''$ by $1\frac{1}{16}''$; deck beams: laminated spruce, $2\frac{3}{4}''$ by $\frac{7}{8}''$; transom: marine plywood, $1\frac{1}{4}''$ thick, reinforced in way of the outdrive mounting plates; stem and keel: laminated mahogany, the former $4''$ by $3\frac{1}{2}''$ and the latter $3\frac{1}{2}''$ by $3\frac{5}{8}''$.

Three Volvo Aquamatics were fitted on *Trident* for her first race (Cowes-Torquay, 1962), from which she had to retire early on owing to hull damage, as I have already mentioned in an earlier chapter. I was not altogether happy with Don's decision to mount three engines on the boat, since I felt that she would be trimmed too much by the stern and, consequently, would not be very comfortable in rough going. Anyway, after this first race Don removed one of the engines and *Trident* was as a result very much more pleasant to handle. It is interesting to note that the difference in speed between the twin and triple engine installations was only $2\frac{1}{2}$ knots (35 knots with two engines, and $37\frac{1}{2}$ knots with three) for an additional 120 or so HP. This can of course be explained by the extra weight of the third engine, and also by the greater appendage drag of the supplementary underwater unit.

Trident won her class in the 1963 Cowes-Torquay event, and has had many other successes since.

I was particularly pleased with *Trident* as a boat, for she appeared to me to be the ideal small, nippy craft for fast cruising; Don in fact on many occasions popped across the Channel in her for lunch in France. I think that it is also true to say that she influenced quite a few designers, since many boats resembling her general configuration were produced both in Europe and in the United States of America.

See Figs. 8/a, 8/b, 8/c.

SETTIMO VELO S

Length overall	— 24′0″ (m. 7.31)	*Deadrise transom*	— 30°
Length waterline	— 20′0″ (m. 6.10)	*Weight*	— 2.8 tons
Beam maximum	— 8′11″ (m. 2.72)	*Engines*	— Twin MerCruisers, with outdrives,
Beam chine	— 7′4″ (m. 2.24)		450 HP
Draught hull	— 1′8½″ (m. 0.52)	*Speed*	— 40 knots

For a detailed description of this boat see Chapter III.

The military version of *Settimo Velo* can be found in Chapter VIII, II Work Boats.

See Figs. 9/a, 9/b, 9/c.

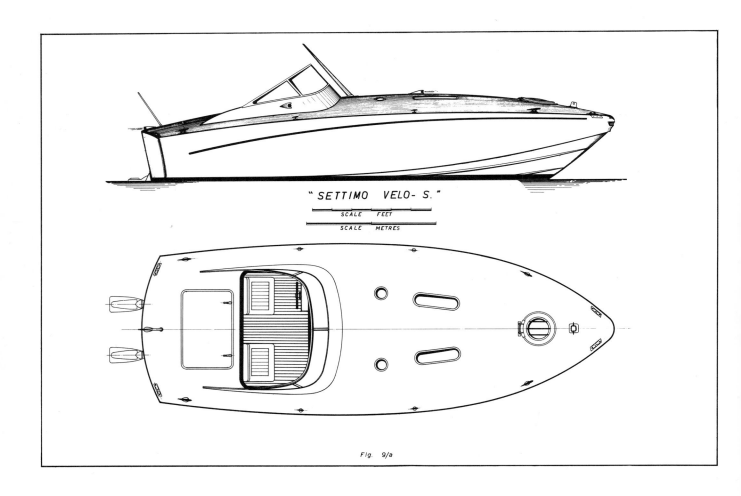

"SETTIMO VELO-S."

SCALE FEET
SCALE METRES

Fig. 9/a

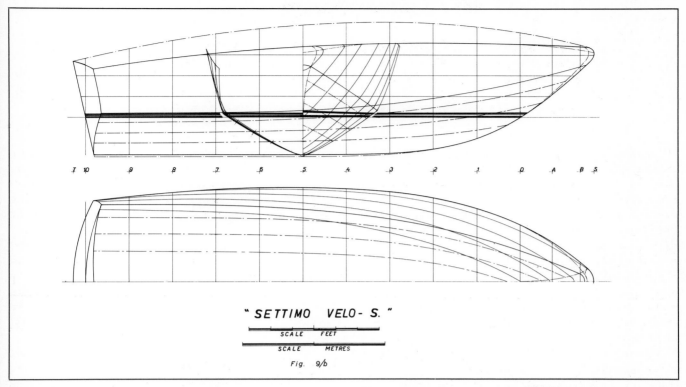

" SETTIMO VELO- S. "

SCALE   FEET

SCALE   METRES

Fig. 9/b

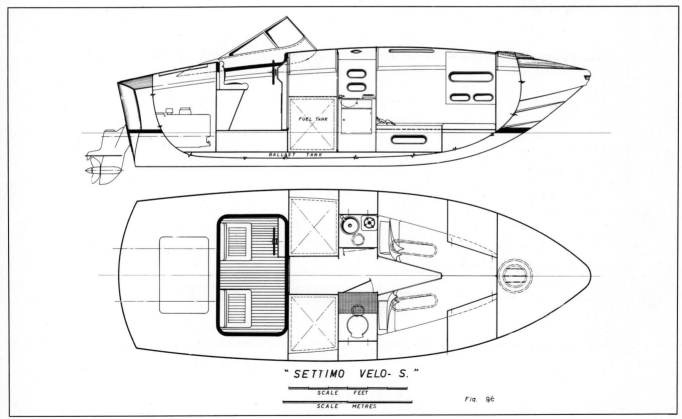

FUEL TANK

BALLAST TANK

" SETTIMO VELO- S. "

SCALE   FEET

SCALE   METRES

Fig. 9/c

ULTIMA DEA

Length overall	—	*36′ 0″ (m. 10.79)*
Length waterline	—	*32′ 2″ (m. 9.80)*
Beam maximum	—	*12′ 6″ (m. 3.81)*
Beam chine	—	*10′ 4″ (m. 3.15)*
Draught hull	—	*1′ 10″ (m. 0.56)*

Deadrise transom	— *22°*
Weight	— *7 tons*
Engines	— *Triple 5.4 litre Maserati 1290 HP*
Speed	— *46 knots*

Ultima Dea was a good boat for her day. She was very comfortable and certainly very strong. On the negative side, the mechanical installation was possibly too complicated to be trouble-free. There was a vast amount of piping since the heat exchangers and the oil tanks were detached from the engines; each shaft line had a thrust bearing which had to be cooled. The exhaust pipes were about the most complicated I have ever been associated with; it took two highly qualified metal beaters about a month to make them. They were tuned exhausts following a very precise drawing and all were water-jacketed.

When the water-jackets were full of water these exhausts were understandably very heavy, and as a consequence we had to resort to solid mounts, al-although Giulio Alfieri (Maserati's Chief Engineer) wanted to fit the engines on flexible mountings. This in turn presented other problems, since the blocks of these engines were of special light alloy and there was a danger that the mounting studs might pull out of the blocks. A steel cage had, therefore, to be prepared which was then secured to the engine by means of the sump bolts as well as by those for the normal legs.

For the earlier trials we had to start the engine on soft sparking plugs, warm them up, and then switch over to the hard racing ones. This was an operation which required quite a lot of time as there were forty-eight plugs to change. Fortunately we eventually managed to find another type of sparking plug which did not require changing, but we had to be very careful not to run the engines too slowly for any length of time (such as on leaving or entering port) as these plugs had a tendency to oil up. It was all quite a party.

The Maserati engines were, however, a beautiful piece of engineering work and certainly put out an enormous amount of power for their capacity, giving over 430 HP for 5.4 litres.

The hull of *Ultima Dea* was of laminated mahogany. Inside I had placed longitudinal stringers of spruce, so as to reinforce the bottom; these stringers coincided with the outer spray strakes and, apart from being glued to the hull, were bolted through to these strakes with specially made stainless steel bolts. I felt that in this way there was no risk of either the spray strakes or the inner stringers coming adrift, but evidently the bolt-holes through the outer strakes (bolt diameter: 5 mm) created a weakness as we found that the strakes were cracking right across where the bolts were placed. After this experience I never used any type of fastening on spray strakes other than gluing. See Figs. 10/a, 10/b, 10/c.

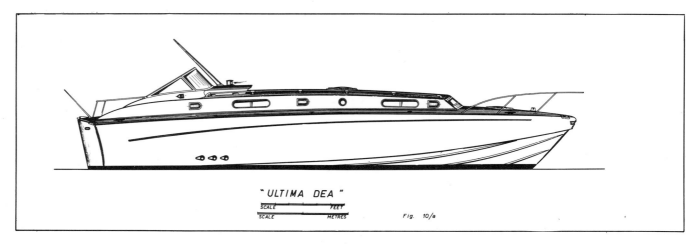

"ULTIMA DEA"

SCALE FEET
SCALE METRES

Fig. 10/a

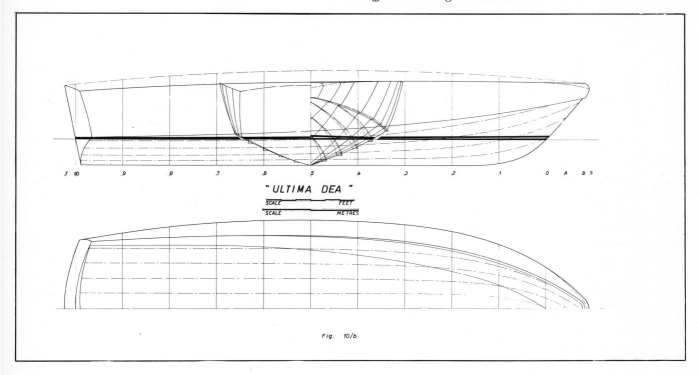

I 10   9   8   7   6   5   4   3   2   1   0   A   B S

" ULTIMA DEA "

SCALE   FEET
SCALE   METRES

Fig. 10/b

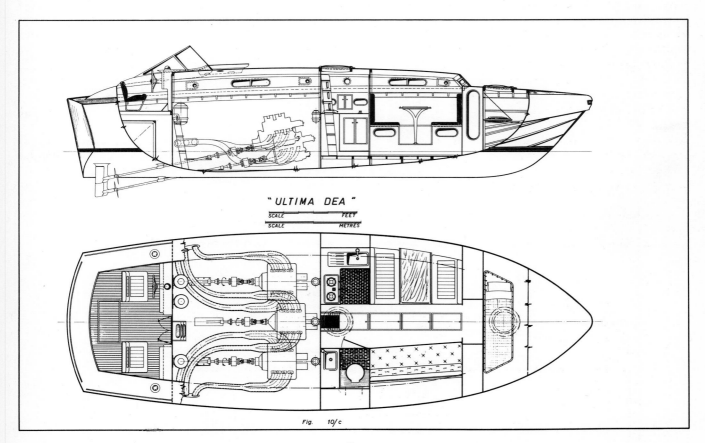

" ULTIMA DEA "

SCALE   FEET
SCALE   METRES

Fig. 10/c

F

LEVI 27 CORSAIR

Length overall	— 27'0" (m. 8.23)		Deadrise transom	— 23°
Length waterline	— 23'0" (m. 7.01)		Weight	— 3 tons
Beam maximum	— 9'0" (m. 2.74)		Engines	— Twin Volvo Penta Aquamatic
Beam chine	— 7'4" (m. 2.24)			300 HP
Draught hull	— 1'7" (m. 0.48)		Speed	— 33 knots

The Levi 27 was not designed purely as a racing boat, but as a fast, comfortable, family cruiser which could also be used for occasional racing. In the event, quite a few of the early boats produced by Thomas Wilks of Viking Marine and by David Cheverton took part in the Cowes-Torquay races.

I designed this boat towards the end of 1963 for Cheverton-Viking. The prototype, *Inertia*, was built of laminated wood for Bert Shead, Don's father. She also served as a plug for the mould for subsequent craft, which were produced by Viking Marine of Gosport; these later boats were built of glass reinforced plastics using the spray method of construction. The internal joinery work, on the other hand, was of wood and was done by David Cheverton, who was also responsible for the finish of the boats.

In my opinion the Levi 27 was an outstandingly good-looking boat, a personal verdict which was confirmed when Farrant Gillham's *Corsair* won the Cowes-Torquay Concours d'Elegance on two occasions. Incidentally, she also won the production class in the 1966 Wills International.

See Figs. 11/a, 11/b, 11/c.

An out-and-out racing craft was also produced by Viking Marine for the partnership John Dalton/Don Shead, called *Alto Volante*. The hull of this boat was identical to that of the production *Corsair*, but a special deck mould was made with a very low, practically non-existent cabin top.

Alto Volante was powered with a pair of Ford Interceptor 427 cu. in. engines with special high risers. These engines were fitted aft driving two-bladed steel propellers through V-drives. She was very fast for her day, although she never had any success in the various races she took part in, mainly owing to mechanical troubles.

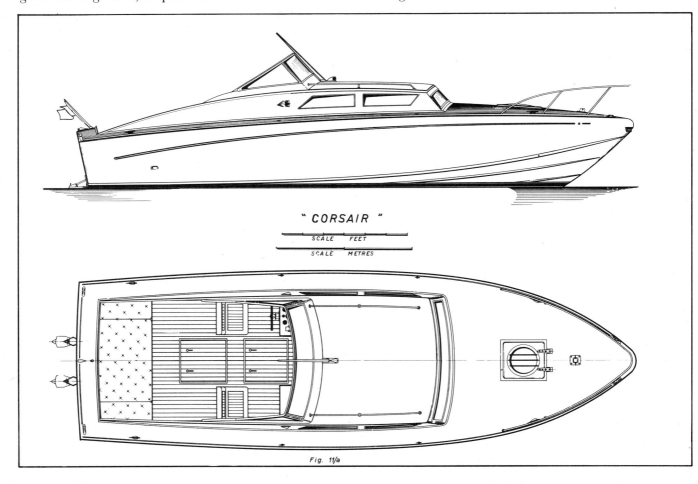

"CORSAIR"

SCALE FEET

SCALE METRES

Fig. 11/a

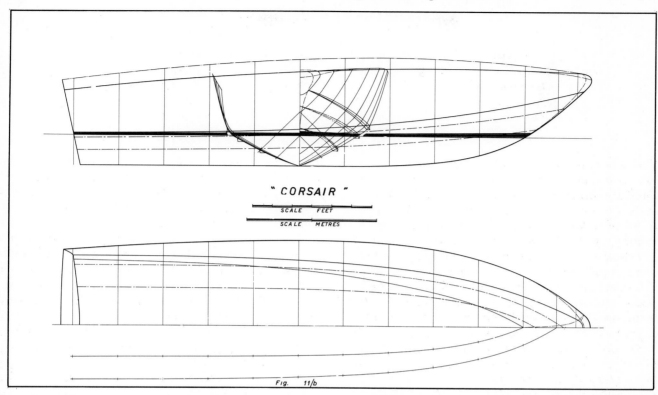

" CORSAIR "

SCALE FEET

SCALE METRES

Fig. 11/b

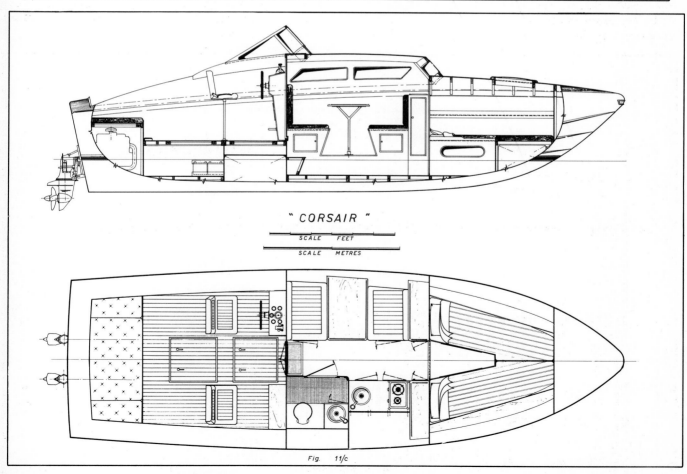

" CORSAIR "

SCALE FEET

SCALE METRES

Fig. 11/c

SPERANZELLA SECONDA

Length overall	—	*32′ 0″*	*(m. 9.75)*
Length waterline	—	*27′ 6″*	*(m. 8.38)*
Beam maximum	—	*10′ 6″*	*(m. 3.20)*
Beam chine	—	*8′ 8″*	*(m. 2.64)*
Draught hull	—	*1′ 10¾″*	*(m. 0.58)*

Deadrise transom	—	*25°*
Weight	—	*4·8 tons*
Engines	—	*Twin Interceptor, Holman &*
		Moody, 800 HP
Speed	—	*46 knots*

Speranzella Seconda was the last "pre Delta" racing boat I designed, She was also one of the most pleasant boats I raced in, after transom flaps were fitted.

Speranzella Seconda was a development of *'A Speranziella* being longer, lower, and generally cleaned up, and having more deadrise. Appearance-wise she was rather a distinctive-looking boat.

Her first race was at Cowes in 1964 (racing under number "One"). We were very well placed in that first race, running quite happily amongst the leaders (*Surfrider, Lucky Moppie, Jackie S*), when suddenly oil flew out from the engine hatches. We had burst a high-pressure oil pipe. This pipe was chafing on the engine bearer and I do not know how we had not noticed it before.

We had trouble again in the 1965 Viareggio-Bastia race, with a sick engine for the latter half of the race which forced me to throttle back rather abruptly as soon as I could after crossing the finishing line in second place, a short way behind *Lucky Moppie*. Immediately after throttling back I felt the boat

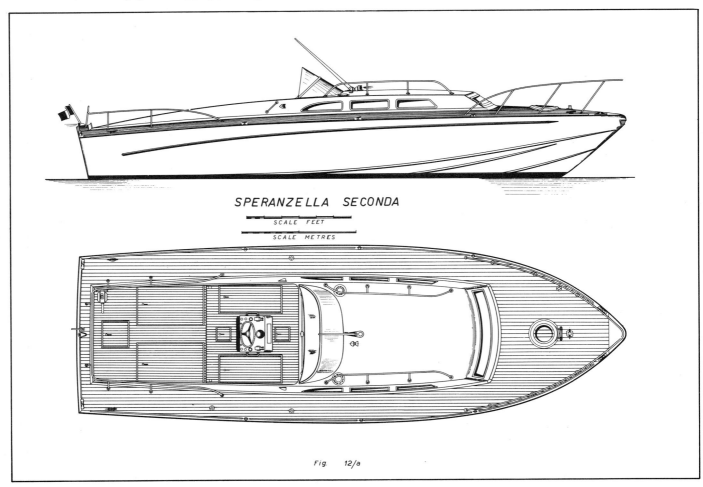

SPERANZELLA SECONDA

SCALE FEET

SCALE METRES

Fig. 12/a

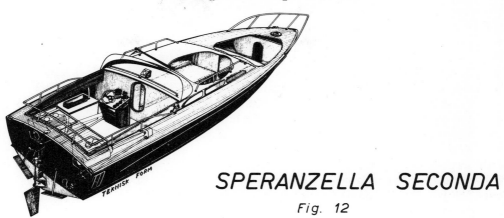

SPERANZELLA SECONDA

Fig. 12

steering very awkwardly, but it was not till a few minutes later we realized that water was gushing in through the stern tube; we had lost a propeller shaft complete with propeller. Some Corsican divers found it later that afternoon, to my surprise as I had felt it was like looking for a needle in a haystack. I was not even sure at what moment we had lost it, though clearly it must have been somewhere over the finishing line after my sudden throttling back. When spotted it was 120 feet down in deep mud, luckily clearly visible since the shaft had the propeller still on it and it stood up like a palm tree.

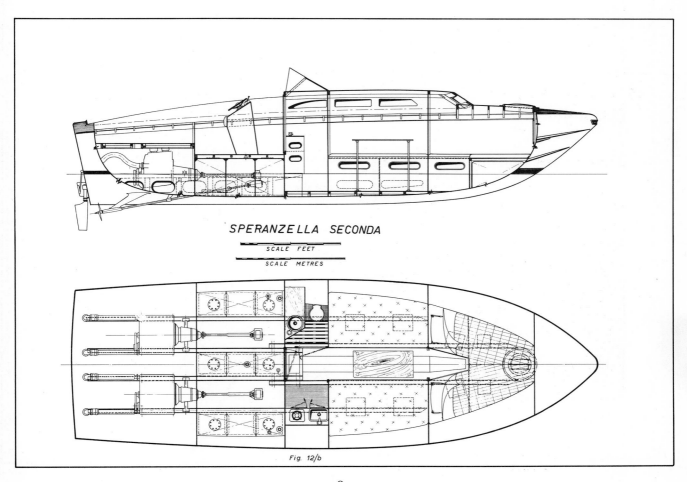

SPERANZELLA SECONDA

SCALE FEET

SCALE METRES

Fig. 12/b

We were therefore able to race again next day, on the return leg to Viareggio, but shortly after the start our sick engine finally died on us in clouds of smoke.

In spite of these initial disappointments, *Speranzella Seconda* proved a reasonably fast boat and took part in many international events, including a Miami-Nassau where she was placed 4th in the hands of Attilio Petroni and Vincenzo Balestrieri. Her engines were changed for this race to a pair of 427 cu. in. Holman and Moodys.

We took a pair of retractable rudders with us to Miami, but we did not have time to try them out in Italy before leaving. These retractable rudders consisted of shallow boxes of stainless steel housing blades which could be raised or lowered, rather like a centreboard, by turning a shaft in a tubular stock. The idea was to reduce rudder drag by raising the blade when the boat was running straight and by lowering it before applying helm for a turn.

I tried these rudders before the race and was running along the measured mile in Miami parallel to Biscayne Boulevard, with the rudder blades retracted, when the wash of a passing boat suddenly upset the balance of *Speranzella Seconda*. She veered violently and we narrowly missed finishing up on the boulevard itself, where no doubt we would have been handed a speeding ticket as we were going quite a lick at the time. Needless to say the idea of retractable rudders was dropped after this experience.

Many fast cabin cruisers were subsequently built around this hull, which at that time was possibly the fastest production cabin cruiser in the world. The standard boat was fitted with a pair of 427 cu. in. Interceptor engines on a straight through shaft, which gave a speed of over 42 knots. The original racing boat was sold a few years later to Count Walter Pasquini, who had her converted into a very comfortable cabin cruiser with a hard top over the steering position. I still see her occasionally during the summer in various Italian west coast ports.

See Figs. 12, 12/a, 12/b, 12/c, 12/d, 12/e.

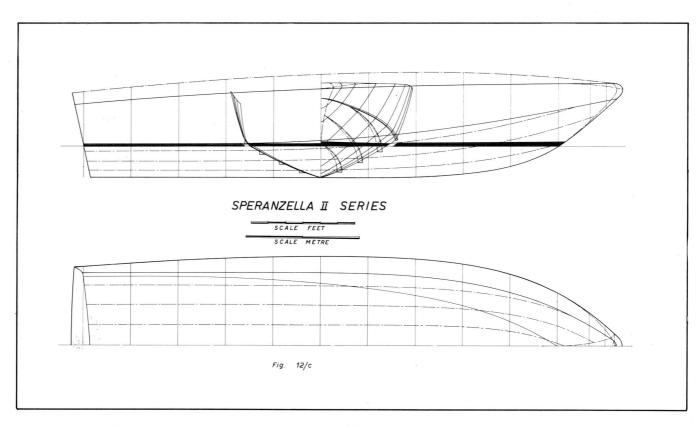

SPERANZELLA II SERIES

SCALE FEET

SCALE METRE

Fig. 12/c

SPERANZELLA II SERIES (Cabin Cruiser)

SCALE FEET

SCALE METRES

.Fig. 12/d

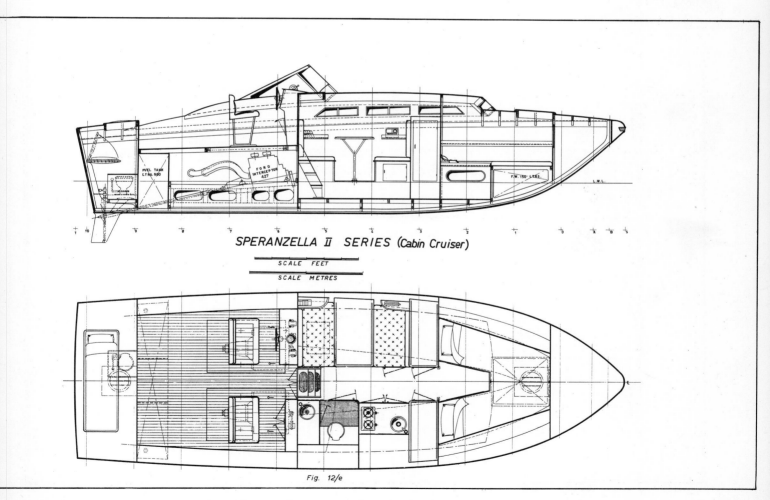

SPERANZELLA II SERIES (Cabin Cruiser)

SCALE FEET

SCALE METRES

Fig. 12/e

Length overall	— *36' 0"* *(m. 10.97)*	*Deadrise transom*	— *25°*
Length waterline	— *31' 6"* *(m. 9.60)*	*Weight*	— *4 tons*
Beam maximum	— *10' 3½"* *(m. 3.14)*	*Engines*	— *Twin Daytona 1050 HP*
Beam chine	— *8' 0"* *(m. 2.43)*	*Speed*	— *58 knots*
Draught hull	— *1' 10¾"* *(m. 0.58)*		

Surfury was designed to what are now known as the Class C 1 rules. When I started on these drawings early in 1965, open class boats were not permitted to race in Europe, and for that reason we had to allow for a six foot headroom in the cabin. I modelled the lines of *Surfury* around this height dimension, keeping in mind that I was aiming at the cleanest possible shape in order to reduce air resistance to the minimum. The cabin top was, therefore, almost semi-circular in shape when seen in cross-section and very heavily sloped in front where it met the deck.

In the first design I prepared I had a continuous reverse sheer from stem to stern, but in the final design Charles Gardner agreed to my cutting away that portion of the deck aft which ran over the tanks since this permitted quite a substantial reduction in weight. The side decks aft were in fact the top of the tanks.

Charles Gardner wanted the design to be based on an installation involving a pair of Daytona engines fitted in tandem. I had never previously designed a boat with a tandem arrangement, and as far as I know there were only two boats in existence at that time which had this sort of mechanical link-up (both of them in America). But this was a wise decision on Charles' part, certainly as far as speed was con-

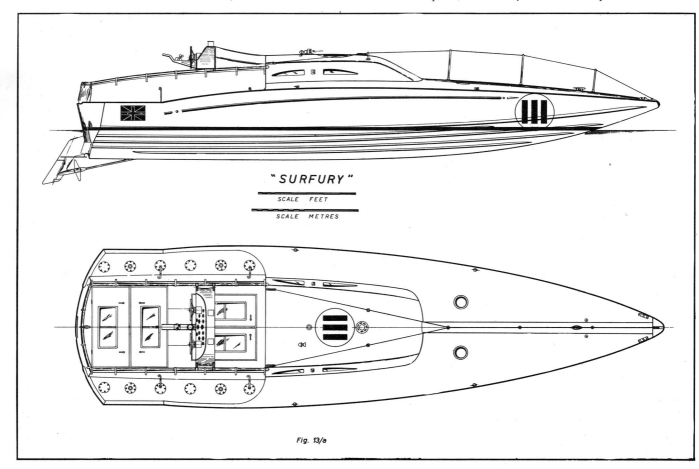

"*SURFURY*"

SCALE FEET

SCALE METRES

Fig. 13/a

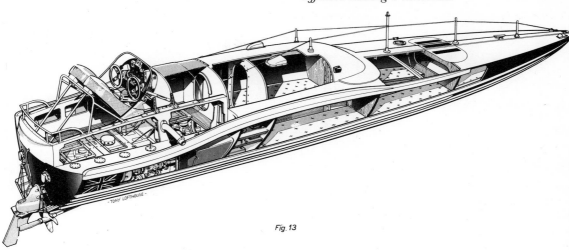

Fig. 13

cerned, since the reduction in appendage drag was equivalent to installing another 200 HP or so at the speeds we were contemplating.

Surfury had a cold moulded hull consisting of four $\frac{1}{4}$″ thicknesses of cedar laminates, with a total thickness of 1″. The hull shell was laminated right through from the keel rabbet to the sheer without any break at the chine. The cabin top moulding was also made in this way, having no break at the corner bars. The

longitudinals were of spruce, and the deck and internal joinery work of plywood. The complete specification is printed in the appendix for those who are interested in further details.

It is, I feel, worth mentioning here that the break in the sheer gave rise to a weakness which became apparent during a rough race in the United States. This weakness was due to the fact that the gunnel members were not continuous, although several

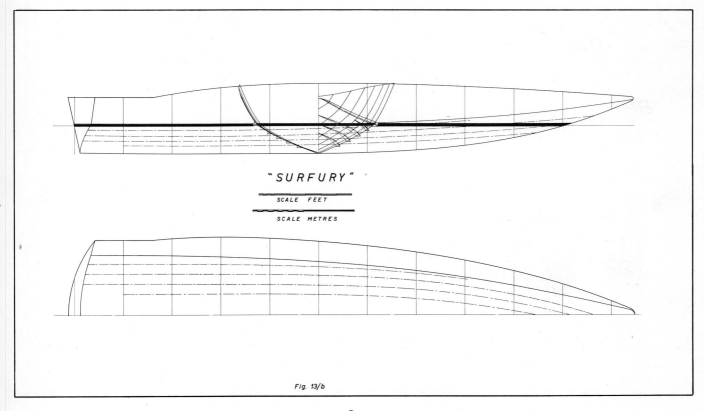

"*SURFURY*"

SCALE FEET

SCALE METRES

Fig. 13/b

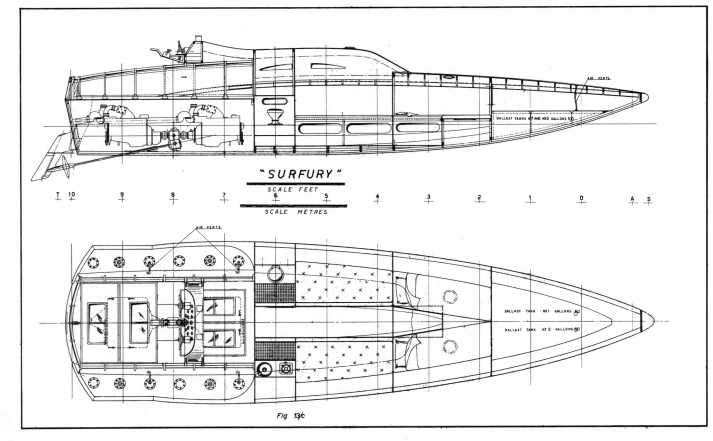

"SURFURY"

SCALE FEET

SCALE METRES

Fig 13/c

knees were located at the break with the object of tying up this longitudinal discontinuity. The defect was cured by applying an external gunnel which ran from the bows to the transom.

The design of *Surfury* was a particularly satisfying job for me since I had tried something new . . . and it had worked. She is also a successful boat, though

here a lot of the credit must go to Charles Gardner for the painstaking care he puts into preparing her for races, not to mention the driving skill of both himself and his brother Jimmy.

Many other boats followed this first example of the Delta line, but *Surfury* has always had a very special significance for me.

See Figs. 13, 13/a, 13/b, 13/c.

DELTA 28

Length overall	— *28′0″ (m. 8.53)*		*Deadrise transom*	— *26°*
Length waterline	— *22′8″ (m. 6.91)*		*Weight*	— *3 tons*
Beam maximum	— *9′0″ (m. 2.74)*		*Engines*	— *Twin Daytona 1050 HP*
Beam chine	— *7′0″ (m. 2.13)*		*Speed*	— *60 knots*
Draught hull	— *1′8″ (m. 0.51)*			

Delta 28 has already been mentioned at some length in Chapter V. She was built by Souter's and, like *Surfury*, was a laminated wooden hull, although in her case three inner laminates of obeche (wawa)

were used with an external laminate of cedar. The thickness of each laminate was $\frac{7}{32}''$, making a total thickness of $\frac{7}{8}''$. The deck was also cold moulded with four thicknesses of obeche, each $\frac{5}{32}''$ thick. All the longitudinal members were of spruce, including the keel and hog. She was powered with the same tandem arrangement Daytonas as *Surfury*.

Delta 28 was one ton or so lighter than her predecessor and her top speed was well over 60 knots. A somewhat laconic telegram arrived at my house in Lavinio after her first trials: "Early trials very satisfactory with speed not inferior to that of *Surfury*". I had been waiting on tenterhooks for the first results of trials, and although this telegram certainly allayed any anxiety I might have felt it did not, on the other hand, reveal any of the detailed information I had hoped for!

The main problem with this boat was that she was extremely difficult to control at high speed in any sort of chop; she would veer off unexpectedly and at the same time roll at an alarming angle.

Various changes were made to her rudder right from the beginning (she was launched with a standard Daytona zip strut like *Surfury*). Later the depth of the rudder was also extended and this did seem to improve matters. An air rudder was tried too, but did not give very convincing results; it was a clumsy appendage which was even a nuisance in certain conditions of sea and wind, acting rather like a small sail, and was therefore dispensed with. When the boat eventually changed hands, Charles Gardner did a lot of experimenting and managed to damp out a great deal of the directional instability by increasing the length of the flaps.

Charles had quite a successful season with *Delta 28* in 1967 after carrying out these modifications. Later he went a step further and lengthened the planing surfaces aft of the transom, changed the shaft angle, and moved the rudder right aft of the extension (where the flaps too were located). I understand that *Delta 28* was very much more manoeuvrable after these final modifications, as well as being a better sea boat; there was, however, some sacrifice in speed.

Analysing the causes of this directional instability, I came to the conclusion that two basic factors were:
(1) that *Delta 28* was too short for a tandem arrangement, which placed her centre of gravity too far forward;
(2) that, as she was very light, she felt the torque far more than *Surfury*, even though the engines were

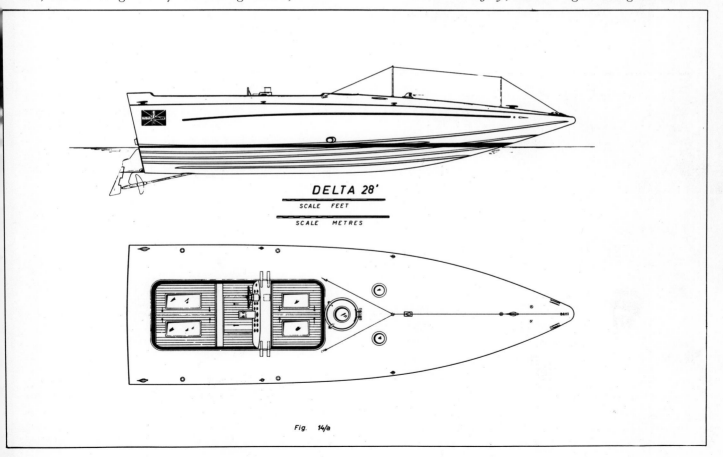

DELTA 28'

SCALE FEET

SCALE METRES

Fig. 14/a

DELTA 28'

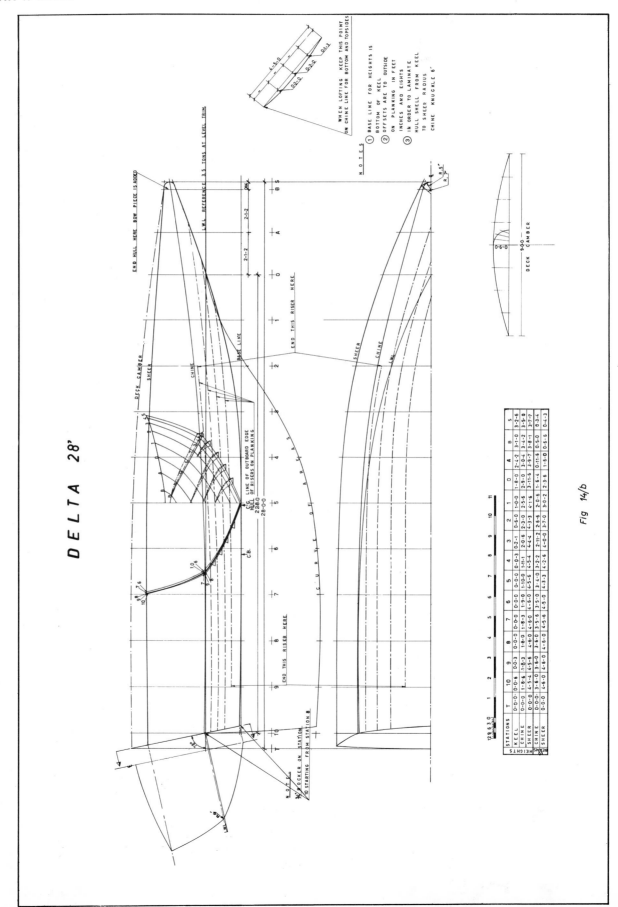

Fig 14/b

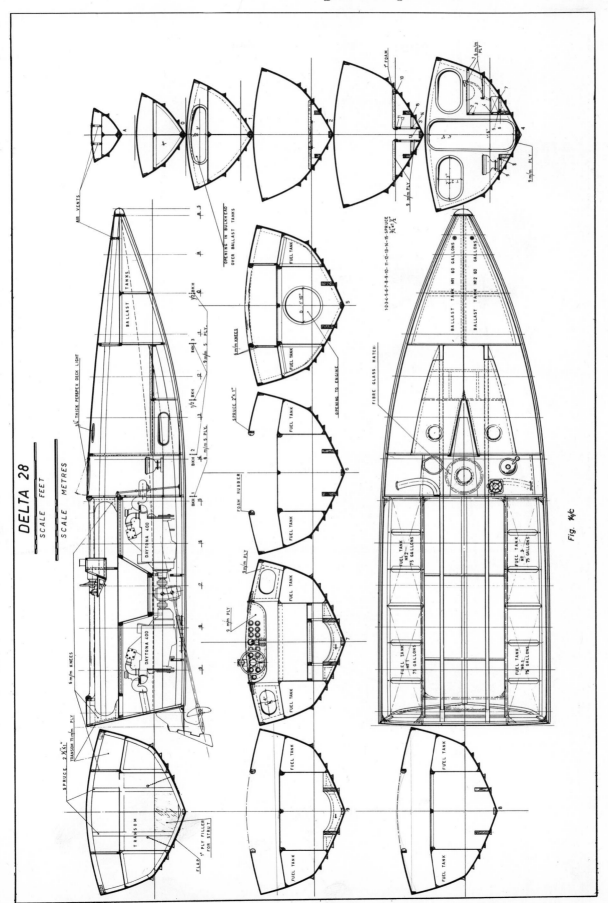

DELTA 28'

	STATIONS	T	10	9	8	7	6	5	4	3	2	1	0	A	B	S
HEIGHTS	KEEL	0-0-0	0-0-6	0-0-3	0-0-0	0-0-0	0-0-0	0-0-0	0-0-3	0-2-1	0-6-0	1-0-0	1-8-0	2-4-2	3-1-0	3-2-6
	CHINE	0-0-0	1-8-6	1-8-3	1-8-0	1-8-3	1-9-0	1-10-0	1-11-1	2-0-6	2-3-0	2-5-6	2-9-0	3-0-4	3-4-2	3-5-0
	SHEER	0-0-0	4-5-4	4-5-6	4-6-0	4-6-0	4-6-0	4-5-6	4-5-4	4-4-4	4-3-3	4-1-6	3-11-6	3-9-7	3-8-1	3-7-7
1/2 BEAMS	CHINE	0-0-0	3-6-0	3-6-0	3-6-0	3-5-6	3-5-0	3-4-0	3-2-2	2-11-2	2-6-6	2-0-6	1-6-4	0-11-6	0-5-0	0-3-4
	SHEER	0-0-0	4-6-0	4-6-0	4-6-0	4-5-6	4-5-0	4-3-3	4-2-6	4-0-0	3-7-0	3-0-2	2-3-6	1-6-0	0-6-6	0-4-3

Fig 14/b

DELTA 28

SCALE FEET

SCALE METRES

Fig. 4/c

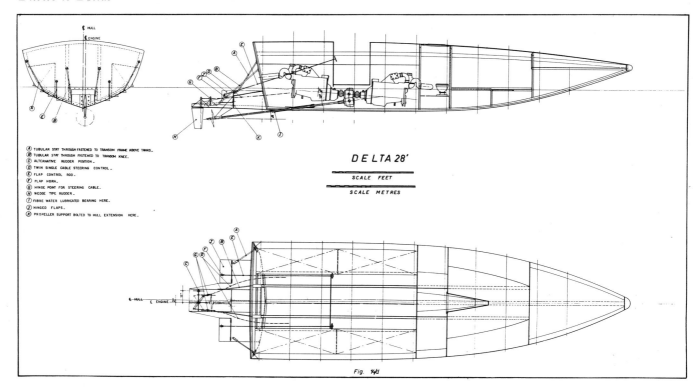

A TUBULAR STAY THROUGH FASTENED TO TRANSOM FRAME ABOVE TANKS.
B TUBULAR STAY THROUGH FASTENED TO TRANSOM KNEE.
C ALTERNATIVE RUDDER POSITION.
D TWIN SINGLE CABLE STEERING CONTROL.
E FLAP CONTROL ROD.
F FLAP HORN.
G HINGE POINT FOR STEERING CABLE.
H WEDGE TYPE RUDDER.
I FIBRE WATER LUBRICATED BEARING HERE.
J HINGED FLAPS.
K PROPELLER SUPPORT BOLTED TO HULL EXTENSION HERE.

DELTA 28'

SCALE   FEET

SCALE   METRES

Fig. 14/d

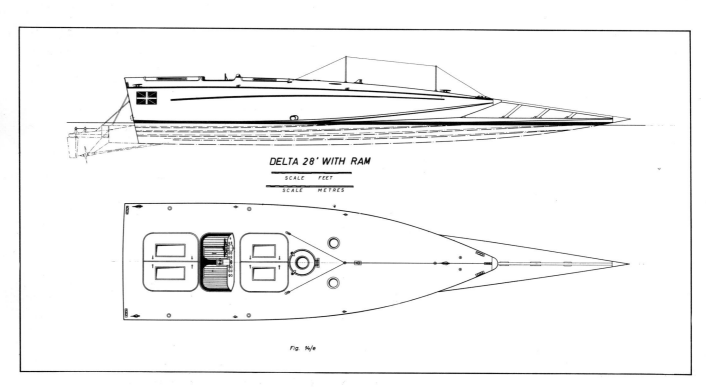

DELTA 28' WITH RAM

SCALE   FEET

SCALE   METRES

Fig. 14/e

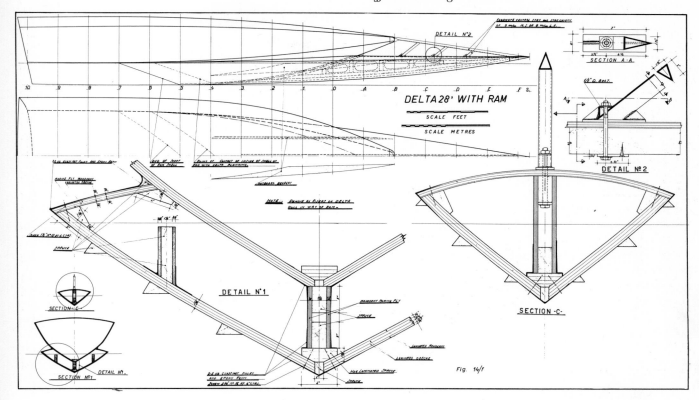

DELTA 28' WITH RAM

DETAIL Nº 2

DETAIL Nº 1

SECTION -C-

Fig. 14/f

offset to counteract this effect. Any torque correction of this sort, however, can only be right for a certain range of speeds, and the more sensitive the boat, the more limited is the range.

A year or so before we built *Delta 28* I remember going out on trials in Nassau with Dick Bertram and Sam Sarra (at that time Daytona's Chief Engineer) in Sam's 23 foot *Holocaust*, which was fitted with a tandem arrangement. The boat was very fast and near its top speed ran into the same alarming rolling phenomenon which we had experienced with *Delta 28*, a phenomenon which could be eliminated only by reducing speed. To damp this rolling Sam had fitted two ingeniously designed hydraulic flaps on either chine about amidship; these could be retracted right into the hull when not in use (rather like the retractable undercarriage on aeroplanes). I watched the boat from another craft while Sam ran her up and down several times, and I noticed that the flaps were all too often right out of the water. I do not honestly feel, though, that even if these flaps had been placed further aft (where they would have been more in contact with the water) they would have cured the rolling.

It is hard to say what the answer is to this problem. A different rudder design could, in my opinion, help quite a lot, as could also the location of the rudder in relation to the slip-stream. This last is extremely important. If the rudder is actually located in the slip-stream it generally pays to have it as far away as possible from the propeller; another solution is to place the rudder outside the slipstream altogether, which gives a possible increase in top speed although incurring some loss of manoeuvrability.

As far as *Delta 28* is concerned, Charles Gardner is continuing with further experiments; these include the superimposition of a new ram-shaped bow, the object of which is to lengthen the hull and provide a means of piercing the crest of the waves. It will be interesting to see the results*.

See Figs. 14/a, 14/b, 14/c, 14/d, 14/e, 14/f.

* The ram-shaped bow has been tried out since I wrote this description of *Delta 28*. I have been told that her rough-water performance is now better than that of *Surfury*, although there is an appreciable reduction in top speed. This is understandable, since applying the ram has increased both weight and wetted surface—the latter, owing to the forward shift of the centre of gravity as well as to the flattening of the buttock lines forward.

It is worth noting that no problems have arisen to date over yawing in following seas; this was one of the negative aspects I feared might accompany the superimposing of a ram.

MERRY-GO-ROUND

Length overall	—	36′ 9″	(m. 11.20)	
Length waterline	—	31′ 6″	(m. 9.60)	
Beam maximum	—	10′ 6″	(m. 3.20)	
Beam chine	—	8′ 0″	(m. 2.43)	
Draught hull	—	1′ 10¾″	(m. 0.58)	

Deadrise transom	— 25°
Weight	— 5 tons
Engines	— Twin Cummins 1100 HP
Speed	— 52 knots

As I have already mentioned in Chapter V, the hull of *Merry-go-round* was actually moulded on the plug of *Surfury*. The same sort of construction was also used. The laminated cedar shell was 1″ thick, the longitudinal members were of spruce, and the decks were lined with cedar laminates in an attractive herring-bone pattern. *Merry-go-round* was finished with varnished topsides and deck, and looked very distinctive indeed.

Merry-go-round was powered with two special Cummins VY-370 N racing marine diesel engines, each rated at 550 HP at 3,000 r.p.m. The diesels were fitted aft in the hull and drove the propellers through Walter V-drives which were fitted with direct drive gears. The propellers were placed very close together (unusually so for that time) so as to get them deep down into the water. To achieve this with the minimum misalignment on the universal joints of the intermediate shafts, the engines were placed converging towards the V-drives, and the V-drives themselves were inclined 15° so as to get the propeller shafts closer to each other.

The transom was raked forward 30° from the vertical in order to lengthen slightly the planing surfaces of the hull and permit the centrally mounted rudder to be well aft; at the same time this solution cut away the additional hull weight which would have been unavoidable with a vertical or outward raked transom. The central transom mounted rudder was wedge-shaped in section, built of stainless steel, and hollow.

The accompanying profile drawings show the boat with and without a cabin top. Sir Max Aitken wanted this dual solution, since he wished both to race a flush-decked boat in the Miami-Nassau and to have a cabin cruiser for the Cowes-Torquay event. The latter modification was never actually carried into practice since open boats were permitted to race that year.

In March 1966, a relatively short time after her launching, Sir Max captured the world diesel record in *Merry-go-round* with a speed of 60·21 m.p.h. over the measured mile of Southampton Water. After gaining the record Sir Max was reported as saying, "I felt very safe. The boat requires no modifications. She is a great tribute to the team of men who produced her."

She was later shipped over to the United States for the Miami-Nassau race, but unfortunately was dropped on to the quayside while being unloaded and suffered quite a lot of damage. She took part in the race notwithstanding, but had to retire.

Merry-go-round changed hands in 1967 and was renamed *Thunderfish III*. The Cummins diesel engines were replaced by a pair of Daytona petrol engines. Driven by Don Shead, *Thunderfish III* won the 1967 Wills International Trophy, but later that year Don had a very lucky escape when the boat caught fire with full tanks and was a total loss.

See Figs. 15/a, 15/b.

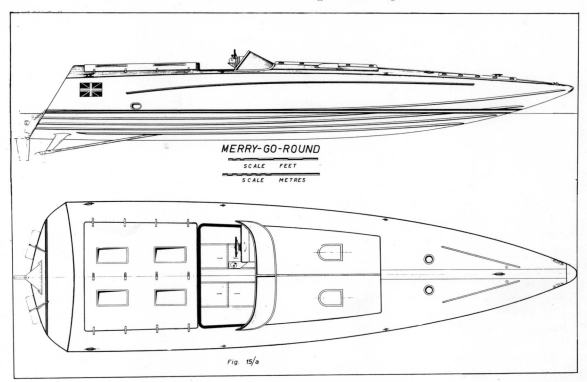

MERRY-GO-ROUND

SCALE FEET

SCALE METRES

Fig. 15/a

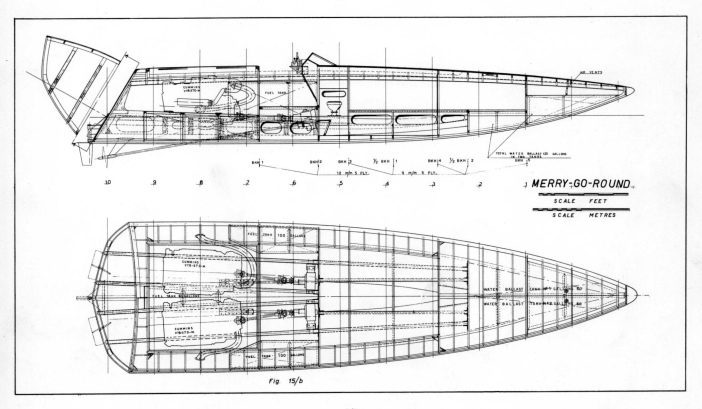

MERRY-GO-ROUND

SCALE FEET

SCALE METRES

Fig. 15/b

G

ULTIMA VOLTA

Length overall — 36′ 6″ (m. 11.12)	*Deadrise transom* — 25°
Length waterline — 31′ 6″ (m. 9.60)	*Weight* — 4.8 tons
Beam maximum — 10′ 8″ (m. 3.20)	*Engine* — Carraro V 12 SS diesel, 850 HP
Beam chine — 8′ 0″ (m. 2.43)	*Speed* — 49 knots
Draught hull — 1′ 10¾″ (m. 0.58)	

Ultima Volta and *Delta Blu* were built at the same time by a team of Anzio craftsmen who later set up their own yard, Cantiere Delta. This yard has subsequently built a great number of boats to my design, and I may say have made an excellent job of them. They have considerable experience in building fast craft and a thorough knowledge of the weaknesses which often crop up in racing boats.

The hull design of *Ultima Volta*, and of many other boats which were to follow her, was very similar to that of *Surfury*, with some minor modifications such as the positioning of the risers, degree of "rocker", outline of sheer, and so on. This was the first time that I introduced poplar into the construction of my boats. I had carried out numerous tests with samples of laminated mahogany, cedar, and poplar, as well as of mixed timber panels (such as obeche cores with harder external laminates), and I found that the strength/weight ratio of poplar was very promising. I have continued to use poplar on many racing boats and on a few really fast pleasure craft with satisfactory results.

Although *Ultima Volta* never actually completed a race (she only raced twice: in the 1966 Dauphin d'Or at Les Embiez, and in the 1967 Viareggio-Bastia), she was an unusual boat and deserved better luck. She was powered with a single 12 cylinder 32-litre Carraro diesel engine putting out around 850 HP at 1800 r.p.m., and on trials I managed to clock a speed of 49·2 knots.

As I wrote to the owner, Gianni Agnelli, I was not very happy with these trials as there was not enough time to do a really systematic series of tests; anyway, they had to be suspended as there was considerable

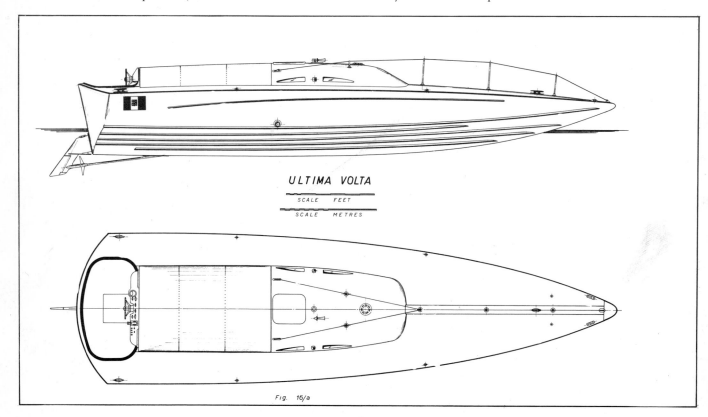

ULTIMA VOLTA

SCALE FEET

SCALE METRES

Fig. 16/a

vibration and over-heating of the V-drive. The vibration was cured by changing the design of the propeller strut, and the over-heating overcome by reducing the misalignment of the universal joints to the V-drive.

On subsequent trials it was interesting to note the effect played by the rudders on the speed. I had adopted an unusual rudder arrangement on this boat since I wanted to remove it from the slipstream; in fact there were two rudders, one on either side of the propeller. Trials were done first with two rudders and then only with one, trying out the port and starboard rudders alternately. There was a difference of some two extra knots when one of the rudders was removed; when each rudder was tried on its own, manoeuvrability seemed to be better with the port rudder than with the starboard one.

The propeller had a right-hand rotation and, following the same line of reasoning mentioned in connection with several earlier single-screw boats, I had placed the engine with V-drive, and with shaft line to starboard so as to offset the torque effect. A point worth mentioning is that, in the beginning, it was not at all easy to get the boat on to the plane. The problem was to match the propeller to the power curve of the engine before and after the turbo-

chargers came into play.

The first propeller we tried did not permit the engine to arrive at the revolutions necessary to bring the turbochargers into action. To make matters worse, the moment when the turbochargers should have come into action coincided with the critical take-off speed of the boat—i.e. the speed with which the boat starts to climb over the hump prior to settling into planing trim. All that happened, therefore, was that we waddled in the water with our bows way up in the air, and the wider we opened the throttles the more thick black smoke poured out of both side exhausts. The cockpit was right aft in *Ultima Volta* and after half an hour of this performance we all looked like chimney-sweeps. On one occasion someone on shore even called out the local fire brigade on seeing the huge, dense columns of inky smoke which were floating around Anzio Bay.

There was, of course, one way of getting the boat up on to the plane, but it was a rather complicated performance which consisted of, first, squirting compressed air into the propeller at the critical moment which allowed the r.p.m. to increase since the propeller was turning in a bubble of air and then, as the boat got over the hump, gradually turning off the compressed air when the boat would continue

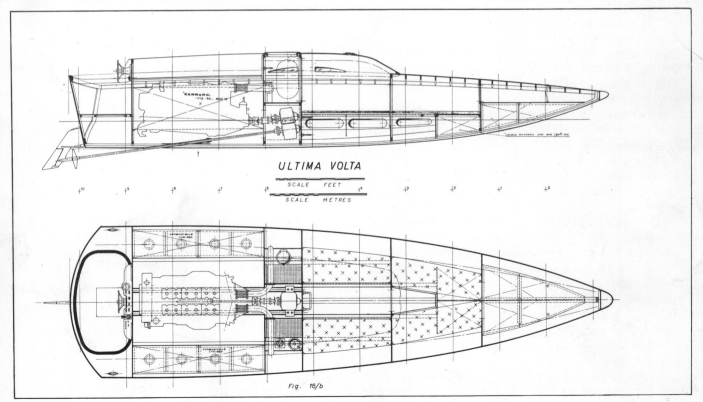

ULTIMA VOLTA

SCALE FEET

SCALE METRES

Fig. 16/b

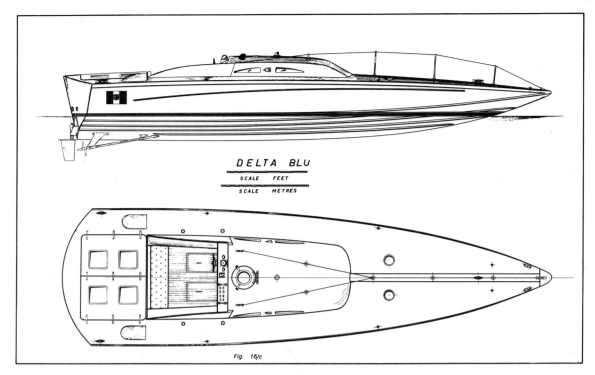

DELTA BLU

SCALE FEET

SCALE METRES

Fig. 16/c

to gain speed. We seemed to empty compressed air bottles at quite a rate, not to mention the fact that getting her on the plane was a jerky business which not only set the crew's nerves on edge but also required some careful timing and was heavy on the transmission. In fact the air had to be turned off at the right moment, when there would be a sudden drop in r.p.m. as the propeller bit into solid water, coupled naturally with a convulsive jerk.

Fortunately we quite soon managed to find a suitable propeller to overcome this problem without any compromise on the top speed of the boat. *Ultima Volta* was an exhilarating boat, and it certainly was an unusual pleasure to be speeding along at over 45 knots without the customary scream of high r.p.m. engines.

The cockpit position right aft made *Ultima Volta* a particularly agreeable ride in rough weather, although it was impossible to work the throttles in the same way as with a petrol engine. In my opinion, this inability to increase and decrease speed with the minimum of time-lag, so as to play the waves, is the principal reason why diesel boats have not yet produced any startling results in racing, not even in rough weather when one would suppose that they would be at their best*.

The V-drive was made by the same manufacturers as the engine, and I had asked them for three sets of

multiplication gears which would give the propeller 3500, 4000 and 4500 r.p.m. As it happened, we settled for 4000 r.p.m., which was a happy compromise, and we managed to clock the top speed of 49·2 knots mentioned earlier with a $17\frac{1}{2}''$ diameter by $21\frac{1}{4}''$ pitch propeller.

Personally I felt that the V-12 cylinder Carraro engine was a sound piece of engineering work. The main trouble which plagued this boat, and regrettably gave her rather an indifferent press, was the difficulty of finding the right material for the cylinder head gaskets. These kept blowing continually. For my money, had this problem been solved in those early stages, *Ultima Volta* would have proved to be one of the most reliable powerboats competing at that time.

Delta Blu was made off the same mould as *Ultima Volta*. She was fitted with two 525 HP Daytona engines installed right aft and driving two propellers through V-drives, but the main difference between these two boats lay in the cockpit position which in *Delta Blu* was just forward of the engines.

Delta Blu won the Dauphin d'Or at les Embiez in 1966, after coming in second a couple of weeks earlier at Viareggio. See Figs. 16/a, 16/b, 16/c.

* Diesel powered boats, with engine capacities near the 2000 cu. in. limit, are necessarily big boats and therefore naturally have an advantage over small craft in rough going.

DELTA SYNTHESIS

Length overall	—	*40′ 0″*	*(m. 12.19)*	
Length waterline	—	*34′ 9½″*	*(m. 10.60)*	
Beam maximum	—	*9′ 6″*	*(m. 2.90)*	
Beam chine	—	*7′ 0″*	*(m. 2.13)*	
Draught hull	—	*1′ 10½″*	*(m. 0.57)*	

Deadrise transom	— *28°*
Weight	— *4 tons*
Engines	— *Twin Daytona, 1050 HP*
Speed	— *55 knots*

Cantiere Partenocraft started building this forty-foot Delta in Naples at about the same time that *Ultima Volta* and *Delta Blu* were on the stocks in Anzio.

Delta Synthesis was more radical than *Surfury* as far as the lines were concerned. She was narrower, longer and had more deadrise. Built of poplar, she was powered with the same model of Daytona engine which was installed in *Delta Blu*; in fact, the engine arrangement, position of the V-drives, shaft angles, and so on were very similar in these two boats.

During the first trials carried out in Naples I felt confident that we had arrived at something interesting, for the boat had a very good turn of speed and was particularly soft-riding. This was unquestionably due to her increased deadrise and additional length.

Delta Synthesis had rather the unfortunate début which I have already described, but nevertheless showed her potentiality during the 1967 Cowes-Torquay race when she placed 2nd to *Surfury*. Incidentally, she was heavily criticized for the excessive way she porpoised through the water in that smooth race. While I do not wish to deny that she was built with excessive "rocker" in the bottom, the transom flaps were perfectly capable of overcoming the porpoising quite easily and I had ample occasion to verify this. When fully applied, the flaps were able to depress the bows to a point where they were practically level with the surface of the water. I feel that insufficient time may possibly have been spent in perfecting the driving technique on this boat. It is not easy to know what is the best trim for optimum speed unless a lot of meticulous speed trials are done. Heavy porpoising can produce a very high engine r.p.m., which need not necessarily mean a very high forward speed. The propellers of a boat which porpoises heavily may come out of the water frequently, even in calm conditions, and show an extremely

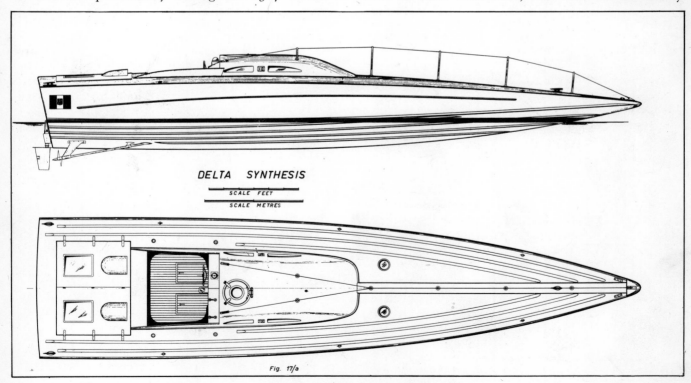

DELTA SYNTHESIS

SCALE FEET

SCALE METRES

Fig. 17/a

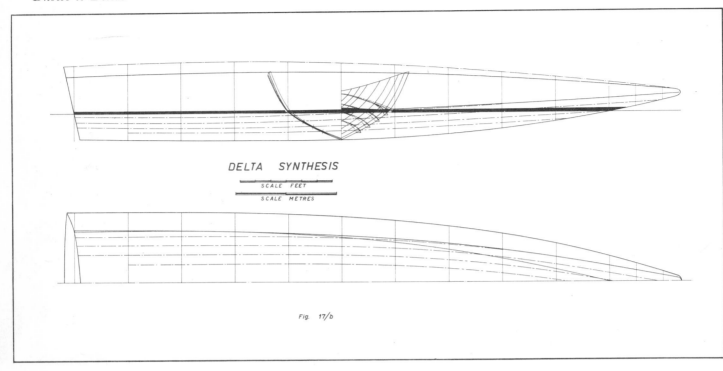

DELTA SYNTHESIS

SCALE FEET

SCALE METRES

Fig. 17/b

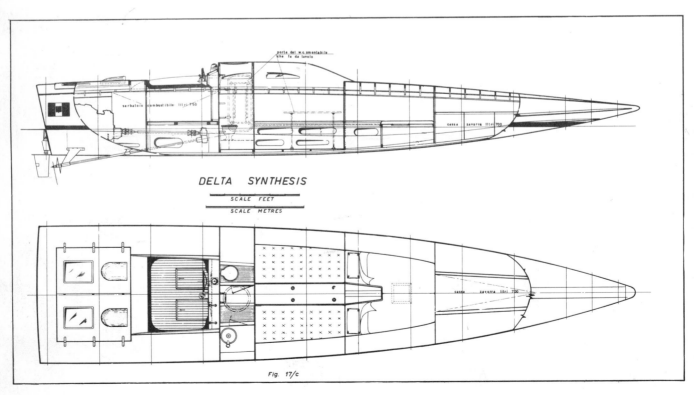

DELTA SYNTHESIS

SCALE FEET

SCALE METRES

Fig. 17/c

high r.p.m., while slightly lower revolutions with less porpoising, and therefore, more propeller in the water, might possibly give higher speeds; the continuous changing of the propeller angle to the water must also be taken into account, since it considerably reduces propulsive efficiency. I suspect that *Delta Synthesis* was being driven by her rev. counters.

I had noticed that the decks of these early Class I Delta boats were subject to quite a strain. A moment's reflection revealed the reason for this. The hull of a boat behaves under stress rather like a girder, the stiffness of which depends on its depth. These Deltas were long and low and, therefore, more prone to flexing than a hull like *'A Speranziella*, which was short and high (it has in fact been described as a "high-walled hull"). *'A Speranziella* had a ¼″ plywood deck which never showed any signs of weakness, whereas the early Deltas showed signs of failure even with decks of ⅜″ or more.

Delta Synthesis was even longer and lower (at least in the freeboard), and particular attention was therefore necessary to the longitudinals high up, such as gunnels and carlings, and to the deck. I doubled up the gunnels, increased the deck thickness, and in addition placed long stringers over the deck, some of which extended from the transom right up to the bows. During trials I could actually see the bows flexing, like the wing-tips of a large aeroplane in flight;

however, we were within the elastic limits of the materials concerned and never ran into any serious trouble on that score.

I personally never had the opportunity of timing *Delta Synthesis* over a measured course, but I would say that her top speed when trimmed out properly was in the region of 55 knots. During the trials I did on this boat we were using Italian Radice propellers (14″ diameter × 17½″ pitch) and were able to turn these at just over 5000 r.p.m. (we had a multiplication gear in the V-drive), so that even with a slip of over 20% 55 knots was possible.

It is particularly important to arrive at the right compromise with the propeller when using a turbocharged engine, such as the Daytonas installed on *Delta Synthesis*. In this case, the maximum permitted engine r.p.m. was 4800, with a boost not exceeding 10 lbs per square inch. During these trials the boost readings on the engines were around 8 lbs and the propellers could, therefore, have been loaded a bit more, with some slight increase in speed but no doubt with more likelihood of blowing up the engine.

Delta Synthesis was also one of the first boats in which I used a rudder incorporating the water pick-ups for cooling the engines. In this way the pick-ups were as low as possible and there was never any risk of the engines suffering through lack of cooling, even if the hull leaped out of the water.

See Figs. 17/a, 17/b, 17/c.

HYDROSONIC SPECIAL

Length overall — 32′ 0″ (m. 9.75)	Deadrise transom — 26°
Length waterline — 26′ 3″ (m. 8.00)	Weight — 3.6 tons
Beam maximum — 10′ 0″ (m. 3.05)	Engines — Twin 8-litre BPM Vulcano 800 HP
Beam chine — 7′ 10½″ (m. 2.40)	Speed — 53 knots
Draught hull — 1′ 10¾″ (m. 0.58)	

Hydrosonic Special was the second Class I offshore racing powerboat which I designed for Cantiere Partenocraft. She qualified for the open category.

Built of cold moulded wood construction, *Hydrosonic Special* was a good deal shorter than *Delta Synthesis*. The object was to have a second string, powered this time with Italian engines, The engines adopted were the 8-litre BPM Vulcano, each rated at 400 HP at 4500 r.p.m.

I wanted to get a good power to weight ratio and a boat which would compare well speedwise with *Delta Synthesis*, even though she had some 250 HP

less installed; hence her reduced dimensions. She was not, in fact, as fast as *Delta Synthesis* though not far off, but she was a good sea boat. She narrowly missed a 3rd place in the 1967 Cowes-Torquay race, retiring a short distance from the finish. It was a great pity that this happened as otherwise it might have been a hat-trick for my designs that day. The boat was driven in this race by the South African Mike Trimming and his crew were the eminent circuit and Class III racing pilot, Lady Arran, and the well-known yachting journalist, Jack Knights.

Hydrosonic Special was towed into Torquay with

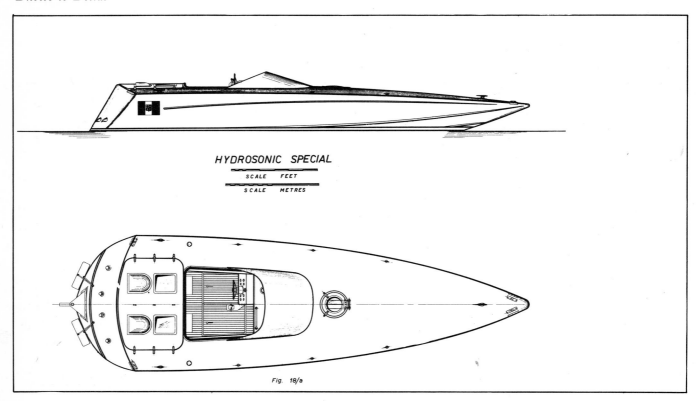

HYDROSONIC SPECIAL

SCALE   FEET

SCALE   METRES

Fig. 18/a

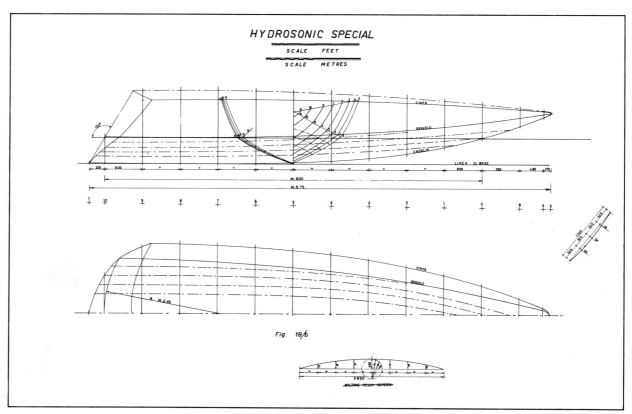

HYDROSONIC SPECIAL

SCALE   FEET

SCALE   METRES

Fig. 18/b

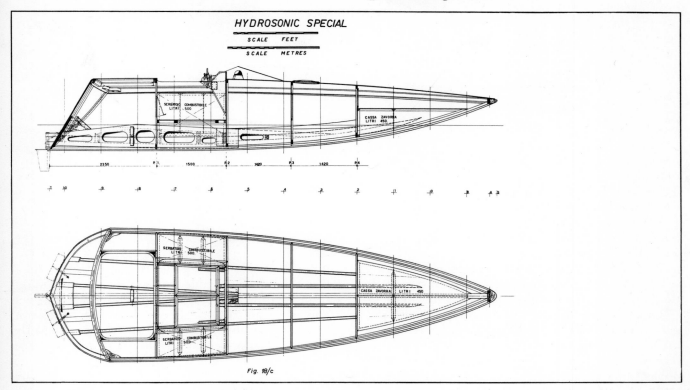

HYDROSONIC SPECIAL

Fig. 18/c

quite a lot of water in her. Nevertheless, Mike Trimming told me later that he was sure he could have finished the race had he not run out of fuel, even though the transom had come adrift from the planking where the rudder was secured to it (the boat had a centrally mounted transom rudder). I inspected the damage afterwards and found a gaping hole which, in my opinion, had been caused by the rudder hitting some object in the water; even so, no water would have entered the hull had the boat been able to maintain planing speed. Why the boat ran out of fuel I really do not know; the design capacity was for 1000 litres, adequate for completing the course. Possibly the tanks were not filled to capacity.

An out-of-the-ordinary feature on *Hydrosonic Special* was the heavily raked forward transom; I did this so as to place the propellers and rudder as far back as I could without actually increasing the length of the hull (and therefore with minimum increase of weight).

See Figs. 18/a, 18/b, 18/c.

DIMPI SEA

Length overall	— *31'0"*	*(m. 9.45)*	*Deadrise transom* — *26°*	
Length waterline	— *25'9"*	*(m. 7.85)*	*Weight*	— *3.5 tons*
Beam maximum	— *8'9¼"*	*(m. 2.68)*	*Engines*	— *Twin 8-litre BPM Vulcano, 800 HP*
Beam chine	— *7'0"*	*(m. 2.13)*	*Speed*	— *57 knots*
Draught hull	— *1'8"*	*(m. 0.55)*		

It was a great pity that I did not know, when I was designing this boat, that the threatened cube regulation would not come into force in the U.I.M. rules. There had been talk early in 1968 of bringing in a rule which would restrict the minimum volume of a boat by requiring it to conform (in the case of a Class I boat) to a cube having a length of 12', a width of 6' and a height of 2'9". This cube had to fit into the skin or shell of the hull, ignoring structural members, and below transverse lines joining the underside of the deck at the cockpit carlings, or their equivalent.

Quite frankly, whilst I understood that this prospective rule was being formulated for reasons of safety, I felt that a restriction of this type did not leave sufficient freedom to designers, one of whose objects after all is to create new hull shapes. I wrote to one of the U.I.M. officials at the time, pointing out that restricting the internal volume of a boat did not

necessarily imply additional safety. Surely what was more important was a sound hull shape, irrespective of hull width or height. I was delighted to hear afterwards that this proposal had been turned down by the U.I.M. Committee—very wisely too.

However, when I started the design of *Dimpi Sea* there was still the possibility of the rule being accepted, and the prospective owner, Paolo Siviero, understandably wanted me to design a boat which would be valid not only for the 1968 season but also subsequently. Paolo Siviero incidentally has a long and successful record in circuit racing having won, among other important races, the "Cento Miglia del Lario", he also formed part of the *Ultima Dea* crew in 1962.

Dimpi Sea was, therefore, designed around the famous cube, which I may say just fitted into my lines drawing very snugly. Speedwise, the boat was

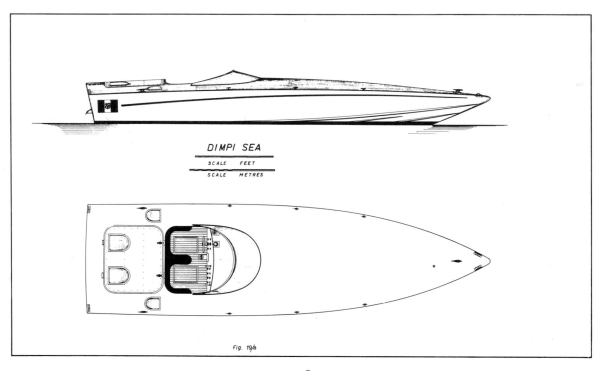

DIMPI SEA

SCALE   FEET

SCALE   METRES

Fig. 19/a

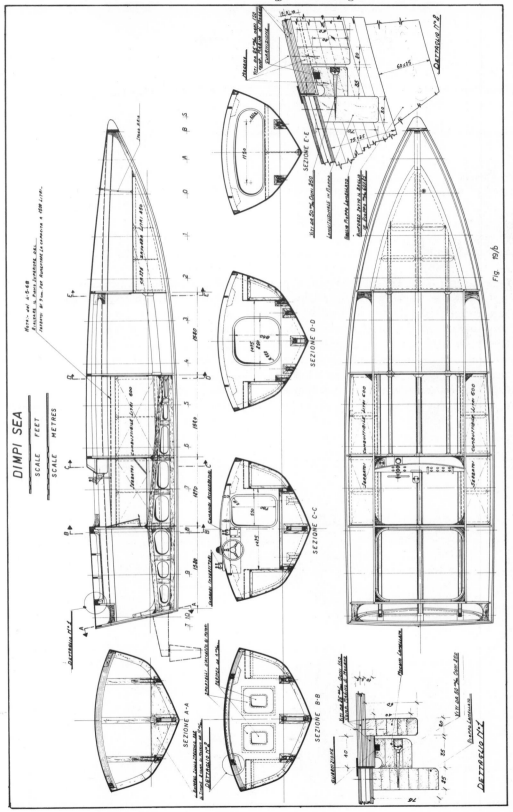

Fig. 19/b

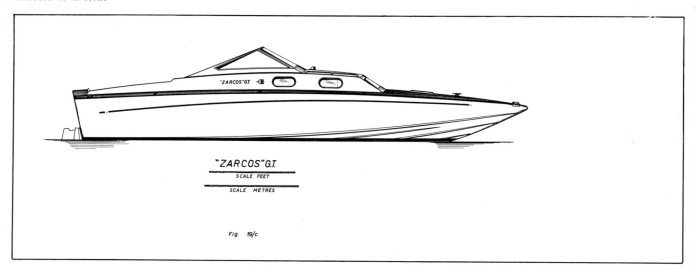

"ZARCOS" G.T.

SCALE FEET

SCALE METRES

Fig. 19/c

a complete success right from the start. With a pair of BPM engines similar to those fitted on *Hydrosonic Special* I clocked a speed of just over 57 knots.

In this design I narrowed the width between shaft centres a further four inches less than in *Hydrosonic Special*, so as to get the propellers still deeper into the water. The shaft angle too was reduced from 10° to 9°. The propellers extended beyond the transom and the central rudder was placed well aft, supported by a long stainless steel box the bottom of which was clear of the water when the boat was planing.

These changes, minor as they may seem, resulted in quite a bit more speed. *Dimpi Sea* was a delightful boat to handle and gave one complete confidence even at full speed. I am sure that the positioning of the rudder well aft had a lot to do with this. Had I not had the cube regulation hanging over me I would have lowered the freeboard considerably and thus gained more speed without any detrimental effect on her safety. Aerodynamic drag becomes an important consideration at speeds of around 60 knots. For this very same reason we had decided to dispense

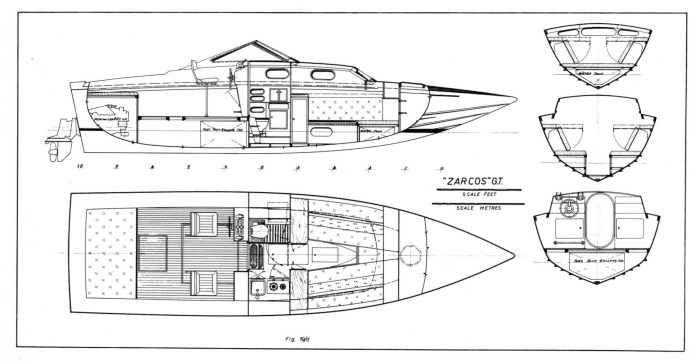

"ZARCOS" G.T.

SCALE FEET

SCALE METRES

Fig. 19/d

with any form of windshield.

Dimpi Sea was built by Cantiere Scorza of Fiumicino in laminated poplar and was completed in time for the 1968 season. She took part in only two races, both of which were a great disappointment. In the first, at Viareggio, a rag found its way into one of the water intakes shortly after the start and caused the over-heating of one engine. In the second, at Les Embiez, again shortly after the start, a stern gland coupling came adrift and resulted in a rapid ingress of water into the hull which forced her to retire.

It has always been my experience, however, that a boat seldom does very well in her first season; it

inevitably seems to take one or two seasons to discover all the bugs.

See Figs. 19/a, 19/b.

Cantiere Scorza produced a G.T. model on the mould of *Dimpi Sea*. The construction of this production craft was very similar to the racing prototype, with a laminated hull shell without any framing other than the bulkheads. With a pair of 250 HP MerCruiser petrol engines with outdrives *Zarcos G.T.* is capable of a speed close on 40 knots; the fuel capacity is 130 gallons, which gives this fast cruiser a range of around 170 miles.

See Figs. 19/c, 19/d.

BILL BULL

Length overall	— 33′0″ (m. 10.05)		*Deadrise transom*	— 26°
Length waterline	— 27′0″ (m. 8.23)		*Weight*	— 3.2 tons
Beam maximum	— 8′7″ (m. 2.60)		*Engines*	— Twin BPM Vulcano 800 HP
Beam chine	— 7′0″ (m. 2.13)		*Speed*	—
Draught hull	— 1′8¼″ (m. 0.515)			

At the time of writing, *Bill Bull* has never actually raced.

She was launched at Anzio towards the end of the 1969 season. Earlier that year I had designed a fast

pleasure boat, *Barbarina*, for the late Count Mario Agusta (see Chapter VIII). During one of my frequent visits to the Agusta helicopter factory, Count Agusta asked me whether I would like to design a

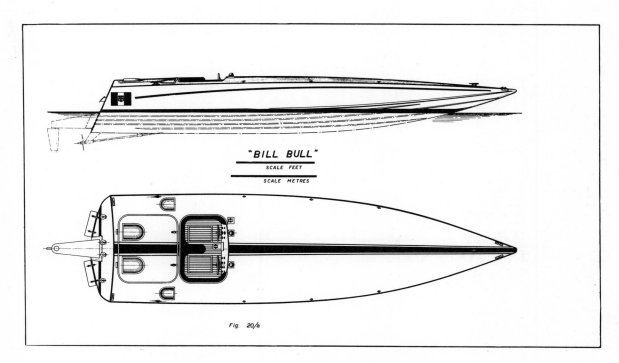

109

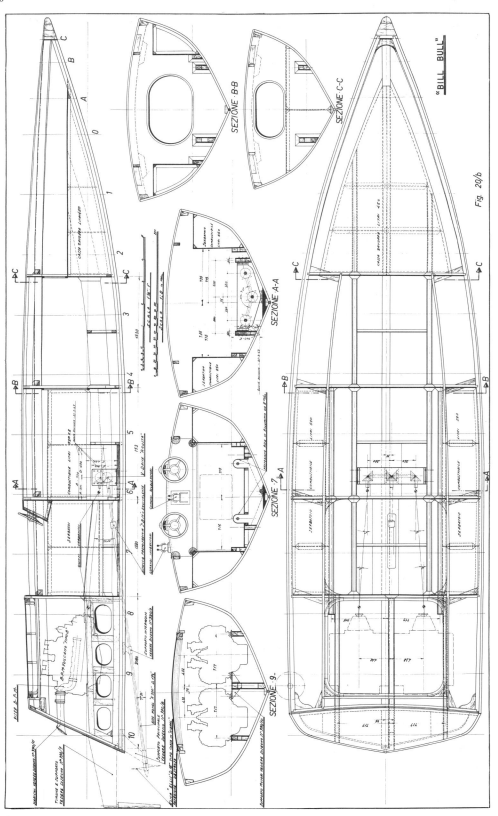

Class I offshore racing powerboat, to be powered with Italian propulsive machinery. I took up the suggestion with alacrity, since not only was Mario Agusta a person who radiated great enthusiasm when it came to boats (which were obviously his chief hobby), but his younger brother, Corrado Agusta, was to drive the finished craft. I might add that Mario Agusta was World Vice-president of the U.I.M. and President of the Federazione Italiana Moto Nautica; his untimely death late in September, 1969 was a very sad blow to all who knew him.

While discussing the design of *Bill Bull* in its early stages, I had asked him whether he would be prepared to design and produce a special V-drive for the boat, based on my schematic requirements. What I wanted to do was to fit two 400 HP BPM petrol engines aft and couple them to a single V-drive, thus running a single shaft. There is nothing new, of course, in connecting two engines to one V-drive, but the system normally adopted is the tandem arrangement, such as was used both in *Surfury* and in *Delta 28*. In this case, however, I wanted both engines aft so as to get the centre of gravity well aft too, and in consequence have greater potential top speed as well as avoiding the steering problems we had already experienced with *Delta 28*.

The design and building of this V-drive was done in record time, and was a most beautiful piece of engineering work—understandable in view of the fact that the Agusta factories are used to working to extremely close limits in producing helicopters and high-performance motor-cycles. The racing version of these motorcycles has swept the board in recent years in the 500 c.c. races in the hands of Giacomo Agostini.

The drive was also V-shaped when seen in section, the V being almost identical to the deadrise of the hull where it was installed. The input flanges of the engines were located at the top ends of the V, then a couple of shafts (with bevelled gears on either end) ran down the arms of the V to a single output flange, which was coupled to the propeller shaft. The shape of this gearbox necessitated a dry sump, which in turn required one oil pump to recover the oil and another to lubricate the bevel gears. The oil when recovered was fed through an oil cooler into a separate tank.

Bill Bull was entered for the 1969 Cowes-Torquay Race, but she never made an appearance on account of oil overheating problems connected with the V-drive. Considerable time was spent trying out different oil coolers, which had to be specially made, and this understandably delayed matters. Nevertheless, her speed potential was good. This was largely due to the single shaft arrangement, coupled with a c.g. position well aft, and to the unusually low inclination of the propeller shaft. It remains to be seen, however, whether *Bill Bull* can compete successfully against boats with similar power but with outdrive propulsion, where it is possible to vary the thrust line and trim out the boat for optimum speed (when weather conditions permit). The drawback of a fixed propeller shaft line is that the boat's trim cannot be varied with the thrust of the propeller. A conventional propeller shaft line, however flat it is, also cannot lift the boat out of the water (thereby reducing wetted surface) to the same extent as the horizontal, or indeed negative, thrust line which is possible with racing outdrives today.

Incidentally, I feel that it is a pity for the sport that at the time of writing there is only one company which produces outdrives capable of taking the sort of power installed in a front-line powerboat.

The accompanying drawings show the layout of this boat and also the V-drive.

See Figs. 20/a, 20/b.

(2) *CLASS III*

During the past seven years Class III powerboat racing has become extremely popular in Great Britain, and no doubt it will become so on the Continent too once the rules governing this class are accepted by the Union Internationale Motonautique. Incidentally these rules were further modified in 1968 by the Royal Yachting Association Offshore Racing Committee and industrial or automobile engines are now permitted as well as purely marine installations.

In my opinion this class of offshore powerboat deserves a lot of encouragement. Financially, these craft cost a fraction of the bigger offshore boats; transport is not a problem as they can quite easily be loaded on to a normal boat trailer; their fuel consumption is modest compared with Class I and II boats; and finally, by virtue of their size, they do not need to be stored in boat yards during the winter months but can be housed in a garage. This makes matters much simpler for those owners who like tinkering about with their boats in their spare time.

Class III racing started in May, 1962 with the Putney-Calais-Putney race. This race was initially a trade proving-ground for offshore outboard driven craft, and it still remains the Class III classic although engines are now of all types, with inboards catching on. It was the longest offshore race in the world (220 miles) until the Bahamas 500 came into existence. By 1967 there were eight races for the National Championship series, with an average length of around 80 miles.

Class III racing is subdivided into various categories, and here again there is the possibility of satisfying those who have only moderate means but want nonetheless to compete in the offshore racing field. Class III A, for example, includes craft with engines of 500 c.c. and up to and including engines of 850 c.c., while Class III E (the last subdivision) includes craft with engines of over 2000 c.c. and up to and including 3000 c.c. The overall length of these boats is also a good deal less than that of Class I and II boats. The lowest category of Class III (III A) need only have a minimum overall length of 14 feet, while at the other end of the class category III E has a minimum overall length of 16 feet. There are, of course, no limits relating to maximum overall length, always keeping mind however the trailability problem.

Owners of craft in any of these categories can win the "Motor Boat and Yachting" Class III Drivers Championship since the points are awarded on the basis of category and not overall results. This gives even the smaller boats a chance of winning, as was the case for instance in 1967 when Frank Jutton won the first championship in his 15'4" craft *Merlin*.

There is yet another aspect of this type of racing which I think is rather interesting; the scale trials of boats of relatively small dimensions can prove extremely useful, purely from a designer's point of view, for the successful designing of larger boats, e.g. Class I and II.

Many of the larger Class III boats also race in Class I and II events such as the Cowes-Torquay, where they can use more powerful engine installations. In 1967 three of them came 5th, 6th, and 7th at Cowes.

In conclusion, all the Class III boats described below (with the exception of *Strale*) have been built by Double M Hulls (Melly and Merryfield), who prefix the boats they build to my design with the cipher "MM". Due credit must be given to them for the patient work put into these boats which has contributed so much to their numerous successes.

LEVI 17

Length overall	— 17'0"	(m. 5.18)
Beam maximum	— 4'10½"	(m. 1.50)

Beam chine	— 4'0"	(m. 1.22)
Deadrise transom	— 25°	
Engine	— Various	——

Mongaso was the original prototype 17' offshore version of the 16' circuit hull, moulded from a modified 16' plug. She was built for Mike Beard and had fore and aft seating.

Volare was one of the production hulls made for James Beard a year later off the same plug; the only difference between the two hulls was in the seating arrangement which in *Volare* was side-by-side, as dictated by the 1966 rules.

Both boats were of laminated wood construction, similar to the smaller 16s but generally strengthened.

Both boats have also recorded speeds of up to 50 m.p.h. in calm conditions and averages of 30 m.p.h. even in rough races.

Mongaso and *Volare* have won a lot of races, and *Volare* not only won the National Class III Drivers' Championship in 1966 but also narrowly missed winning the "Motor Boat and Yachting Championship" in 1967, when she finished 2nd with *Vertigo* 3rd.

See Fig. 21/a.

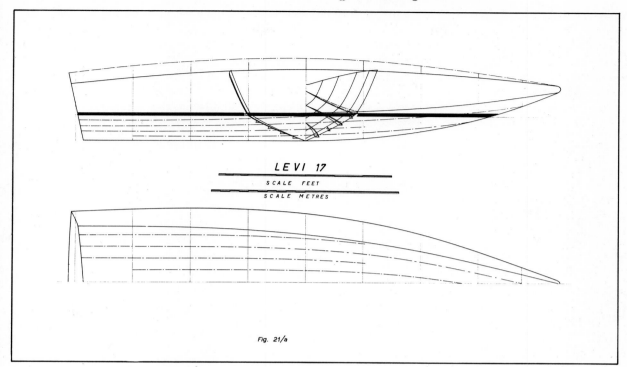

LEVI 17

SCALE FEET

SCALE METRES

Fig. 21/a

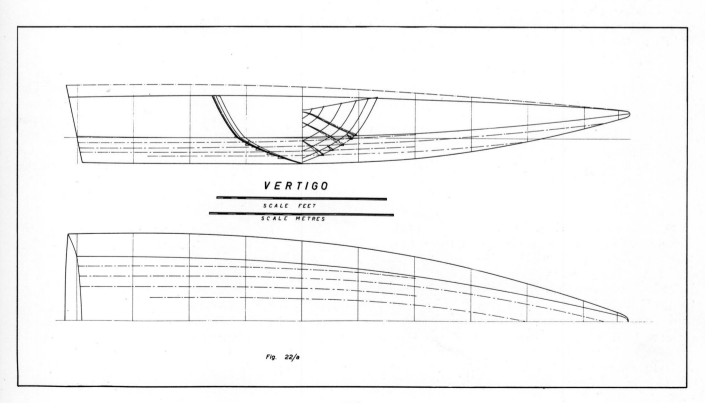

VERTIGO

SCALE FEET

SCALE METRES

Fig. 22/a

113

H

LEVI 20

Length overall	— 20′0″ (m. 6.10)		Beam chine	— 4′8″ (m. 1.42)
Length waterline	— 16′0″ (m. 5.03)		Draught hull	— 0′11½″ (m. 0.29)
Beam maximum	— 6′4″ (m. 1.93)		Deadrise transom	— 22°
			Engines	— Various

Vertigo was the prototype 20′ offshore hull owned by Keith Horseman. This hull was very fast in light seas, but had a lack of buoyancy forward and too much "rocker" aft.

Vertigo Too was also owned by Keith and was made, along with its sister *Towmotor*, at the beginning of 1968. These two hulls were more heavily built, with increased buoyancy at the bow and re-reduced "rocker". Although twin 950 Mercurys were used on the prototype and twin 1000 Mercurys on *Vertigo Too*, their performance was roughly the same with a maximum of 55 to 60 m.p.h. under best conditions; *Vertigo Too*, however, could maintain a better average in heavier seas. These two boats were also fitted with electro-hydraulic trim tabs. *Towmotor*

was fitted with a pair of Johnson G.T. 115s.

The steering on these offshore boats is by stainless steel cable and ball bearing pulleys with 2:1 reduction, the two motors being linked together by two rigid tie rods bell-jointed at the front and rear of each motor.

In 1967 an 18′6″ circuit boat was also produced from this set of lines, the prototype being called *John's Son*. This craft was powered with the Johnson G.T. 115 engine. In the same year, John Reed and Clive Curtis drove her in the Paris Six Hour Race; she proved to be one of the faster hulls in her class during that race, though the way she handled was not altogether satisfactory.

See Fig. 22/a.

FAT CAT

Length overall	— 20′4″ (m. 6.20)		Wing area	— 102 sq. ft. (9 5 m²)
Beam maximum	— 8′6″ (m. 2.60)		Deadrise transom	— 35°
Beam chine			Engines	— Twin Mercury 200 HP
(hulls)	— 2′4″ (m. 0.71)			

In 1966 I produced several designs of powered catamarans involving the ram wing concept. One of these was Lady Aitken's *Fat Cat*.

This craft was also built by Len Melly and John Merryfield and started her racing career in Class III in 1966. Basically, the geometry of this boat was as follows: two 20′ symmetrical heavily vee-ed hulls

joined together with an aerofoiled section wing. The two hulls were of laminated construction and had the usual longitudinal risers, in this case three per side, the last being the chine. The beam of these hulls was governed by the width required to get a person into them, since the pilot sat in one and the navigator in the other.

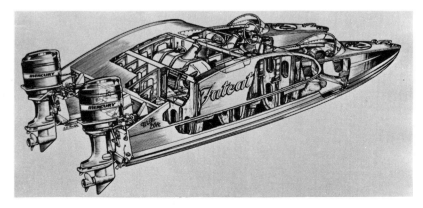

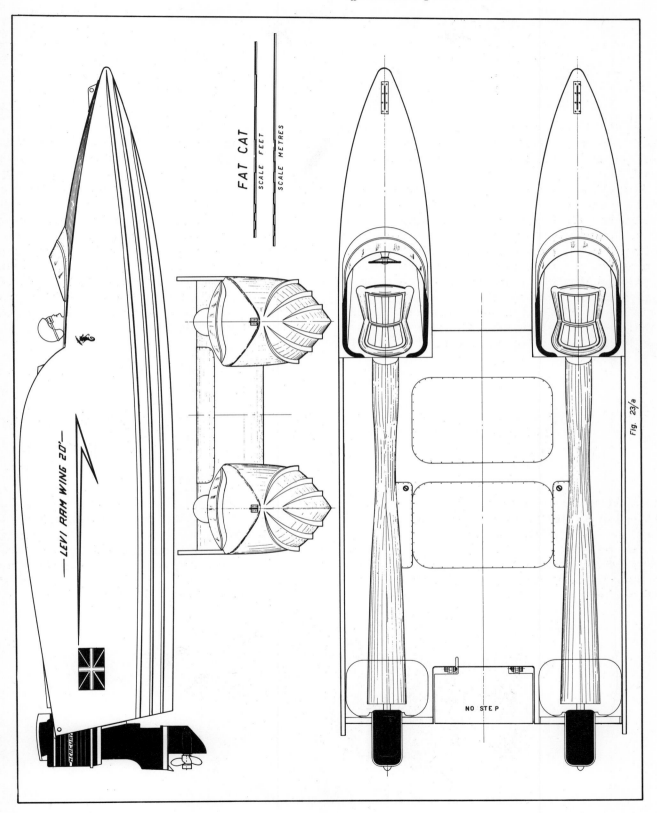

FAT CAT

SCALE FEET

SCALE METRES

— LEVI RAM WING 20' —

NO STEP

Fig. 23/a

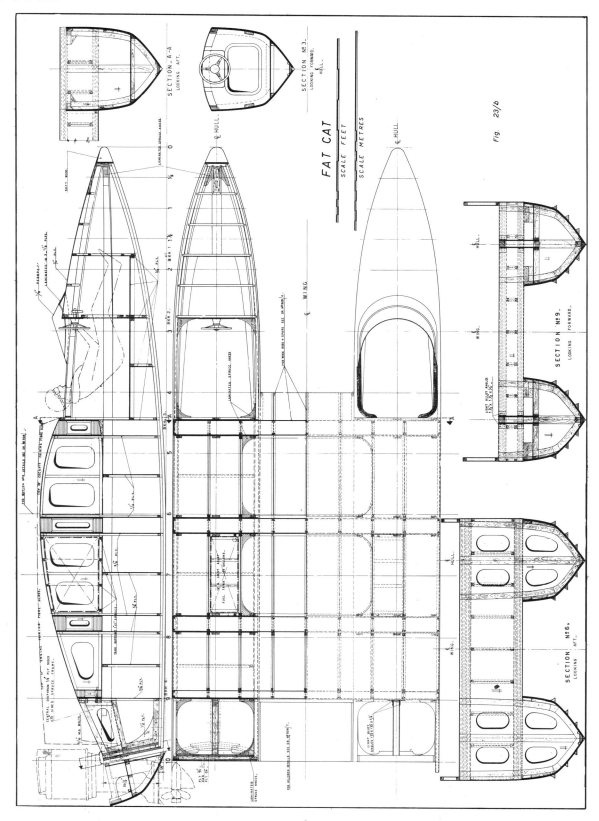

FAT CAT

SCALE FEET

SCALE METRES

Fig. 23/b

SECTION A-A
LOOKING AFT.

SECTION N° 3.
LOOKING FORWARD.

SECTION N° 9.
LOOKING FORWARD.

SECTION N°6.
LOOKING AFT.

Class III rules call for a minimum plan cockpit opening of 2' by 2'6" per person, consisting of either a single cockpit 4' by 5' fore and aft or two individual cockpits 4' by 2'6" fore and aft. I had selected the two cockpit arrangement, for structural reasons, and planned to place them in the hulls since I wished to situate the main spar tying up the two hulls between the two cockpits. The thickness ratio of this aerofoil tie-up was governed by the minimum depth rule, which required 18" at any point within the opening. The minimum cockpit dimensions could not, however, be fitted into the hulls themselves so I had to locate official openings in the wing. Since nobody would, in fact, be sitting in these latter cockpits, they were covered over (as permitted by the rules), thus making it possible to have a true aerofoil section.

The idea behind the ram wing design was to obtain aerodynamic lift at speed, reducing in this wise the wetted surface of the hulls. I had placed fences at the wing extremity in the original design in the hope of increasing lift, and I had also placed a flap at the trailing edge of the wing between the two floats for the same reason. In addition, it was hoped that this flap would make it possible to vary the trim aerodynamically. Both refinements were subsequently removed, since they did not prove really beneficial (possibly the speeds were not sufficiently high) and, in fact, were only an added complication.

I think I placed too much importance on a sturdy structure, with a resulting increase in weight. One of the problems with these multi-hulled craft is to get a sound tie-up between the two floats, and it could well be that I exaggerated on this point. The more deadrise you can put into a hull the smoother it is in rough conditions, and in fact I have been told that *Fat Cat* was one of the best rough water hulls in Class III.

Lady Aitken, who is one of the most qualified women offshore racing pilots competing today, also raced this boat in several Class II events adopting a three-engined installation; the third engine was mounted on the trailing edge in the centre of the wing.

See Figs. 23, 23/a, 23/b.

RAM WING 21

Length overall	— *21' 0" (m. 6.40)*	*Wing area*	— *104 sq. ft. (9.7 m²)*
Beam maximum	— *7'11" (m. 2.40)*	*Deadrise transom*	— *18°*
Beam chine	— *7'11" (m. 2.40)*	*Engines*	— *Twin Evinrude 230 HP*

This design was a development of *Fat Cat*, with quite a few modifications.

In 1967 there was a change in the Class III rules concerning cockpit openings. Four individual cockpits were now permitted, which made it possible to locate these in the hulls and, consequently, employ a thinner wing section. I used a modified U.S.A. 35-B aerofoil, which has a 12% thickness ratio, and flattened the underside from 15% of the chord to the trailing edge. The thinner section and the lower hulls have considerably reduced the frontal area; this should result in a noteworthy reduction of aerodynamic drag.

Some rather dogmatic statements have been made on the question of where the centre of pressure (C.P.) should be on these craft in relation to the centre of gravity (C.G.). Not long ago I read a report prepared by a team of experts following tests on a Ram Wing to my design, which concluded by declaring that the design was not a workable proposition on account of the fact that the C.P. was aft of the C.G. This would seem to imply that craft of this kind can only work satisfactorily if the C.P. is forward of the C.G.

I can only think that this conclusion was reached by following aircraft theory; but aeroplanes can— and do—fly quite happily with the C.P. aft of the C.G. (for instance, the *Monsoon* which is described in Chapter X).

There is admittedly a close analogy between ram wings and aeroplanes when it comes to the question of equilibrium. For this reason, two other main forces, thrust (T) and aerodynamic and hydrodynamic drag (D), must be taken into consideration. Hydrodynamic drag causes the nose down attitude. Without going into a detailed explanation here (see Chapter IX, unlimited record breakers), it can be said that the best location for the C.P. depends on the magnitude and position of the forces involved.

On a relatively slow craft of this type, for example, higher speeds may be possible with a C.P. located well forward which will lift the bows and reduce

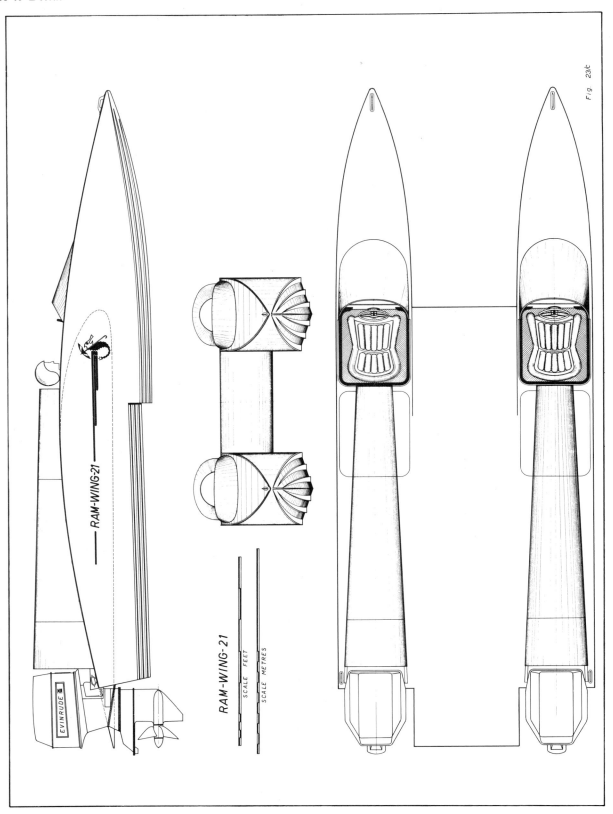

RAM-WING-21

RAM-WING-21

SCALE FEET

SCALE METRES

EVINRUDE

Fig 23/c

wetted surface. The same C.P. location on a faster boat, however, could cause excessive lift of the bows with the risk of an eventual capsize.

In the case of this particular ram wing I have located the wing further aft in relation to the hull in order to get the C.P. nearer the C.G. The deadrise has been reduced by nearly half, which should increase the speed even if it makes the boat harder riding. Transverse steps have also been incorporated in the hulls. The reasons for this latter modification are twofold: first, to try and cut down the wetted area, and second (perhaps more important), to

reduce pitching since there will be four areas of contact with the water instead of two. The reduction of pitching is particularly desirable in a ram wing as the wing will operate more efficiently when there are small variations around its optimum angle of incidence. Fine adjustments to obtain the optimum angle of incidence or trim of boat can be achieved by means of flaps placed on the trailing edges of the steps as well as on the transoms.

Lastly, the construction of this ram wing has been considerably simplified, so as to produce a lighter and a cheaper structure. See Fig. 23/c.

STRALE

Length overall	— 20′8″ (m. 6.30)	*Draught hull*	— 0′11½″ (m. 0.29)
Length waterline	— 16′9″ (m. 5.10)	*Deadrise transom*	— 22°
Beam maximum	— 6′3″ (m. 1.90)	*Engine*	— MerCruiser 140 HP (2966 c.c.)
Beam chine	— 4′8″ (m. 1.43)		

In 1967, as the result of the growing popularity of Class III racing in England, I wrote a series of articles for Italian nautical journals on the lines of "Why not this Class for the Mediterranean too?". I

regret to say that this proposal did not gain a great deal of support, but nevertheless Gaetano Petrone, owner of S.A.P.R.I., a Salerno yard, asked me to prepare a Class III design for him for Category E.

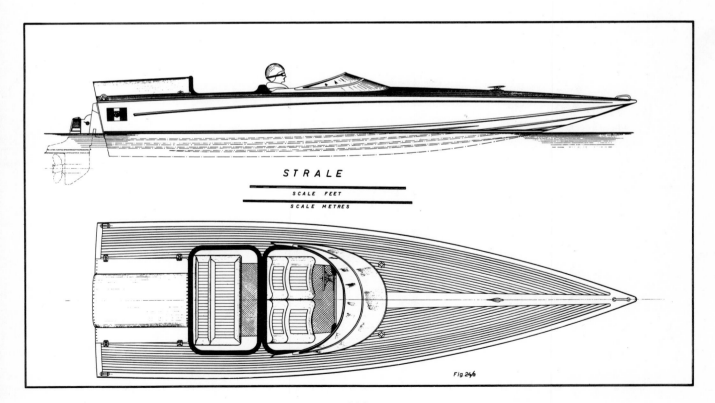

STRALE

SCALE FEET

SCALE METRES

Fig. 24/a

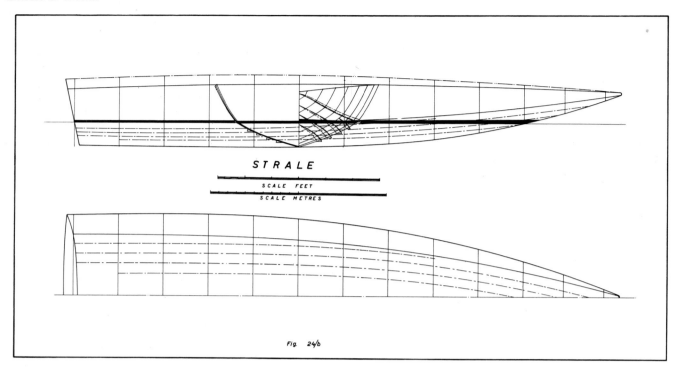

STRALE

SCALE FEET

SCALE METRES

Fig. 24/b

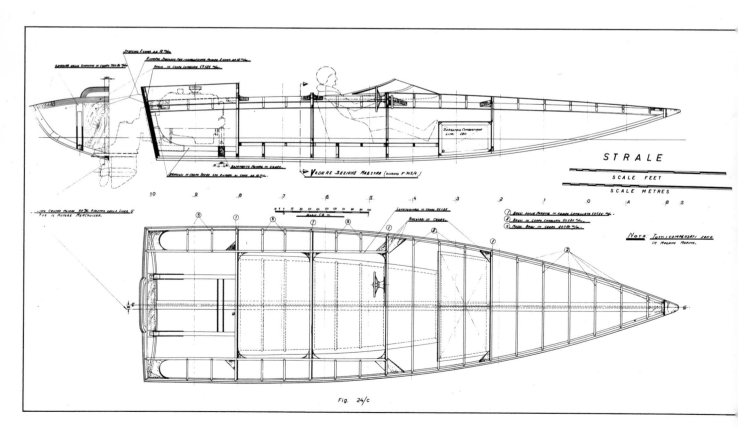

STRALE

SCALE FEET

SCALE METRES

Fig. 24/c

A few years earlier I had produced a set of drawings for him of a small cabin cruiser (now being built in glass reinforced plastics), and I was delighted to hear of his interest in a Class III boat as his workmanship on the earlier design had been first-class and I knew he would make an excellent job of this craft also.

The boat was named *Strale* (which means "arrow"). The prototype in laminated timber was used, after completing trials, as the plug for the subsequent production hull in glass reinforced plastics. In their standard version these boats are powered by a single 140 HP MerCruiser with sterndrive, which has an engine capacity to the limit of the Class III rule (2966 c.c.). She has proved to be very fast and handles well.

Irrespective of whether Class III is or is not adopted in the Mediterranean, I think that this type of boat should prove popular with anyone who is looking for a fast and exhilarating runabout for water-skiing, etc.

See Figs. 24/a, 24/b, 24/c.

CHAPTER VIII

Fast Pleasure Craft
and Work Boats

*T*here is no question that the designs of my fast pleasure craft and work boats in recent years have been influenced in no uncertain manner by the experience gained in designing, building, and racing offshore powerboats.

Before the advent of the deep deadrise hull developed by Raymond Hunt and myself, there was a selection of warped plane and constant section low and moderate deadrise planing hulls to choose from which, although capable of fairly high speeds, could only maintain these in calm weather. Small high speed pleasure cabin cruisers, or indeed work boats, were not therefore very popular or much in demand. Obviously once one had had rather a rough ride at around 30 knots in choppy water one tended to turn back with relief to slower displacement craft, or even to go in for sailing.

I do not think I would be far wrong in saying that whilst eight or ten years ago there were only a handful of yards in the world producing fast deep deadrise cruisers, today there are probably more yards building this type of craft than the earlier conventional shallow deadrise models.

In recent years, too, enormous strides have been made in the development of marine propulsion. Where power to weight ratios have improved considerably, engines are more compact and diesel machinery has in particular become the order of the day for the bigger fast cabin cruisers and work boats. This rapid progress in hull and machinery design has made it possible to meet the ever-increasing demand for high speed both in pleasure and in work.

The designing of pleasure craft and work boats presents a series of problems somewhat different from the racing models I have mentioned earlier. For instance, these boats are more often required to have adequate volume within the hull so as to produce a comfortable layout in the case of purely pleasure craft, and passenger or stowage space in

the case of work boats.

There is generally a preference for diesel machinery on the larger boats in both these categories, and, therefore, more weight for an equal amount of horse-power. The range of operation of these craft can also be much greater and more fuel therefore has to be carried, as well as more water, stores and so on.

There are, then, two major factors to face which conflict with speed: more volume of boat and more weight to propel. The designer must take these important factors into consideration; he must in fact produce a hull with the right measure of compromise. Frequently one of the greatest pitfalls in designing these boats is under-estimating their loaded weight, with consequential effects on the calculated speed.

Plate 32   The author at the controls of the fast commuter Cinquanta.

122

Plate 33 . Cinquanta *on trials in Anzio Bay; a top speed of over 55 knots was obtained.*

Plate 34   Day cruiser Sagitta *in Salerno Bay.*

I personally have had occasion to utilize a variety of materials for the construction of these craft, including wood, light alloy, glassfibre and even steel; I have also employed different techniques of construction with these materials. There is endless scope for experimentation in this connection, with the ultimate aim of achieving the lightest possible structure with the required strength for the purpose. Costs, of course, can vary considerably according to the materials employed.

My preference in the case of a wooden hull is for a laminated shell utilizing as little framing as possible, as this not only produces a visually uncluttered interior but also gives more actual room. This form of construction certainly makes the internal fitting-out much easier, and I think that it need not be unreasonably expensive compared with other types of construction if it is carried out by a yard with experience in this kind of work.

Light alloy, on the other hand, has not proved as popular as wood for the smaller boats though I think it is an excellent material which is worth further investigation. The aircraft industry today, after all, where the problems of weight and strength are of paramount importance, uses almost nothing else for its structures. The corrosion aspect of this material for marine use is possibly a deterrent, but there are an infinite number of light alloys produced today which have exceptional corrosion-resistant properties if certain basic rules are observed. There has also been great progress in the development of protective coatings.

The various methods of glassfibre construction seem to be gaining ground very rapidly, and quite understandably. This material is particularly suited to production boats where moulds are necessary, and it also offers other noteworthy advantages such as reasonably low maintenance costs, the possibility of engineering light and strong structures by means of sandwiches, and last but not least complete liberty of shape, which if applied intelligently can add considerable rigidity of form. Unfortunately we often see boats today, even produced by well-known designers, which appear to ignore this fundamentally important characteristic; craft with slab-sided hulls or straight-sectioned bottoms which have absolutely no rigidity inherent in them, and therefore have to be built with greater thicknesses or, alternatively, beefed up with framing in order to stop the drumming of their numerous flat panels. A further advantage of glassfibre, which should not be forgotten, is that it permits a considerable reduction in the employment of highly skilled (and therefore expensive) labour.

Steel has evident disadvantages for planing craft. The main snags are weight and liability to corrosion, although corrosion is becoming less of a problem today as the result of the excellent synthetic protections now available. Stainless steel is the obvious solution, but the cost of this material is a serious deterrent to its use.

The future will no doubt offer many other interesting materials and methods of construction.

The question of styling is extremely important in the two categories of boat under discussion, and in particular in the case of pleasure craft. This requirement in fact is usually high on the list when a prospective buyer is contemplating a new boat.

Styling is undoubtedly greatly influenced by individual taste, but there are nevertheless certain classic shapes which do not tire the eye as quickly as other more extreme forms. The boat can, for instance, be styled with crisp, angular motives or else have a series of rounded forms and in both cases look equally well-balanced and pleasing.

Here again the right measure of compromise has to be worked out in the basic concept, a balance for instance between internal volume and external appearance. Height within the hull is very nice to have even if unnecessary; those extra inches of headroom make all the difference to a feeling of well-being and have an important psychological effect. On the other hand, every inch of reduction in sheer makes the boat look that much slimmer and more elegant externally. There are, of course, many ways of creating optical illusions by means of cove lines, colour play, and so on, but basically the right sort of proportions are essential to producing a thoroughbred craft.

I feel that one should try to be very sincere with oneself on the subject of styling. I am often carried away by all sorts of futuristic lines which are not, strictly speaking, very practical and which are, in some cases, a major headache to produce. Panoramic windows in the bridge, for instance, may look nice (and have been done very successfully), but they can be expensive and also a nuisance if the wrap round portion happens to be within eye range of the helmsman. The same criticism applies to heavily raked windshields. Masts and air intakes often contribute to spoiling the profile of a boat, while misplaced or badly-proportioned ports can be responsible for ruining the appearance of an otherwise pleasantly styled craft. Bridges, too, require a particular

Plate 35   80 ft. light alloy cruiser Cohete *built by Cantiere Rodriguez of Messina. (Photo Armone Messina).*

Plate 36   43 ft. patrol boat of the Super Speranza class.

measure of balance between height and length and between forward and aft rakes.

To sum up, designers should be careful to avoid changing basic shapes purely for the sake of producing something new and different, great though the temptation may be. Generally speaking, functional practical styling is also pleasing to the eye.

In the following pages I will describe some examples of the many pleasure boats I have designed, ranging from small runabouts and day cruisers to larger cabin cruisers and commuters. A small section on work boats (in particular, patrol boats) will follow.

SPERANZA MIA

Length overall	— *38′6″ (m. 11.75)*	*Deadrise transom* — *10°*
Length waterline	— *35′0″ (m. 10.66)*	*Weight*	— *7 tons*
Beam maximum	— *12′0″ (m. 3.66)*	*Engines*	— *Twin Perkins S6M diesels*
Beam chine	— *10′0″ (m. 3.05)*	*Total 200 HP*	

Speranza Mia has already been described at some length in Part I, Chapter I.

The hull lines of *Speranza Mia* have unquestionably "aged", but nevertheless I continue to get periodical requests for the drawings of this boat from various countries. Her styling was both functional and simple, and this may well be the reason why she still generates interest even at the distance of some fifteen years from her designing.

You can get to know a boat's personality really well by sailing in her. I covered many thousands of

miles in *Speranza Mia* and found her a thoroughly practical craft, ideal for long-distance cruising. Her lay-out was rational and compact—the man at the helm, for instance, in no way felt isolated from the rest of the crew, the cook hardly had to move at all in order to serve meals, and yet, if anyone wished to sleep, the forward cabin was quite private. Also, if any work had to be carried out on the engines, this could be done without in any way disrupting life on board. These (and other) details can be seen on the accommodation plan. See Figs. 25/a, 25/b, 25/c.

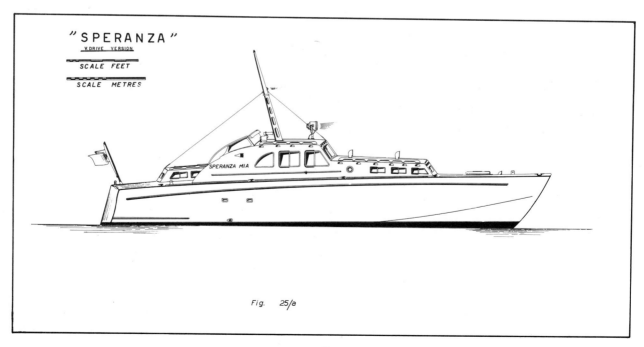

"SPERANZA"
V DRIVE VERSION

SCALE FEET

SCALE METRES

SPERANZA MIA

Fig. 25/a

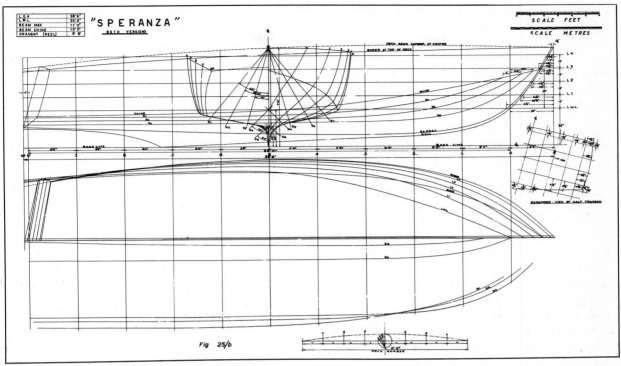

L.O.A	38'6"
L.W.L.	35'0"
BEAM MAX	11'11"
BEAM CHINE	10'0"
DRAUGHT (KEEL)	2'9"

"SPERANZA"
BOTH VERSIONS

SCALE FEET

SCALE METRES

Fig 25/b

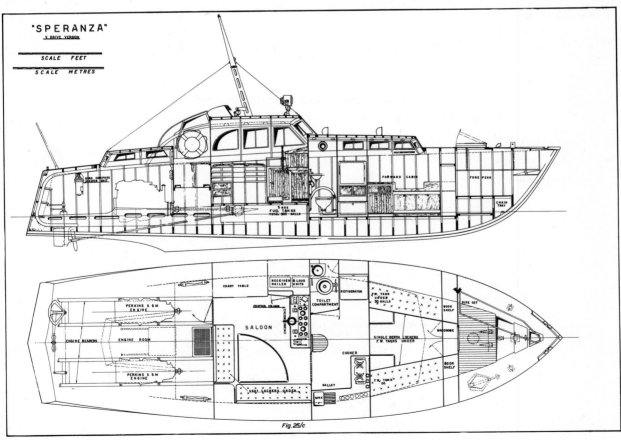

"SPERANZA"
V. DRIVE VERSION

SCALE FEET

SCALE METRES

Fig.25/c

127

TRIANA LEVI 25

Length overall	— 25′ 0″	(m. 7.62)	*Draught hull*	— 1′ 6½″	(m. 0.47)
Length waterline	— 21′ ½″	(m. 6.41)	*Deadrise transom*	— 25°	
Beam maximum	— 8′ 11″	(m. 2.72)	*Weight*	— 3 tons	
Beam chine	— 7′ 4″	(m. 2.24)	*Engines*	— Twin Volvo Aquamatic 240 HP	

The yachting press, particularly in Great Britain, gave this small cabin cruiser very full coverage when she first came on the market in 1968.

Her origins lie in *Trident* (cf. p. 114), although the overall length of *Triana*'s hull has been increased by two feet and the layout of the boat has been completely redesigned. I feel that she is altogether a thoroughly up-to-date, practical, fast cruiser even though her basic hull lines date back six or seven years.

Triana has been described as a supremely efficient and comfortable craft, combining speed and safety. She has been produced with a variety of power plants and can hold her own speedwise with most boats of her class. With a pair of Volvo 120/200 Aquamatic engines of 120 HP each, and a standard fuel capacity of 90 gallons, she has a comfortable continuous cruising speed of over 20 knots and a range of approx. 175 miles. One happy touch: despite her low cabin top (which is largely responsible for her rakish appearance) there is a full six foot headroom below.

The credit for *Triana*'s success must be given both to Messrs. Tyler of Tonbridge, who were responsible for the glassfibre structure (built under Lloyd's supervision), and to Howard Symmons of Trident Marine, who has made such a thorough job of studying her layout and producing a great many practical solutions which have made life on board that much more comfortable.

See Fig. 26.

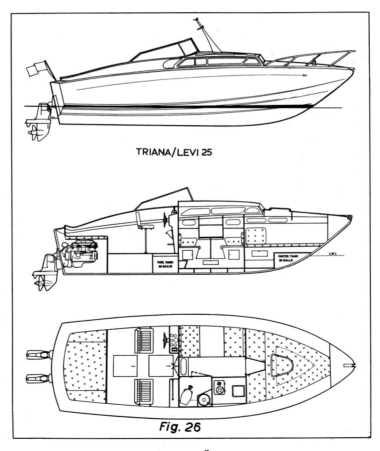

TRIANA/LEVI 25

Fig. 26

DELTA 24D

Length overall	— 24' 0"	(m. 7.32)	Draught hull	— 1'5$\frac{1}{4}$" (m. 0.44)
Length waterline	— 19' 4"	(m. 5.90)	Deadrise transom	— 21°
Beam maximum	— 8' 10"	(m. 2.70)	Weight	— 2.8 tons
Beam chine	— 7' 2$\frac{1}{2}$"	(m. 2.20)	Engines	— Twin MerCruiser 240 HP

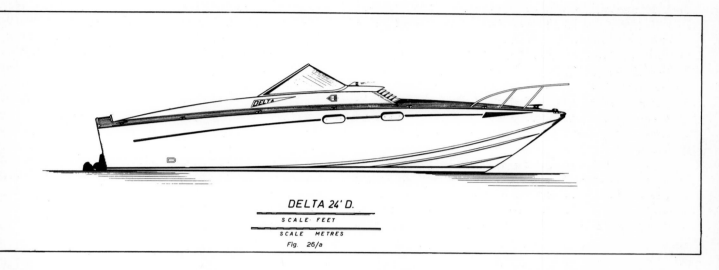

DELTA 24' D.

SCALE FEET

SCALE METRES

Fig. 26/a

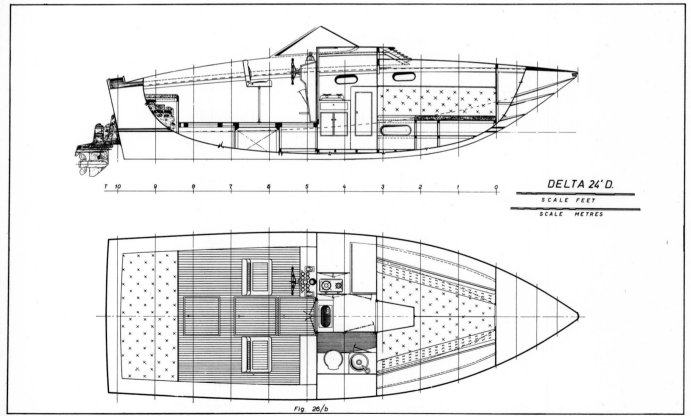

DELTA 24' D.

SCALE FEET

SCALE METRES

Fig. 26/b

I designed *Delta 24D* for Cantiere Delta of Anzio (hence her name). This day cruiser was built entirely in wood, having a cold-moulded laminated hull; the decks were also laminated and covered with teak laid in narrow strips. The prototype was powered by a pair of 120 HP MerCruiser engines with out-drives, giving a maximum speed of around 30 knots. The standard model is being powered with a pair of 160 HP MerCruiser engines, with a maximum speed just short of 40 knots. The fuel capacity is 350 litres (approx. 77 imp. gallons), and the cruising range around 150 miles.

The prototype was put through some fairly rough weather on trials and proved very satisfactory, having a soft entry as well as being extremely manoeuvrable. In following seas she held her course without any need for correction, there being no tendency to yaw. She was also remarkably dry even in quartering head seas.

Delta 24D has one rather unusual feature in her superstructure: a louvered motif in the forward section which is, in fact, a ventilator incorporating a water trap and effectively ventilating the cabin. See Figs. 26/a, 26/b.

ZARCOS 12

Length overall	— 39′5″ (m. 12.00)	*Draught hull*	— 2′0″ (m. 0.60)
Length waterline	— 33′4″ (m. 10.15)	*Deadrise transom*	— 22°
Beam maximum	— 12′6″ (m. 3.80)	*Weight*	— 8 tons
Beam chine	— 10′4″ (m. 3.15)	*Engines*	— *Twin Perkins diesel 330 HP*

This 12 metre hull, produced in laminated timber by Cantiere Scorza of Fiumicino, was designed as a small luxury cabin cruiser with an eye to long-distance cruising in the Mediterranean. To date, several of these boats have been built and their performance has been highly satisfactory; I would even go so far as to say that *Zarcos 12* is an unusually efficient and successful design.

Zarcos 12 is by no means a light boat; she is very generously fitted out and no great effort was made to save on weight, but in spite of this she is capable of a maximum speed of over 24 knots with a pair of turbocharged 165 HP Perkins marine diesel engines, and a continuous cruising speed of 20 knots. The range of the boat, with standard fitted fuel tanks, is over 300 miles.

The internal layout was designed by an interior decorator and is typical of the modern trend to call in a styling specialist as part of the design team. See Figs. 27/a, 27/b.

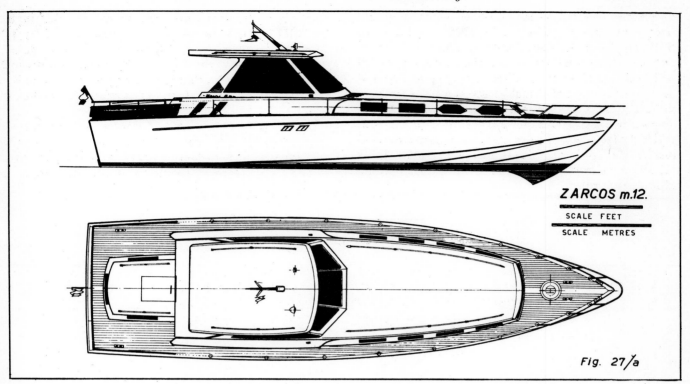

ZARCOS m.12.

SCALE FEET

SCALE METRES

Fig. 27/a

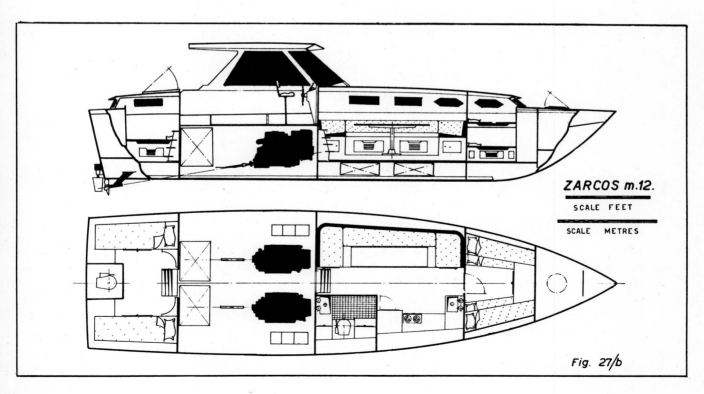

ZARCOS m.12.

SCALE FEET

SCALE METRES

Fig. 27/b

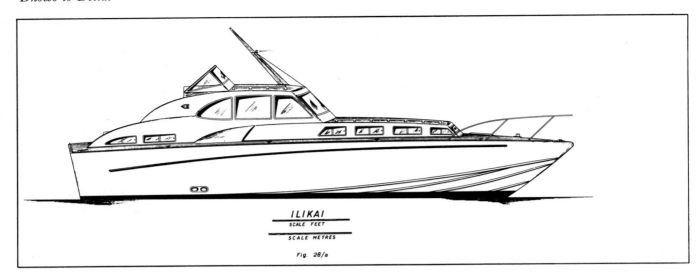

ILIKAI

SCALE FEET

SCALE METRES

Fig. 28/a

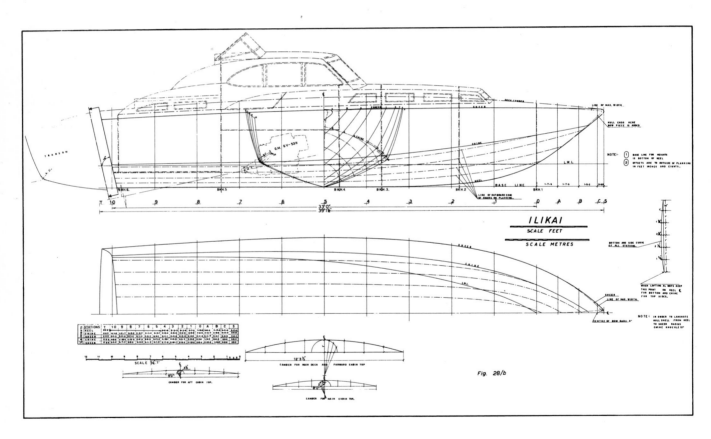

ILIKAI

SCALE FEET

SCALE METRES

Fig. 28/b

ILIKAI

Length overall	— 39′ 2″	(m. 11.94)	*Draught hull*	— 1′ 10″ (m. 0.56)
Length waterline	— 33′ 0″	(m. 10.06)	*Deadrise transom*	— 22°
Beam maximum	— 12′ 3½″	(m. 3.75)	*Weight laden*	— 9 tons
Beam chine	— 10′ 1½″	(m. 3.09)	*Engines*	— *Twin Cummins diesels 560 HP*

I prepared this design for Chas Western of Auckland, New Zealand. Chas had already built one boat in New Zealand to my design, a 38′6″ hull called *Resolution* based on the original *Speranza Mia*. *Ilikai* was a bigger boat of deep V form. I think Chas' own description (written for a New Zealand journal) cannot be bettered and I am quoting some excerpts here.

"*Ilikai*'s hull is actually round bilge. It is of four quarter-inch hand picked strictly moisture controlled heart kauri laminations. There is not a rib or stringer inside; the planing battens form stringers outside. The result is a light exceptionally strong hull which does not distort when lifted from the mould and no internal space is lost to frames, ribs or stringers. What a difference it makes when painting or fitting out. It is all clear "cubic", but every tank, bulkhead, planing batten and so on, plays a clearly defined part in establishing the strength and absorbing the stresses which are associated with the boat."

"At rest the bow is lower than the stern. The very good reason for this is that under way you must have first class visibility. When planing the bow lifts, visibility is superb and due to the lift of the bow, waves never break on board."

"From a manoeuvring point of view the boat can be steered with a finger and thumb on a wheel spoke in any sea condition. There are no problems with yawing. In harbour, or berthing at mooring or wharf, the large propellers act like tracks on a crawler tractor. . . . The boat will turn 'on a sixpence' and in light winds can even be encouraged to travel sideways!"

Ilikai is powered by a pair of 280 HP supercharged Cummins diesel engines, giving a top speed of around 28 knots and a cruising speed of 24 knots. Her range is over 300 miles.

See Figs. 28/a, 28/b, 28/c.

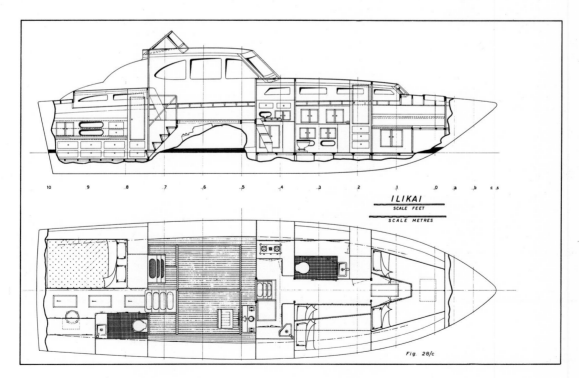

ILIKAI
SCALE FEET
SCALE METRES

Fig. 28/c

COHETE

Length overall	— 79′9″	(m. 24.30)	*Draught hull*	— 3′3½″ (m. 1.00)
Length waterline	— 69′0″	(m. 21.03)	*Deadrise transom*	— 16°
Beam maximus	— 25′6″	(m. 7.77)	*Weight*	— 60 tons
Beam chine	— 22′4″	(m. 6.80)	*Engines*	— Twin CRM diesels 2100 HP

I was responsible for the hull lines of this eighty foot luxury sea-going motor yacht, which was constructed by Cantiere Rodriguez of Messina in light alloy (Peraluman AG4). Cantiere Rodriguez were also responsible for installing the machinery, electrical equipment, and so on, while Cantiere Navaltecnica

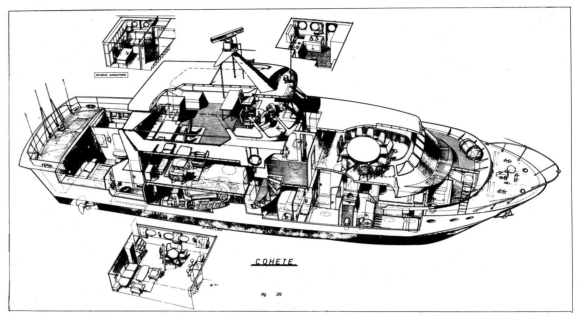

Fig. 29

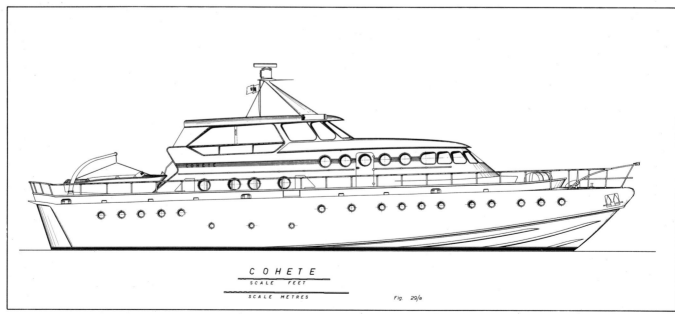

COHETE

SCALE FEET

SCALE METRES

Fig. 29/a

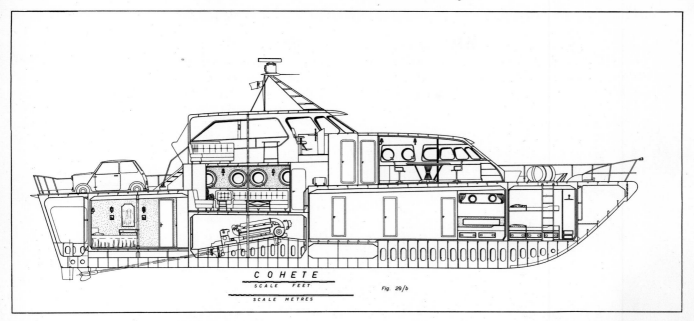

C O H E T E

SCALE FEET

SCALE METRES

Fig. 29/b

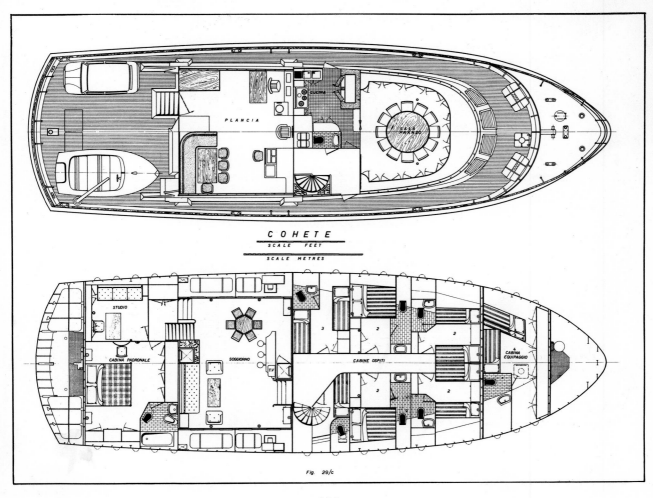

C O H E T E

SCALE FEET

SCALE METRES

Fig. 29/c

of Anzio did all the fitting out and the woodwork including teak decks.

Cohete is a moderate deadrise hull, powered with twin 1050 HP C.R.M. diesel engines and carrying 13 tons of fuel and 2 tons of fresh water. On trials, when the displacement was 60 tons, a maximum speed of 24 knots was obtained. Her continuous cruising speed is between 18 and 20 knots.

During the preliminary design stage extensive model testing was carried out in the hydrodynamic test tank at Rome. The position of the spray rails was changed several times in the course of these tests—in one series they were even removed altogether. The results were interesting, in that there was an 11% difference in maximum speed between the worst and the best tests, the worst being with no strakes at all. It has often been said that spray strakes have virtually no value <u>at</u> low speed length ratios ($V = 2 \cdot 5 \sqrt{L}$ to $V = 3 \sqrt{L}$), but in this particular case we found that on the contrary they contributed in a positive manner to increased efficiency.

See Figs. 29, 29/a, 29/b, 29/c.

SONNY 14

Length overall	— 14′0″	(m. 4.27)
Length waterline	— 11′4″	(m. 3.45)
Beam maximum	— 6′2″	(m. 1.88)
Beam chine	— 4′8″	(m. 1.43)

Draught hull	— 0′9¼″	(m. 0.23)
Deadrise transom	— 18°	
Weight	— .35 tons	
Engine	— Evinrude 90 HP	

Sonny 14 is a fourteen foot runabout, powered with an Evinrude 90 HP inboard engine with outdrive unit, designed with several objects in mind: water-skiing, pottering around in sheltered waters, yacht's tender, and so on. The prototype in fact was the yacht's tender of M.Y. *Cohete*.

See Figs. 30/a, 30/b, 30/c.

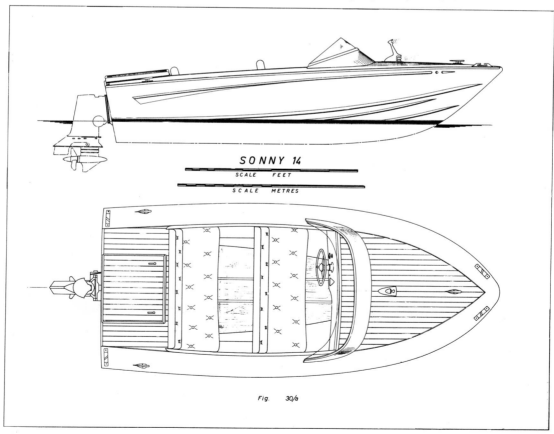

SONNY 14

SCALE FEET

SCALE METRES

Fig. 30/a

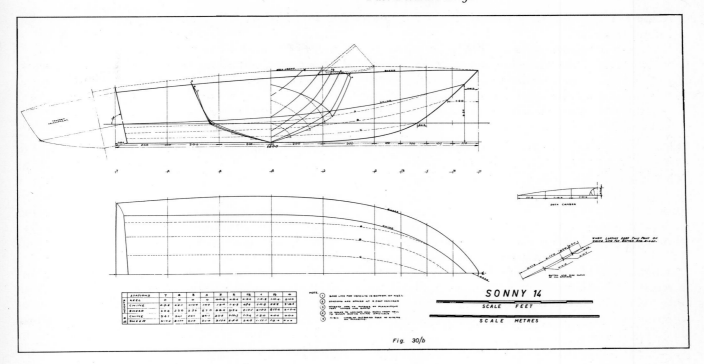

Fig. 30/b

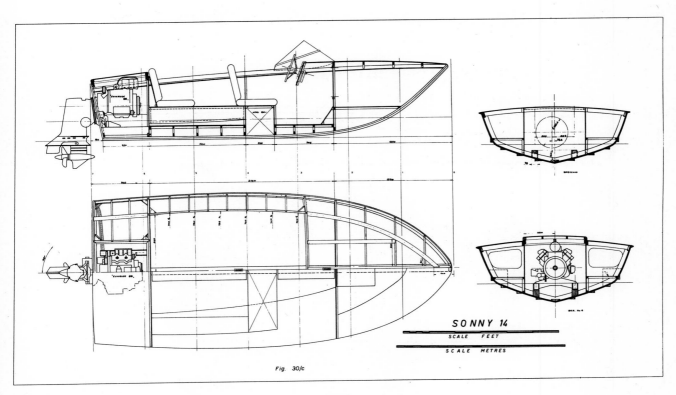

Fig. 30/c

ZARCOS 16

Length overall	— *53′6″ (m. 16.30)*	*Deadrise transom*	— *22°*
Length waterline	— *43′8″ (m. 13.30)*	*Weight*	— *22 tons*
Beam maximum	— *16′9″ (m. 5.10)*	*Engines*	— *Twin GM 12V-71 diesel,*
Beam chine	— *13′0″ (m. 3.96)*		*1000 HP*
Draught hull	— *2′8″ (m. 0.80)*	*Speed*	— *25 knots*

This 53 foot luxury cruiser is the most recent of a string of designs I have prepared for Cantiere Scorza. The hull lines are similar to those of *Zarcos 12* (see p. 131, which incidentally was the first design I produced for this yard.

The prototype *Zarcos 16* was completed a short time ago, and on trials proved both fast and comfortable. Her sea keeping qualities are excellent, and I imagine that life on board must be very pleasant as a result of all the meticulous attention to detail put into her. The accommodation was styled by an interior decorator who has obviously studied the layout with great care.

Zarcos 16, like the other production cruisers in the Zarcos series, is a laminated structure in wood, but in her case longitudinal framing has been adopted on the bottom and top sides owing to the dimension of the hull shell.

The propulsive machinery consists of a pair of G.M. 12V-71 diesels, developing 504 HP each at 2300 r.p.m.; the engines are equipped with 2:1 reduction gear and drive 31″ diameter propellers. Her top speed is 25 knots and her continuous cruising speed just on 21 knots. The fuel capacity is 660 gallons, giving a range at cruising speed of around 380 miles.

Yachts of these dimensions are becoming increasingly popular in the Mediterranean. I imagine that this popularity is due to the fact that boats of the size of *Zarcos 16* provide both home comforts and the adventures of travel. No problems exist in finding hotel accommodation when in port, a difficult business at the height of the summer season, while they are capable of negotiating adverse weather without those on board having to rough it too much.

See Figs. 31/a, 31/b, 31/c.

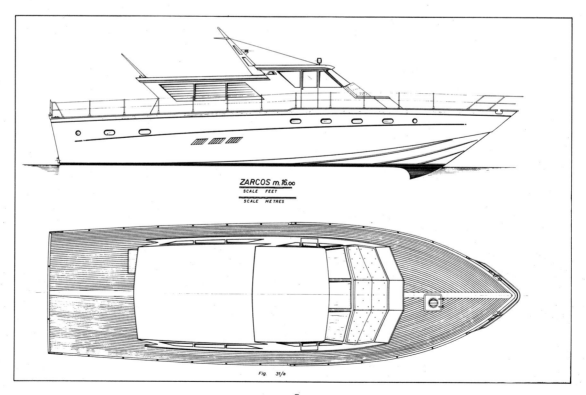

ZARCOS m. 16.00
SCALE FEET
SCALE METRES

Fig. 31/a

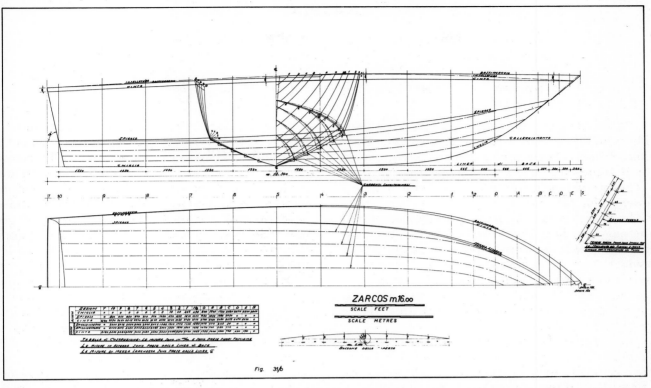

Fig. 31/b

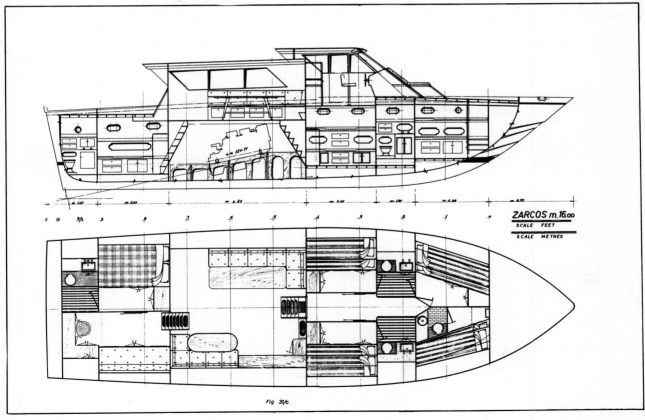

Fig 31/c

SAGITTA

Length overall	—	*24′ 7″ (m. 7.50)*	*Draught hull*	— *1′ 3″ (m. 0.38)*
Length waterline	—	*19′ 2″ (m. 5.85)*	*Deadrise transom*	— *21°*
Beam maximum	—	*7′ 10″ (m. 2.40)*	*Weight*	— *2.7 tons*
Beam chine	—	*6′ 6″ (m. 1.98)*	*Engines*	— *Twin MerCruiser 320 HP*

Sagitta was designed for a Salerno boatyard, Cantiere Sapri; her hull lines were based upon my Delta configuration, although of course the Delta shape is not so radical as it is in my racing powerboats.

The unusual feature of the lines drawing is a pronounced flat section at the chine; the object of this was to make the boat more stable laterally when at rest. The superstructure was also stream-lined as much as possible, in order to reduce windage.

Built in glass reinforced plastics with internal joinery work in wood, the prototype was powered by a pair of 160 HP MerCruiser engines with outdrives which gave a maximum speed of close on 40 knots. A fuel capacity of 400 litres (88 imperial gallons) ensured *Sagitta* a cruising range of approx. 175 miles.

Incidentally, I feel that this boat could well give a very good account of herself in offshore racing in Class C2, although the deadrise aft is on the shallow side.

See Figs. 32/a, 32/b.

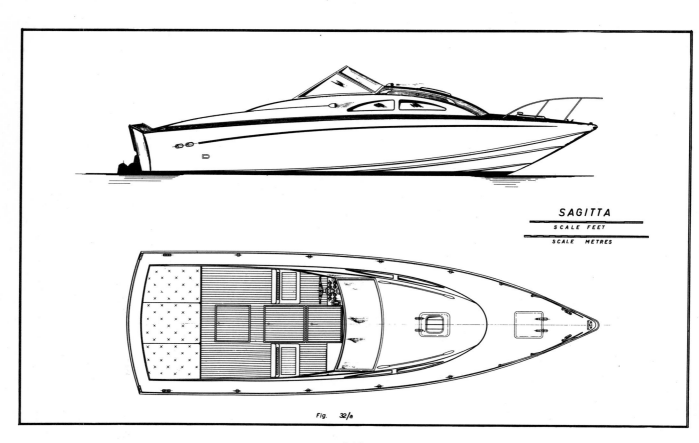

SAGITTA

SCALE FEET

SCALE METRES

Fig. 32/a

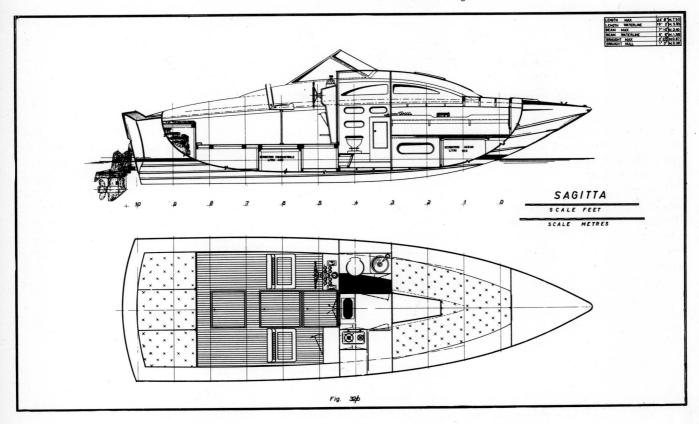

LENGTH MAX	24' 8" m 7.50
LENGTH WATERLINE	19' 2" m 5.85
BEAM MAX	7' 10" m 2.40
BEAM WATERLINE	6' 6" m 1.98
DRAUGHT MAX	2' 2" m 0.67
DRAUGHT HULL	1' 3" m 0.39

SAGITTA

SCALE FEET

SCALE METRES

Fig. 326

DELTA 38

Length overall	— *38' 0"*	*(m. 11.58)*	*Draught hull*	— *1' 10¾" (m. 0.58)*
Length waterline	— *31' 8"*	*(m. 9.65)*	*Deadrise transom*	— *25°*
Beam maximum	— *10' 9"*	*(m. 3.27)*	*Weight*	— *5.5 tons*
Beam chine	— *8' 0"*	*(m. 2.43)*	*Engines*	— *Twin Daytona, 1050 HP*

Towards the end of 1966 I was delighted to be asked to produce a design for Merrick Lewis of Alliance, Ohio. That year, Merrick had competed in all the major European races with his *Thunderbolt*, a 28 foot formula powered by two 525 HP Daytona engines, and had a successful season with wins both at Famagusta in Cyprus and Viareggio in Italy.

What Merrick really wanted for this new design was a boat which was fast enough to win races but at the same time could adequately house his crew on board. He felt that if his crew "lived in" he would have no problems over finding hotel rooms, getting to and from the port, and so on. The dual requirements of speed and acceptable living accommodation are not easily compatible in an out-and-out racing craft—especially when this has to compete

against open category boats. However, I think that the compromise I drew out for him was reasonably well balanced.

Delta 38 was built by Cantiere Delta in Anzio. She had comfortable quarters for the crew but I never saw her running as she was shipped to the United States for the installation of her engines, mechanical gear, etc. I cannot, therefore, judge her speed capabilities, but I have no reason to believe that she was a particularly slow boat since the hull lines were based on the already well-tried *Surfury*, and we had also paid great attention to economy in weight and aerodynamic cleanliness. The craft was not as low as I should have liked, owing to the crew's cabin, but the shape of the superstructure was well streamlined and offered good penetration. I was also

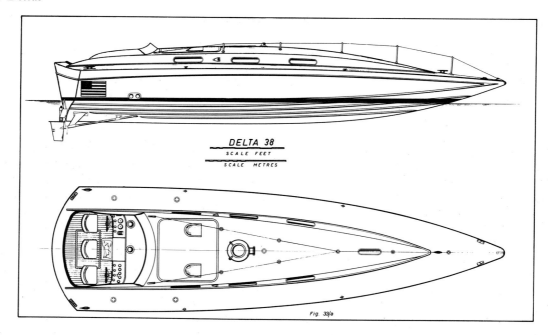

DELTA 38
SCALE FEET
SCALE METRES

Fig. 33/a

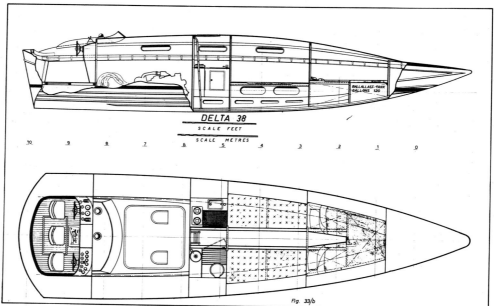

DELTA 38
SCALE FEET

10   9   8   7   6   5   4   3   2   1   0

SCALE METRES

BALLAST-TANK
GALLONS 120

Fig. 33/b

not very happy, from a pure speed standpoint, about the installation of the engines on straight through shafts just aft of amidship, but one of Merrick's main requirements had been for the driving cockpit to be right aft and the engines, therefore, obviously had to be moved forward.

I heard no more of *Delta 38* after she left Italy, other than the news that she sank during a race in the United States in 1967.

The concept underlying this boat was sound: the improvement of fast cabin cruisers as a breed in the light of what could be learned from racing them. *Delta 38* also started a new design trend for me, that of the fast commuter.

Soon after *Delta 38* was completed I designed yet another craft on very similar lines, and for almost identical purposes, *Delta Tiger*. This hull was built by the same yard in Anzio and was powered by a pair of 525 HP Daytona engines which also were fitted on straight through drives.

G. CINQUANTA

Length overall	—	*37′0″*	*(m. 11.28)*	*Deadrise transom* — *26°*	
Length waterline	—	*31′8″*	*(m. 9.65)*	*Weight*	*— 4.8 tons*
Beam maximum	—	*10′5″*	*(m. 3.18)*	*Engines*	*— Four 8-litre BPM Vulcano*
Beam chine	—	*8′0″*	*(m. 2.43)*		*1280 HP*
Draught hull	—	*1′10¾″*	*(m. 0.58)*		

Towards the end of 1967 Gianni Agnelli commissioned me to study the design of a fast, reliable craft for commuting purposes. The boat had to be capable of negotiating mixed weather conditions at high speed with an acceptable degree of comfort (the maximum speed required was 55 knots). No cabin was needed, although in the final design a space under the foredeck was utilized for a couple of berths, a lavatory, and a wash-basin.

I found the design of this boat a most interesting exercise for not only were the requirements unusual, but there were also many ways in which they could be met. In addition, this was the beginning for me of a new type of collaboration in producing a design, where styling specialists contributed in many ways to improving the appearance of the finished product.

I decided eventually on a length of 37 feet for the *G. Cinquanta*, based on my Delta configuration, since I felt that this would be the best compromise between the various conflicting requirements. The craft was to be flush-decked and to have four engines,

each independently driving a propeller. I had naturally also contemplated a tandem arrangement whereby the four engines would be coupled to two shafts, a solution which would have been undoubtedly more efficient and have given a higher maximum speed owing to reduction of appendage drag, but after due consideration I decided to adopt the first solution for reasons of reliability. I also felt that the maximum required speed of 55 knots could be obtained satisfactorily with four independent shafts (and four propellers). I came to this conclusion after having studied some tank test data I had on *Ultima Dea*, the Maserati-powered triple screw racing craft built some five years earlier.

We selected the normal 8-litre (500 cu. in.) Italian BPM Vulcano marine petrol engines for the power plant; these engines were rated at 320 HP each at 4000 r.p.m., giving us a total of 32 litres (2000 cu. in.) and 1280 HP, and were chosen for their reliability, compactness and excellent power to weight ratio (the engine blocks etc. were made of

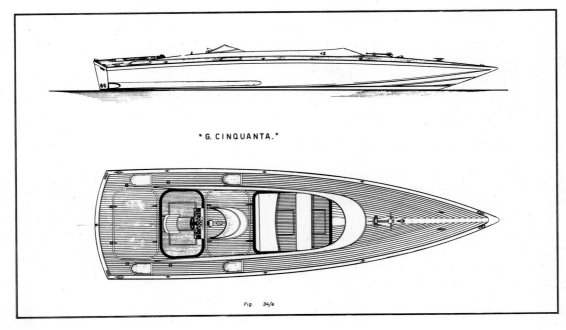

" G. CINQUANTA."

Fig. 34/a

143

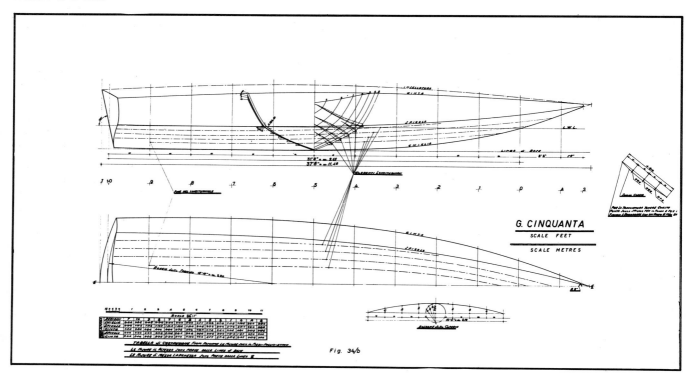

G. CINQUANTA

SCALE FEET

SCALE METRES

Fig. 34/b

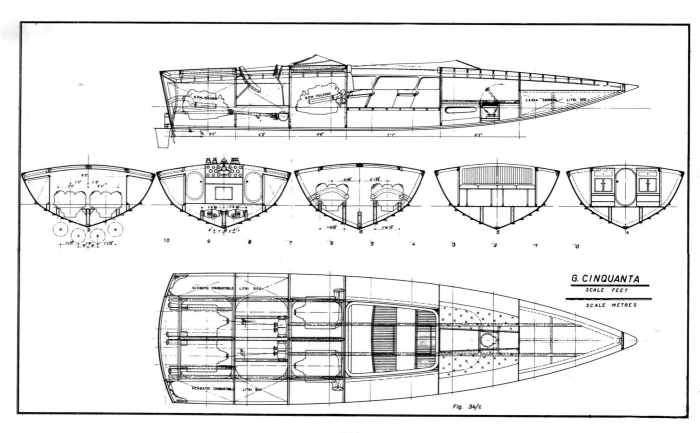

G. CINQUANTA

SCALE FEET

SCALE METRES

Fig. 34/c

light alloy). One pair of these engines was installed aft, driving the two inboard central propellers through BPM V-drives which incorporated 25% multiplication gears. The other, forward pair drove the outboard wing propellers with straight through shafts and direct drive gear. The diameter and pitch of the wing propellers were, therefore, greater than those of the central propellers. The forward engines were to be used for manoeuvring and for slow running; this worked out particularly well since manoeuvring was facilitated with the widely positioned wing propellers, acceleration was good owing to the large diameter, and at slow running speeds the straight through shafts eliminated any backlash noise which might have occurred had the propellers been driven through V-drives at low r.p.m. The two central screws could, therefore, be shut off on entering port and only the two other ones adopted, in the same way as 4-engined airliners utilize only two engines when taxying.

Since one of the requirements was comfort at high speed in rough water, I adopted a deadrise at the transom of 26°. This deadrise was maintained for a short length aft and then increased towards the bows. All sections were convex in form, since the hull was to be a laminated wood structure and I wished to adopt a continuous lamination from keel to sheer in order to obtain a light structure with maximum rigidity of form. The deck was also laminated, which eliminated the necessity for deck beams. As the topsides were to be varnish finished, a fifth laminate was applied to these which was pressed on without tacking strips so as to avoid the possibility of seeing any staple holes through the clear varnish finish.

The craft was built at Anzio by Cantiere Delta who made an excellent job of the woodwork; this is in fact of the very highest order. The hull was finished with synthetic paints and varnishes especially studied by Veneziani of Trieste, one of the top Italian firms specializing in this field. These synthetic varnishes and paints incorporated polyurethane and epoxy resins, giving a durable and high gloss finish. Silicone pastes were also prepared for the bottom in an experiment (which proved successful) to see if they would be more efficient speedwise than anti-foulings and, at the same time, equally effective against marine growth. The deck was finished in teak laid in narrow strips parallel to the sheer and caulked with a neoprene compound.

Four fuel tanks, for a total capacity of 1600 litres (350 imperial gallons), were built into the hull aft (two on each side). They were made of plywood and lined with glassfibre. This solution not only reduced the amount of space required for this quantity of fuel, but also contributed to the strength of the hull structure. This fuel capacity gave *G. Cinquanta* a range of over 300 miles at a cruising speed of around 35 knots.

The steering cockpit was situated between the four engines, with the driving position on the centre line of the boat and all the controls and instruments placed in a beautifully styled console designed by Pininfarina of Turin. The wheel operated hydraulically a single deep transom mounted rudder. The driver was provided with a very comfortable adjustable backrest-cum-seat into which he could lean in a position rather similar to that adopted on some of the bigger racing powerboats. Pininfarina were particularly successful in their styling of the forward cockpit, which in its attractive simplicity rather resembles the interior of an executive aircraft with its smart side-racks, concealed handholds, and luxurious upholstery.

I had adopted a double solution for protecting the cockpits from wind and spray: a heavily raked laminated wood wind deflector in front of the forward cockpit tapering away along the sides until well aft of the rear cockpit, and an elliptical perspex screen in front of the helmsman very similar to those on Formula 1 racing cars. When I saw Gianni after his first full season's cruising in *G. Cinquanta*, during which he covered about 2000 miles, he told me that he was perfectly satisfied with her performance, with one exception. The windshield in front of the steering position did not give the driver sufficient protection; at speed the driver's cheeks tended to be depressed, and it was quite an effort to keep one's eyes open at all.

I had made the original shield low so as to offer the least possible wind resistance. I think that this would have worked all right had the boat been flush-decked without any forward cockpit opening, but as it was I suspect that the deflector round the forward cockpit caused a turbulence which prevented the windshield from receiving a clear flow of air. A new windshield was therefore designed and fitted.

This is yet another example of the compromises which are constantly necessary between conflicting design problems.

G. Cinquanta's engine compartments were both carefully insulated with extremely light soundproof material in order to keep the boat as quiet as possible. Cowls were fitted to conduct the exhaust gases right aft to the transom, since the exhausts of the forward

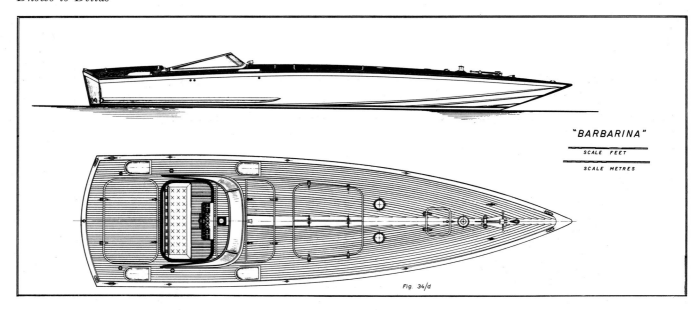

"BARBARINA"

SCALE FEET

SCALE METRES

Fig. 34/d

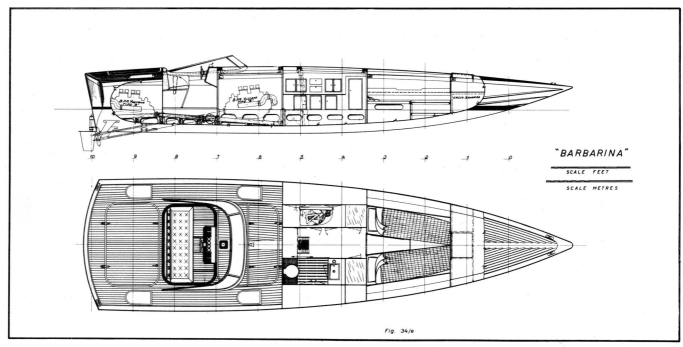

"BARBARINA"

SCALE FEET

SCALE METRES

Fig. 34/e

engines were led out of the sides of the hull about amidships. This arrangement has proved very effective in reducing exhaust noise. Cooling water for the four engines was provided by two scoops situated on either side of the hollow wedge-shaped central rudder.

The transom was fitted with electric-hydraulic flaps and a 500 litre (110 imperial gallons) capacity ballast tank was located forward, so as to be able to vary the trim of the boat. Both these devices contributed in good measure to make life on board more comfortable, especially in the forward cockpit, when *G. Cinquanta* was running fast in choppy seas.

G. Cinquanta was completed and launched early in June, 1968. Trials were particularly successful and trouble-free; only once were the propellers changed, and the promised speed of 55 knots was exceeded. The boat was actually capable of over 30 knots at

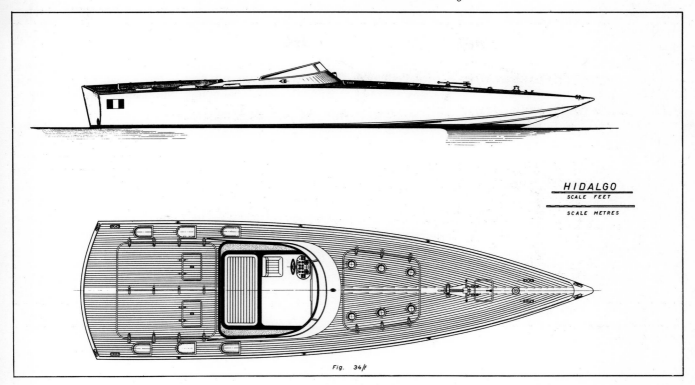

HIDALGO
SCALE FEET

SCALE METRES

Fig. 34/f

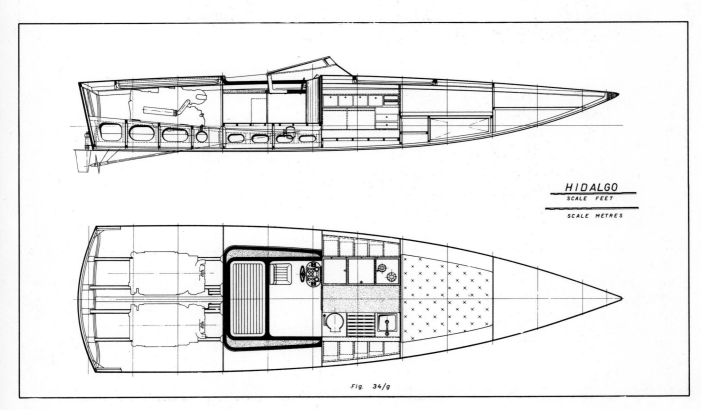

HIDALGO
SCALE FEET

SCALE METRES

Fig. 34/g

2000 r.p.m. on all four engines, 37 knots at 2500 r.p.m., and 43 knots at 3000 r.p.m. I was especially pleased that she planed quite easily and did a speed of around 25 knots with either the two forward or the two stern engines. This meant that in the event of any one, or two, of the four engines being unserviceable the boat was still capable of maintaining a high cruising speed and could enter port without difficulty.

A nautical writer in Italy has dubbed *G. Cinquanta* "a boat for following offshore races . . . ahead of the winner". Well . . . I don't know about that, but she is probably one of the fastest pleasure boats in existence.

Following *G. Cinquanta* I designed a further two boats along the same lines for two industrialists from North Italy, the late Count Mario Agusta and Roberto Olivetti. Count Agusta's *Barbarina* was launched in May, 1969 at Anzio and was another four-engined commuter with the same engine layout as the prototype, although this time the competition BPM Super Vulcano engines were installed giving

approximately 400 more HP and a top speed of over 60 knots. Roberto Olivetti's *Hidalgo* followed her into the water a month later; she is powered by a pair of 370 HP Cummins marine diesel engines fitted right aft and driving the propellers through BPM V-drives, and has a maximum speed of over 40 knots. Both boats were built by Cantiere Delta.

An interesting feature of these two boats is the cabin accommodation, which is situated under a flush deck. The object of this is to have a low profile when navigating, combined with the possibility of giving headroom and ventilation to the cabin when required by opening specially fitted hatches on deck. This idea seemed to me to be quite functional, since these craft were to be used in the Mediterranean during the summer season (when it can be extremely hot and close at night in port), and in fact it has proved successful. Privacy is ensured by stretching specially made awnings over the hatches when they are open.

See Figs. 34/a, 34/b, 34/c, 34/d, 34/e, 34/f, 34/g.

QUASAR

Length overall	— 17′8½″ (m. 5.40)	Deadrise transom	— 18°
Length waterline	— 13′5″ (m. 4.10)	Weight	— 0.8 tons
Beam maximum	— 6′3″ (m. 1.90)	Engine	— Alfa Romeo Giulia 1600 c.c., 77 HP
Beam chine	— 4′9″ (m. 1.44)	Speed	— 32.8 knots
Draught hull	— 1′5½″ (m. 0.44)		

In 1968 Ing. Luigi Castoldi of the BCS Engineering Company asked me if I would be prepared to design a runabout around a water jet unit he had himself produced. He sent me data on the speeds achieved with his unit on various standard craft used as test beds (results which compared very favourably with those obtained with conventional propulsive machinery, both inboard and outdrive), and suggested that I came to Milan to witness some trials myself.

I travelled up to Milan without feeling particularly convinced about the merits of this method of propulsion, since I had been associated in previous years with water jet units which quite frankly had not given very happy results. After witnessing trials on the artificial lake at Milan, however, I had to admit that this particular unit was extremely efficient on the boats being demonstrated, although I still had some reservations on the performance we could expect at sea, especially with a bit of a chop.

The reason for this scepticism was that I felt that the water intake would be frequently ventilated by air when the craft was riding high on the wave crests, making it impossible to maintain any sort of speed. One of the problems with these water jets in heavily loaded boats is that acceleration from standstill has to be done gradually, since if at any time a depression occurs on the suction side of the water tunnel the entire system can stall completely, and it is then necessary to start all over again. I felt that in open water we would run into this inconvenience every time the tunnel was ventilated, or partially ventilated. However, when the prototype of this runabout was later tested at Anzio on a roughish day, I was delighted to see that there was no need at all for any deceleration even after the boat had taken completely to the air. I suppose what actually happened was that, upon re-entry, the high forward speed rammed a column of water into the intake and the boat was thus able to carry on quite happily without

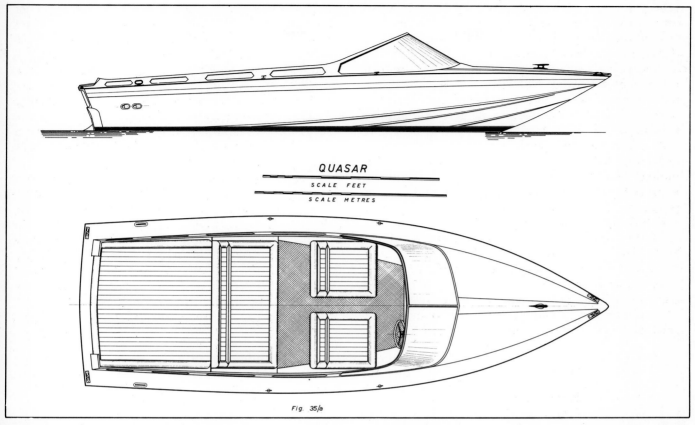

QUASAR

SCALE FEET

SCALE METRES

Fig. 35/a

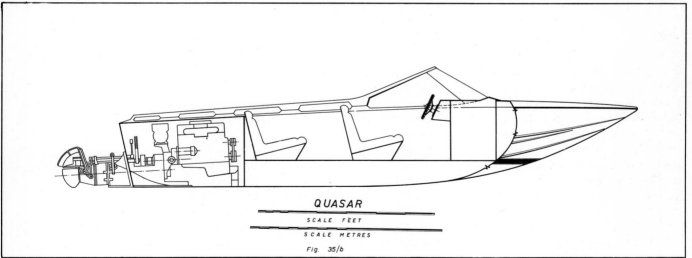

QUASAR

SCALE FEET

SCALE METRES

Fig. 35/b

any loss of speed.

Luigi Castoldi has, to my mind, made a wonderful job of this most interesting jet unit. He powered the standard production form with a 1750 c.c. Alfa Romeo motor-car engine, which he marinized himself (very successfully), and has also produced a more powerful version with the 3-litre Ford engine as well as several alternatives with other power plants.

He asked me to prepare the hull design because he wished to market his jet unit complete with a suitable boat; as he explained to me, a good measure of the success of this propulsive system lies in the proper choice of craft and in the correct installation of the unit. I am convinced that his reasoning is 100%

right.

Castoldi is incidentally a cousin of the famous aircraft designer Mario Castoldi, who was responsible for the *Macchi-Castoldi 72* seaplane which held the world air speed record from the Schneider Trophy era right up to the last war.

The *Quasar* is yet another example of a boat where the services of a styling expert have been employed; in this case the motor-car body designers Ghia of Turin, who styled the deck, windshield, instrument panel, and seats. They did an excellent job, as can be seen from the drawings; the hallmark of the specialist is clearly visible.

For those who are interested, the speeds obtained on trials with different loadings were as follows (carried out on a boat with the Alfa Romeo Giulia 1600 c.c. engine developing 77 HP at 5100 r.p.m.):

Boat speed	Weight
60·5 km/h	785 kg
57·5 km/h	890 kg
55 km/h	995 kg
52·5 km/h	1120 kg

This table shows the extremely high efficiency of Castoldi's water jet unit.

See Figs. 35/a, 35/b.

WORK BOATS

As I have already mentioned in the introduction to this chapter, possibly the most important feature of a pleasure boat is the accommodation—coupled with the styling. In a fast work boat, on the contrary, these requirements take second place and the designer's main task is usually to work out a compromise between speed and strength. Compared with pleasure boats (which may do only a few hundred hours' running in the whole year), patrol boats and so on do thousands of hours and go out in all kinds of weather; they are also subject to tremendous wear and tear, since at times they have to dock in places where facilities can be anything but ideal.

The designer of a work boat must take into consideration too the fact that these craft are sometimes run by crews working in shifts, which may account for a diminution of pride in the maintenance and appearance of their craft. In extreme cases, advantage may also be taken of the fact that it is difficult to allocate responsibility for any damage due to negligence. In other words, the designer has to make sure that the craft can take a fair amount of punishment.

I have chosen to illustrate here as examples of work boats I have designed, the coastal patrol boat versions of the 25 foot *Settimo Velo*, the 36 foot *Speranza*, and the 43 foot *Super Speranza*, as well as a 56 foot Sports Fisherman (even though this is not truly a work boat in the strict sense of the word).

SETTIMO VELO

Length overall	— 25′ 0″	*(m. 7.62)*	
Length waterline	— 21′ 0″	*(m. 6.40)*	
Beam maximum	— 8′ 11″	*(m. 2.72)*	
Beam chine	— 7′ 4″	*(m. 2.24)*	

Draught hull — 1′ 6½″ *(m. 0.47)*
Deadrise transom — 25°
Weight — 4 tons
Engines — *Twin MerCruiser 450 HP*

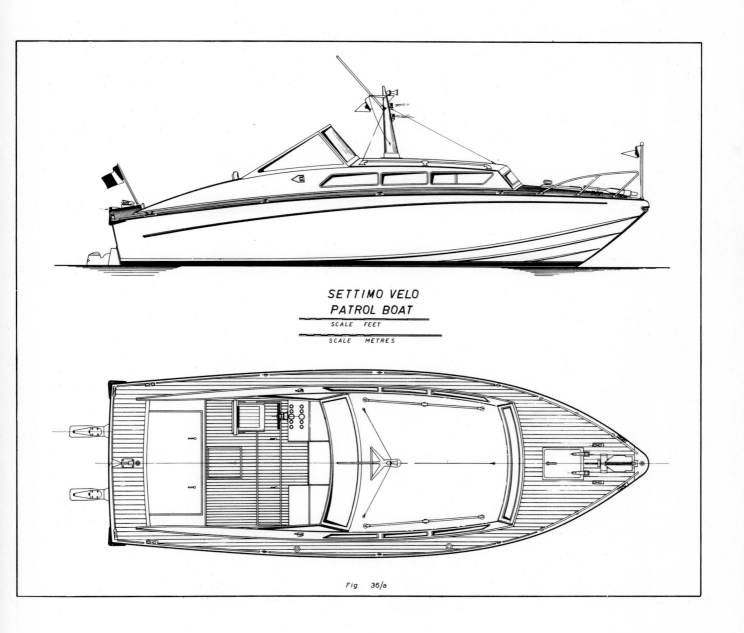

SETTIMO VELO
PATROL BOAT

SCALE FEET

SCALE METRES

Fig. 36/a

151

SPERANZA

Length overall   — 36′ 0″ (m. 10.97)   Draught hull   — 1′ 10″ (m. 0.56)
Length waterline — 32′ 2″ (m. 9.80)   Deadrise transom — 22°
Beam maximum — 12′ 6″ (m. 3.81)   Weight   — 8 tons
Beam chine   — 10′ 4″ (m. 3.15)   Engines   — Various up to 800 HP total

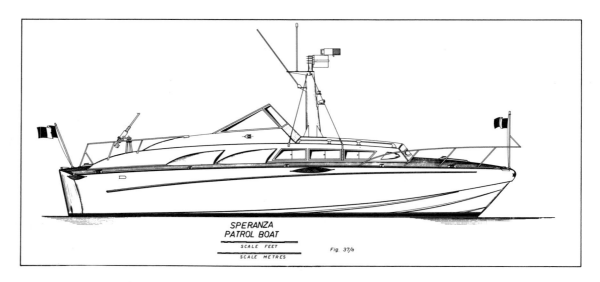

SPERANZA
PATROL BOAT

SCALE FEET
SCALE METRES

Fig. 37/a

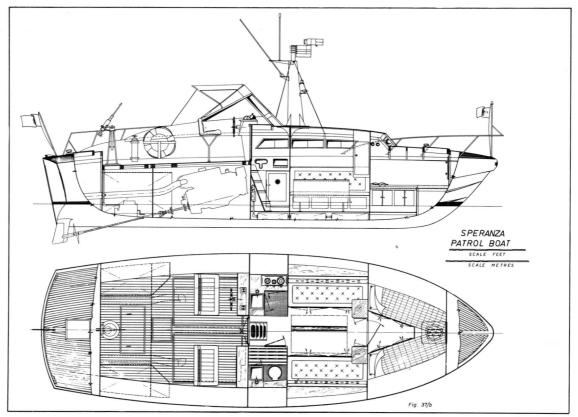

SPERANZA
PATROL BOAT

SCALE FEET
SCALE METRES

Fig. 37/b

SUPER SPERANZA

Length overall	— 43′0″ (m. 13.10)	*Draught hull*	— 2′4½″ (m. 0.72)
Length waterline	— 36′6″ (m. 11.12)	*Deadrise transom*	— 23°
Beam maximum	— 15′4″ (m. 4.68)	*Weight*	— 12 tons
Beam chine	— 12′6″ (m. 3.81)	*Engines*	— Various up to 800 HP total

These three types of patrol boat were built at Anzio by Navaltecnica. *Settimo Velo* and *Speranza* were produced for the Italian Customs Authorities, while *Super Speranza* was originally designed for the Harbour Office Authority. Many of these craft have been built subsequently for other organizations, such as NATO, or for air-sea rescue work and so on.

A particularly interesting phenomenon cropped up during the trials of the 25 foot *Settimo Velo*. These boats were powered by a pair of 225 HP MerCruiser engines with outdrive propulsion units. Light alloy propellers had had to be adopted so as to avoid bi-metallic erosion, since the casings of the underwater units of the drives were made of this material; standard propellers also had to be used for reasons of easy replacement. The yard was tied down to a contractual speed of some 38 knots in fully loaded conditions, while the fuel capacity was considerable (500 litres).

During the first trials the boats proved very slow in getting over the planing hump, even in ideal conditions, and on occasions failed to get over it at all when there was a strong head wind and resulting choppy sea. On reaching a certain speed (below the hump) the boats would just wallow in the water with their sterns well down and their bows pointing skywards; the propellers would then stall (i.e. turn in a bubble of air). The problem was further complicated by our having to use standard propellers only. However, after thinking the matter over, I decided to try cupping the propellers (bending over the trailing edge); this fortunately had the desired effect and the boats planed without any difficulty in any conditions of loading as well as with strong head winds and choppy seas.

Another problem then arose: severe cavitation erosion occurred on the back of the propeller blades at the root, reaching a depth of over $\frac{1}{8}$″ of after only a

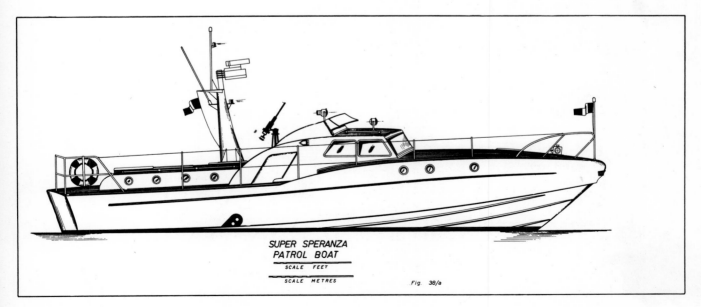

SUPER SPERANZA
PATROL BOAT

SCALE FEET

SCALE METRES

Fig. 38/a

few hours' running. (The propellers incidentally were two-bladed.) We were pushed for time as the delivery date was approaching, so this puzzle had to be solved pretty rapidly. I therefore decided to drill a $\frac{1}{4}''$ hole right through the root of the blade, using the deepest part of the cavitational erosion as the centre of the drilled section. If the face showed no signs of cavitation, I reasoned, why not connect the face with the back so that a passage could be made for the high-pressure water from the face to reach the low-pressure at the back? This experiment proved to be the answer as there was no further trouble of this kind.

Another interesting point to be solved arose from the fact that the outdrives had had to be mounted fairly far apart, since the engines were V 8s. During high-speed turns the outboard propeller would come right out of the water; this not only caused over-revving of the engine but also reduced the thrust on the outboard side so that the boat straightened up. A series of see-sawing manoeuvres, with the outboard propeller alternately leaving and re-entering the water, were necessary in order to do a complete U turn. This disadvantage was rectified very simply by fitting chine wedges.

These wedges stretched from the chine to the first riser and, in tight turns, reduced inboard list, kept the outboard propeller in the water, and enabled the boat to complete a continuous turn without difficulty. When the boat was running straight at high speed, the wedges were clear of the water and had no effect on the trim.

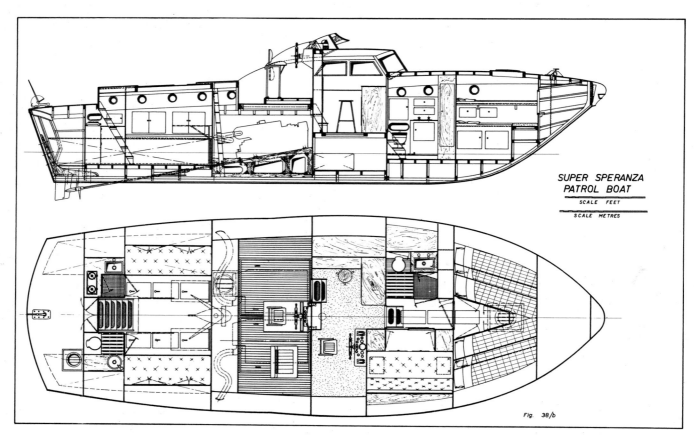

SUPER SPERANZA
PATROL BOAT

SCALE FEET

SCALE METRES

Fig. 38/b

LEVI 56

Length overall	— 56'6" (m. 17.20)	*Engines*	— *Twin GM 16 V-71 N diesels*
Length waterline	— 48'7" (m. 14.80)		*1400 HP*
Beam maximum	— 17'9" (m. 5.40)	*Maximum speed*	— *30 knots*
Beam chine	— 15'3" (m. 4.65)	*Cruising speed*	— *22 knots*
Draught hull	— 2'9" (m. 0.85)	*Range at cruising*	
Deadrise aft	— 20%	*speed*	— *450 miles*
Weight	— 24 tons		

This 56 foot Sports Fisherman was designed for Mr. J. W. Mitchell of South Africa, and is currently under construction in Cantiere Delta's yard. The requirements were for a boat which could be used both as a sports fisherman and as a comfortable cruiser. The accommodation had to include three two-berth cabins, and the owner also wanted a boat capable of maintaining high speeds in rough weather. For this reason one of my reasonably high deadrise hull designs was adopted, while the length of 56 feet seemed a good compromise for easy cruising in adverse sea conditions.

One of the problems with deep vee hulls is lateral tenderness; this causes them to roll when they are stopped or proceeding slowly, particularly when there is top hamper. It was necessary to give this aspect careful attention since a sports fisherman spends a considerable part of its time trawling at

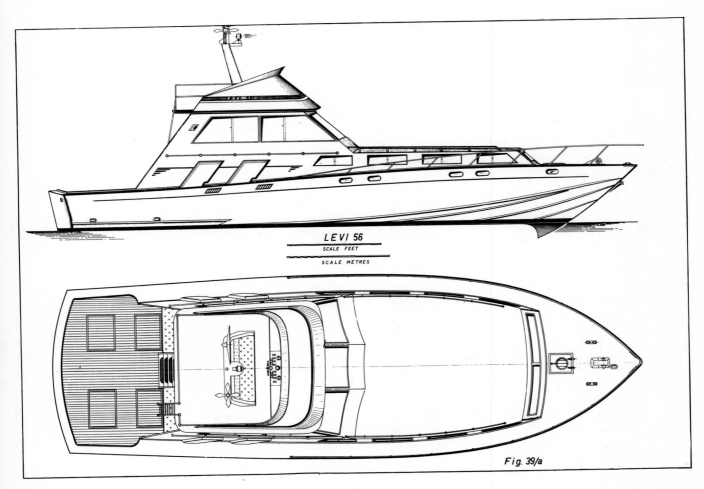

LEVI 56
SCALE FEET
SCALE METRES

Fig. 39/a

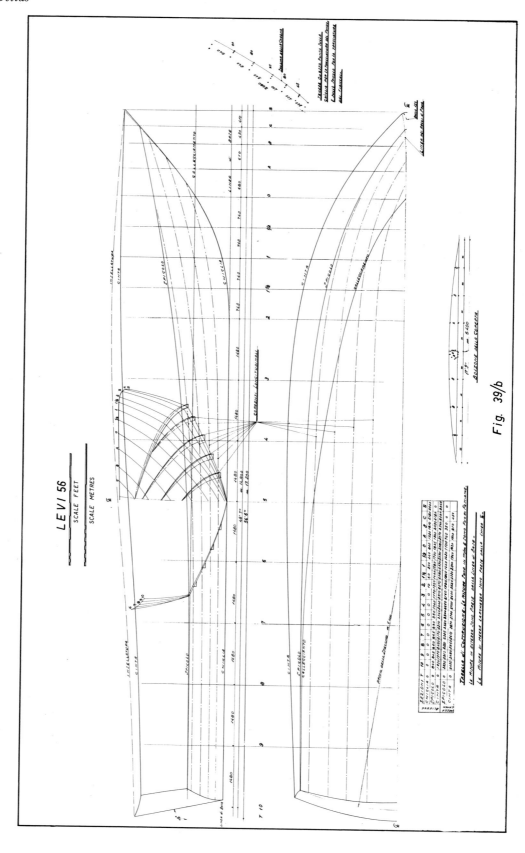

LEVI 56

Fig. 39/b

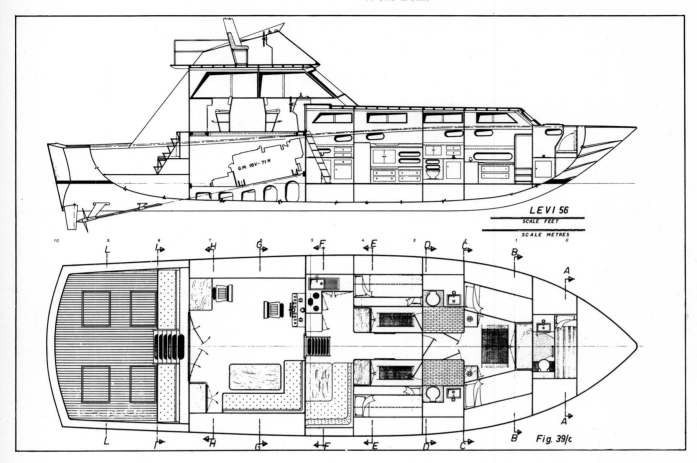

LEVI 56
SCALE FEET
SCALE METRES

Fig. 39/c

reduced speed. The aft planing surfaces of this design are not, therefore, extremely vee-ed although adequate deadrise has been provided in the impact area to reduce pounding.

The craft has an S-shaped sheer in order to keep the freeboard low aft for gaffing and landing the catch without difficulty and high forward to obtain maximum space for accommodation without a break in the deck-line. A continuous sheer line is both lighter and eliminates the possibility of any weakness.

The hull is of laminated mahogany, framed with laminated longitudinal stringers; the deck is teak, laid in narrow widths parallel to the sheer. Fillets of glass cloth and epoxy resin are being applied so as to

ensure a good tie-up at keel, chines and sheer joints.

The craft is to be powered with a pair of GM 16 V-71 N marine diesel engines, with a maximum rating of 700 HP each at 2300 r.p.m., in order to obtain the 30 knots required as maximum speed. The continuous rating of 490 HP each will give a cruising speed of around 22 knots, while the fuel capacity of 800 gallons (3,600 litres) will give a range of 450 miles at cruising speed. The craft is also to be fitted with all the latest electronic equipment, including automatic pilot, long-range radar, and even sonar.

See Figs. 39/a, 39/b, 39/c.

CHAPTER IX

Aerodynamic Hull Shapes

*I*n this chapter I am dealing with a particular breed of craft which are greatly influenced by aerodynamic lift. Obviously any craft, even mono-hulled, that skims over the water at high speed is affected by this phenomenon, but I intend here to examine only those boats which are designed to make use of aerodynamic lift by their forward motion, either as a means of lifting the vehicle or, as in the case of record breakers where forward speed is extremely high, of keeping it on the water. I mentioned in an earlier chapter that a great many of the characteristics of the Delta design were dictated by the effect aerodynamics had on monohulls at high speed; but the magnitude of the forces involved on the Deltas are relatively low compared with those on the craft I am going to describe now.

A number of designs fall into this category. There are, for example, catamarans, three-point suspension hydroplanes, side-wall craft, and ram wings. These are all multihulled craft and are rather similar to one another, as we will see presently. In addition there is the winged monohull, a relatively new concept which I predict may well become very popular.

The geometrical configuration of a catamaran concept offers many interesting advantages. First, a vast choice of hull shapes—for instance very deep deadrise, far more than is possible with monohulled craft whose lateral stability diminishes rather rapidly once the higher angles of deadrise are reached; with the catamaran we have two or more hulls and, as a result, a wide platform and good lateral stability. Secondly, a wide deck configuration which offers a good deal more space, at least as far as area is concerned. Thirdly, asymmetric hull shapes which can be used to advantage in creating efficient tunnels to generate lift, thus reducing wetted surface and, consequently, increasing speed.

In the past, owing to the comparatively low speed of these boats, the question of ventilating the bottom

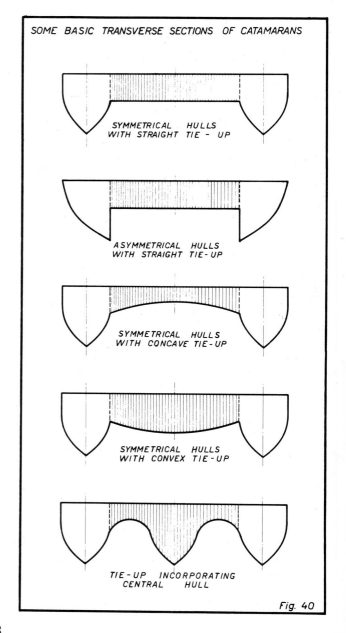

SOME BASIC TRANSVERSE SECTIONS OF CATAMARANS

SYMMETRICAL HULLS WITH STRAIGHT TIE-UP

ASYMMETRICAL HULLS WITH STRAIGHT TIE-UP

SYMMETRICAL HULLS WITH CONCAVE TIE-UP

SYMMETRICAL HULLS WITH CONVEX TIE-UP

TIE-UP INCORPORATING CENTRAL HULL

Fig. 40

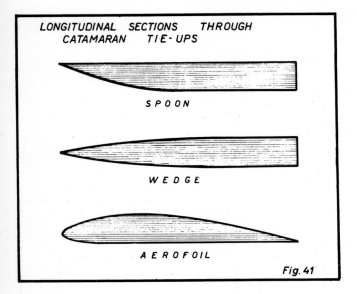

LONGITUDINAL SECTIONS THROUGH CATAMARAN TIE-UPS

SPOON

WEDGE

AEROFOIL

Fig. 41

pension hydroplane is merely an asymmetrical twin-hulled catamaran with an extension to the central tunnel, or if we want to look at it another way, a catamaran with a portion of the two aft hulls removed.

Again, the basic difference between a conventional powered catamaran and a ram wing lies in the variance in the longitudinal section of the tie-up between the hulls; in the former it approaches a wedge, while in the latter it has an aerofoil section (see Fig. 41).

and generating lift was possibly not given a great deal of consideration, and I do not suppose mattered much anyway at that time. Now, however, with the advent of more powerful and lighter engines, speeds are increasing and aerodynamic considerations are becoming more important.

I suppose that the Hickman *Sea Sled* was one of the first types of high speed powered craft which could be said to qualify in this category. The *Sea Sled* was a partially tunnelled craft, which could best be described as an inverted vee hull with a flat or near flat section at the transom. From all accounts, although I have never had occasion to test one myself, she was a particularly good sea boat in rough weather, and was also reputed to be fast. I do not know to what extent her speed was influenced by the surface propeller, but certainly the ventilation generated by the tunnel must also have helped in reducing wetted surface. The *Sea Sled*'s ability to provide a comfortable ride at speed in choppy conditions could be explained by the cushion effect produced by the tunnel, particularly forward. I cannot help feeling, however, that those flat sections aft would be particularly uncomfortable on re-entry if these craft were pushed at the speeds which today cause boats to fly out of the water.

Catamarans of all types are now being built with a great variety of shapes. The basic forms of some of these craft are shown in Fig. 40, while the various shapes the tie-ups can take both in transverse and in longitudinal section can be seen in Fig. 41.

As can be seen from Fig. 42, a three-point sus-

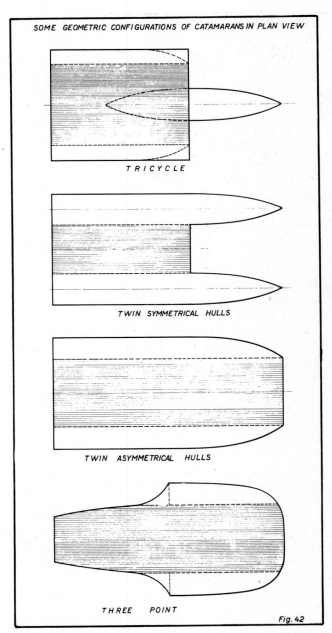

SOME GEOMETRIC CONFIGURATIONS OF CATAMARANS IN PLAN VIEW

TRICYCLE

TWIN SYMMETRICAL HULLS

TWIN ASYMMETRICAL HULLS

THREE POINT

Fig. 42

Dhows to Deltas

"Catamaran" is perhaps rather a misleading term. The word comes from Tamil (*katta-maram*) and mean *tied tree*. It would seem, therefore, that all multi-hulled craft are really *catamarans*, but the term in powerboats has come to be attached to one type only: a twin-hulled craft with a rectangular platform tie-up. Generally, this rectangular platform starts at or near the bows and ends at the transom.

The three-point suspension hydroplane has the same basic geometry with asymmetric hulls or sponsons, but in this case the centre section (the tie-up section) is extended beyond the transom of the twin hulls. The side wall craft is the same again, except that the shape of the hull is based on twin keels which form a closed tunnel. The ram wing, as

we have already mentioned, differs in that the centre section tie-up has an aerofoil section.

Unlimited record breakers today are also multi-hulled craft which can take two different plan view geometries; either the conventional two points forward and one point aft, or the reverse (which is sometime appropriately termed the tricycle configuration).

Examples of these various types of aerodynamic vehicle are described in more detail below, accompanied by explanatory drawings. Understandably, most of the examples are racing craft since very high potential speeds are possible with these hull forms, but other types are also mentioned which are suitable for pleasure or for work.

1. *WINGED MONOHULLS*

I referred in Chapter VI to a possible category of monohull craft with lifting aerodynamic fins. The U.I.M. rules, as they stand at the moment, forbid this type of boat, but I am including it here nevertheless as a potential formula for increasing the speed of monohulled craft.

In my opinion, a well-designed boat of this type could prove superior to the catamarans seen on racing circuits today. I am basing this assumption on the fact that only one hull would be skimming

over the water instead of two, and that there would therefore be an appreciable reduction in wetted surface. Without question, one of the main problems in such a craft would be its inherent lateral instability, but I feel that this could be overcome by properly designed wings with the right amount of dihedral built into them—or even by the adoption of differential ailerons on the trailing edges of the fins.

Lateral tenderness also tends to make it more

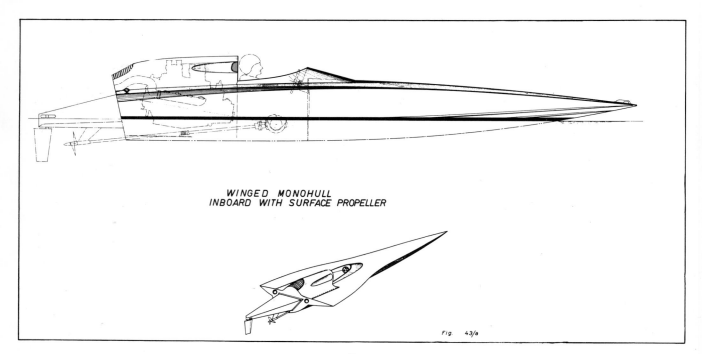

WINGED MONOHULL
INBOARD WITH SURFACE PROPELLER

Fig. 43/a

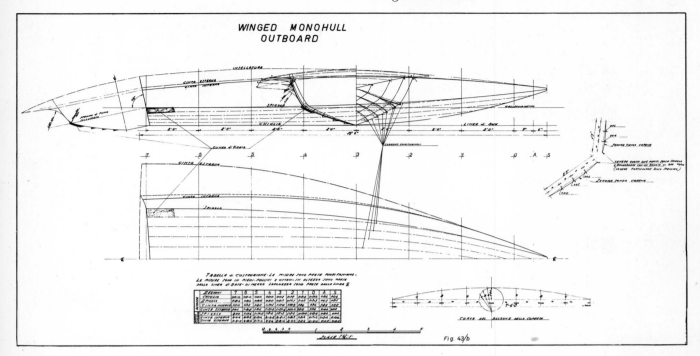

Fig. 43/b

difficult to execute tight turns, such as are sometimes necessary in circuit racing, without the inboard wing digging into the water and without running the risk of the boat turning an involuntary cartwheel. Catamarans have the edge here on this type of monohull, since they are capable of extremely tight high speed turns, but I think a lot could be done by the judicious use of chine wedges; these wedges would only be in contact with the water on turns, and would have the effect of preventing the winged

monohull from listing any further once they had come into action.

The drawings reproduced illustrate two types of circuit racer one of which is currently under construction. No trial data are as yet available but it will be interesting to see the validity of this design, since there might possibly be a future for this type of craft for high speed travel in models other than those for pure racing.

See Figs. 43/a, 43/b.

CANARD 21

A hull equipped with aerodynamic lifting fins (such as has been described on p. 194) must rely on water contact, even if only occasionally, for longitudinal and trasverse equilibrium as well as for any change in direction. These moments of contact with the surface of the water, brief though they may be, are bound to slow the craft down and it will therefore be necessary to lift the hull clear of the water altogether before greater speeds can be achieved. This however raises question of controlling the boat while it is in the air.

The obvious answer is to equip the hull with aircraft air surfaces (wing, tailplane, rudder) either in the conventional configuration (tailplane and rudder aft) or else in the canard geometry shown here. The wing would have to be located well aft in order to get

the right relationship between the centre of pressure and the centre of gravity. This would require a boom for the tail surfaces in the case of a conventional configuration, and for this reason in my opinion the Canard offers a simpler, lighter, and more compact solution (the hull, in effect, also serves as fuselage).

The hull is wide and reasonably flat aft so as to give good lateral stability at rest, dispensing with wing-tip floats; this will simplify construction and also reduce weight and aerodynamic drag. There seems to be no point, either, in having pronounced deadrise in a hull which is to operate clear of the water.

The question is whether pilot reflexes will be quick enough to keep a boat like this on an even keel

161

L

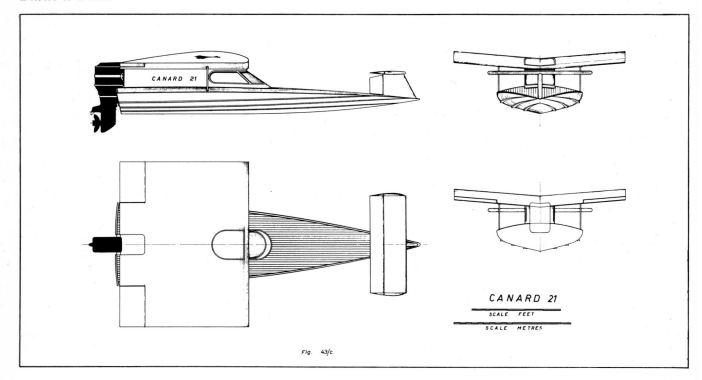

CANARD 21

SCALE FEET

SCALE METRES

Fig. 43/c

a foot or so above the water. What one really needs, I suppose, is automatic controls, but this would make the craft quite an expensive little toy.

2. CATAMARANS

An immense number of catamaran hulls are being produced today both for racing and for pleasure. Runabouts and small open cruisers are plentiful, but as yet no serious attempt has been made to tackle larger sizes of fast powered cabin-cruisers utilizing multihull designs. Of course there have been a few isolated examples of sizeable craft of this type, but they have generally been designed with a specific purpose in mind.

As I see it, these large powered cabin cruiser catamarans can be divided into two categories; first, the relatively slow craft—which can be called the non-aerodynamic variety—and second, those which proceed at a sufficient speed to generate aerodynamic lift. The first category need not necessarily be limited to displacement craft but can also include vessels which, although they have sufficient speed to plane, do not generate enough aerodynamic lift to qualify them for the second category.

Certain advantages and disadvantages are com-mon to both categories. By virtue of the geometrical form, we automatically have tremendous space to play with in comparison to a monohulled vessel of equal length. We are able, therefore, to incorporate an enormous amount of accommodation in this type.

There is too a wide liberty in the choice of hull forms, since these multihulled craft have considerable beam and consequently are very stiff stability-wise. We know that deep-vee-ed vessels are softer riding than flat ones, but there is a limit to the amount of deadrise which can be incorporated into a mono-hulled vessel (owing to the tender stability character-istic); there is no such restriction with the catamaran from the purely stability point of view, although an excessively high deadrise will affect optimum speed negatively and give rise to problems of exaggerated angle of incidence, etc. A catamaran can, in fact, be designed to be extremely soft riding, assuming that the tunnel or tunnels are sufficiently high above the surface of the water to avoid the possibility of wave impact.

The high initial stability characteristic adds to the comfort of those on board in certain conditions of sea—and also permits ample superstructures to be designed without greatly prejudicing the stability of the craft. High superstructures should be avoided whenever possible, in order to reduce windage, but there are cases when height is essential for the efficient functioning of a boat (e.g. towers on certain types of Sports Fisherman).

These advantages apply to both categories of catamaran, but the really fast catamaran can claim two additional ones—increased speed as a result of the lift generated in the tunnel and, to a certain extent, shock-absorbent properties deriving from the high pressure air between the hulls.

Generally speaking, where there are advantages there are also disadvantages, and in fact these powered cabin cruiser catamarans have quite a few negative aspects. For instance, there are numerous structural problems arising from their immense beam. Great attention has to be paid to getting a good tie-up between platform and hulls, and so on. All this means that producing such a craft commercially would almost certainly prove quite an expensive business; not only is there more material involved, by reason of the larger area, but there is also the question of producing a light structure of consider-able strength, employing a number of principles used in the aircraft industry. A light structure is of particular importance in connection with the fast catamaran as a large measure of its success depends on weight saving.

Higher superstructures too are needed in catamarans in order to provide the same amount of headroom as is available in monohulls, since the floor height in the main section has to be on top of the tunnel. This has the disadvantage of creating more windage.

Slamming will occur under the tunnel at low speed in lumpy weather, when the hulls are well immersed and there is no high pressure in the tunnel. This may possibly prove to be the greatest disadvantage of all, since there will obviously be times when slowing down is unavoidable. A possible solution to this drawback might be to undulate the flat surface of the centre section tie-up in a longitudinal sense.

Yet another disadvantage could be the difficulty of finding sufficient berthing space in crowded ports, since a catamaran requires something like twice the width of a normal vessel of the same size.

However on the whole I think the advantages outweigh the disadvantages, and I am sure that we will be seeing quite a few examples of powered cabin-

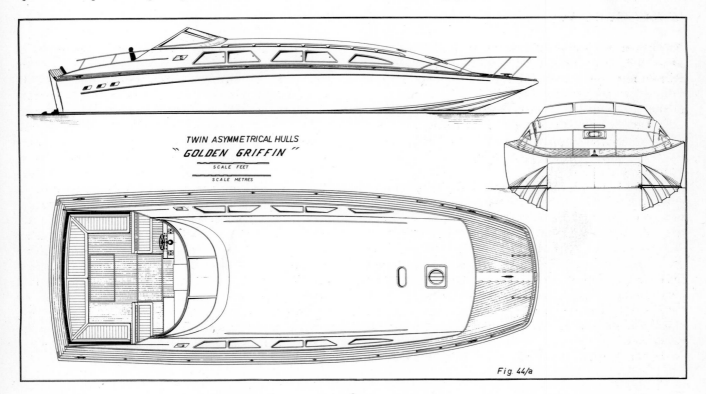

TWIN ASYMMETRICAL HULLS
"GOLDEN GRIFFIN"
SCALE FEET
SCALE METRES

Fig. 44/a

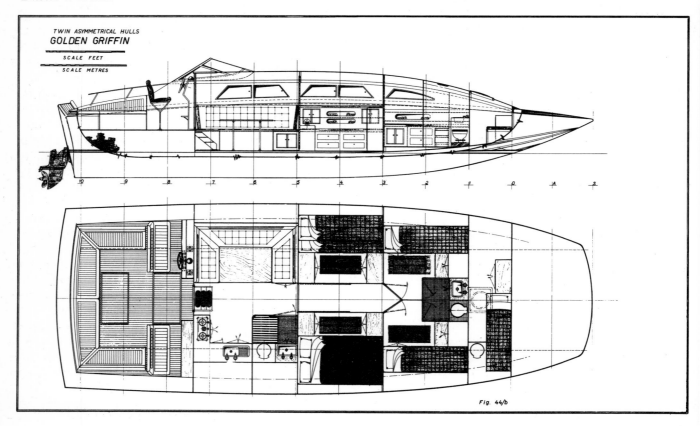

TWIN ASYMMETRICAL HULLS
GOLDEN GRIFFIN
SCALE FEET
SCALE METRES

Fig. 44/b

cruiser catamarans in the near future—particularly as it does seem possible to combine high speed, smooth riding qualities, and exceptional comfort in the same craft. We have of course been trying to achieve all these characteristics in monohull vessels too, but I feel that we have only done so by applying a notable measure of compromise and by sacrificing one or other of these qualities.

To illustrate the second category of catamaran (i.e. the aerodynamic lift variety) I have prepared a design study of a cabin cruiser—*Golden Griffin*—which, with adequate power, could be made to exceed well over 40 knots and still ride comfortably over fairly choppy seas. Since this is only a design study, a certain amount of practical testing will obviously be necessary before arriving at the successful realization of such a craft. The drawings of this craft are reproduced here.

Golden Griffin's principal dimensions and characteristics are as follows:

Length overall	— 40′0″	(m. *12.5*)
Length waterline	— 34′0″	(m. *10.35*)
Beam maximum	— 15′0″	(m. *4.60*)
Draught	— 2′0″	(m. *0.60*)
Tunnel height	— 2′0″	(m. *0.60*)
Head room	— 6′6″	(m. *1.92*)
Engines	— *Twin 400 HP outdrive*	
Range	— *200 miles*	

See Figs. 44/a, 44/b.

3. *RAM WINGS*

A ram wing can be either a twin or a triple float craft; in the latter case, it can conform to the tricycle pattern or to the conventional two forwad and one aft, joined together by a platform with an aerofoil section.

The American glider and aircraft manufacturers, Switzer, have done a great deal to develop these very fast craft. As far as I know, the Switzer ram wings have always been twin hull vehicles, but experimental trials were carried out on a triple-hull craft in Japan in 1963 by the Kawasaki Aircraft Company. Several other experiments have been made at various times, in some cases by large aircraft concerns, and it will be interesting to see what the future trend will be for this type of boat.

Air controls, such as rudders and flaps, are often used on ram wings for both pitch attitude and directional control. I am told that, on the Switzer craft, the outboards on the hull extremities also contribute in some measure aerodynamically to directional control at high speed.

The main difference between the ram wing and the catamaran lies in the cross-sectional shape of the central tie-up. In the ram wing this is an aerofoil of proven aerodynamic properties, which has been tested in wind tunnels so as to ascertain such details as centre of pressure location, lift/drag ratio, and so on. The depth of this aerofoil is limited and there is, therefore, very little useful space for accommodation in the central section. For this reason the hulls are normally used for living space, contrary to the catamaran where the centre section has more depth along its length, and where little importance is given to the lift generated by the deck area, so that apertures for cockpits, etc., can be made without any difficulty.

From an aerodynamic point of view the ram wing is unquestionably superior to the catamaran, since more lift is possible for a given wing area owing to the sophisticated section of the tie-up. Ram wings could well become popular for offshore racing, fast pleasure cruising, or even for workboats.

Another point worth remembering about this type of craft is the importance of the location of the

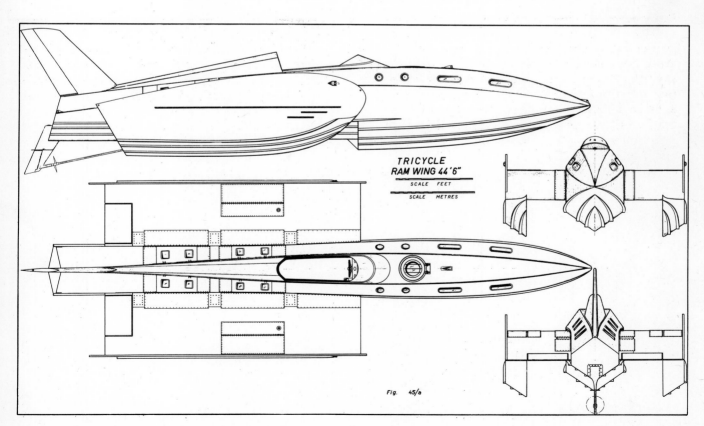

TRICYCLE
RAM WING 44'6"

SCALE FEET

SCALE METRES

Fig. 45/a

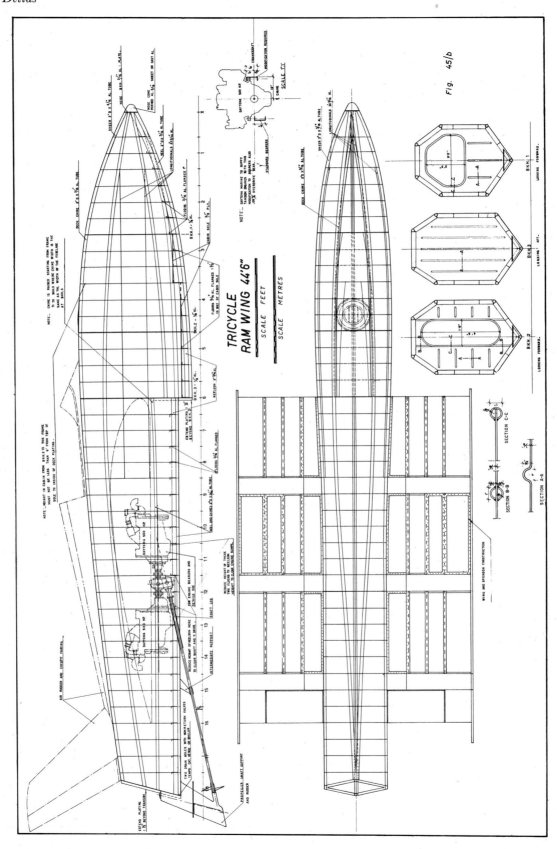

TRICYCLE
RAM WING 44'6"

SCALE FEET

SCALE METRES

Fig. 45/b

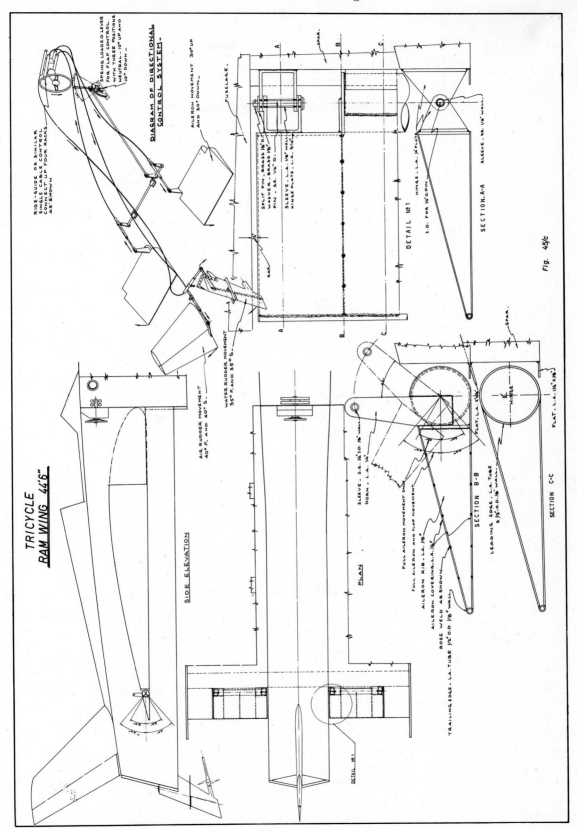

Fig. 45/c

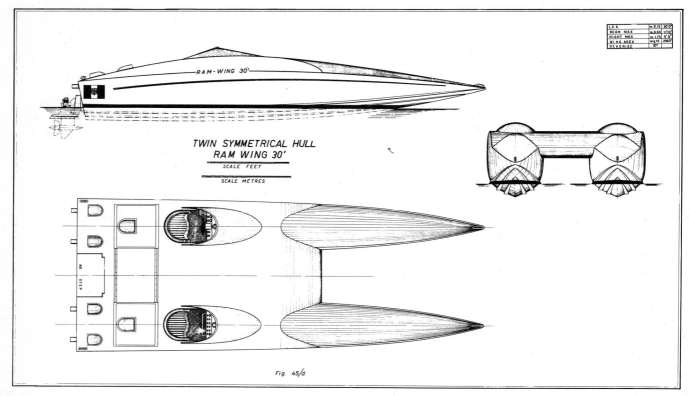

L.O.A.	m.9.15	30'0"
BEAM MAX	m.3.60	11'10"
HIGHT MAX	m.1.75	5'9"
WING AREA	mq.19	206ft²
DEADRISE	30°	

RAM-WING 30'

TWIN SYMMETRICAL HULL
RAM WING 30'
SCALE FEET
SCALE METRES

NO STEP

Fig. 45/d

centre of gravity in relation to the centre of pressure, if optimum results are to be obtained, in particular with longitudinal stability. An aerofoil section should also be selected which has, amongst other attributes, a small movement of the centre of pressure, since the incidence of the aerofoil is subject to constant variation when the trim of the boat alters on running over uneven water surfaces.

Reproduced here are a tricycle arrangement ram wing and a more conventional two-float version for offshore racing, which I prepared some years ago for clients in the United States and in Italy. As far as I know, neither of these craft was ever built.

See Figs. 45/a, 45/b, 45/c, 45/d.

4. SIDE WALLS

I began to think about the feasibility of a side wall—cum—ram wing craft early in 1960, and even prepared a design study of a fast military patrol boat along these lines for a foreign government (which in the event came to nothing). However, apart from the fact that it would have been an expensive experiment, which might not have turned out satisfactorily, I was not entirely convinced of the utility of the craft for their particular needs. One of the requirements, in fact, was that the boat had to present a small target, which did not seem to me to work in with the basic concept of a craft that relied for efficiency on coming out of the water and virtually gliding on a cushion of air. This was anything but synonymous with a low profile.

Even though the proposal did not materialize, I put in a lot of time working out various details and made a lot of drawings, one of which is reproduced.

I hoped that the forward speed of this arrangement would be sufficiently high to generate the aerodynamic lift necessary to reduce the wetted surface and permit even greater speeds. As can be seen from the drawing, the twin keels formed an enclosed tunnel, thereby increasing the pressure below the centre section and enabling more lift to be generated. In theory, therefore, such a craft should be an efficient, fast load-carrier.

See Fig. 46/a.

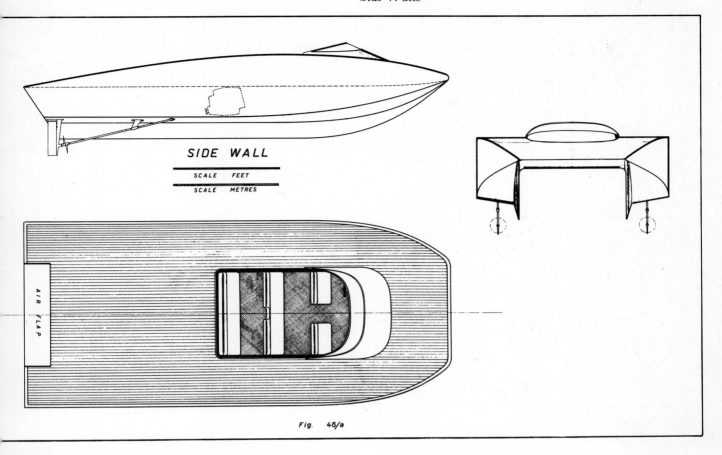

SIDE WALL

SCALE FEET

SCALE METRES

AIR FLAP

Fig. 46/a

5. *THREE-POINT SUSPENSION HYDRO-PLANES*

This is yet another aerodynamic hull shape, which was first developed by the American designer, Apel. As I mentioned in the introduction to this chapter, the three-point suspension hydroplane is really a variation on the catamaran with the centre section longer than the two hulls. An interesting feature of this configuration, at least as far as the water-propeller versions are concerned, is that the third point, on which the craft rests at high speed, is a portion of the propeller, which is situated right aft.

Three-point suspension hydros are extremely efficient for high speeds in calm water, since the wetted area is reduced to a minimum and in some cases to just a few square inches of sponsons); the appendage drag is very low as only about half the propeller and a minimal part of the rudder are actually in the water.

I have already described a 1300 c.c. three-point suspension hydroplane in Chapter VI (Circuit Racers), so I am reproducing here the lines drawing of a 900 kg racer which I designed recently. A model will be tested in a wind tunnel, after which, if the tests are successful, construction will start on the full scale craft. One of the objects of this design is to have a crack at the 900 kg world record, which now stands at 241·7 km/h*. Unlike the ordinary three-point suspension hydros, in this case the centre section is an aerofoil.

One of the main problems of these craft when running at record speeds is the ever-dreaded take-off. It is hoped that extensive wind tunnel testing will help to arrive at the correct compromise of lift, since excessive lift causes take-off while insufficient lift increases the wetted surface on the sponsons, with a corresponding reduction in speed.

See Fig. 47/a.

* This world record has been held since 1953 by Achille Castoldi, whose brother Luigi designed the water jet unit described on p. 181.

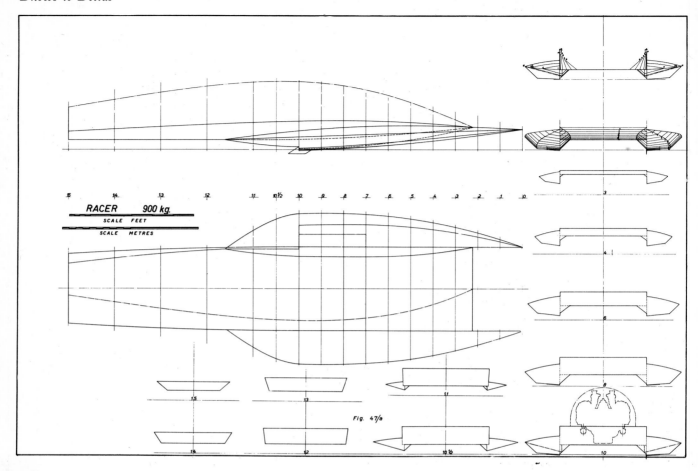

RACER   900 kg.
SCALE FEET
SCALE METRES

Fig. 47/a

6. *UNLIMITED RECORD BREAKERS*

Donald Campbell's tragic death on January 4th, 1967 left all sportsmen and speed enthusiasts with a deep sense of loss, for not only was he an extremely charming person but also one of those people who pursued speed with tremendous determination and courage.

The problems connected with these record-breaking boats have always intrigued me enormously, though perhaps more from the design point of view than from any wish to pilot them. I have, in fact, been contemplating the design of such a boat for some time, and for this reason have studied a lot of the available material on the subject.

A designer with considerable experience in this field today is Commander Peter Du Cane. Through the years Peter and I have had many interesting discussions and exchanges of ideas on the principal design aspects of offshore powerboats and circuit racers. Upon hearing that I was studying a possible

future boat for the record, he at once offered to help by putting at my disposal all the data he had available. Peter was, of course, responsible for the design of both Sir Malcolm Campbell's *Bluebird II* and John Cobb's *Crusader*. Incidentally, *Crusader* (which in my opinion is one of the most fascinating designs ever made for an attempt at the water speed record)

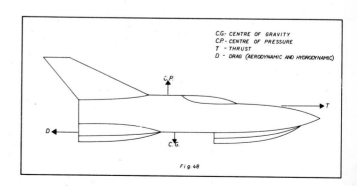

C.G.- CENTRE OF GRAVITY
C.P.- CENTRE OF PRESSURE
T - THRUST
D - DRAG (AERODYNAMIC AND HYDRODYNAMIC)

Fig. 48

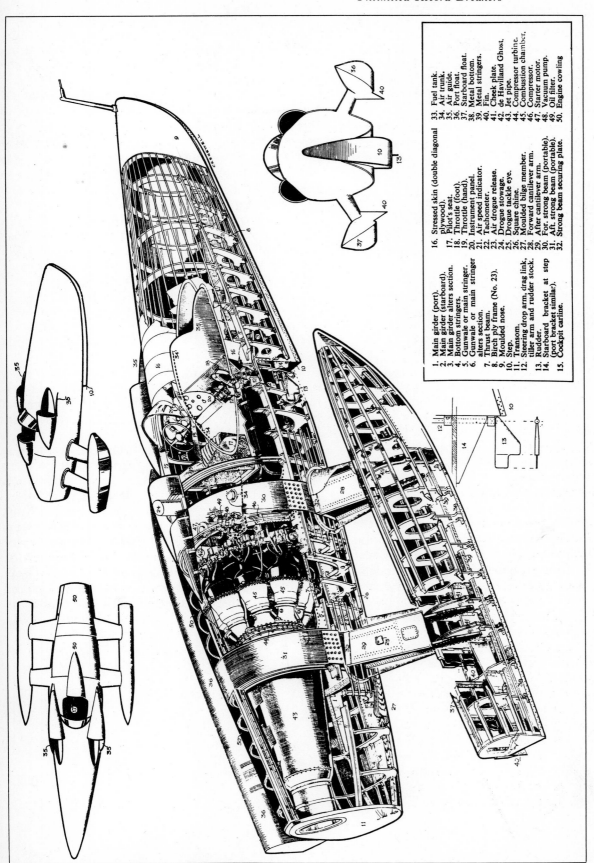

1. Main girder (port).
2. Main girder (starboard).
3. Main girder alters section.
4. Bottom stringers.
5. Gunwale or main stringer.
6. Gunwale or main stringer alters section.
7. Thrust beam.
8. Birch ply frame (No. 23).
9. Moulded nose.
10. Step.
11. Transom.
12. Steering drop arm, drag link, tiller arm and rudder stock.
13. Rudder.
14. Starboard bracket at step (port bracket similar).
15. Cockpit carline.
16. Stressed skin (double diagonal plywood).
17. Pilot's seat.
18. Throttle (foot).
19. Throttle (hand).
20. Instrument panel.
21. Air speed indicator.
22. Tachometer.
23. Air drogue release.
24. Drogue stowage.
25. Drogue tackle eye.
26. Square chine.
27. Moulded bilge member.
28. Forward cantilever arm.
29. After cantilever arm.
30. For. strong beam (portable).
31. Aft. strong beam (portable).
32. Strong beam securing plate.
33. Fuel tank.
34. Air trunk.
35. Air guide.
36. Port float.
37. Starboard float.
38. Metal bottom.
39. Metal stringers.
40. Fin.
41. Cheek plate.
42. de Havilland Ghost,
43. Jet pipe.
44. Compressor turbine.
45. Combustion chamber,
46. Compressor.
47. Starter motor.
48. Vacuum pump.
49. Oil filter.
50. Engine cowling

Plate 37   John Cobb's Crusader, designed by Commander Peter Du Cane, was one of the most fascinating designs ever made for an attempt at the water speed record.

was the first record-breaker designed exclusively for propulsion by gas turbine.

I spent a weekend with Peter in Northumberland early in 1967, when he took a great deal of trouble in showing me the extremely detailed tests which had been carried out on both working models and models in wind tunnels. I immediately realized that the problems were far more complex that I had suspected. It was clear from some of the figures I saw that the forces involved were of great magnitude, and it was also obvious that in such a design all factors must be evaluated with meticulous care.

I personally would prefer not to advance any opinion as to why Donald Campbell's *Bluebird* took off. Even today, nearly three years later, I have no further details on this unfortunate disaster and I do not therefore feel qualified to discuss it.

One of the major problems with these boats is clearly the danger of take-off. Let us for a moment examine the main forces acting upon a boat of this type when it is propelled through the water at high speed (see Fig. 48).

These are:

(a) the resultant of the forces of gravity acting downward through the centre of gravity;

(b) the resultant of the aerodynamic forces acting upward through the centre of aerodynamic lift;

c) the thrust acting forward at a certain height;

d) the drag (aerodynamic and hydrodynamic) acting backward at varying heights.

Assuming that the centre of gravity is very near the centre of aerodynamic lift, the only righting couple is the thrust in relation to the drag, if the former is above the latter. As velocity increases, the magnitude of the centre of aerodynamic lift also increases. If this is forward of the centre of gravity it tends to lift the bow, whereas if it is aft it tends to lift the stern. Also, as velocity increases, the wetted area is reduced to a point where the hull is barely touching the water and the drag becomes almost entirely aerodynamic. Drag is, therefore, exerted higher up on the hull than at lower speeds, reducing the nose-down couple between thrust and drag. Clearly, in the final analysis, the solution of the problem lies in aerodynamics.

Referring back to John Cobb's *Crusader*, it should be remembered that Du Cane began the design of this boat in 1949 and that the craft was doing over 200 m.p.h. on Loch Ness in 1952 when it disintegrated and John Cobb, another very fine sportsman, was killed. On this occasion the disaster was not due to take-off, but I understand it was due to a failure of the forward sponson on hitting a wave pattern.

It is interesting to note that Du Cane adopted a tricycle configuration in this design, i.e. one float ahead and two aft (see Plate 37). I personally feel that this solution is extremely valid for turbine or rocket propelled craft. It enables the centre of aerodynamic lift to be further aft and, therefore, reduces the possibilities of involuntary take-off, although even with this configuration the aerodynamic figures, at relatively low angles of incidence, are of incredible magnitude.

The present record holder, Lee Taylor's *Hustler*, is yet another remarkable boat. The geometry is rather similar to that of a three-point suspension hydroplane, although the 30'6" craft has an extremely low profile and is, in fact, needle-nosed.

The diminutive size of this record-breaker can be gathered from the following dimensions: 30'6" in length, *Hustler* has a beam of only 8' with a maximum height to the top of the tail of 4'10". The all-up weight, with driver and fuel, is 5000 lbs and the thrust put out by the Westinghouse J-46 turbojet engine is 6200 lbs. With this thrust/weight ratio Taylor clocked the record speed of 285 m.p.h., beating the former record held by Campbell of 277 m.p.h. A braking device, in the form of a parachute, is used at the end of the run; this is carried in the air fin.

CHAPTER X

Yachts and Aeroplanes

I should like to end the Design Section of this book by returning to my two first loves—sailing and flying.

One of my main ambitions soon after I was de-mobilized was to design and build a cruising ketch of some 30′ or so and sail her around the world. In those days my book-shelves were full of volumes about men who had circumnavigated the globe, either single-handed or with a small crew. I knew by heart the courses followed by such celebrated sailors as Joshua Slocum in his yacht *Spray*, and sincerely admired both the high qualities of seamanship shown by Voss with his overgrown dug-out and the hardiness of Gerbault, that ace fighter pilot and tennis player who also sailed single-handed round the world and finally ended his days on a Pacific island.

Robinson's cruise in the *Svaap* was, for me, a most satisfying feat by someone who had realized his his greatest ambition while he was still young—as was also the case with Dwight Long. Harry Pidgeon particularly captured my imagination when he built single-handed (at I believe the age of forty-four) his 35′ yawl *Islander*. in which he sailed round the world several times. Pidgeon was eventually shipwrecked in the Pacific, but built himself another boat and continued cruising to a ripe old age. The sea had obviously captured him completely.

Although I often thought about these men who actually did what they most wanted to do, I per-sonally never managed to follow in their wake. This is a sad admission, I know, but I imagine that many yachting enthusiasts find themselves in the same position—that is, having to fit in their sport with their normal way of life.

Circumstances prevented me from building a boat and sailing round the world in it, but I did manage to do the next best thing and design these fascinating craft.

While I was still in India, I designed three classes of racing dinghy and a Junior Offshore Group yacht which were built by our yard at Bombay. Two of these classes of racing dinghy were for the Military Academy on Lake Kharakvasla near Poona. One was modelled on the restricted class rules of the Merlin Rocket, while the other was an 18′6″ design which turned out particularly well. They were known respectively as the *Eagle* and *Excalibur* classes. The sails for these boats were made of Egyptian cotton in our own yard; I might add that they were lofted by me with a book close to hand called *How To Make Your Own Sails*. They were not too bad considering that the cloth was not really meant for sail-making and that I was rather groping in the dark when it came to such details as stretch allowance or the amount of curvature to be given to the luff and foot.

I had a drawing-board at home in Bombay and tackled quite a number of design competitions during my spare time. My first attempt was a 27′6″ LWL seagoing yacht with 10′ 3″ beam for *Yachting World* in 1957. All designs had to be named and I called mine *Coriander*. I was both surprised and de-lighted to receive a Mention and a very encouraging letter from the editor, congratulating me on my design and commenting that he liked curry himself!

I prepared designs for quite a few other competi-tions in the next two to three years. Three of them are reproduced in the following pages, *Funtoo*, *Tarragon*, and *Fez*, accompanied by my comments at the time and those of the competition judges.

I referred earlier to two other yachts, *Hermitage* and *Dany* (see Chapter I). These are not the only sail boats I have designed since my arrival in Europe, but they do represent two extreme contrasts in size—*Hermitage* being a 50 ton displacement yawl and *Dany* a One Ton Cup design sloop—and for that reason I am including them here.

Exactly how our yard in Bombay entered the

aviation field with a glider order for the Indian Government, I cannot now honestly remember; but I think that some officials of the Indian Ministry of Aviation had got to hear of our production of sculls, pairs, and fours for rowing clubs. The construction criteria of these craft are not unlike those of a glider. A *best boat*, for instance, is quite a tricky piece of workmanship; ours had a planking thickness of around $\frac{1}{16}''$ and was glued throughout, with no metal fastenings at all apart from those of the riggers and slides.

The first gliders we were commissioned to produce were built to a design provided by the technical department of the Ministry of Aviation; they were single-seater affairs for training purposes and very much resembled a *Grunau Baby*. As far as I remember, they were non-aerobatic.

I nearly had a fit when I watched our prototype being tested by the Chief Gliding Instructor for India. I had suggested, somewhat nervously, that the pattern for the preliminary set of trials should not impose too heavy a load on the structure, but to my horror, after casting away the winch line, he promptly dived the machine and did two consecutive loops. . . . I had yet another shock when he landed and realized that he had not even bothered to harness the parachute, for which we had provided a recess in the backrest of the cockpit. He certainly had more faith in our creation than I did!

I think it was the work with these gliders which started me off on the idea of building an aeroplane. I had always wanted to design and build my own 'plane, but an additional motive now spurred me on. At that time, all light aircraft in India were imported—apart from a couple of prototypes made by the Hindustan Aircraft Factory. The object of these prototypes was to reduce, and if possible eventually eliminate, the need for importing small aircraft and thus save valuable foreign currency, which at that time was rather an acute problem in India. What struck me as illogical was the fact that these prototypes were entirely made of materials which were unobtainable in India and therefore had to be imported—

for example, 4130 chrome moly tubing, aircraft light alloy, etc. I intended to build my aeroplane as far as possible in indigenous materials, and did in fact utilize Himalayan spruce for the structure which, though a little heavier than Sitka spruce, proved perfectly satisfactory for the job.

I thought I would get a pat on the back for this enterprise, but things never work out as one expects. Had I known the multiple difficulties which building an aircraft entailed from the bureaucratic point of view, I am not at all sure I would have embarked on the project in the first place. Amongst other things, I was told—halfway through the construction—that the building of aircraft was on the prohibited industries list for private companies. Fortunately my good friend Paul Poberezny of the Experimental Aircraft Association in the United States (an organization which has now grown to gigantic proportions and of which I was then, and still am, a member) helped me out by writing a personal letter to Pandit Nehru, who was Prime Minister of India at that time. I was eventually allowed to test fly from a disused airfield miles out of Bombay.

The *Monsoon* went through her initial stage of testing (50 hours flying time with a minimum of 100 landings) with no trouble at all. Even I flew her without difficulty and she stood up well to rather rough treatment on my first landing when I dropped her from quite a height. The stall characteristics too were extremely good, with no tendency to drop a wing.

Incidentally she was called *Monsoon* as we started her construction during the monsoon season. I left the prototype behind in India, but I have had requests for quite a number of sets of her plans since those days and she still seems to be generating a lot of interest among amateur builders.

I designed the *Mongoose* comparatively recently. The object here was to produce a relatively simple, inexpensive single-seater aircraft which could be powered with the popular Volkswagen air-cooled motorcar engine.

FUNTOO

Length overall	— *30'0" (m. 9.14)*		*Sail area*	— *323 sq. ft. (30 sq. m.)*
Length waterline	— *24'0" (m. 7.31)*		*Displacement*	— *3·75 tons*
Beam	— *8'9" (m. 2.59)*		*Iron ballast*	— *1·5 tons*
Draught	— *4'9" (m. 1.45)*		*Engine*	— *Penta F12A, 5½ HP*

Funtoo tied with G. van der Stadt and H. Glacer designs for the first place, in *Svenska Kryssarklubben's* 18th design competition in 1957.

The competition called for a boat of the coast cruiser type fit for touring and open sea racing, which would at the same time be suitable for amateur construction and cheap to build.

I therefore designed a transom sterned hull with a single chine which could be planked with plywood. This is about the simplest and most economical type of hull for building by amateurs.

To quote my remarks at the time: "The side and bottom sections are straight for simplicity and although the hull is not strictly developed, there will be no difficulty in planking it in plywood, provided some curvature is given to the bottom frames at Sections No. 0 to 3. The amount of curvature required is shown on the Lines Drawing, but from a practical point of view it would be advisable to erect these frames with straight edges, clamp the fore foot plywood to the rabbet and chine, and allow it to take its natural curve, then measure the amount of curve required and glue suitable filling pieces to the outside of these frames.

"The bottom of the hull has been drawn to give good initial stiffness and sufficient deadrise has been incorporated to produce a sea-kindly yacht. The ballast ratio is fairly high which will permit her to

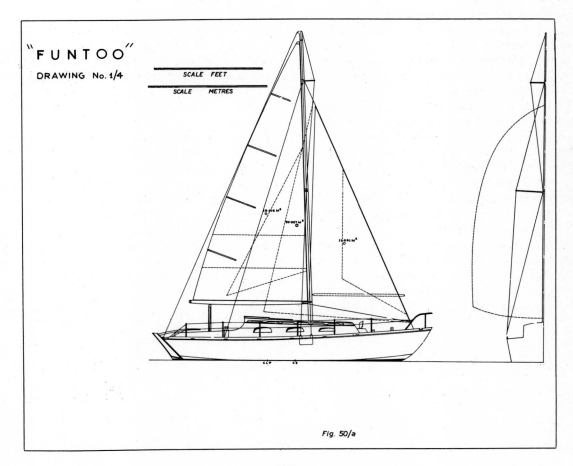

"FUNTOO"

DRAWING No. 1/4

SCALE FEET

SCALE METRES

Fig. 50/a

stand up well to her sail area and make good head-way even in a blow. The lateral plane, which is well aft, should make her easy to keep on her course and thereby conserve some of the helmsman's energy in offshore racing.

"The coach roof has been kept as simple as possible and provides as much head room and space as can be given to a hull of this size and type.

"To give adequate ventilation, a Cowl ventilator has been placed at the fore end of the cabin with two mushroom ventilators on the aft deck and the inside of the hull has been kept free of awkward corners. The gunwales for this reason have not been carried to the deck, which will permit air to circulate around them.

"The fore peak, which is easily accessible, is large enough for storage of crew's gear, cordage and sails, and the bulkhead in this compartment can be utilized for hanging waterproofs."

The jury's comments on *Funtoo* were as follows:

"*Funtoo* is the biggest of all the boats entered. . . . It is a comparatively heavy and sturdy boat with small sails apparently intended for rougher weather than our summer winds. The designs are not much elaborated and there is no construction description. The constructor's exposition is clear and illustrative. As to the lines, there is not much to criticize; the prow might perhaps have been a little less peaked. The rig is small, the shrouds may be unnecessarily thick and double under-shrouds are desirable. A design for the spar is missing. The fixtures include four quite spacious bunks, those astern are, however, difficult to get at and the ribs intrude too much on the forward ones. There is no arrangement for comfortable sitting. The clothes closet is 70 cm high, whereas 97 cm is desirable. Afore there is plenty of room, the ventilation arrangements are good and there is no wonder they do not think of heating in Bombay.

"The sitting space is of the seaworthy—from the

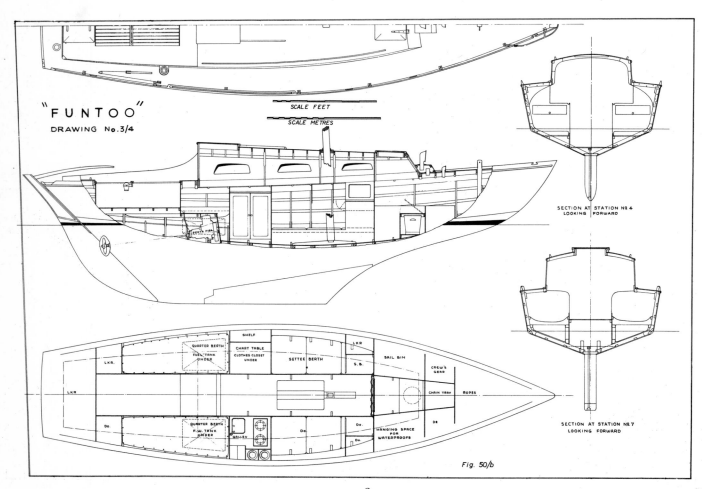

"FUNTOO"
DRAWING No. 3/4

SCALE FEET
SCALE METRES

SECTION AT STATION No. 4
LOOKING FORWARD

SECTION AT STATION No. 7
LOOKING FORWARD

Fig. 50/b

point of view of the boat—but uncomfortable and unprotected type, where you sit on deck with a low frame behind your back. The constructor has chosen 10 mm plywood for planking and deck, because it is easier to handle for amateur builders. The other, lighter boats have 12 mm, which is perhaps more suitable for a boat of this size with regard to the hard

sea cruisings. The building method is good, but the hatches will hardly be tight if fixed in the way indicated.

"*Funtoo* is a good boat in its way, but it is not what we meant and expected."

See Figs. 50/a, 50/b.

TARRAGON

Length overall	— *35'6" (m. 10.80)*	*Sail area (RORC)*	— *545 sq. ft. (50·6 sq. m.)*
Length waterline	— *27'6" (m. 8.40)*	*Displacement*	— *8·3 tons*
Beam	— *10'2" (m. 3.10)*	*Iron ballast*	— *3·1 tons*
Draught	— *5'9" (m. 1.75)*	*Engine*	— *Parsons Prawn*

Tarragon won the second prize in *Yachting World's* 1958 designing competition for a yacht suitable for

club ownership and able to sleep five in port.

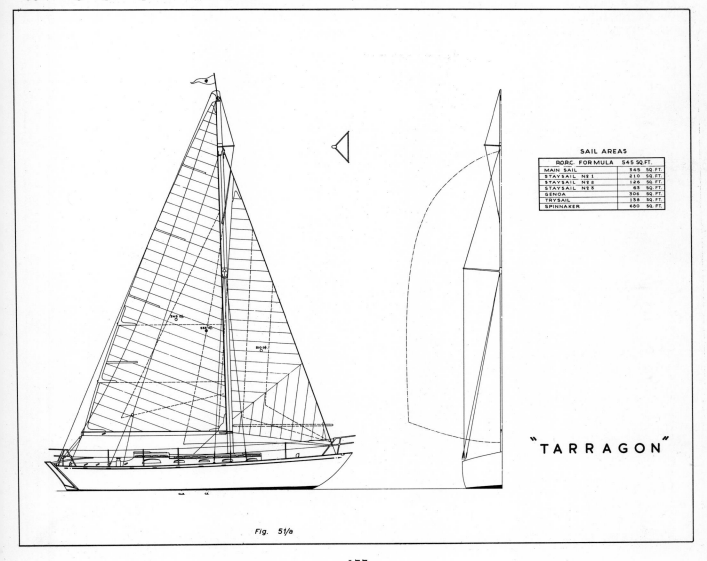

SAIL AREAS

R.O.R.C. FORMULA	545 SQ.FT.	
MAIN SAIL	345	SQ.FT.
STAYSAIL Nº 1	210	SQ.FT.
STAYSAIL Nº 2	126	SQ.FT.
STAYSAIL Nº 3	63	SQ.FT.
GENOA	306	SQ.FT.
TRYSAIL	138	SQ.FT.
SPINNAKER	680	SQ.FT.

"TARRAGON"

Fig. 51/a

Designer's Remarks:

"A club yacht which has to satisfy the needs of a variety of sailors both for cruising and racing is perhaps a far more difficult compromise to achieve than a yacht built to an owner's specific requirements, or to a definite rating rule. *Tarragon*, in my opinion, will strike a happy medium as a club yacht. A waterline length of 27′6″ will provide adequate sleeping accommodation for five while in port, but could be easily sailed when short-handed with a crew of two.

"It is true that a beam of 10′2″ is a great deal more than is usual for a yacht of this length in Europe where beam, apart from being expensive, is associated with poor windward performance. This trend is not followed in America, where building costs are even higher than in Europe, and where these yachts have proved efficient on all points of sailing. Therefore, I do not feel that *Tarragon* will

suffer on this account if well sailed in offshore races, but will have the definite advantage of more accommodation and better stability. This latter quality should be particularly welcome to both the inexperienced and the man who wants to cruise with a young family, and should be worth the additional expense of greater beam.

"The rigging is extremely simple, and although I have specified runners to ensure a tight forestay, the mast is sufficiently stout and well stayed to dispense with them while cruising when optimum performance is not required.

"The lateral plane, which is well aft, should make her easy to keep on her course in following and quartering seas, and conserve some of the helmsman's energy in offshore cruising and racing.

"The coachroof is simple to construct, the sides and fronts being perpendicular, and is carried through past the mast so as to provide headroom in

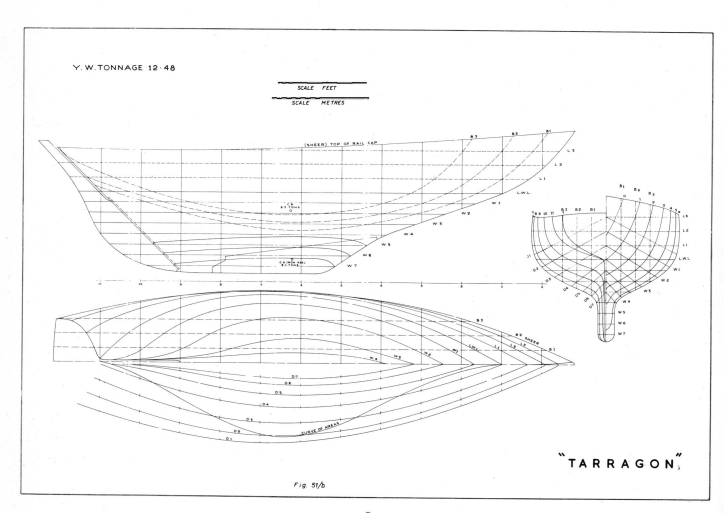

Fig. 51/b

the forward cabin. The two bulkheads which are on either side of the mast will give the required stiffness in that part of the hull.

"For an auxiliary motor I have specified the Parsons "Prawn", which is a light engine for the power it delivers and will be capable of driving *Tarragon* at her maximum economical speed with about two-thirds power. This will leave sufficient in reserve to negotiate a strong adverse tide when the necessity arises. The engine will be equipped with an additional dynamo, which will feed batteries of suitable capacity to cope with the navigation and internal lighting.

"*Tarragon* is not designed to any rating rule, but I have borne in mind the R.O.R.C. rules in respect of mast height, aspect ratio, overlap of head sails, and size of spinnaker to avoid considerable penalties being imposed on her rating."

Editor's Comments:

"The judges considered that *Tarragon* ranked little below Alan Gurney's design which won the competition. . . . Renato Levi has chosen a size and type of hull similar to that which was the subject of the previous competition, in which he was mentioned.

"One of the largest of the entries, *Tarragon* is 27′6″ on the waterline and 10′2″ beam. A transom stern is considerably cheaper to build than a counter, so that the cost to the club would probably not be so much greater than for one of the smaller yachts, and there are distinct advantages in the layout made possible by the bigger hull.

"A forward overhang 5′ long suggests that the bow is somewhat out of proportion to the transom stern. Without the damping effect of a counter, a buoyant bow is apt to produce a violent pitching motion in a steep head sea. In other respects, the lines of *Tarragon*'s hull are well conceived and drawn with few inaccuracies. Having a 10′2″ beam, 5′9″ draft and a ballast keel of over 3 tons, she will not suffer from lack of stability. With displacement of 8·3 tons, one does not have to bother too much about the weight of gear and stores carried.

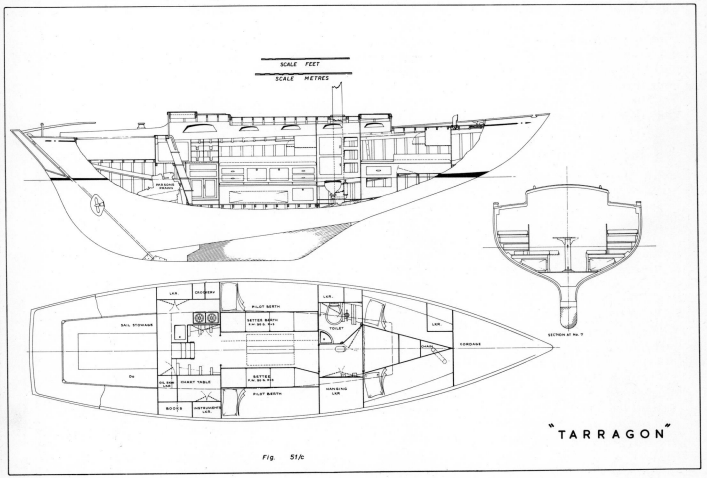

Fig. 51/c

"The fore-and-aft lines of *Tarragon* show easy curves in the forebody, and the point of maximum beam on the waterline is about 57 per cent aft of the waterline end. The bilge diagonal is well balanced, although the lower levels could be improved if the garboard diagonal were not biased so far aft. However, she ought to be a well-balanced and seaworthy hull.

"*Tarragon*, like many of the other entries in this competition, suffers from lack of sail. We have become used to yachts with small sail areas in this country, partly because of the climate and partly because designers have had an idea that the R.O.R.C. Rule is hard on sail area and have competed with each other in reducing the draperies of their models—in a strong breeze this does not matter, in light airs there are many excuses.

"*Tarragon* is a big lump of a boat, and yet she has less sail than an under-canvassed ocean racer, presumably to cater for the club novices. If they are the only members who will be interested in her, she will soon be in a poor way. Why not have 2′ on the mast, 3″ off the boom, a masthead foretriangle and 1″ on the base of the foretriangle; and a small mainsail for the beginners? The boom would then clear the permanent backstay, the yacht, with 85 sq. ft. more area, would be more interesting to sail.

"The judges considered that *Tarragon*'s accommodation is well arranged for a club yacht, whether she is being used for family cruising with children, mixed parties of adults or offshore racing. It would have been difficult to arrange this if she had been smaller and to provide also an adequate galley and chart table. More might have been made of the toilet compartment, particularly if the mast had been further aft, but one must not design one's sail plan around the lavatory compartment. No anchor winch has been allowed for, and a sampson post should be placed forward instead of the cleat which has been provided for the anchor chain. Ventilation is very poor, only one ventilator is shown and that is of the 'water-injection' type. A Parsons 'Prawn'—it would be a 'Scampi' now—is suitable as an auxiliary and will be powerful enough.

"Construction is generally well planned, but the coachroof and deck ought to be braced more strongly in way of the mast. The beam shelf is rather light for a yacht of this type. Use of wood floors throughout is to be commended in a hull to be planked with mahogany, but it does mean that the water tank cannot be placed under the cabin sole. Also, some builders never seem able to find suitable oak crooks.

"Most of the criticisms of *Tarragon* are points of detail which can be altered. Renato Levi can feel pleased that his general conception was so apt for a club yacht and that he has designed a beautiful yacht with a good lines plan."

See Figs. 51/a, 51/b, 51/c.

FEZ

Length overall	— 30′0″ (m. 9.14)	Sail area	— 321 sq. ft. (30 sq. m.)
Length waterline	— 24′0″ (m. 7.31)	Displacement	— 3·1 tons
Beam	— 8′6″ (m. 2.60)	Fin and ballast	— 1·3 tons
Draught	— 5′0″ (m. 1.52)	Engine	— 5 HP

I prepared the design of *Fez* for the designing competition organized in 1958 by *The Glasgow Herald*; the rules asked for a cruising yacht for four people to sail the West Coast of Scotland, the price to be aimed at being £1000.

The winning design was produced by Alan Buchanan—a lovely 21′ waterline sloop—and the runner-up was an equally attractive boat of practically identical dimensions designed by A. K. Balfour. My own design was based on *Funtoo*'s hull, but I changed the underwater profile of the keel, etc., and went to town on the plyglass method of construction (already mentioned on page 23). This method of construction was very fully described by Mr G. F. Findlay, Yachting Correspondent of *The Glasgow Herald*, in the publication *The £1000 Yacht* which I feel is worth quoting here:

"Novelty is the outstanding feature of the 24′ waterline sloop *Fez* from Bombay. Her method of construction in plywood and plastics has been patented in India, and patent applications have been filed in Great Britain and in other countries.

"It was evolved by Mr. Renato Levi because the all-glassfibre yacht has proved too expensive, and moulded plywood required large quantity production to make it an economic proposition. He thinks that plywood hulls are the cheapest method of building yachts today, and his method involves joining the plywood panels with fillets of resin-impregnated glass fibre mat, which gives the same

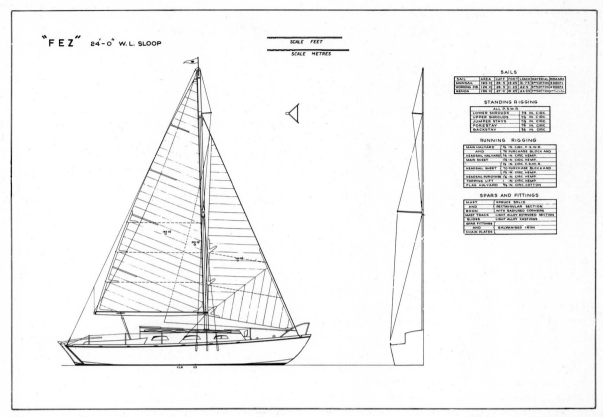

"FEZ" 24'-0" W. L. SLOOP

effect as capping the edges with an angle of metal.

"The advantages Mr. Levi claims for this method are that a very light but sturdy, water-tight hull can be built by unskilled labour more cheaply than by conventional methods because of the great reduction in the quantities of timber and fastenings required thus saving in building time.

"The essence of the construction of *Fez* is that the glass fibre mat makes waterproof joints possible by sealing the end grain of the plywood, one of the weaknesses of this material. The plywood edges to be joined are left rough and the recommended chine joint has two stringers at the corner, the inboard edges of which have a chamfer of 45° for the full length, thereby avoiding hand shaping.

"These stringers not only stiffen the plywood but locate the position of the chine, and in the same way a plywood backbone for keel and stem fix the profile shape of the hull. As epoxy resins are expensive in India, Mr. Levi uses a mixture of coarse sawdust and the cheaper urea formaldehyde resin as a filler, to fill the edges of the plywood and round off the joint. On top he then applies two or three layers of chopped strand glass fibre mat (weighing 2 oz. per sq. ft.) impregnated with resin. Increasing the num-

ber of layers in the fillet increases the strength of the joint until it is greater than the plywood itself. On tests, the wood broke before the joint, which remained intact.

"These details are for one-off construction, and the plywood keel and inner chines could be replaced by thickened reinforcing fillets of fibre glass if two or three boats were being built from the same mould. Standard sizes of materials have been kept in mind, and the bottom of the hull does not exceed 4'—the standard width of a sheet of plywood. Similarly, the fin keel can be made from steel sheet 10' × 4' and this metal fin is also bonded to the planking. It is advisable first to sandblast or pickle the steel and then apply a jell coat on which the glass fibre mat can be bonded in the usual way.

"Although he has had good results bonding glass fibre with adhesive resins to metal, the designer believes that in view of the abnormal strain to which the fin keel joint would be subjected if the yacht went aground, the fin keel should also be bolted through to mild steel 2" × 2" angles on the heavy oak floors of the yacht. The cylindrical ballast keel, cast in two halves, is bolted to the forward edge of the steel fin and gives *Fez* a draft of 5'.

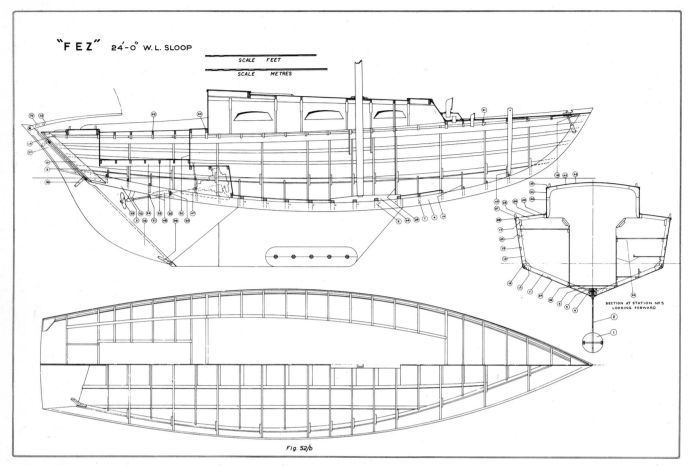

"FEZ" 24'-0" W.L. SLOOP

SCALE FEET

SCALE METRES

SECTION AT STATION N°5
LOOKING FORWARD

Fig. 52/b

"With this method of building, the moulding technique differs for different joints, because on side and overhead work there is a tendency for the resin to creep away. One should avoid overhead work by building the hull, which is very light without the fin and ballast, upside down. All the joints except the steel fin fillets can be finished, the hull turned over, the steel fin placed in position and the inside fillets on it completed. The only overhead work still necessary would be the outside fillets on the fin. The designer found that the resin could be kept in overhead joints by stapling the glass fibre to the work, brushing the resin into the glass mat and placing a strip of thin polythene over it while it was curing. After the resin has cured, the polythene is removed, leaving a smooth finish and where necessary the fillets can be trimmed with a hand plane.

"So much space has been given to describing the novel plywood and plastics construction of *Fez* that little has been said about the yacht herself. From the plans her form and layout can be envisaged, but the feature about which I have misgivings is the tre-mendous triangular gap between the fin keel and the rudder. When *Fez* is sailing to windward, the water disturbance from the high pressure leeward to the low pressure windward sides of the fin, cannot but have serious effects on the sailing performance. For all that, the design of this yacht incorporates some worthwhile new ideas and therefore fulfils one of the reasons for promoting the competition."

With reference to Mr. Findlay's remarks in this last paragraph concerning the disturbance caused by the fin keel to the rudder, I cannot unfortunately offer any concrete evidence to disprove his criticism as no boat (as far as I know) has ever been made to this design. However, I do feel that even if there were any such disturbance it would be limited to the lower part of the rudder, and would also be over a small area only, so that the windward sailing performance should not be affected very seriously. The clearance between the fin and the top area of the rudder is, after all, pretty conventional by today's standards, when the general trend is towards detached keels and rudders.

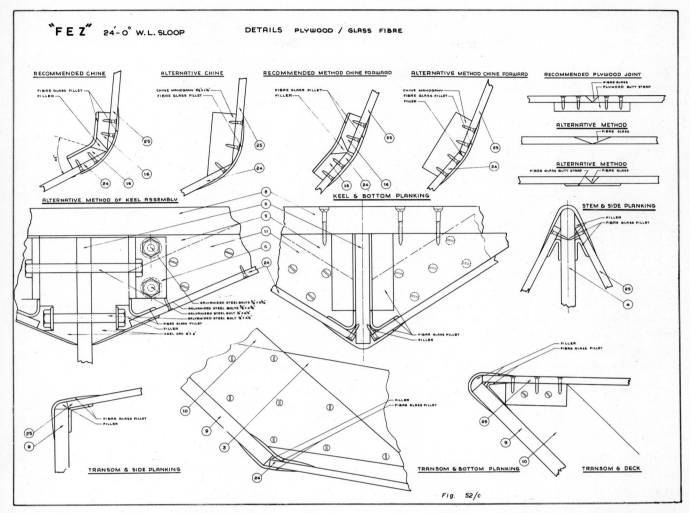

Fig. 52/c

Finally, as far as the plywood and plastics method of construction is concerned, I well remember thinking at the time as I studied the various details that this was going to be either God's gift to yachts-men or suitable material for the nearest wastepaper basket.

See Figs. 52/a, 52/b, 52/c.

HERMITAGE

Length overall	— 73' 0" (m. 22.25)		Sail area RORC	— 2588 sq. ft. (240.9 sq. m.)
Length waterline	— 52' 10" (m. 16.10)		Displacement	— 50 tons
Beam	— 16' 5" (m. 5.00)		Iron ballast	— 18 tons
Draught	— 9' 10" (m. 3.00)		Engine	— Cummins diesel, 300 HP

Hermitage is the largest yacht I have designed to date. The original object of the design was for a very comfortable cruising boat which would be capable of long, fast passages when the wind permitted. The rig also had to be simple, so as to reduce the crew to a minimum.

A month or so after the keel had been laid, how-ever, the owner decided that he would also like the boat to race in some of the more important Mediter-ranean events, such as the Giraglia. This meant changing the rig to an out-and-out racing rig.

I was particularly happy that this branch of the

design work was in the extremely capable hands of John Illingworth and Angus Primrose. They produced an extremely workmanlike and powerful rig, "powerful" because the hull lines were not ideally suited to racing. *Hermitage* was very full-bodied forward, and her construction too was more that of a purely cruising boat than that of a cruiser-racer; in addition, for reasons of economy, an iron ballast keel had been adopted.

With this rig *Hermitage* was second over the finishing line in her first Giraglia, missing a 1st by a matter of minutes. I was later told by a member of her crew that *Hermitage* could have pipped the winner if they had not miscalculated a tack at the end of the race.

Rather an amusing incident occurred during the construction of the iron ballast keel. I was scratching my head over the numerous difficulties I felt sure we were going to meet in casting such an enormous piece of iron—the keel was to be 21 feet long, 2 feet wide, well over 3 feet in depth, and weighing 18 tons. I had had unfortunate experiences in the past with annoying defects on small castings (such as fuel filler caps, cleats, and bollards) when, after hours of machining, blowholes would appear or shrinkage defects would

prevent a clean finish. I could imagine only too well what might happen with a casting of this magnitude; among other things, we had straight-through bolt holes which required cores of up to 3 feet in length. It would obviously be a devil of a job to keep these cores straight during the process of pouring the molten metal.

A casting of this size could only be done by one of the big Italian foundries at Terni. The day the foundry technician came to see me I was ready with a long list of recommendations and cautions, but I was only half-way through when he interrupted with an "Okay, okay—when do you want it?". After ten days, in fact, I had a casting which was perfect in shape, dimensions, and weight; the shrinkage allowance was spot on and the bolt holes were straight and true throughout.

Serious racing is an extremely expensive business for a boat of this size; in addition there is the difficulty of finding a skilled crew capable of working as a team to handle the considerable surface of sail involved. Understandably, therefore, *Hermitage* has not done a great deal of racing—though she has won quite a number of times.

See Figs. 53/a, 53/b.

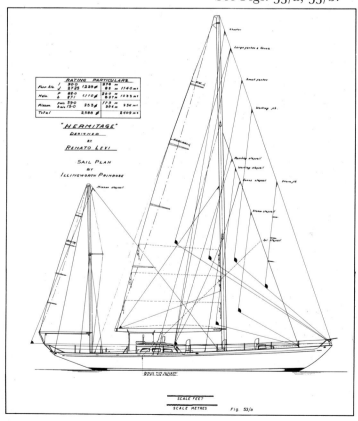

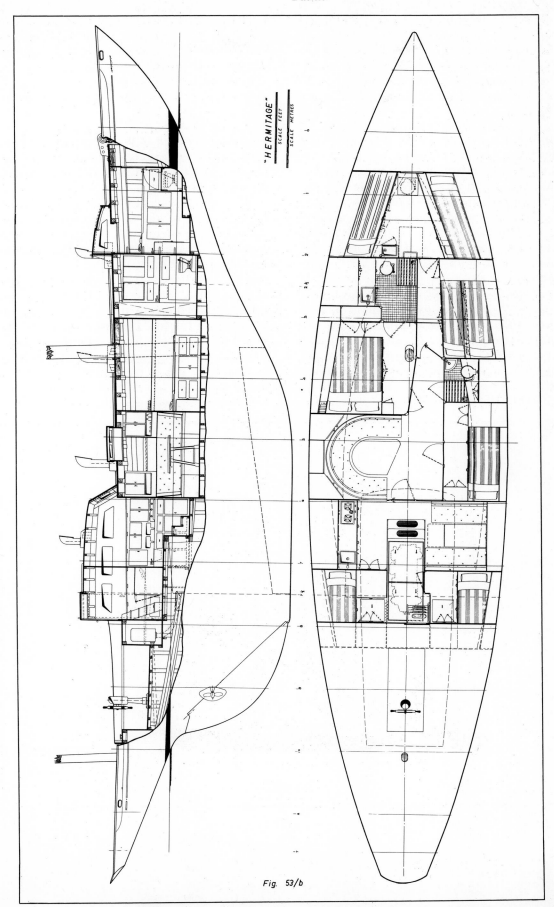

Fig. 53/b

DANY

Length overall	— *37′0″*	*(m. 11.28)*	*Sail area RORC*	— *527 sq. ft. (48·93 sq. m.)*
Length waterline	— *27′0″*	*(m. 8.23)*	*Displacement*	— *6·5 tons*
Beam	— *10′8½″*	*(m. 3.26)*	*Fin and ballast*	— *3·2 tons*
Draught	— *6′0″*	*(m. 1.83)*	*Engine*	— *Farymann auxiliary diesel, 18 HP*

Dany, a One Ton Cup yacht (22 RORC rating) was launched at Anzio early in October, 1968.

I had actually begun the design towards the end of 1967, but nearly a year passed before she was completed owing to various changes which had to be made, not to the basic hull form itself but to other aspects such as the sail plan, fin keel, and deck arrangement. The object of these changes was to try and include the most up-to-date technical refinements possible in the design.

This class of yacht is becoming increasingly popular and, as a result, the competition in One Ton Cup racing is very stiff indeed. In addition it was over five years since I had designed *Hermitage* and I was, therefore, particularly anxious to produce a craft which would, I hoped, be capable of standing up to the competition.

Dany's 37 foot hull is a laminated wood construction

of mahogany built in four laminates; the frames and deck beams are also of laminated mahogany, while the deck itself is made of teak laid in narrow widths parallel to the sheer.

The underwater profile has the familiar detached keel and skeg rudder arrangement which nowadays seems to have become almost universal. The fin keel is equipped with a trim tab, which also seems to be very usual these days, but the uncommon feature of this fin and ballast is perhaps the fact that the fin consists of a steel plate and the ballast, which is of lead, is torpedo-shaped, made in two halves, and bolted onto the fin. The total weight of the fin and keel is 3·2 tons, which puts the ballast ratio at 49%, since the displacement of the boat is 6·5 tons.

The trim tab is controlled by a separate tiller below the main tiller which can be operated either simultaneously with the main tiller or disconnected

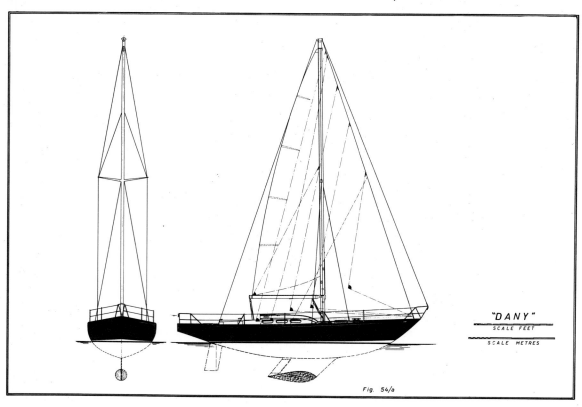

"DANY"

SCALE FEET

SCALE METRES

Fig. 54/a

and used separately.

As I have already mentioned, the keel was one of the elements which underwent a change, partly as the result of a very interesting article I read in the French magazine *Bateaux* written by E. Ravilly. The article described a number of fin keel arrangements which were tank tested prior to selecting one for Eric Tabarly's *Pen Duick III*. In the end I adopted a fin and ballast keel which was rather similar to the one chosen for Tabarly's boat.

Another rather unusual feature of *Dany* was the result of a half-joking suggestion made by her owner; the entire cabin top, in fact, can be opened as it hinges on the aft bulkheads—the idea being to enjoy maximum possible ventilation on those hot, still, summer nights which are so typical of the Mediterranean. In practice this solution proved most efficient, even as far as waterproofing was concerned since the top has a very generous overlap at the sides, as well as large gutters on the corner bars which drain off any water finding its way between the top and the cabin sides. There is also a generous water trap forward.

Dany has an extensive wardrobe of sails (some eleven in all), made by the well-known American firm of sail-makers, Hood of Marblehead. Here again there is rather an unusual feature—the somewhat large overlap of the ghoster and genoa which have a foot of 180% of the fore-triangle (J). David Coggins of Hood had many invaluable suggestions to make on the geometry of the sail plan; I am quoting here one of these suggestions which was adopted.

"Regarding the storm trysail, I am trying something new, although it is not what I would directly classify an experiment. I have altered dimensions slightly, whereby I have increased the luff to 17′ and increased the leech length accordingly. In addition, we are installing four battens which you should take extreme caution with to be certain you have the adequate strength and have included a slight roach. Also, there is a slight foot skirt, although nothing excessive that would cause any problems; as in this way, with the general revisions, we are simulating a loose-footed main. I think the storm trysail is probably the one sail in the inventory that is used very rarely, and from experience in the past, it has been definitely advantageous to increase the area conforming more closely to a small mainsail."

The spars were made of light alloy by Sparlight of England, and I think the roller reefing is worth a particular mention. The roller reefing mechanism is

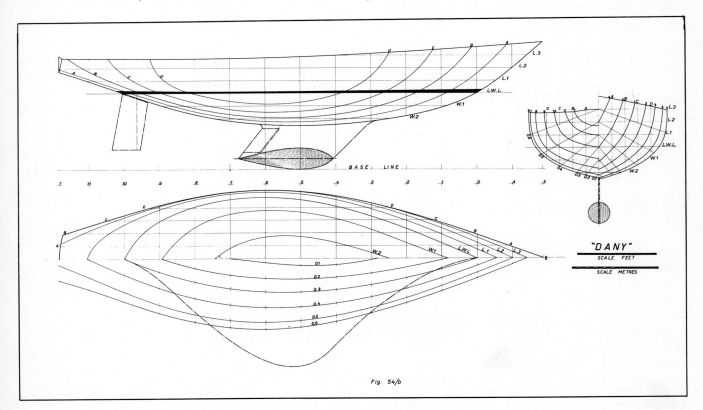

Fig. 54/b

in fact placed through the mast, and roller reefing is effected from the forward side of the main mast. This permits the luff of the mainsail to remain close to the mast throughout its length. It is a very much neater job all round, and I gather the system was first tried out by the same firm on Dick Carter's successful yacht *Tina*.

Dany has a Farymann auxiliary diesel engine of 18 HP, placed off centre, which gives her a speed of 6–7 knots.

The boat is very comfortably fitted out with four single berths and one double, as well as a spacious galley and toilet compartment.

Unfortunately *Dany* was launched at the end of the season and there was no chance of ascertaining her real possibilities, although she showed promise in the various trials carried out.

See Figs. 54/a, 54/b.

AEROPLANES

MONSOON

General dimensions			Pilot and		
Span	— 25′ 0″		Passenger	— 340 lbs	
Length	— 20′ 3″		Luggage	— 12 lbs	
Height	— 5′ 4″				
Wing area	— 111 sq. ft.		Performance		
Gross weight	— 1300 lbs		Engine		
			(Continental)	— 85–8F	
				85 HP at 2575 R.P.M.	
Weights			Propeller	— 5′ 6″ diameter	
Empty weight	— 827 lbs		Top speed	— 130 M.P.H.	
Fuel	— 100 lbs		Cruising speed	— 115 M.P.H.	
Oil	— 8 lbs		Landing speed	— 45 M.P.H.	
			Rate of climb	— 800 F.P.M.	

The prototype of the *Monsoon* was a twin-seat cantilever low wing monoplane, built in India and first flown in November, 1960. She was built entirely of wood and her design was kept simple, consistent with a clean appearance and good aerodynamic qualities. To give an example of the simplicity of construction, the wing and tail plane had constant section chords which reduced considerably the number of jigs necessary to build these components.

The aircraft was stress loaded, and the structure proved entirely satisfactory during the tests.

Flight tests proved very satisfactory, so much so that detailed "as fitted" working drawings were prepared.

My ultimate objective in designing the *Monsoon* was to provide a safe, rugged, simple and smart looking aircraft which could be built at low cost by the amateur equipped with average woodworking knowledge.

Prospective builders may ask why the weight of the aircraft is higher than many others of similar type; the answer is that the prototype was built of an Indian spruce which is a good deal heavier than the Sitka spruce recommended for general use. The maximum and cruising speeds given are also those obtained on the prototype—with a home made wooden propeller. No doubt these figures could be improved by using a more efficient propeller.

The basic fuselage is a four longeron structure of Pratt Truss design. The main longerons are 1″ × 1″ spruce, and the upright and diagonal members are 1″ × ¾″ spruce. All gussets are ⅛″ plywood, and the bulkheads are also covered with the same thickness of plywood. The turtle deck formers are laminated spruce. The two sides of the fuselage are first made on a jig and then joined together by means of the bulkheads and cross members. Since the top longerons of the sides are perfectly straight, aligning the two sides before joining them is simplified by building the fuselage upside down. Once the basic box structure of the fuselage is completed, the turtle deck and back are added. The entire front portion of the fuselage from the cockpit to the firewall is covered with ¼″ plywood whereas the turtle-back is faired with nine spruce stringers. The entire fuselage is fabric covered.

The wing is a one-piece monospar structure consisting of main spar, secondary spar, and false spar. The leading edge from the main spar is covered with plywood to form the D spar. The aerofoil used is the NACA 23012 and the chord throughout the wing is of constant section. There are thirty-one wing ribs in the whole wing, twenty-nine of which have the same outline; the remaining two are smaller and are those at the wing tips. The construction of the wing ribs is straightforward; they are made of top and bottom members in spruce, with upright and diagonal bracings held together by plywood gussets. Fibreglass was used in the prototype to cover the wing tips, so as to give a cleaner appearance, but fabric can be used here as for the rest of the wing.

The main spare is a hollow girder, consisting of laminated spruce compression and tension members (which should be laminated in a jig) and incorporating the 4° dihedral and 2° twist (which is the washout of the wing). These top and bottom members are joined together by means of plywood cross webs and plywood sides which complete the box. The short secondary spar is a simple girder with a top and bottom member of solid spruce and a plywood web. The false spar is of solid laminated spruce construction.

The ailerons are of constant section and of simple construction, having a plywood nose covering, and are hinged onto the false spar.

The whole wing, and the ailerons, are fabric covered.

The elevator and stabilizer have a constant section chord using a symmetrical aerofoil section. The stabilizer consists of a main and a secondary spar; these are built up of top and bottom members of spruce and a plywood web. There are ten ribs having the same outline, two diagonal ribs and one central nose rib. All the ribs are of web construction, having spruce top and bottom members. The whole stabilizer

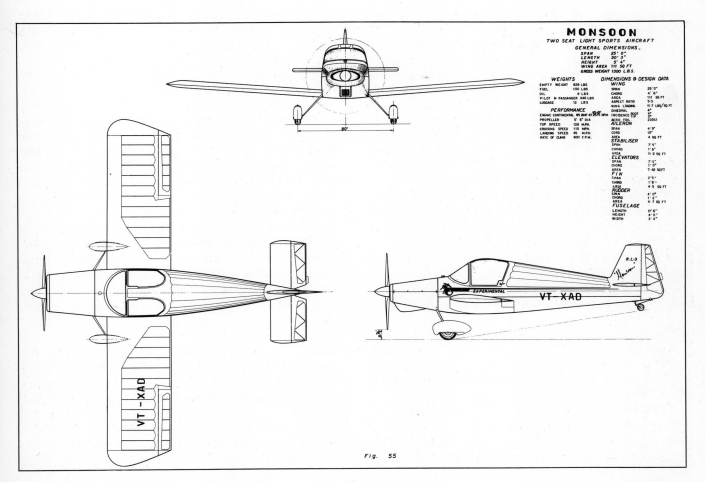

Fig. 55

is covered with 1·5 mm skin, while the tips are of expanded polyvinyl chloride plastic foam.

The elevator is ribbed diagonally and is hinged to the secondary spar of the stabilizer by means of three hinges; it has a 1·5 mm plywood covering over the nose and is entirely covered in fabric. The tips of the elevator are also shaped of polyvinyl chloride plastic foam.

The fin and rudder are of similar construction to the stabilizer and elevator. The fin has five web ribs of symmetrical aerofoil section and are of varying chord widths. The main and secondary spars are built up as for the elevator and the entire fin is covered with 1·5 mm plywood; the tips are also of polyvinyl chloride plastic foam. The rudder is braced with diagonal web ribs and the nose and base sections are plywood covered.

The rudder is hinged to the secondary spar of the fin, which also forms the end of the fuselage, by means of three hinges, and is entirely covered with fabric.

The layout of the undercarriage is conventional, with the main landing wheels forward and a tail wheel.

The main landing gear is of the torsion bar design and consists of high tensile tapered spring steel rods raked aft. The function of this type of landing gear is to flex in a fore and aft direction. These torsion bars are secured to the base frame of the engine mount with two $\frac{1}{2}''$ diameter aircraft bolts. The diameter of these spring steel rods is $1\frac{3}{8}''$ at the shoulder tapered to $\frac{7}{8}''$ before the brake collars. The main landing gear wheels are 500 × 5 and should be equipped with either hydraulic or mechanical brakes.

The tail wheel assembly is of the coil spring type; this spring is contained in a tube and is compressed by a rod or piston at the end of which is welded a fabricated yoke made of steel tubing in which the tail wheel is secured. The tail wheel is connected to the base of the rudder by means of a tube, and enables good steering while on the ground. The connection between rudder and tail can, further-more, be easily unlocked for parking purposes.

The engine mount consists of a tubular steel frame upon which are welded the various engine mount supports. The bracing of the engine mount supports follows conventional practice. Four steel plates are welded at the four corners of the engine mount frame; these plates are drilled out for the securing bolts which pass right through the firewall and secure the engine mount to the fuselage. Inside the firewall there are four metal knees which are bolted to the four longerons of the fuselage so that all the loads in this area are well distributed. The base of this engine mount frame receives the under-carriage legs.

The engine cowling is made of light gauge air-craft quality aluminium and fibreglass. The fibre-glass components are the carburettor air intake, the nose piece of the cowl, and the spinner; the aluminium parts are the top and bottom members of the cowl itself.

The flight controls are laid out for side by side operation. All controls are actuated by means of aircraft quality cables, although the elevator con-trols have one section at the tail and another in the cockpit which are actuated by means of push rods connected by cables.

The prototype *Monsoon* was fitted with toe brakes on the rudder pedals.

The windshield and canopy doors are made of $\frac{1}{8}''$ plexiglass. The windshield is secured to the turtle deck by means of an aluminium angle; aft it is fixed to a semicircular tubular structure. The frame of the canopy doors is made of tubular steel and is hinged forward on the windshield tubular structure. A simple pin hinge enables the canopy doors to be removed if required.

While the plexiglass of the windshield has simple curvature in it and can be easily shaped by gentle heating, the plexiglass canopy doors have com-pound curvature in them and must be stretch mould-ed. This operation must be done on a mould.

See Fig. 55.

MONGOOSE

General dimensions		Weights	
Span	— 20′0″	Empty weight	— 360 lbs
Length	— 15′9″	Fuel	— 45 lbs
Height	— 4′8″	Oil	— 5 lbs
Wing area	— 82·33 sq. ft.	Pilot	— 170 lbs
Gross weight	— 600 lbs	Luggage	— 20 lbs

Performance

Engine	— Volkswagen 36 HP at 3700 R.P.M.	Cruising speed	— 85 M.P.H.
		Landing speed	— 30 M.P.H.
Propeller	— 4′0″ diameter	Rate of climb	— 500 F.P.M.
Top speed	— 95 M.P.H.		

Mongoose's system of construction is very similar to that of *Monsoon*, with the exception that in this design I reduced the number of building jigs to the minimum. Even the diagonal ribs of the elevator are built on the same jig.

The wing proved the most difficult component to make in the *Monsoon*, and the main spar was the trickiest element of all—particularly when it came to assembling it with the necessary twist for the washout. The wing tip fairings were also fibreglass covered, and moulded in situ on a male mould; this necessitated a great deal of very careful workmanship in order to get a good finish. The *Mongoose*'s spar had no twist and her wing tips had no fairings, which I am sure would have made things much easier when it came to building her.

The wing washout was not actually eliminated on the *Mongoose*, but the twist was to be obtained by erecting the ribs on the spar with a gradual reduction of incidence towards the wing tip, and not by warping the spar itself. The NACA 23012 aerofoil section has some excellent characteristics, such as a very small centre of pressure movement; but it has also rather an awkward stall in that it is very sudden. The washout ensures that the stall starts at the root of the wing, and therefore permits satisfactory aileron control in the early stages; it also makes the stall progressive, giving the pilot some warning.

See Fig. 56.

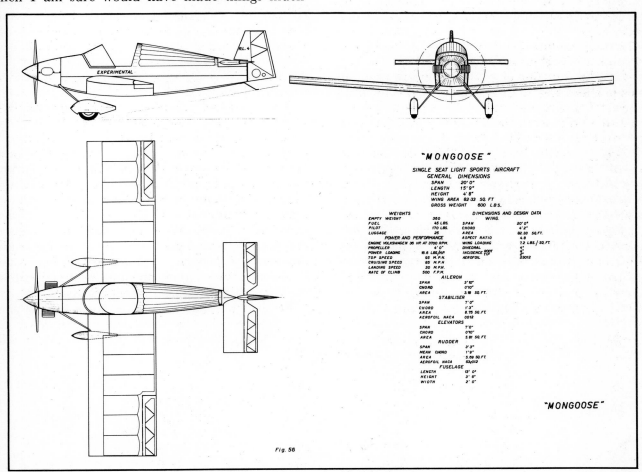

Fig. 56

Introduction to Part III

As I have already mentioned in the preface this is not intended to be a text book, but this third part deals with the theoretical and practical considerations underlying the design of fast craft.

It is not possible to condense into a few chapters all the arguments dealing with a vast subject such as this. I will in fact only explain the more important factors governing the performance of these boats and will only touch on theory when this is necessary to explain a particular point.

Throughout the ages speed has fascinated mankind and the sea is probably the only place left to us where we can freely experience this pleasure.

The desire to create is a fundamental instinct in all of us. Today fast cars and aeroplanes are the product of a highly specialized industry offering little possibility for a technical contribution from the amateur. With fast boats we are a long way away from this state of sophistication and the enthusiast can contribute in many ways to their development.

The object of this section of the book is to give the ever growing enthusiastic following of powerboats a better understanding of the fundamentals behind their design. If it helps too in providing food for thought for the development of new ideas this will be another worthwhile reason for expressing these thoughts and opinions. The field is wide open for such ideas, not only on hull design but on use of materials, methods of construction and so on. What is perhaps most exciting is that we can still as individuals make these valuable technical contributions. The design of fast craft is more of an art than a science where intuition plays a big part in a successful innovation and perhaps one of the greatest assets a progressive designer has today is a "nose" for sensing what must work. A good knowledge of naval architecture and engineering are a great help and of course experience is probably the key to the whole affair since progress in every design field is based upon past results.

It is impossible to predict how long this state of affairs will last but inevitably as progress continues there will come a time when only large industries will be able to finance the research necessary in every aspect of this field and the design of these craft will be the product of many specialists.

In the final chapter I will speculate on the shape of things to come, and will discuss the three pigeon holes open to us for really high speed in rough water; Under, Over or Through.

Included in the appendices is a most valuable contribution by Peter Du Cane and Klaus Suhrbier on propellers. I particularly appreciate their collaboration and the material they have supplied on such a vast subject, is to my mind, very complete and clear. The choice of propellers for fast craft is all to often a rather hit and miss affair. For this reason the theory underlying the design of propellers will be found most interesting to those who wish to know more about this fascinating subject.

Finally I have included in the index the complete specification of "Surfury" as a record of how a front-line racing powerboat was built in the middle sixties.

Part Three

CHAPTER XI

Design Considerations for High Speed Offshore

*I*t is a characteristic of any design innovation that it is accompanied by advantages and disadvantages; a successful design break-through can be said to be one where the former outweigh the latter. I think that the deep deadrise hull is possibly one of the very few instances where little can be said on the negative qualities, eclipsed as these are by the positive attributes of this hull form.

It is unthinkable that a really fast offshore powerboat today, either for pleasure or racing, should have anything but a deep deadrise or deep vee hull. Yet, when this type of hull was first introduced some ten years or so ago, there were understandably many people who were not convinced that these new boats were clearly superior to the more conventional warped plane or constant section shallow (or moderate) deadrise forms.

I am surprised, however, that so much is still being said, or written, in criticism of this basic hull shape. Naturally there are good and bad examples of any type of hull, but after all only successful examples should be taken into consideration if we wish to arrive at a fair comparison. Criticisms such as "Yes, but they do require an awful lot of power to push them", "They roll like hell", or (from builders) "Those spray strakes are a headache to put on" do not, in my opinion, detract in any way from the real merits of the deep vee hull form. Furthermore, these criticisms do not take into consideration the full picture; spray strakes, for instance, may be a headache constructionally but, quite apart from their necessity from a performance stand-point, they do contribute to the overall stiffening of the hull bottom and thus enable a reduction in the structure elsewhere (e.g. thickness of hull skin, framing, and so forth).

Some clarification is necessary here of terms such as warped plane, constant section (or monohedron), and deep vee, which are all too often used misleadingly in describing the various types of hull.

This may be due to the lack of any clear-cut defining line between one hull form and another, or to a measure of unfamiliarity with the subject; the fact remains that there is frequently an inexactness in applying these terms. A moderately vee-ed hull with a few risers placed on the bottom thus finds itself at times quite wrongly labelled a deep vee.

In these pages I will adopt the following classification for fast powerboats, where by "fast" I mean craft having speed/length ratios of over 5 $\left(\dfrac{V}{\sqrt{L}} > 5\right)$.

(1) *Warped plane*: a hull having a fine entry fanning out to flat or near flat sections at the transom.

(2) *Constant section or monohedron*: a hull having constant section planing surfaces aft (angle of planing surfaces up to $15°$ or so).

(3) *Deep vee*: a hull having an angle of deadrise of over $20°$ at the transom, with or without constant sections but with longitudinal strakes.

Speed in calm conditions

Perhaps the greatest criticism levelled at deeprise hulls is that they need a lot of power to plane, and that their speed potential in calm conditions is not as high as that of the warped plane or shallow deadrise form. This argument stems quite naturally from the theory that a flat plate is more efficient for planing than an inclined one.

Yet in recent years offshore races have shown that speed wise the deep deadrise hull has an advantage over the warped plane or shallow deadrise hull even in calm weather, since some of these races took place in conditions which theoretically should have been all in favour of the latter.

The answer undoubtedly lies in the fact that while these shallow deadrise hulls can achieve higher speeds in calm conditions at the lower speed/length ratios (say, under $\dfrac{V}{\sqrt{L}} = 5$) this is not the case with the higher speed/length ratios.

Briefly, and in simple terms, planing is due to lift being exerted on the hull bottom by deflecting a mass of water downward. The main factors governing the magnitude of lift are forward speed, effective lifting area of bottom, and hull incidence. It follows, then, that as speed increases either area or incidence, or both, will be reduced to lift a given weight. To attain equilibrium when planing, the longitudinal position of the centre of hydrodynamic lift remains the same in relation to the longitudinal centre of gravity (LCG) due allowance being made for the thrust component.

For purposes of comparison it is assumed that the different types of hull under consideration have the same weight, the same size and aspect ratio at rest, and the same LCG well aft. The thrust, depth, and angle are also the same.

In the early stages of planing, the greater effective lifting area of the flatter planing surfaces permits the shallow deadrise hull to plane more rapidly and with a shallower angle of incidence than the deep deadrise form. Getting over the planing hump is also achieved more easily, and therefore with less expenditure of power. As speed increases both types of hull reduce their angle of incidence. At the higher speeds we are dealing with, this reduction of incidence is greater in the case of the warped plane or shallow deadrise hull than in the deep deadrise form since the flat or near flat planing surfaces of the former offer ultimately little possibility of reduction in wetted area and no possible reduction in wetted beam. In fact, there

comes a point when the well vee-ed forward sections, which contribute little or nothing to lift, are forced into the water, thus increasing wetted length, and the boat can become unstable both vertically (porpoising) and laterally (leaning). Resistance at this moment is also increased owing to the very shallow angle of incidence, which is substantially less than the optimum (Fig. 57).

In the case of deep deadrise hull the evolution of events as speed increases is somewhat different. Here, the effective lifting area is reduced owing to the decrease in wetted beam caused by the hull lifting bodily out of the water. The hull assumes a greater angle of incidence so as to obtain the required hydrodynamic lift upon this reduced effective lifting surface, while in its turn the greater incidence reduces the wetted length (Fig. 58). It is possible that at around the same relatively very high speeds the deep vee form may have more planing wetted surface (frictional resistance) proportional to 1/cos B (Fig. 58), and that from this point of view it may be less efficient but the greater planing angle of incidence will be nearer the optimum and the gain from this, therefore, will be greater than the loss arising from the possibly slightly increased wetted surface (Fig. 58).

This does not take into consideration the effect played by spray strakes on these deep vee hulls in reducing planing area and in changing trim, both factors which contribute in an uncertain manner to the efficiency of this hull form at high speed. I will be dealing with this point however in more detail a

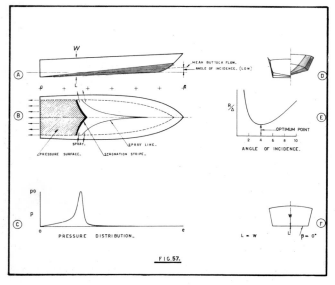

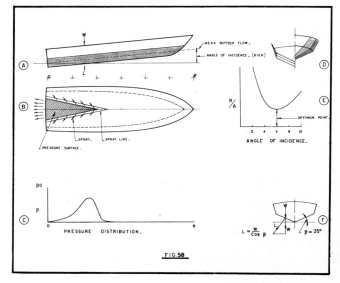

bit further on in this chapter, when I will also, as a matter of interest, touch on the desirability of flattening the planing surfaces for exceedingly high speeds $\left(\dfrac{V}{\sqrt{L}} > 20\right)$.

Merits in rough water

A simple explanation of the deep deadrise hull's ability to maintain high speeds in rough water lies in the fact that, at the high speed/length ratios referred to here, these boats are bound to leave the water partially or entirely on coming into contact with a wave, and the point of impact upon re-entry is often right aft. It follows that if the stern section is flat these impact loads will be much greater than if it is angled; the warped plane and shallow deadrise hulls, therefore, have to slow down sooner than the deep deadrise form.

Even if we assume that conditions are not rough enough for the craft to take to the air, we still have a more uncomfortable motion in the hull with flat planing surfaces. If we look at the pressure distribution diagrams (Figs. 57 and 58), we can see that there is a greater concentration of pressure in the case of the flat-bottomed hull; any changes in trim, due to the surface of the water, will in this case be corrected more abruptly, producing a violent impact motion and subjecting the hull structure to considerable strain. The deep forward sections in the regions of the bows, which are usually associated with warped plane hulls, are also liable to render the craft very wet, even if these sections are flared.

Deep deadrise hulls, too, offer better directional stability than the shallow deadrise forms; this may be of relatively minor importance when the craft is reaching or beating, but it is an essential attribute when running before following seas. The pronounced difference in lift between the aft and forward sections of shallow deadrise hulls (flat stern and fine bows) can in given conditions produce a noteworthy oscillation of the centre of lateral resistance.

This extreme lack of balance between the stern and bow sections results in a forward shift of the centre of lateral resistance when the hull is running down from the crest of the wave into the trough. The bows tend to dig in to the wave in front, with a resultant temporary slowing-down even though the propellers are still driving. At this point the stern is prone, owing to the extreme forward position of the centre of lateral resistance in relation to the centre of gravity, to slew off either to port or to starboard. Unless this yawing movement is checked immediately by rudder correction (assuming that this is possible), the boat will broach to and, in extreme cases, the stern will overtake the bows with conceivably dangerous effects.

The introduction of a skeg often helps on these hulls by bringing the centre of lateral resistance further aft, since it presents a vertical surface in the stern portion of the boat which reduces the rapidity of the yaw. Even with this appendage, however, it is often extremely exhausting and nerve-racking keeping these boats on course. I have myself had occasion to verify this when driving boats of this type to my

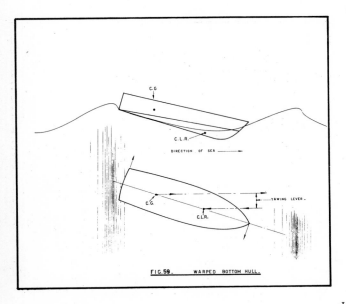

FIG. 59. WARPED BOTTOM HULL.

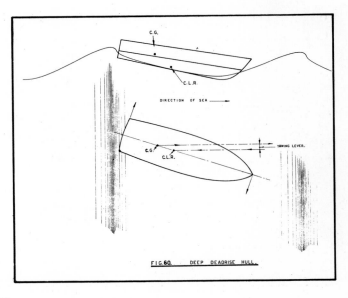

FIG. 60. DEEP DEADRISE HULL.

design in adverse weather conditions; the experience was anything but pleasant.

The deep deadrise hull does not suffer from this directional instability since it has relatively full-bodied sections forward and heavily vee-ed sections aft. Figures 59 and 60 show the difference in behaviour of the two types of hull in the conditions described.

Smoothness in turns at high speed is yet another positive merit of the deep deadrise hull. This attribute can be explained partly by the fact that, with the varying conditions of trim which may occur during a turn owing to the uneven surface of the water, the longitudinal movement of the centre of lateral resistance is small compared with that of the shallow deadrise hull. In effect this means that the various forces which act upon a craft when turning, change very little in relation to each other in the case of the deep deadrise hull. The turn is therefore more controlled.

This smoothness in turning is also due to the phenomenon of inboard bank (Fig. 61). Inboard bank is pronounced in the case of the deep deadrise hull where the transverse pressure distribution under the hull permits the centrifugal force to be well contained by the forces exerted upon the hull by rudder or rudders, and there is no tripping effect by the outboard chine which is well clear of the water. In very heavily vee-ed hulls the inboard bank may be excessive, causing such inconveniences as propellers coming out of the water, but this can be checked quite easily by means of chine wedges. These wedges come into play only on turns, and have the effect of checking the bank.

In the case of the flat-bottomed hull, on the other hand, there is a tendency to bank outward (Fig. 62), with a resulting digging in of the outboard chine which can in extreme cases lead to actual capsizing. The digging-in effect can be reduced to some extent by bevelling the chine, but the defect cannot be eliminated completely. Unusually deep rudders are also often necessary to offset this tendency.

So far I have dealt with the various advantages of the deep deadrise hull, such as maintenance of high speed in rough water, directional stability, smoothness in turning, and so forth, I also mentioned very briefly the important part played by spray strakes in the performance of these deep vee hulls. I would now like to discuss these in more detail, as well as touching on some other points of interest.

Spray Strakes

Spray strakes, or longitudinal risers as they are sometimes termed, are normally placed on the bottom of deep deadrise hulls. A great deal has been said about the number, positioning, proportion, and cross-sectional shape of these risers. As a general rule, there are three to four per side, placed parallel to each other aft in the planing area, varying in length and triangular in cross section. Designers associated with the deep deadrise hull naturally have their different theories and preferences, but there are nevertheless some basic considerations which should be kept in mind.

The principle underlying the function of spray strakes, in so far as pure planing is concerned, is that of generating lift by deflecting downwards a mass of

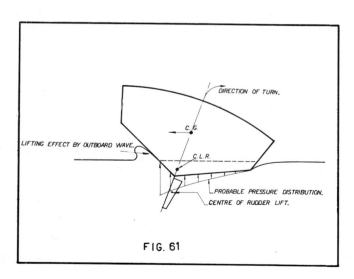

FIG. 61

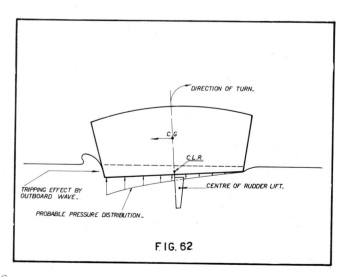

FIG. 62

196

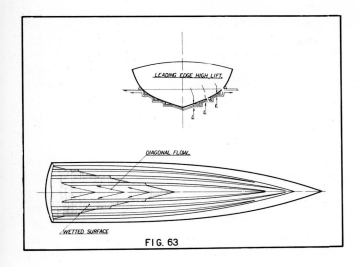

FIG. 63

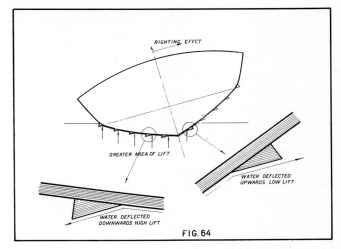

FIG. 64

water which passes under them (Fig. 63). It must be borne in mind that the flow under these strakes is diagonal, and that consequently the whole of the inboard or leading edge of the strake is the part which is subjected to maximum lift. For this reason it is an erroneous belief that the portion of the spray strake which is well submerged has little or no effect on the lift. On very fast craft, especially offshore racing powerboats, these spray strakes are cut short in the aft planing area; their general tendency is therefore to be foreshortened nearest to the keel and become progressively longer towards the chine. This is done in order to reduce lift in the stern area, as excessive lift aft can cause a reduction in the angle of incidence and a consequent increase of wetted area. At the same time there seems to be another advantage: fast boats of the type I am refering to often fly out of the water, re-entering on their stern planing surfaces, and the absence of spray strakes aft makes this re-entry smoother.

Spray strakes also have secondary uses. In the bow region, for instance, they reduce wetted surface and throw down spray. They contribute too in some measure to directional stability, since the vertical portions act as a series of small fences; any directional change generates a difference in the balance of pressure underneath the hull, thus bring the craft back on course. Rolling at high speed is also automatically and rapidly corrected (Fig. 64), since a greater area of riser in the water causes more lift on the side inclined into the water than on the other—and this has a righting effect.

On the negative side, it can be said that spray strakes make a hull harder riding. For this reason, assuming that a hull requires a given area of risers,

this area should preferably be sub-divided into many strakes, so as to break up the abruptness of the impact loads on these flat surfaces and, at the same time, offer the additional advantages of enabling the hull (according to its various loadings and speeds) to lift from one riser to another in more gradual steps. Also, as I have already mentioned before when referring to the reason for the lift generated by these risers (due to their changing the direction of the water flow), lift can be augmented by increasing the number of leading edges as long as these receive a clear flow of water with no interference or shadow from one riser to the next.

It is impossible to be categorical over the number and positioning of these strakes but, in very general terms, a greater area of strakes is necessary to increase the planing efficiency of slow craft, whereas on very fast craft a reduction in area can give better results as far as speed is concerned, and certainly will make the boat softer riding since the intensity of impact loads increases with speed. Likewise, logically, the more deadrise a hull has the more area of strakes is necessary.

Apart from this consideration of increasing planing efficiency, attention must also be paid to the positioning of the strakes in relation to appendages, particularly propellers. Several cross-sectional shapes have been adopted for these risers, but in my opinion possibly the most efficient is the triangular form with the underside horizontal to the water. Here again, on slower craft, incidence on the bottom surface of the strake can possibly increase efficiency.

Sections
There are three basic shapes which the sections of

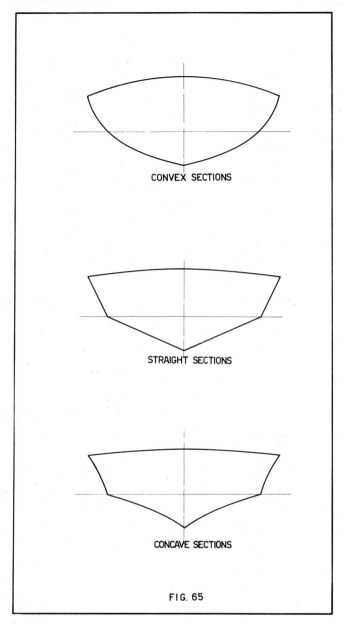

CONVEX SECTIONS

STRAIGHT SECTIONS

CONCAVE SECTIONS

FIG. 65

would be the logical answer. With convex sections it is also possible to eliminate any break at the chine, thus obtaining a continuous shell from keel to sheer. In my opinion convex sections on the bottom of the hull also render the craft less prone to hard slamming when it falls on its side (Fig. 66).

It is a popular belief that the task of planking a plywood hull or plating a metal one is much simplified if the sections are straight; this is incorrect. Certainly producing the framing, if athwartship, will be a quicker job if the section of the bottom and top-sides do not have any curvature in them, but the point is that to plank or plate a hull without any compound curvature in the panels it is necessary to have a degree of convexity in the framing where the sections change shape rapidly such as occurs, for instance, below the chine, in the region of the forefoot. For this reason the lines must be developed using cylindrical or conical projections. Employing a series of cones gives much more latitude to the hull shape and at the same time makes it possible to incorporate some convexity into the bottom and top-side panels, thus stiffening the hull, improving its appearance and perhaps even reducing its weight. Fig. 67 shows the lines of a 39′ deep vee cruiser intended for light alloy or plywood construction. As can be seen the lines are developed around six cones, three for the bottom and three for the top-sides.

In the case of really fast light alloy hulls where

high-speed hulls can take as far as bottom and top-sides are concerned, irrespective of whether they are shallow or deep deadrise: concave, straight, or convex. Naturally there are also variations on these three (Fig. 65).

From a purely structural standpoint, I cannot find any merits in concave or straight sections for the bottom or for the top-sides. These shapes do not have the rigidity of form offered by convex sections and, therefore, require heavier structures to stiffen up the flat panels. If a boat were contemplated in laminated timber, for example, convex sections

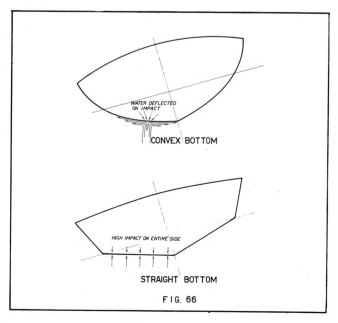

WATER DEFLECTED ON IMPACT

CONVEX BOTTOM

HIGH IMPACT ON ENTIRE SIDE

STRAIGHT BOTTOM

FIG. 66

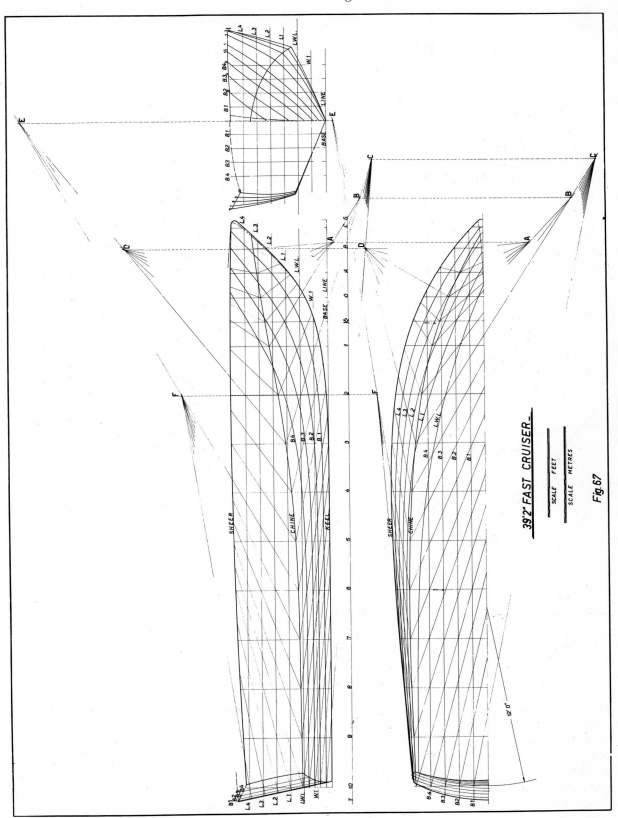

39'2" FAST CRUISER

SCALE FEET

SCALE METRES

Fig. 67

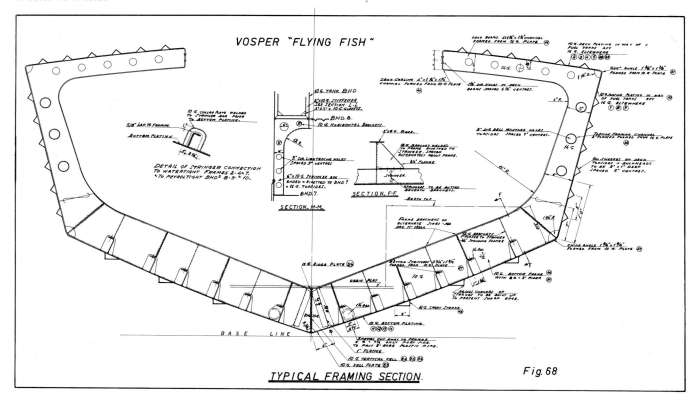

VOSPER "FLYING FISH"

TYPICAL FRAMING SECTION.

Fig. 68

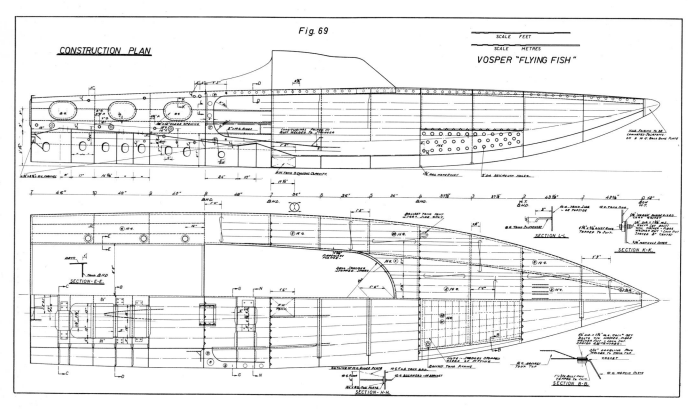

Fig. 69

CONSTRUCTION PLAN

VOSPER "FLYING FISH"

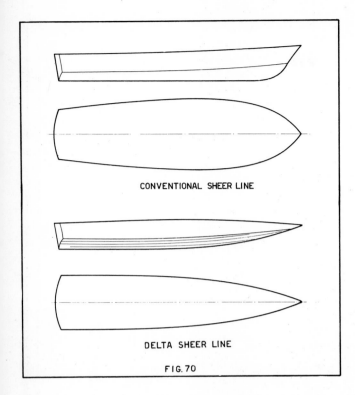

CONVENTIONAL SHEER LINE

DELTA SHEER LINE

FIG. 70

it is desirable, for weight saving reasons, to use comparatively light gauge plating which would necessitate a considerable amount of framing to obtain the required stiffness, resorting to corrugating of the plating is an excellent way of stiffening the panels with a minimum addition of weight. (Fig. 68.) This shows a typical framing section of the Vosper "Flying Fish". This craft was designed by Peter Du Cane and was, as far as I know, the first light alloy offshore racing powerboat to adopt corrugations as a means of stiffening light gauge plating. The structure of this boat was most ingenious in many other ways and employed a lot of the techniques used in aircraft construction. Fig. 69 shows the construction plan.

Aerodynamics
Great attention should be paid to aerodynamic cleanliness in designing these hulls, especially when really high speeds are contemplated. Apart from contributing to increased velocity, aerodynamic cleanliness renders a craft much more manageable in strong winds. High, flared bows, which are all too often in evidence in many designs today, have no justification in that they are prone to generate aerodynamic lift in the bows, thereby causing awkward flying characteristics. They also do not contribute in any way to keeping the spray down, since

Design Considerations
spray deflection must be achieved under the hull; they move the aerodynamic centre further forward in cross winds, necessitating greater helm correction; they obstruct visibility at the more acute angles of incidence; and appearance-wise, in my opinion, they are distinctly old-fashioned. For all these reasons I prefer to see the top-sides with reverse sheer, such as I developed in my Delta form (Fig. 70).

Reducing Deadrise for High Speeds
Earlier on I touched on the desirability of reducing deadrise again for very high speeds $(V \div \sqrt{L} => 20)$ in the interest of efficiency. The exact reason for this is somewhat obscure, or at any rate has not been conclusively proved, but it seems probable that an aerodynamic factor is involved. As speed increases, the aerodynamic forces become understandably greater (they increase, in fact, in proportion to the square of the speed); there comes a moment when flatter sections aft can generate more aerodynamic lift and, therefore, reduce wetted surface. In any event, the efficiency of these relatively flat surfaces is much improved by incorporating longitudinal steps, which have the effect of reducing wetted surface (beam) as speed increases (Fig. 71). However, since we seem to be a fairly long way away from these speed/length ratios at the moment for offshore craft, this point is mentioned here only as a matter of interest. In any case, flat deadrises which are efficient for these speeds would be quite unsuitable for rough open water.

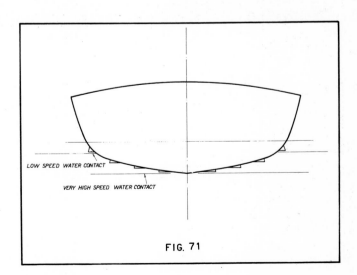

LOW SPEED WATER CONTACT

VERY HIGH SPEED WATER CONTACT

FIG. 71

Negative Aspects

So far I have only indicated the positive qualities of deep vee hulls, without mentioning the negative aspects. The latter all stem from the basic fact that deep vee hulls are tender. When at rest, or travelling slowly, they have a tendency to roll and are also very sensitive laterally, listing very easily with any athwartship change of weight. With the wind on the beam at high speed they are prone to list to windward; this list becomes more pronounced as speed, deadrise, or height or freeboard (particularly forward) are increased, owing to the fact that rudder correction is necessary so as to keep the boat on course in cross winds.

Single screw deep deadrise hulls also have a noticeable torque problem which is not easy to overcome. This torque correction can be done either dynamically or physically—or by a combination of the two.

These disadvantages in the deep vee hull, however, seem a small price to pay in return for the very definite assets which it offers for fast open water performance.

Finally, the craft as a whole will have its own distinctive appearance; this can vary considerably according to personal taste (whether it is that of the designer, the yard, or the owner). "De gustibus non disputandum est", but nevertheless I cannot help feeling that in designing these craft the accent must be placed above all on efficiency. Any line or idea which is dictated by a precise function looks right and, even if it may not appeal at first, must eventually be accepted.

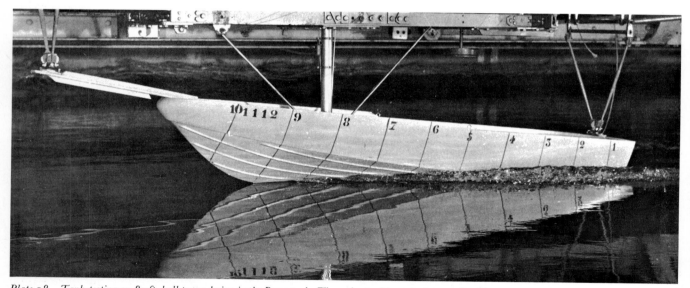

Plate 38   Tank-testing an 80 ft. hull to my design in the Rome tank. The scale speed is equivalent to 26.26 knots.

CHAPTER XII

Producing the Design

There are two ways in which a designer can approach the task of preparing a new design. He may either do so at the request of a client, or he may have an idea which he wishes to develop. In the latter case he is only responsible to himself for what he designs, and therefore has complete freedom to incorporate any number of new ideas which the average client, understandably, may not be prepared to accept owing to the inevitable element of uncertainty. This is without doubt the most satisfying course to follow for a designer who has genuinely new ideas. Nothing gives a greater sense of achievement than producing something which is really revolutionary, or even unusual which gives the desired results.

In practice, however, the greater part of new designs are prepared upon request, and the designer is therefore responsible for interpreting his clients' requirements in the best way he can? Often too much is demanded; often the designers themselves are too ready to accept requirements which they are not certain that they will be able to fulfil. It is essential at this stage that all aspects of the design are carefully analysed to ensure that the finished product will satisfy the clients' wishes.

It is immaterial whether the boat is intended for pure racing, pleasure, or work; in each case a certain degree of compromise will be necessary. In the case of a racing boat, for example, there might be a compromise between size and speed; for a given engine installation a small boat will have a higher power to weight ratio than a big one. The smaller boat will therefore be faster in calm weather but unable to maintain a high speed in rough water, whereas the bigger (longer) heavier boat will have the advantage in rough going but lack the speed of the smaller craft in calm conditions. In the case of a pleasure or work boat, the compromise could be between size and cost, speed and weight, and so on.

With a racing boat the conflicting necessities, are perhaps fewer; the aim is to win a race, or a series of races, and the designer is often given a free hand as to the size, type of construction, and often even the kind of machinery and transmission to be installed. Selecting the most suitable propulsive machinery is not always an easy task; although in recent years, in the case of front-line offshore power-boats results have clearly shown that it is necessary to fit outdrives with variable thrust mechanism in order to be competitive.

The designer must use his judgement as to the likely weather conditions in which the boat will be racing and this can be a risky business. A boat designed exclusively for racing in the English Channel would require to be more rugged than one designed for use in the Mediterranean during the summer season. Yet there have been races in the English Channel in a flat calm, just as there have been off-shore races in the Mediterranean in rough weather; but these are more the exception than the rule.

The small proportion of racing boats which appear in the numerous international events, need to be designed with a different criterion in mind; they must be good all rounders, capable of negotiating all kinds of weather conditions and showing up well in them, and it is perhaps here that the designers' skill is most evident. Apart from every other consideration the boat will be up against the giants of the sport, and therefore must be meticulously studied in all its details. Every weight saving refinement must be incorporated so as to produce a sturdy and yet a light structure. This tends to be an expensive business with the use of new materials, methods of construction, etc. In cases such as these, being backed by an owner who understands and is prepared to meet the bill for such refinements goes a long way to assisting in a successful creation.

Last but not least these boats are designed around

a set of rules drawn up by a national or international authority.

In a pleasure boat, the most important consideration is generally the accommodation; what sort of accommodation is needed, for how many people and how it is to be laid out. Next in importance comes the maximum and cruising speeds desired, the type and power of machinery to be installed, the type of construction most suitable, the styling and so on.

One cannot argue about taste as this varies a great deal from person to person. It is a question here of blending in one's own style with the clients' taste. Likewise one cannot be dogmatic about size since this again is not only influenced by practical considerations but also by personal criteria as well as, perhaps even more important, what the client is prepared to spend on his boat.

I will use here the 38′ fast commuter "Hidalgo" as an example to show the way I set about producing a design. I have already referred to this boat in the design section but will go into more detail here. I particularly enjoyed designing this boat for Roberto Olivetti for two main reasons; his ideas from the start were crystal clear, as it was equally clear that the outcome was going to be an extremely functional craft with a very clean appearance.

Briefly his requirements were: a fast diesel powered cruiser capable of maintaining a good speed even in rough conditions with an acceptable degree of comfort. The craft had to have sufficient range to cruise freely about the Mediterranean. Comfortable living accommodation was to be provided for two people and the boat's dimensions had to be such that it could easily be handled in port by one person (himself) for he did not wish to carry a paid-hand on board.

As far as the accommodation was concerned, he rightly reasoned that, in a fast boat such as he wanted, it was not practical to go forward into the cabin when the craft was underway. The cabin therefore would only be used when the craft was not in motion, i.e. anchored in port or stationary at sea. Furthermore he particularly wanted a low and very clean profile so as to reduce windage, and at the same time give the boat an elegant and crisp appearance. I remember vividly on this subject of a low profile that he even suggested that the inflatable dinghy which he wanted to carry should be recessed into the aft deck under hatches.

We discussed all these details at length and quite a clear picture emerged in my mind on the sort of boat that would fulfil all these requirements and what was particularly satisfying was that there were hardly any conflicting requisites. All the pieces of the jigsaw were falling neatly into place; a low profile was possible to reduce windage, since the cabin would not be in use during navigation; the low profile, apart from reducing windage, would also reduce weight which would contribute to more speed.

In fact we came up with an unusual solution

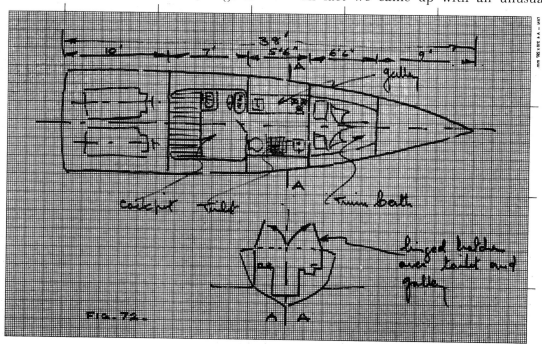

which consisted of a flush deck over the cabin with large hatches which would only be opened when the craft was stationary. This provided the headroom in the cabin, the hatches, which would open in two halves along the centre line of the boat, would form the cabin sides and a light awning which could be stretched over the top would provide shelter and privacy. Furthermore this arrangement would offer excellent ventilation which is so essential in a hot climate. As a rule cabin cruisers of the size we were contemplating are hot and stuffy inside.

There was no doubt in my mind about the hull shape, I was going to use my Delta configuration for three reasons: its high speed potential, distinctive appearance, and proven sea-keeping qualities.

I now had to establish the dimensions of the boat, what power would be necessary to drive the boat at a maximum speed of 40 knots, the fuel to be carried for a range of 300 odd miles and other details of this kind. The speed and range figures were arrived at by reasoning that 40 knots was about the maximum one could expect with standard diesel machinery. Such a performance would permit a continuous cruising speed of 33 to 34 knots. In order to cruise 300 miles would require about 9 hours at the helm—which was considered to be about as much as one would want to do in a day. Furthermore this range would be sufficient to cover the longest hops between refuelling stations.

The proviso was left open to me to check whether this was possible on technical grounds after I had proceeded further with the design.

It was now time to get down to the drawing board so as to crystallize the design and support it with facts and figures.

I like to prepare a very rough outline drawing, usually this is a freehand sketch, of the plan of the boat, bulkheading it off with the various spaces required for cabin, saloon, toilets, engine room, cockpit, etc. Though these drawings are freehand I nevertheless make them to scale, utilizing a scale that does not exceed ten inches. The reason for this is that the eye can see at a glance the whole picture and secondly a small drawing can be produced very quickly, especially if it is done on graph paper. (Fig. 72.)

I selected a length of 38′ for this craft in this preliminary sketch; I felt this was a comfortable size for long cruising, would not be too much of a handful for one person to manage, and would permit me to fit in the engines and the accommodation.

As far as the beam was concerned, Delta forms of this size have a length to beam trio of about 3·5 $(L \div B = 3·5)$ so the beam in this case was taken at 10′9″. This was of course the maximum beam which in this type of hull is situated right aft.

The next step was another freehand sketch, again on graph paper and to the same scale, of the outboard profile. This serves to get an idea of what the boat would eventually look like (Fig. 73).

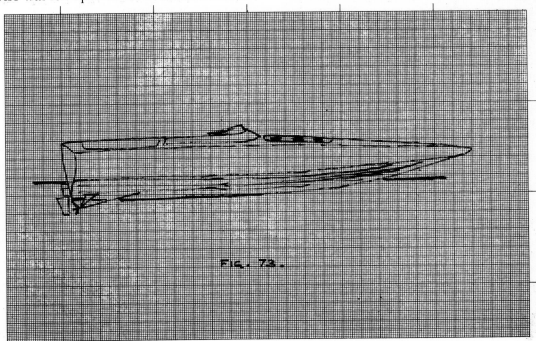

FIG. 73.

At this point several things have to be worked out more or less together. The weight of the boat must be estimated so as to work out the power required. In order to arrive at the light and loaded displacement of the boat an approximate estimate must be made of the engine weight and the variable loads, i.e. fuel, water, crew and provisions. In this case I was able to estimate this quite quickly and fairly accurately from some previous 9 or 10 Delta designs of very similar size which had already been built. I came to the following provisional figures on the weight:

Complete hull structure including internal joinery work and equipment	4480 lbs
2 diesel engines for a total of between 700–800 HP at 8 lbs per HP	6000 lbs
2 complete shaft lines and transmissions	500 lbs
Fuel, water, crew and provisions	3360 lbs
Total light displacement	10980 lbs = 4·9 tons
Total load displacement	14340 lbs = 6·4 tons.

The fuel, water, crew and provisions estimate was arrived at in the following way:

Fuel: for the purpose of this calculation I took the worst condition (which in practice a boat will never meet) i.e. 3000 miles at 40 knots which meant a running time of $7\frac{1}{2}$ hours. Assuming a total of 750 HP were required to propel the boat at this speed, then the fuel consumption per hour would be around 37·5 gallons (5 gallons per 100 HP/hour) or 281 gallons for the $7\frac{1}{2}$ hours running. Actually in the final design I was able to reduce this to 265 gallons for even this capacity left a good margin for safety at cruising speed. Therefore the break up of these variable weights were:

Fuel	265 gallons at 8·66 lbs =	2300 lbs
Fresh water	60 gallons at 10 lbs =	600 lbs
Crew	2 persons at 150 lbs =	300 lbs
Provisions and personal belongings	2 persons at 80 lbs =	160 lbs
	Total	3360 lbs

I now had the approximate weight of the boat and it was necessary to check whether the power I had estimated was sufficient to arrive at the maximum speed of 40 knots. A useful formula for this is:

$$V = K \sqrt{\frac{HP}{W}}$$

Where V is the speed in knots, K is a constant, HP is the shaft horsepower and W is the weight in tons. (2240 lbs.) The accuracy of this formula lies in the correct selection of the K value and here again data and past experience are invaluable. On my designs these K values have varied from 3·3 to a figure of 4. In this respect one of the biggest influences upon this value, assuming the hulls are identical and have approximately the same power loading, is the appendage drag, i.e. number of shafts the boat has. Having built boats with one, two, three and four shafts I was able to hit pretty accurately on a realistic figure for K of 3·6. Taking a cruising weight of 5·65 tons, then:

$$V = 3·6 \sqrt{\frac{750}{5·65}} = 41·4 \text{ knots.}$$

The diesel engines had now to be selected having a horse power as near as possible to 375 each and a weight not exceeding 8 lbs per HP. There was not really an awful lot of choice in this category and after discussing the matter with Olivetti I chose a pair of Cummins VT8-370-M's. These engines, from my point of view, were extremely compact, the weight per HP was within the limits I wanted and though the shaft HP was less than the 375 I had taken in the calculation (probably around 350 shaft HP), I felt we would still get the 40 knots asked for.

Actually on the first trials we clocked a speed of just under 42 knots, but it must be admitted that the boat was not loaded to its full cruising weight, though it was not far off.

The rough sketches that I had prepared seemed to embody the salient requirements of the boat. The next stage was to prepare a preliminary lines drawing so that I could verify the cabin sole height, headroom with hatches closed (though full headroom in the cabin with the hatches closed was out of the question there had to be enough height to enter in a stooped position), position of the engines and other fundamental considerations. It is often necessary to carry out certain changes to the free hand sketches, to ensure that everything fits into the space allotted, that the headroom is adequate, that the deck over the engine department is sufficiently high, and other details of this nature.

The centre of buoyancy (C.B.) must be known in order to place the major weights in their correct position, i.e. engines, fuel, water, etc. The C.B. can be hit on pretty accurately, especially if one has designed similar hulls before, without going into elaborate calculations, although as a precaution this should be worked out. The simplest method I know is to run a planimeter over the underwater area of the sections, plot a curve of areas, and find the centre of gravity of it. To do this an easy method is to cut out a paper pattern of the curve of areas diagram, fold it along the water line into narrow strips and then balance it on a pin.

The C.B. on these Delta hulls of mine is located at about 63% of the water line from the bows. To locate the major weights I referred to earlier, in their correct position, the centre of gravity (C.G.) of the hull structure must be found since this also constitutes a major weight. This can either be done by calculations (weights and moments of all the scantlings) or by plotting a curve of girths diagram of the hull, including the deck and then using the paper pattern process described for the C.B. In practice the latter method gives excellent results.

For convenience the lines drawing is prepared with the aft-running lines of the bottom parallel to the water line, but it does not follow that this will be the ideal trim of the boat. In very general terms, it is desirable on slowish planing hulls where the speed/length ratio is less than $5 \left(\dfrac{V}{\sqrt{L}} < 5 \right)$ to be trimmed by the bow; this enables them to get onto the plane more quickly and when planing do so with a reduced angle of incidence and an increment in speed. Boats such as the one in question where the speed/length ratio is $7 \dfrac{V}{\sqrt{L}} = 7$ the reverse is

the case, for craft at these speeds tend to flatten out and this, owing to an increase in wetted area, reduces their top speed potential. Also a fast hull rushing along with a very shallow angle of incidence can run into steering problems.

For this reason, on this craft I placed the major weights so that the C.G. was well back, it was in fact located at about 7% of the water line length aft of the level trim position of the C.B. This meant that the boat floating at rest would be noticeably down by the stern. (In a state of equilibrium the C.B. will be vertically under the C.G.). The trim of these fast boats is often criticized on aesthetic grounds but one cannot get away from the fact that they perform better when they are trimmed by the stern just as the slower planing craft benefit from being trimmed by the bow.

Probably one of the steps in the design which requires the most care is the sighting of the engines and the shaft lines. In this case, where the engines were located aft driving the propellers through V drives, the positioning of these also had to be worked out. The aim of a correctly positioned shaft line is to reduce as much as possible the shaft inclination and keep the propellers close to the centre line, so that they are deep down in the water, without too much misalignment on the universal joints of the transmission connecting the V-drive to the engine.

In order to position a shaft line it is necessary to

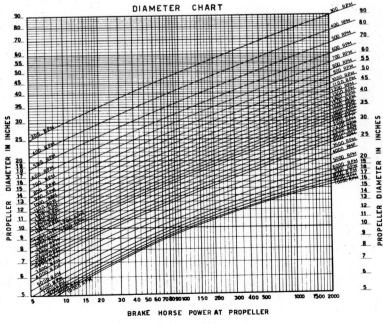

Fig. 74

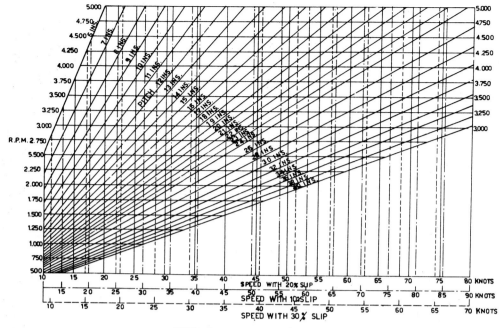

PROPELLER PITCH FOR HIGH R.P.M. AND SPEED

Fig. 75

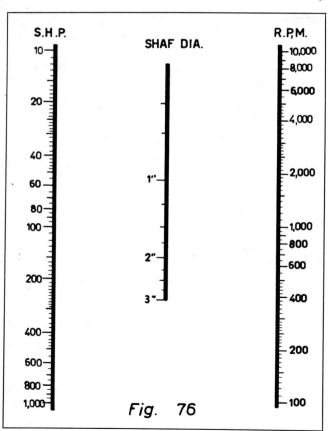

Fig. 76

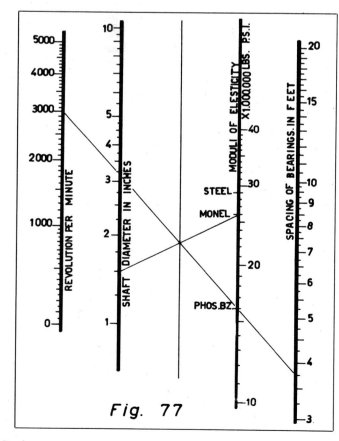

Fig. 77

know the diameter of the propeller, the efficiency of which is greatly influenced by its pitch diameter ratio (P/D), which in the case of fast boats will vary between 1·2 and 1·6. It can be seen therefore, that the correct choice of propeller R.P.M. is important. Often there is not too much choice. In this particular case I adopted a direct drive gear on the engine and V-drive, i.e. 3000 R.P.M. and from the propeller diameter chart (Fig. 74) the appropriate diameter was 17″. Assuming a pitch ratio of 1·2 the pitch would be 20·4″, which in theory would give a speed of just over 40 knots with a 20% slip. For those interested in propeller theory see Appendix I by Suhrbier & Du Cane.

Knowing the diameter (Fig. 75) it was now possible to position the propeller under the hull making due allowance for tip clearance (between tip of propeller and bottom of hull), which in this case was 6″ but which should not be less than $\frac{1}{6}$ of the propeller diameter. Since I had decided to employ a single central transom mounted rudder to reduce drag, I was able to locate the propellers right aft which enabled me to obtain a shaft angle of 9° 30′. My work of placing the propellers as near the centre line as I could, without too much misalignment on the universal joints, was greatly facilitated by using the B.P.M. V-drives which are unusual in that the input and output shafts are side by side, unlike most V-drives where they are one above the other.

The misalignment on the universal joints of the transmission were 2° when seen in plan and 3° in profile; well within the permissible limits.

I selected monel metal for the propeller shafts; this is a nickel alloy which has excellent mechanical properties and is particularly resistant to corrosion since it has a high electrical potential. The correct choice of diameter and bearing spacing had now to be established. These are both mechanical considerations which vary with the choice of material, they can either be calculated or what is quicker and easier is to use the two graphs prepared by the International Nickel Company of New York. The first (Fig. 76) gives the appropriate shaft diameter. It is a question of connecting the RPM to the SHP with a straight line and the intersection on the centre line will be the recommended shaft diameter. In the case of *Hidalgo* I adopted 1½″ shafts. For the correct bearing spacing the second chart (Fig. 77) has to be used in the following way: connect with a straight line the shaft diameter in the second scale to the appropriate metal on the moduli of elasticity scale then, rule a line from the revolutions per minute

scale on the extreme left which passes through the Intersection of the previous line drawn with the vertical line in the centre of the chart and read off on the right the maximum bearing spacing permissible.

Since the distance between the P. bracket and the shaft log bearing in the hull was approximately 8′ it was necessary to fit an intermediate support.

We had already decided in our early discussions that the boat would have a laminated wooden structure as this method is ideally suited for a "one off" construction, it has an excellent strength-to-weight ratio and a very high standard of external finish is possible. Another advantage is that one can dispense with framing on a boat of this size thus obtaining a bit more room inside with a clean and uncumbered appearance.

The layout of the cockpit and cabin was the work of Gae Aulenti, an architect from Milan, very well known for her ability in the interior decorating field. I always enjoy working with specialists of this kind and though she told me it was her first boat interior, it was most interesting to see the way she approached the various problems. The outcome was very functional and pleasing in its simplicity.

All the more important details had been decided now and I proceeded with the main drawings which generally are the following:

1. *Lines Drawing*, complete with table of offsets and fully dimensioned for bow and stern overhangs, including the deck camber drawing and (what is useful to the builders) an outline drawing of the superstructure (if any); (Fig. 78).

2. *Midship Section and Details*, generally including a section through station 5 at twice the scale of the other drawings as well as details of the various parts of the structure such as the keel, chine, sheer, carlin, etc., at full or half scale, together with a description of materials and dimensions of scantlings; (Fig. 79).

3. *Accommodation Plan and Profile*, showing the position of all the berths, tables, cupboards, and other joinery work contained in the craft; (Fig. 34/g).

4. *Sections*, which should be made on every station (and there are generally 10 stations dividing the water line equally); if these principal sections do not pass through any particularly interesting aspect of the accommodation, further intermediate stations may be necessary; these sections are useful not only to the builder, but also to the designer enabling him to complete

P

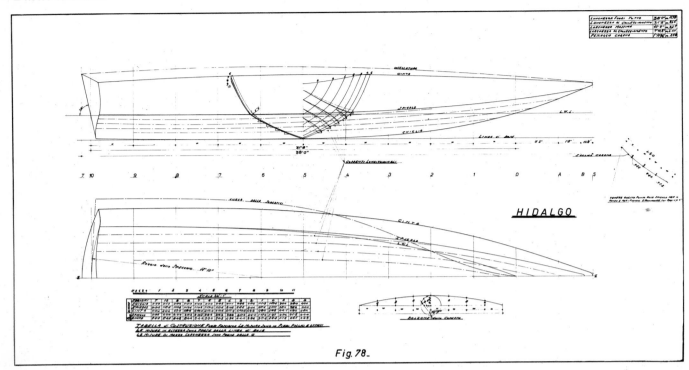

Fig. 78.

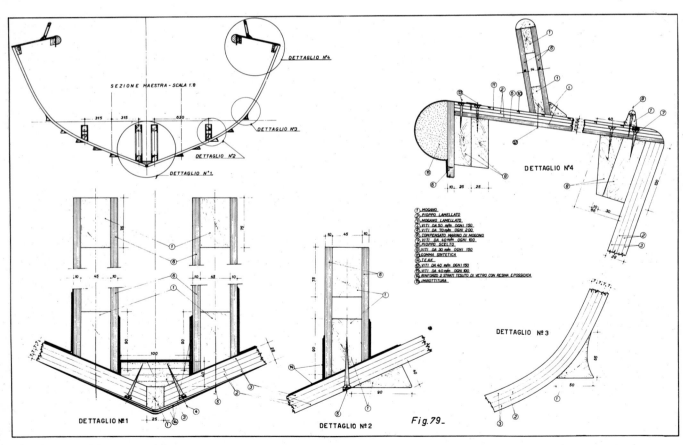

Fig. 79.

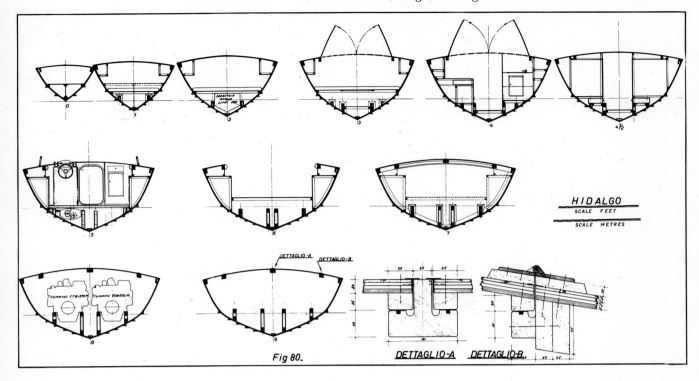

Fig 80.

the construction and accommodation drawings; (Fig. 80).

5. *Construction Drawing in Plan and Profile*, showing position of bulkheads, hull framing, deck beams, superstructure (if any), engine bearers,

cabin sole position and any other structural details; (Fig. 81).

6. *Outboard Profile and Plan*, showing how the deck is to be laid, position of deck fittings, any hull decorations such as cove line, etc. A particularly

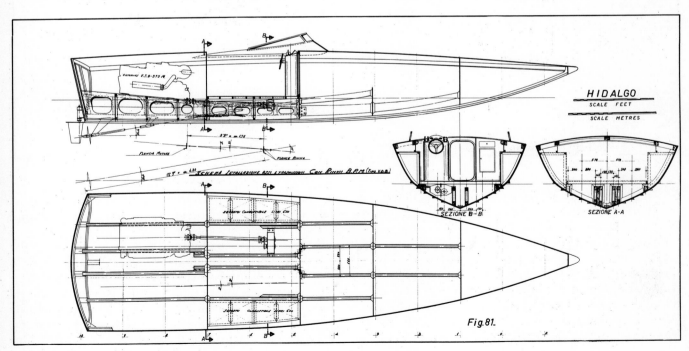

Fig. 81.

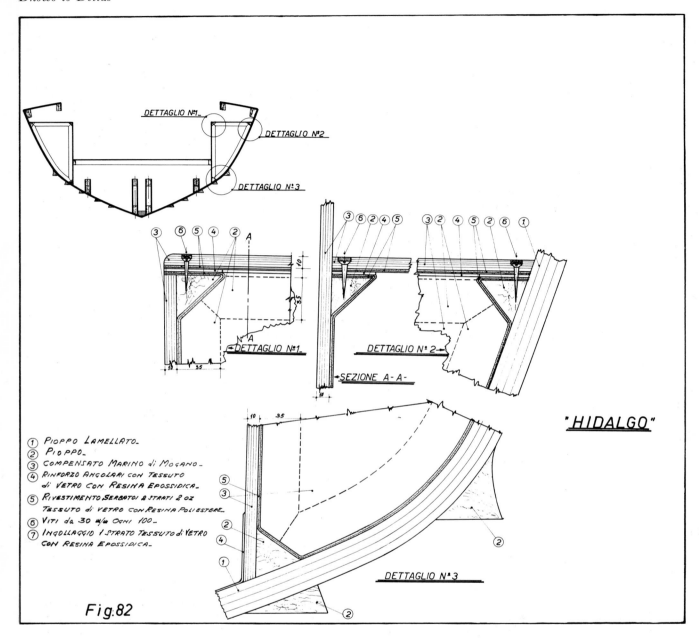

① PIOPPO LAMELLATO.
② PIOPPO.
③ COMPENSATO MARINO di MOGANO.
④ RINFORZO ANGOLARI CON TESSUTO
di VETRO CON RESINA EPOSSIDICA.
⑤ RIVESTIMENTO SERBATOI 2 STRATI 2 OZ
TESSUTO di VETRO CON RESINA POLIESTERE.
⑥ VITI da 30 m/m OGNI 100.
⑦ INGOLLAGGIO 1 STRATO TESSUTO di VETRO
CON RESINA EPOSSIDICA.

"HIDALGO"

Fig. 82

high standard of draughtsmanship is desirable here, though this drawing is not important from a technical standpoint it is perhaps the most looked at in the entire set; (Fig. 34/f).

To complete a design, it is also necessary to prepare detailed drawings of any parts or fittings which cannot be purchased ready-made, and which consequently have to be manufactured either by the yard or by an outside firm. As a rough guide, these would include the following:

7. *Fuel tanks*, specifying materials, methods of construction, dimensions, capacity and so on; (Fig. 82).
8. *Shaft Line*, including drawings of the "P" bracket, intermediate bracket (if any), specifying all materials; (Figs. 83 and 84).
9. *Rudder*, with details of the rudder housing, quadrant or rudder arm, and a diagrammatic sketch showing the link-up between the rudder and the wheel; (not generally necessary for

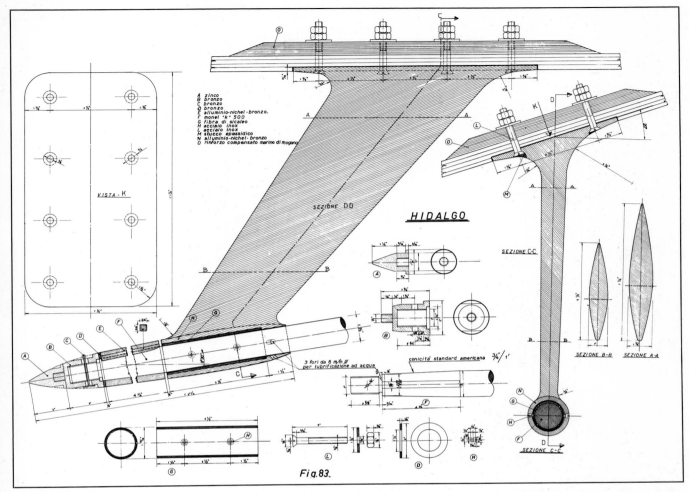

Fig. 83.

hydraulic or single cable steering) (Figs. 85/a and 85/b).

10. *Engine Installation*, showing the method of fixing the engines, location and particulars about the exhausts, water-cooling and fuel lines; (diagrams are generally provided for the latter particulars).

11. *Freshwater Tanks*, including details of their dimensions and a piping diagram (if necessary: on smaller craft the piping is generally so straightforward that this diagram is superfluous).

12. *Electrical Circuit*, although as a rule a wiring diagram is not necessary on small craft if the electrical specification is well detailed; however, there are cases when it is advisable for larger cabin cruisers, particularly where a lot of electronic equipment is installed.

There are times when a good many more drawings are needed, particularly in the larger, more complicated craft; vice versa, they can be reduced to bare essentials in the case of smaller day and cabin cruisers. It goes without saying that the adoption of outdrive propulsion eliminates all the drawings connected with the stern gear and rudders, although in this case an engine installation drawing should be supplied containing particulars on how the engine should be mounted, at what height the cavitation plate should be in relation to the running lines of the hull, and if a single outdrive installation is in question whether this is to be offset to compensate for torque.

Preparing a design may sound rather laborious, but as one gains experience in a particular type of boat the work in practice becomes much simpler. Nevertheless the design of a new boat, especially if the designer and builders are a long way away from each other, as is often the case, should always be sufficiently detailed so as to avoid any unnecessary delays or hitches in the building; a complete set of

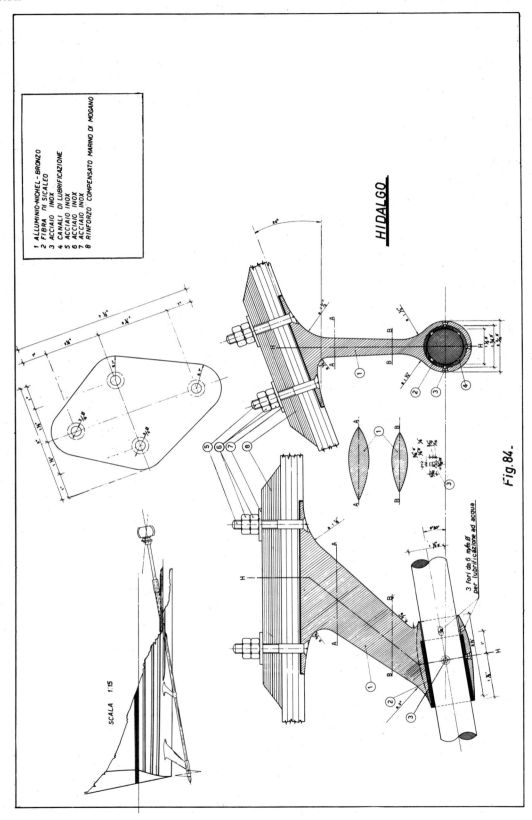

SCALA 1:15

HIDALGO

Fig. 84.-

1 ALLUMINIO-NICHEL-BRONZO
2 FIBRA IN SICALEO
3 ACCIAIO INOX
4 CANALI DI LUBRIFICAZIONE
5 ACCIAIO INOX
6 ACCIAIO INOX
7 ACCIAIO INOX
8 RINFORZO COMPENSATO MARINO DI MOGANO

3 fori da 6 m/m ø
per lubrificazione ad acqua

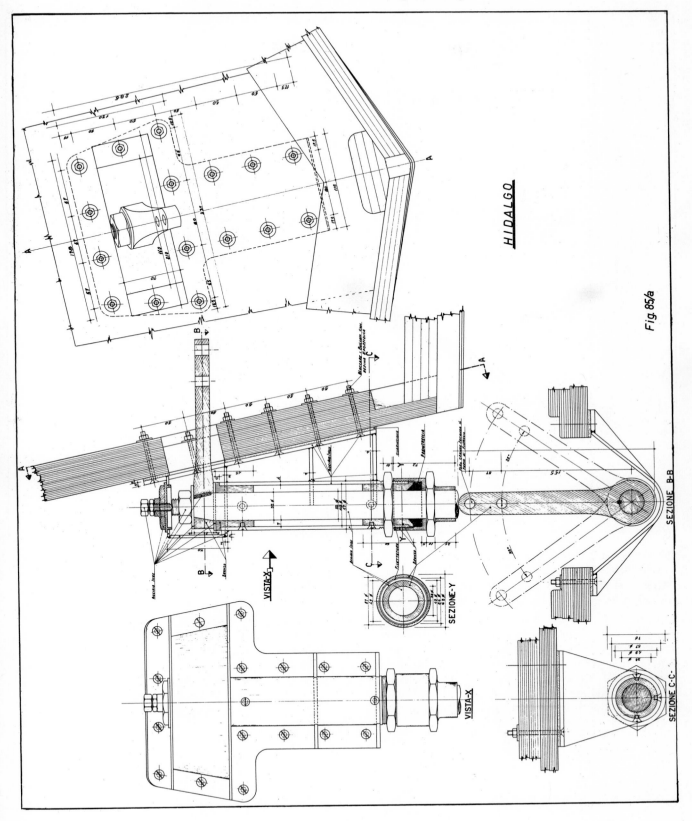

HIDALGO

Fig. 85/a

VISTA-X

VISTA-X

SEZIONE-Y

SEZIONE B-B

SEZIONE C-C-

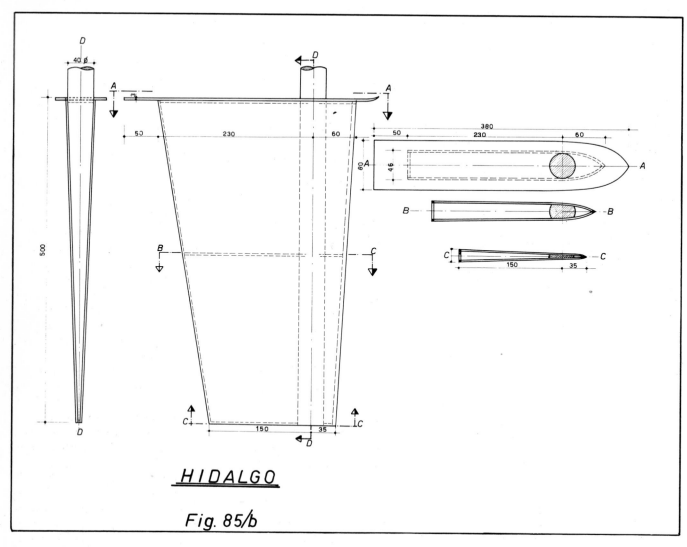

HIDALGO

Fig. 85/b

drawings, therefore, can be time-consuming but worthwhile.

Every designer has his preferences, both as to the materials he specifies and as to the method of dealing with certain portions of the construction; these special features should be clearly described in the specification if the yard building the craft is not yet conversant with the designer's technique. See Appendix II for a typical specification, in this case of *Surfury*, where I felt two specifications were necessary, one for the actual construction of the craft and the other for the mechanical aspect.

As a freelance designer who has the pleasure of working with yards all over the world I have always found close attention to detail pays hand over fist. The extra time spent is amply rewarded when, every now and again, photographs arrive from far away builders showing the excellent work done on a boat to my design—even more when I have the opportunity to visit them myself and actually see these beautifully turned out creations. This is the culminating moment for any designer.

CHAPTER XIII

Speed and the Future

*I*n this final chapter I am going to deal briefly with a few points which might well be kept in mind in the future when designing small high-speed craft for open water, craft which are, say, under 100 feet in length and capable of achieving speeds even in mixed sea conditions which are greatly superior to the fastest we have today.

Modern offshore racing powerboats offer the best examples for assessing the various technical problems which have still to be overcome in this field—even though they are only one branch of the whole class of high speed open water craft—since they are the fastest offshore vessels in existence.

These racing powerboats generally range in size from 30 to 40 feet and are powered by two 7 or 8 litre engines, totalling from 900 to 1200 HP; their maximum speed is around 60 knots, although a few can get close to 70 knots. Even higher speeds have been claimed, but I have never had the opportunity to verify these personally.

It should be noted also that for the moment these high speeds can only be maintained in reasonably good weather conditions; naturally, when the sea is rough, the longer craft have the advantage over the shorter as far as speed is concerned.

At this stage, and I have already mentioned this in the design section, I would like to emphasize the difference between sheltered and open water, as far as meteorological conditions are concerned. Generally speaking, the sea tends to have a long, gentle swell even on a calm day, which can cause a fast-moving boat to fly out of the water. On a lake or river, on the other hand, the chop is short and level, even in rough weather, and the boat stays in the water and goes through the crests of the waves (Fig. 86). The analogy is of a motorcar running on a flat road full of potholes which can nevertheless keep up a high speed since it stays on the road, whereas on a good surface but with long humps it tends to take off from the crests of these unless speed is reduced, with the possibility of serious mechanical damage or loss of control.

For this reason fast offshore craft perforce spend a lot of their time in the air. Particular attention has therefore to be paid when designing these craft to the problem of coping with this flying phenomenon. For instance, the propeller, or propellers, and the rudder, or rudders, should be placed well aft so that they are the last portion of the craft to leave the water and the first to re-enter it. In this way both propellers and rudders are out of the water for the shortest possible time, with a consequent minimum loss of thrust in the case of the former (as well as a reduction of the risk of damage owing to over-revving when out of the water), and in the latter a continuity in the steering which keeps the boat upright and under control.

The design of the underwater hull should also be such that take-off and re-entry are executed with minimum variation in acceleration and minimum impact loads. Logically, this means less wear and tear for both crew and boat and higher velocities are obtainable without undue risk. One of the fundamental factors underlying smoothness on take-off

Calm conditions in open sea with long gentle swell    *Rough conditions in sheltered water with short level chop*

Fig. 86

217

and re-entry is the amount of deadrise in the hull bottom. The more deadrise there is, the more comfortably will the boat ride, although there is of course a limit to the amount of deadrise which can be incorporated, since ultimately this will have a negative effect on lateral stability. The distribution of deadrise along the hull has its effect, too, as also has the attitude which the boat assumes when out of the water and flying through the air.

Attitude can of course be influenced hydrodynamically by the use of transom flaps, variable thrust out-drives, physically by means of water ballast, or—all too often neglected—aerodynamically in the form presented by the hull itself. In the latter case, high flared bows tend to shift the aerodynamic centre forward, with the resultant lifting of the bows. As speed increases these aerodynamic considerations clearly become increasingly important and, if not interpreted correctly, cannot only create awkward flying characteristics and in some cases even serious steering problems, but can also greatly influence forward speed.

No matter what has been done within the above limits to date, however, the fact remains that even the best of these boats are incapable of maintaining their maximum speed when the weather is really rough without incurring structural or mechanical damage, or injuring the crew.

Such is the design situation in which we find ourselves today. Where do we go from here? What is the best answer: UNDER, OVER, or THROUGH the waves.

UNDER

This solution would certainly eliminate several difficulties; perhaps the most important, the fact that the weather would have very little effect upon the speed and motion of the craft. The power required to propel such a body underwater at high speed, however, would be enormous, without taking into consideration all the other engineering complications involved. On the psychological side, too, the thrill of high speed at sea can obviously only be appreciated on the surface.

OVER

In this category we already have today a wide selection of hydrofoil and hover craft, but these vessels seem above all to be suited to definite specific applications, and we are still a long way away from achieving really high speeds with them in rough weather.

We have today a type of craft also which, by virtue of its forward motion, utilizes aerodynamic effect for lift. A particularly successful example of this configuration is the circuit racing catamaran; but these craft cannot be considered as airborne craft as they remain in contact with the surface of the water a great deal of the time, even though this contact is limited to a very small area of the hulls (this contact is necessary to maintain aerodynamic stability). It is this characteristic which limits their high-speed qualities in very rough seas and has up to now prevented any serious break-through being made with these boats for fast rough offshore work.

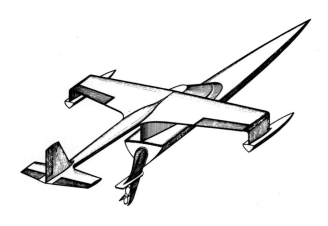

CONVENTIONAL WING BEFORE TAIL

FIG. 87

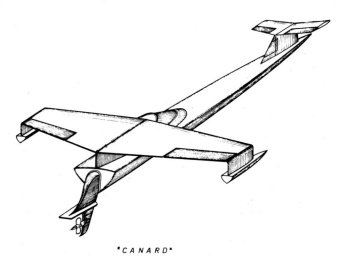

"CANARD"

FIG. 88

THE OVER CONCEPT

FIG. 89

Would a winged hull which lifts right out of the water be a possibility worth investigating? Certainly one could do no better for really high speeds with a minimum of power installed than lift the hull clear of the surface. If the height of the craft could be varied at will above the surface of the water, this would completely eliminate all contact with the sea in rough weather; the possibly dangerous and certainly uncomfortable effects of hull impact would thus be avoided.

The problem here seems to centre on maintaining satisfactory aerodynamic stability when the craft is out of the water. It will clearly be necessary to adopt air controls to pilot such a craft; we must, in fact, think in terms of aircraft design, utilizing proven configurations such as the conventional wing before tail (Fig. 87) or the "canard" (Fig. 88). Of these two solutions the latter seems to me to be the logical one since the hull also serves as the fuselage to support the tail surfaces. In the former case it would be necessary to extend a boom aft so as to obtain the required moment arm for the tail surfaces, resulting in an increase in dimensions, weight, etc.

The question which undoubtedly comes to mind now is: Why not use an aeroplane and be done with it? But this is perhaps a somewhat hasty conclusion.

What advantages would a winged craft in fact have over an aeroplane? First of all, the ground effect factor could be utilized to advantage. (Lift/Drag

(L/D) values of 20 to 25 and even, in some cases, up to 30 can be expected when the ground effect factor is present. This is considerably more than an L/D of around 15 which is about average for an aircraft in normal flight.) Secondly, a water propeller might be more efficient for the speeds in question than an air screw. Against this we have a limited height range, which would necessitate some fairly expensive and sophisticated electronic equipment (gyroscopic controls, etc.) so as to enable the craft to simulate successfully the antics of a bird flying low over the sea and, at the same time, to keep the propeller in the water (Fig. 89). Other complications might be caused by the indispensably long transmissions, which would demand very deep draft (retractable outdrives would probably eliminate this inconvenience). One would also have to adopt folding wings so as to reduce the berthing area in port.

THROUGH

For some time I had been thinking of a craft with a long needle nose for just such an application. In 1967 I prepared my first design study of what I called the "Ram Craft" which should not be confused with the "Ram Wing Vehicles" referred to in the design section. The latter is, of course, essentially an aerodynamic craft and the word "Ram" describes the forcing of an aerofoil sectioned wing through the air. The ram craft, on the other hand,

THE THROUGH CONCEPT

FIG. 90

RAM CRAFT

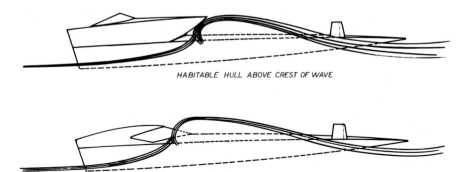

HABITABLE HULL ABOVE CREST OF WAVE

HABITABLE CABIN THROUGH CREST OF WAVE

FIG. 91

is a hydrodynamic vehicle with a configuration incorporating an actual ram such as was a feature of the galleys in Caesar's day. Even in those far off times the rams were not only used as a means of holing and sinking the enemy but also for shattering the stormy seas. It is difficult to think of something new!

I have had occasion since, to prepare numerous other studies based upon the same concept but with different purposes in view.

This type of craft requires considerably more power for a given speed than the "flying" example described above for the "over" concept. It is necessary also to have a fast planing hull with extremely good penetration, and with what I call a neutral hull form, at least in the bow area (Fig. 90); that is to say, a bow so designed that when faced with a wall of water it penetrates it rather than causing the hull to lift. After this initial penetration the bow (ram) would take the rest of the hull with it. The G loadings would be reduced in relation to the fineness of the bow, thus permitting higher speeds with

CORRECTLY TRIMMED

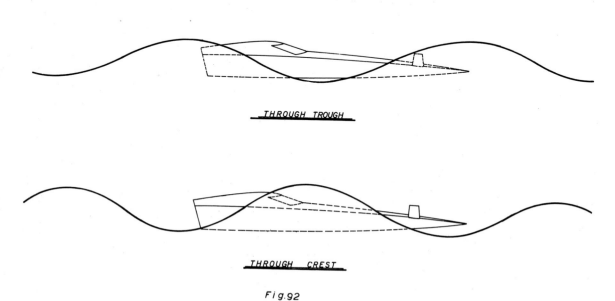

THROUGH TROUGH

THROUGH CREST

Fig. 92

INCORRECTLY TRIMMED

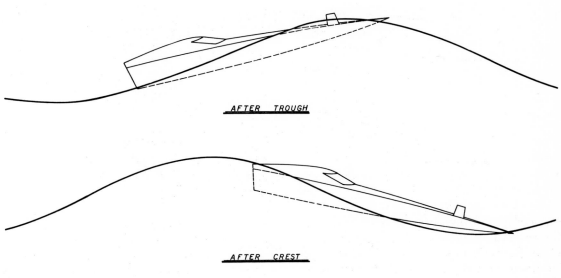

AFTER TROUGH

AFTER CREST

Fig. 93

greater comfort. It is interesting to note here that trials have been done in rough sea conditions on fast craft fitted with the appropriate instrumentation: impact loads of up to 25 G have been recorded in the bow area, which is considerable when one considers that a modern fighter aircraft is designed around the stress factor of 10 G.

Whether the habitable hull volume attached to the ram is designed so as to remain above the crest of the wave or go under it, depends on the purpose for which the boat is built. The former solution would be indicated more for a pleasure craft, whereas the latter seems more applicable in the case of a racing craft or a pure work boat (Fig. 91).

In my opinion, the main problem in producing a successful design of this nature lies in finding a simple system for adjusting the trim to suit various weather conditions. One solution might be the use of variable incidence forward hydroplanes; yet another, a variable incidence ram or a combination of both. Incidentally, the raising of the ram for pure high speed in favourable sea conditions would reduce the wetted surface and, therefore, also be useful in increasing the speed. Unquestionably, variable thrust outdrives would also be most useful for trim

adjustment. If we assume that such a craft is capable of negotiating rough seas at 200 km per hour (108 knots), then the forward distance covered in a second will be approximately 55 metres (180 odd feet); in such a case it is not hard to realize that extremely refined equipment, such as is used in high-speed aircraft when weather conditions are tricky (for example modern automatic pilots), will probably be essential for driving such a craft when split second reactions are required (average pilot reaction is considered to be around one second). If there was an error in manoeuvring at this speed the ram craft could find itself a considerable distance below the surface—with easily imaginable consequences for those on board (Figs. 92 and 93).

This may all sound like something out of the pages of Jules Verne, but I am convinced that there is room for study in this direction.

Experiments are currently under way to try out the validity of this third type of craft which, if successful, might well be the answer to the problem of negotiating rough seas at high speed in a relatively simple manner . . . at least until we come up with something better.

APPENDIX I

Propellers

By K. Suhrbier, Dipl. Ing.* and Commander Peter Du Cane**

1. Introduction

Relatively few types of propulsion devices have normally to be considered for boats and high-speed craft. In all cases the propeller thrust is generated by internal reaction forces based on impulse (momentum) action, which is always attended by loss of kinetic energy and interaction effects. Only propulsion by external forces, either by towing or pushing, would allow a power transmission virtually free of losses. The most common (internal) ship propulsion systems are: water screw propellers—including contrarotating propellers, tandem propellers and ducted propellers—paddle wheels, vertical axes propellers (Voith-Schneider and Kirsten-Boeing propellers), air screws and waterjets. The water screw propeller is the most practical and usually also the most efficient means of propulsion. Air screws and waterjets may have to be considered under special circumstances, such as draught restrictions or possibly for high speeds. The following chapter will mainly deal with conventional and supercavitating screw propellers, however an introduction to the problems of waterjet propulsion is added. Only the basic principles of propeller theory are outlined here. Although considerable progress in propeller theory has been made in recent years, it is probably true to say that most high-speed propellers are designed in a semi-empirical way, often with the use of experimental facilities, such as cavitation tunnels. Modern design methods, such as vortex (lifting line or lifting surface) theory, are employed with full confidence for highly sophisticated propellers, mainly in the subcavitating range. For most practical purposes, however, series data from model experiments are normally used by the designer of small craft. The emphasis of this chapter will be on basic

principles and on this application although it may not always be possible to find the optimum solution, particularly from the cavitation point of view. For further studies on modern propeller theories, which are not within the scope of this article, the reader is referred to the special literature (ref. 1 to 7).

2. Geometry of the Screw Propeller

The main characteristics of the screw propeller are: diameter, pitch (constant or radially varied), expanded or developed blade area, blade thickness, section type, number of blades, size of boss, skew and rake. The blades are either fixed (fixed pitch propeller) or adjustable (controllable pitch propeller).

The screw propeller is built on a helicoidal surface, with constant (or radially varied) pitch P (Fig. 94). The pitch angle ϕ for each radius r can be obtained from:

$$\tan \phi = \frac{P}{2\pi r}. \tag{1}$$

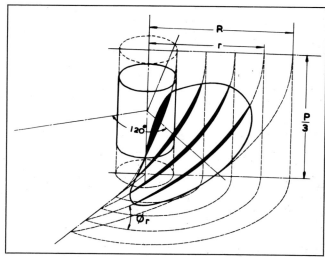

Fig. 94   Propeller blade on helicoidal pitch surface.

* Senior Hydrodynamicist, Vosper Thornycroft Ltd.
** Deputy Chairman, Vosper Ltd.

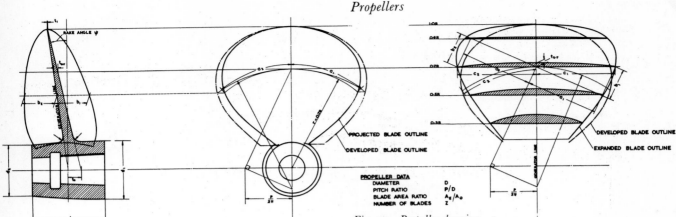

Fig. 95   *Propeller drawing.*

This angle is smaller at the outer radii and greater at the inner, so that the blades appear to be twisted. The pitch can be determined from:

$$P = 2\pi r \tan \phi. \qquad (1a)$$

The propeller drawing is usually commenced with the expanded blade sections for some radii, thus determining the expanded blade area. The blade contour is given by the projected outline as shown in Fig. 95. The outline of the developed area is obtained by turning the cylindrical sections into the plane.

The blade area ratios A_E/A_0 or A_D/A_0, where A_E is the expanded area, A_D the developed area of the blades and A_0 the disc area $\dfrac{\pi D^2}{4}$, are used to define the blade "width". Both have about the same value and are important propeller parameters.

The hub diameter is usually 15% to 20% of the propeller diameter, or for controllable pitch propellers up to 35%. The virtual thickness t_0 at the axis usually varies between 0·045 and 0·06 D and the tip thickness t_1 between 0·002 and 0·003 D. Leading and trailing edges should be well rounded, except for special designs, such as supercavitating propellers. In order to reduce stress concentrations fairing radii are normally applied between the blade and the hub, approximately 0·04 D on the back (suction side) and 0·03 D on the face (pressure side).

3. *Basic Propeller Theory*

The action of a propeller in uniform axial flow can be described in an idealized way by the simple momentum theory (Rankine, Froude). It is based on the assumptions that (1) frictional losses and slip-stream rotation can be neglected and (2) the thrust distribution is even over the "actuator disc" replacing the propeller of the same diameter. By accelerating the water (or air) in this disc, a thrust

is produced as a reaction force equal to the rate of fluid momentum, i.e. the product of mass per unit time and the change of velocity. When V_A is the speed of advance, u_a the velocity increment in the propeller race and m the mass flow passing through the disc, the ideal thrust becomes:

$$T_i = m((V_A + u_a) - V_A) = m u_a. \qquad (2)$$

This can also be expressed by the pressure difference generated by the propeller and the disc A_0 it is acting upon:

$$T_i = \Delta p A_0.$$

It can be shown that the velocity difference u_a at some distance behind the propeller reaches half its value in the propeller disc; hence the mass flow is:

$$m = \rho A_0 (V_A + \frac{u_a}{2}), \qquad (3)$$

with ρ being the density of the fluid. The combination of equations (2) and (3) yields:

$$T_i = \rho A_0 (V_A + \frac{u_a}{2}) u_a. \qquad (4)$$

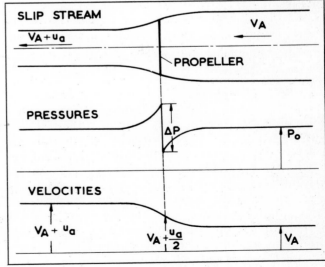

Fig. 96   *Velocities and pressures in the propeller slipstream.*

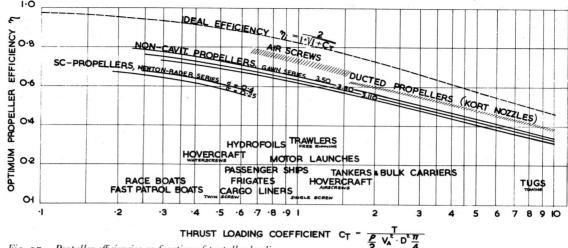

Fig. 97 Propeller efficiencies as function of propeller loading.

According to the screw momentum theory the power P_i absorbed by the propeller is equal to the useful work $T_i V_A$ done on the disc and the kinetic energy $T_i \frac{u_a}{2}$ lost in the race, which is necessary to accelerate the fluid:

$$P_i = T_i V_A + T\frac{u_a}{2}. \qquad (5)$$

Therefore the ideal or so-called Froude efficiency is:

$$\eta_i = \frac{T_i V_A}{T_i V_A + T_i\frac{u_a}{2}} = \frac{V_A}{V_A + \frac{u_a}{2}} = \frac{1}{1 + \frac{u_a}{2V_A}}. \qquad (6)$$

With the thrust loading coefficient

$$C_{Ti} = \frac{T_i}{\frac{\rho}{2} V_A{}^2 A_0} \quad \text{and} \qquad (7)$$

$$V_A + u_a = V_A\sqrt{1 + C_{Ti}} \quad \text{(from (4) and (7))} \qquad (8)$$

the ideal efficiency for unshrouded propellers can also be written as:

$$\eta_i = \frac{2}{1 + \sqrt{1 + C_{Ti}}}. \qquad (9)$$

Equations (6) and (9) are of great practical importance, since they show the effect of the induced velocity and thrust loading respectively, on the efficiency. As can be seen from Fig. 97, a low thrust loading is always advantageous from the efficiency point of view. In general the propeller with the larger diameter (low r.p.m.) and therefore low fluid acceleration is the more efficient one. A propeller producing high thrust on a small propeller disc (high u_a and C_T) will normally have a lower efficiency. However, the optimum propeller diameter is, of course, not infinite as follows from the simplified formulations (6) or (9) ($\eta_i = 100\%$ for $D \to \infty$ and $C_T \to 0$) because viscosity effects are not taken into account. The efficiency according to equation (6) represents an ideal that cannot be surpassed by any propulsion device (screw propellers, waterjets, paddle wheels, etc.) having kinetic energy and frictional losses. It should be mentioned that the momentum theory has been further developed to allow for the rotation in the slipstream of a screw propeller.

Fig. 97 shows the ideal efficiency (equ. (9)) compared with the optimum propeller efficiencies that can be achieved in practice by various propeller types.*

Depending on the propeller loading and subsequently on the velocity increment in the propeller race the slipstream is contracted behind the screw (due to the law of continuity) (Fig. 96), unless the propeller is heavily cavitating.

As the momentum theory does not provide any information for the detail design of the screw, the forces and velocities acting on a propeller blade element have to be considered. It is assumed that the section of each radius r is equivalent to an aerofoil moving with the resultant velocity V_R and the angle of incidence $\alpha = \phi - \beta_i$. The hydrodynamic pitch angle β_i differs from the angle of advance β, since normal to V_R a "downwash" velocity $u/2 = \sqrt{(u_a/2)^2 + (u_t/2)^2}$ is induced in the propeller plane (Fig. 98).

* See also footnote on page 236.

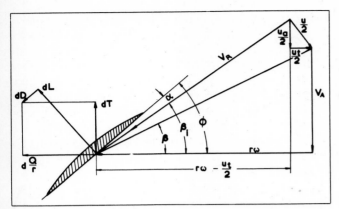

Fig. 98   Velocities and forces acting on a blade element on radius r.

V_A . . . speed of advance (see also equation 21)

$$V_R = \sqrt{(V_A + \frac{u_a}{2})^2 + (r\omega - \frac{u_t}{2})^2}$$

$$\approx \sqrt{V_A{}^2 + (\omega r)^2}$$

$r\omega = 2\pi nr$ rotational speed (on radius r) with shaft speed n.

u . . . induced velocity far behind the propeller with axial component u_a and tangential component u_t,

$\varnothing$ . . . face pitch angle,

β_i . . . hydrodynamic pitch angle,

β . . . angle of advance,

dD . . . drag element,

dL . . . lift element,

dT . . . thrust element,

dQ . . . torque element.

The elementary forces, pressures or the cavitation characteristics of each section can be related to those of 2-dimensional aerofoil data (theoretical or experimental). The forces are resolved in elements of lift dL and drag dD or in thrust dT and torque/r dQ/r. By integrating over the blade the total thrust and torque can be obtained. The propeller efficiency will then be:

$$\eta_0 = \frac{V_A}{2\pi n}\frac{\int_o^R \frac{dT}{dr}dr}{\int_o^R \frac{dQ}{dr}dr} = \frac{TV_A}{2\pi nQ} = \frac{TV_A}{550P_D},\qquad(10)$$

where T is the thrust, Q the torque and P_D is the delivered horsepower on the propeller. High lift/drag ratios (at small angles of incidence) are desirable for good efficiencies.

For modern theoretical propeller design the so-called vortex or circulation theory (developed by Lancaster, Prandtl, Helmbold, Betz, Goldstein,

Lerbs and others) is employed, which allows one to calculate the induced velocities and forces acting on each strip of the blade and to optimize its geometry provided corrections for viscous and some 3-dimensional effects are applied. In this theory the propeller is represented by a system of vortices.

The slip of a propeller, although not used in modern propeller design, may be mentioned here. The real slip—based on advance speed $V_A = V(1 - w)$ (equ. 21), propeller pitch P and shaft speed n—is defined as:

$$S_R = 1 - \frac{V_A}{Pn}.\qquad(11a)$$

The apparent slip—based on the ship speed V and often recorded in the ship's log book—is not really relevant for the ship's performance; it is given by:

$$S_R = 1 - \frac{V}{Pn}.\qquad(11b)$$

4. Cavitation

A phenomenon called cavitation is met on high powered and high-speed propellers (also on pumps and water turbines). If a minimum pressure on the surface of a foil drops below a critical value, at or near to the vapour pressure, the fluid will form a gas filled cavity. This starts at certain speeds and rpm and might cause thrust breakdown, loss in speed, noise, vibration and also erosion on the propeller blades or other appendages. Cavitation, and in particular cavitation erosion, is a serious problem for the designer. Although several theories exist on the nature of this phenomenon, the physical and chemical attack of material is still not fully under-

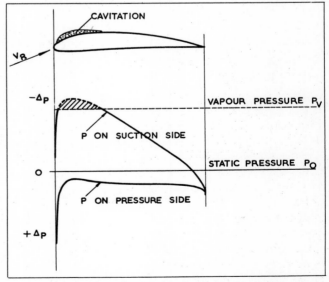

Fig. 99   Pressure distribution on a partially cavitating blade section.

225

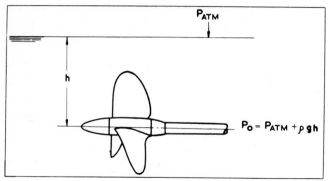

Fig. 100   Static pressure on a propeller.

stood. The cavities, or bubbles, formed in a low pressure region, travel downstream and collapse in an area of higher pressure. This can be associated with high local shocks on the blades, thus causing the above mentioned phenomena. However, apart from the mechanical nature of this process, electro-chemical or corrosive action is often involved or accelerated once the protective surface film has been damaged by cavity collapse. The designer may have to decide whether cavitation has to be completely avoided by choosing the appropriate blade shape, or some cavitation can be allowed, or whether cavitation should be encouraged and a so-called

supercavitating propeller would be advantageous.

The onset of cavitation depends on the pressure drop $\Delta p = p_0 - p_{min}$ somewhere on the blade (due to high velocity or thrust) and the pressure above vapour point $p_0 - p_v$, p_0 being static pressure equal to atmospheric pressure plus the pressure gh due to the propeller immersion. Cavitation can only be avoided if the minimum section pressure p_{min} is greater than the vapour (or critical) pressure of water:

$$p_{min} > p_v.$$

Applying the Bernoulli theorem for the flow around the section, this can be expressed as:

$$\frac{p_0 - p_{min}}{\frac{\rho}{2} V^2} < \frac{p_0 - p_v}{\frac{\rho}{2} V^2}. \qquad (12)$$

The right hand term is the so-called cavitation number σ_0. It can be described as the ratio of the greatest possible pressure drop at a section to the free-stream stagnation pressure $\frac{\rho}{2} V^2$. The criterion for cavitation-free operation can then also be written in the form:

$$\frac{\Delta p}{q} < \sigma_0. \qquad (12a)$$

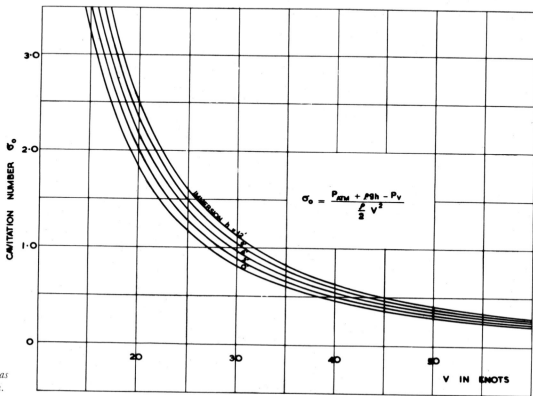

$$\sigma_0 = \frac{P_{ATM} + \rho gh - P_v}{\frac{\rho}{2} V^2}$$

Fig. 101   Cavitation number as function of speed and immersion.

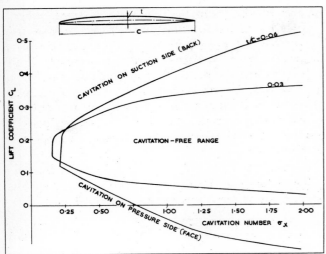

Fig. 102   Typical cavitation inception graph for cambered sections (designed for $C_L = 0.2$).

cavitation number, calculated with the resultant velocity (Figs. 102 and 103). For propellers a representative local cavitation number σ_x for the "equivalent" radius (normally $x = \frac{r}{R} = 0.7$) is often used, which is related to the nominal cavitation number σ_0 in the following way:

$$\sigma_x = \frac{p_0 - p_v}{\frac{\rho}{2}V_R^2} \approx \frac{\sigma_0}{1 + \left(\frac{x\pi}{J}\right)^2} \qquad (13)$$

with the resultant velocity $V_R \approx \sqrt{V_A^2 + (xD\pi n)^2}$ and advance coefficient (equ. 25).

A cavitation diagram obtained by Gawn and Burrill from systematical tests on 3-bladed propellers with segmental sections and $t_0/D = 0.045$ is reproduced in Fig. 103 (ref. 8). For a given $\sigma_{0.7R}$ the highest acceptable thrust loading $\tau_c = \frac{T/A_P}{\frac{\rho}{2}V_R^2}$ can be read off

and the minimum blade area determined:

$$\text{projected area } A_P = \frac{T}{\tau_c} \cdot \frac{1}{\frac{\rho}{2}V_R^2} \text{ or} \qquad (14)$$

$$\frac{\text{expanded area}}{\text{propeller disc area}} = \frac{A_E}{A_0} = \frac{A_P}{A_0}/(1.067 - 0.229\,P/D). \qquad (15)$$

The nominal cavitation number $\sigma_0 = \frac{p_0 - p_v}{\frac{\rho}{2}V^2}$, based on ship speed or speed of advance (see also equ. 21) and propeller immersion, is given in Fig. 101. Foil and propeller data are available from theoretical or experimental work to determine the cavitation-free conditions. They are normally presented as a function of lift (or thrust) coefficient, the thickness-chord ratio and the local (or section)

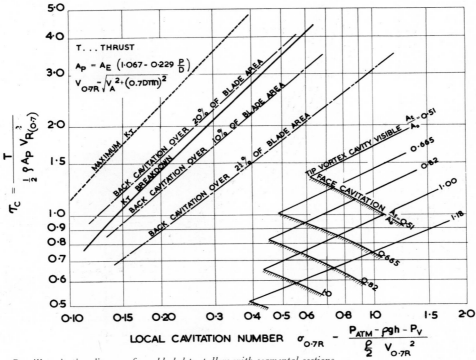

Fig. 103   Gawn-Burrill cavitation diagram for 3 bladed propellers with segmental sections.

The upper permissible limit or margin against cavitation has to be decided. For high-speed boats, the race boats in particular, where blade erosion is less important, a thrust loading τ_c near to the K_T breakdown line may be acceptable (for thrust coefficient K_T see Section 7). It should be borne in mind however that these data have been obtained in uniform axial flow; a cavitation number correction factor between 0·9 and 0·7 is therefore often applied to the calculated σ to allow for shaft inclination, wake peaks, scale effects and manufacturing tolerances. For commercial applications a larger blade area will usually be necessary in order to obtain a τ_c below the cavitation inception line. Higher number of blades and conventional aerofoil sections also require somewhat larger blade areas.

Shock free entrance conditions and therefore more even pressure distributions can be achieved with cambered sections (Section 8), thus leading to a greater cavitation-free range. Propellers calculated by modern vortex theory are in most cases designed with these cambered aerofoils. Cavitation characteristics and efficiencies are improved. The blade area ratio will normally be smaller than that found by the use of Fig. 103.

Earlier cavitation criteria are sometimes based on the thrust loading thrust/area or on propeller tip speed. Maximum permissible thrust loadings T/A_P are, for instance, suggested by K. C. Barnaby (ref. 9), derived from Wageningen Tank (NSMB) data, and may be used for first assessments:

Speed	10 kts	20 kts	30 kts	40 kts
1′ immersion	6·0 lb/in²	8·5 lb/in²	10·4 lb/in²	12·1 lb/in²
5′ immersion	6·7 lb/in²	9·5 lb/in²	11·5 lb/in²	13·5 lb/in²

The expanded blade area A_E can then be determined from equation (15).

The main types of cavitation are "bubble" cavitation, which is regarded as very undesirable, and "sheet" cavitation. The latter more stable type is often tolerated or even encouraged, if cavitation cannot be completely avoided. On a propeller, one distinguishes also between:

    back cavitation (on the suction side),
    face cavitation (on the pressure side),
    tip and root cavitation, etc.

Different materials will respond differently to cavitation attack (Section 8f). Propeller coatings have been tried on several occasions, even with shock-absorbing materials (rubber, etc), but so far

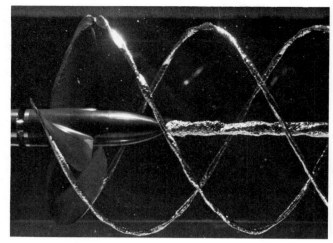
Fig. 104   Tip and hub vortex cavitation.

Fig. 105   Back bubble and tip cavitation.

Fig. 106   Supercavitation.

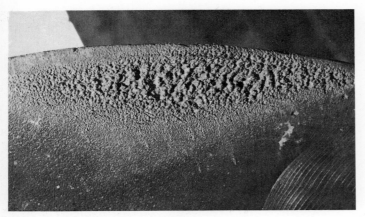

Fig. 107 *Cavitation erosion at blade tip.*

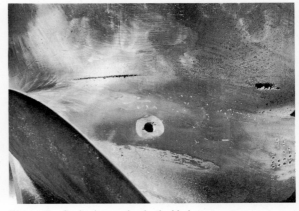

Fig. 108 *Cavitation erosion in the blade root area.*

Fig. 109 *Vosper Thornycroft cavitation tunnel.*

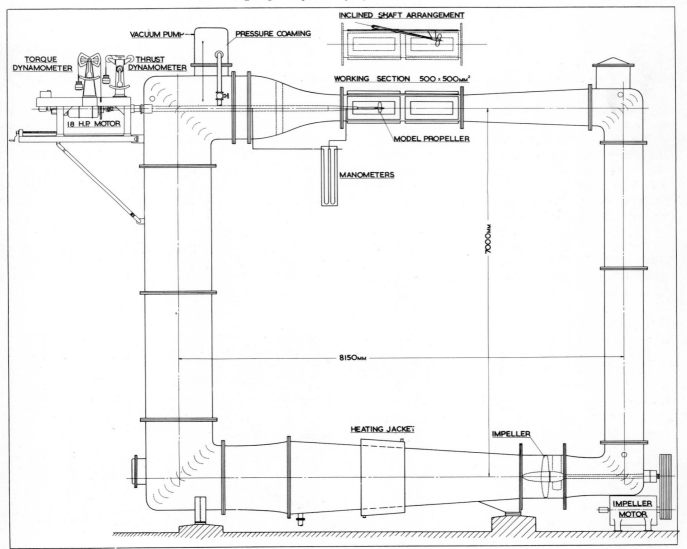

229

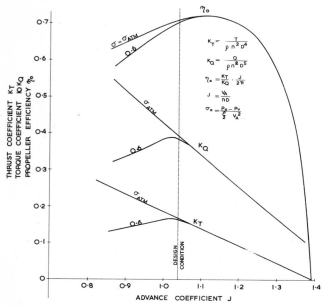

The coefficients shown in the diagram:

$$K_T = \frac{T}{\rho n^2 D^4}$$

$$K_Q = \frac{Q}{\rho n^2 D^5}$$

$$\eta_o = \frac{K_T}{K_Q} \cdot \frac{J}{2\pi}$$

$$J = \frac{V_A}{nD}$$

$$\sigma_o = \frac{P_a - P_v}{\frac{\rho}{2} V_A^2}$$

Fig. 110 $K_T - K_Q - J$ *diagram.*

no successful method has been reported.

The special problems of fully cavitating propellers are dealt with in Section 9.

5. *Model Propeller Testing and Inclined Shaft Problems*
Propeller characteristics as required for design and performance prediction are often determined or checked by model testing. The first applies for all propeller series (Section 7), the second mainly for propellers designed by vortex theory. The majority of such experiments is carried out in uniform axial flow conditions under atmospheric pressure (open water tests in towing tanks). In special cases shaft inclination, the wake of the ship, or even the free water surface may be simulated. A more comprehensive picture of the interaction effects between ship's hull plus appendages and propeller (wake, thrust deduction, hull efficiency and relative rotative efficiency)* can be obtained from towing tank tests at Froude number identity ($F_{N, Model} = F_{N, Ship} = V/\sqrt{gL}$) with a self-propelled ship model. However, simularity of cavitation can only be achieved in a closed depressurized flume (or special tank), a so-called cavitation tunnel (tank). The pressure can be reduced and only then will the pressure drop on a model section normally be sufficient to reach the critical (vapour) pressure and reproduce a cavitation pattern similar to full scale. The experiments have to be conducted at the same or, if a safety margin is required, at a somewhat lower cavitation number, obtained by low tunnel pressure. Velocity, shaft speed, thrust and torque can be measured. Non-dimensional thrust and torque coefficient, K_T and K_Q, are plotted as functions of the advance coefficient J. The effect of cavitation on thrust and torque at $\sigma_o = 0.6$, $J < 1.07$, corresponding to a craft speed of approximately 35 knots, is shown as an example in Fig. 110. Breakdown starts at this condition which could mean that the engine power can not be fully absorbed, unless the pitch is readjusted (controllable pitch propeller) or a higher pitch has been designed to account for this effect. The cavitation pattern can be observed by a stroboscope and the boundaries of cavitation onset may be determined (see also Figs. 103 and 120).

Most propellers of small or fast craft have to operate on an inclined shaft and it is often most desirable to simulate this condition. A test rig suitable for such studies is used in the Vosper Thornycroft

* See also Section 6.

Fig. 111 Forces and velocities in an inclined shaft propeller.

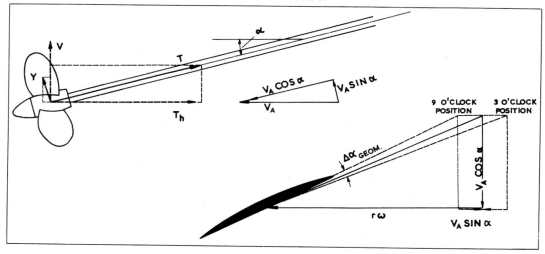

Cavitation Tunnel (Fig. 109). Due to the cyclic variations of the angle of incidence propulsion and cavitation characteristics are affected and rather unfavourable cavitation patterns as well as torque and thrust fluctuations may be experienced. The tangential velocity component ($V_A \sin \alpha$) varies sinusoidally during each revolution; but it should be noted that due to induced velocity effects, the change of the effective angle of attack $\Delta\alpha$ is appreciably smaller than $\Delta\alpha_{geom}$. (Fig. 111). For a right hand propeller the incidence increases in the 3 o'clock position and decreases in the 9 o'clock position, or in other words, the angle of attack will be higher on the descending and lower on the ascending blade. This may lead to either back or face cavitation respectively. A very common problem is the so-called root cavitation erosion (in the blade root area, see for instance Fig. 108). The cavitation-free range will be reduced in oblique flow as compared with axial flow conditions. Vibration and fatigue problems may have to be studied. Furthermore, a vertical force V is generated by the propeller, made up by a thrust component $T \sin \alpha$ and a normal force component $Y \cos \alpha$ (due to the change of incidence), thus: $\qquad V = Y \cos \alpha + T \sin \alpha.$ (16)

This may have considerable influence on the forces and moments acting on a fast craft. The effect of this, including that of the propeller-induced pressure field, on the trim can be substantial and very important on fast boats (ref. 10 and 11). The useful thrust is no longer identical with the axial thrust. The horizontal thrust consists of the horizontal thrust component reduced by a backward component due to the normal force Y, therefore:

$$T_h = T \cos \alpha - Y \sin \alpha.$$ (17)

Generally speaking, a supercavitating propeller will be less influenced by the cyclic variations of incidence, because of the lower lift slope of the SC propeller section.

6. Powering, Propulsive Efficiencies and Hull/Propeller Interaction Effects

For the powering of ships and the dimensioning of a propeller the propulsion components and their interaction effects have to be looked at, also the shape of the resistance curve, which may have a pronounced hump at lower speeds. This could mean that at low r.p.m. the thrust and power required exceeds the thrust or power (torque) available, or that the acceleration of the craft is marginal. In cases, where less torque is available at lower engine r.p.m., this may be met with SC propellers because of the re-

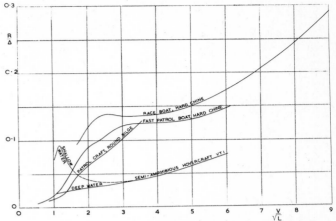

Fig. 112 *Specific resistance curves of fast craft* (R...*naked hull resistance*, Δ...*displacement*, V...*speed*, L...*length*).

latively high pitch absorbing high torque at low speeds.

One has to be careful when discussing or comparing propulsive efficiencies. Unfortunately, the definitions do not always agree. Besides the propeller efficiency η_0, there are the quasi-propulsive coefficient (QPC) and the overall propulsive coefficient (OPC). QPC and OPC may be based on the naked hull or the appendaged hull resistance, or data predicted with different friction or correlation lines (ITTC 1957, Froude, Schoenherr, etc.). Roughness or wind allowances may or may not be included. The breakdown recommended for boats is defined in the following*.

The total installed brake horsepower (BHP) is:

$$P_B = \frac{P_D}{\eta_{Transm.}} = \frac{(1+x)P_E}{QPC \, \eta_{Transm.}},$$ (18)

with $P_D = \dfrac{(1+x)P_E**}{QPC}$ delivered horsepower at the propeller (DHP),

$P_E = (P_{Eo} + \Delta P_E)$ effective (or towing) horsepower of naked hull plus appendages (EHP), from model tests,

$P_{Eo} = \dfrac{R_o V}{550}$ effective horsepower (EHP), obtained from naked hull resistance R_o,

ΔP_E ...increment of effective horsepower due to appendages,

QPC...quasi-propulsive coefficient (or propulsive efficiency η_D),

$\eta_{Transm.}$....transmission efficiency, allowing for gear box and shaft bearing losses,

$1+x$...model-ship correlation or prediction

*Not all "efficiency" terms defined here are real efficiencies in the correct physical sense, but they are widely used as such in this field.
** This definition has been adopted by the International Towing Tank Conference 1960 and the British Towing Tank Panel 1965.

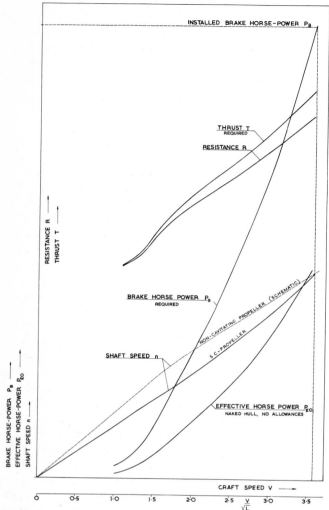

Fig. 113 Performance prediction for a semi-displacement craft.

factor, allowing for scale effects, roughness, aerodynamic drag, weather conditions, steering etc., to be obtained from analysis of trials data of similar craft or to be estimated (often between 1·05 and 1·1, in special cases less than 1·0).

The quasi-propulsive coefficient is determined by:

$$QPC = \frac{(1+x)P_E}{P_D} = \eta_0 \eta_H \eta_R, \qquad (19)$$

with η_0 ...propeller efficiency in uniform axial flow,

$\eta_H = \dfrac{1-t}{1-w}$ hull efficiency,

$\eta_R = \dfrac{\eta_B}{\eta_0}$ relative rotative efficiency,

η_B ...propeller efficiency behind the ship,

$t = \dfrac{T-R}{T}$ thrust deduction fraction (see equ. 22),

$w = \dfrac{V-V_A}{V}$ wake fraction (see equ. 21),

T...total propeller thrust,

$R = (R_0 + \Delta R)(1+x)$ total resistance, including allowances for appendages, roughness, wind, etc.,

ΔR...appendage resistance.

Instead of using equation (18) it is often preferred, in particular in the boat design field, to calculate the brake horsepower P_B (or BHP) from the naked hull effective horsepower P_{Eo} (or EHP) and the overall propulsive coefficient OPC:

$$P_B = \frac{P_{Eo}}{OPC}. \qquad (18a)$$

The overall propulsive coefficient can be defined as:

$$OPC = \eta_0 \eta_H \eta_R \frac{1}{1+b}\frac{1}{1+x}\eta_{Transm.} \qquad (20)$$

$$= QPC \frac{1}{1+b}\frac{1}{1+x}\eta_{Transm.},$$

with $1+b = \dfrac{R_0 + \Delta R}{R_0} = \dfrac{P_E}{P_{Eo}}$ appendage resistance factor (for $\dfrac{1}{1+b}$ the term "appendage efficiency" is sometimes used).

The naked hull resistance R_0, the appendage resistance ΔR and efficiency elements η_H and η_R may be determined by model tests or other methods. If propeller efficiencies near 65% are expected, the overall propulsive coefficients of small craft may be in the order of

$$OPC = 0·50 \ (0·45 ... 0·55).$$

For the propeller calculation it is necessary to know the speed of advance (or entrance velocity) V_A of the propeller behind the ship (retarded flow). The difference between ship speed V and advance speed V_A is the so-called wake. According to Taylor the speed of advance is defined as:

$$V_A = V(1-w). \qquad (21)$$

For boats and high speed craft the wake fraction w is normally small and may be between 0 and 0·1.

If the thrust curve of the craft is to be determined, it has to be realized that the ship resistance in the propelled condition is increased due to the propeller action (the flow field at the stern is affected by the propeller) and/or that in the case of the inclined shaft the axial thrust is not identical with the horizontal thrust (Section 5, equ. 17). The so-called thrust deduction factor t (in the order of 0·05 to 0·10 for many boats) has therefore to be determined. The thrust is:

$$T = \frac{R}{1-t}. \qquad (22)$$

The thrust required can also be obtained from:

$$T = \frac{550 P_E (1+x)}{(1-t)V} = \frac{550 P_D}{(1-t)V} \, QPC. \qquad (22a)$$

On very fast boats (race boats, etc.) relatively large appendages (mainly shafting) can affect the overall performance quite considerably and these definitions may become somewhat meaningless. It may be impossible to differentiate between the naked hull model resistance and appendaged resistance, or to predict the full scale resistance at all with any confidence, because of the large scale-effect on the appendages, and also because of the entirely different behaviour of the model in the two conditions. Trim and rise (heave) and therefore also the hull resistance depend to a large extent on the appendage forces lift and drag (which cannot always be expected to be similar on model and full size craft because of the different Reynolds numbers).

This is demonstrated in Fig. 114, where a naked and an appendaged race boat model tested at $V/\sqrt{L} \approx 10$ in a towing tank is shown (ref. 12). In this case resistance for the appendaged model was less than for the naked hull because of the lift provided by the appendages (shafting) and the subsequent reduction of hull drag.

This extraordinary situation may be borne in mind when data are predicted or analysed. In spite of these difficulties, it should be said that in most cases valuable information can be obtained from experiments, both resistance and propulsion tests, including resistance experiments with appendages fitted.

For further studies on the whole subject of propulsion and interaction effects the various handbooks of Naval Architecture (ref. 1, 4, 5, 9, 13) are recommended, in particular also the papers by Hadler (ref. 10), and De Groot (ref. 14).

7. *Selection of a Propeller from Systematical Model Series Data*

A number of systematic propeller model series (families of propellers of geometrically similar shape) have been tested in towing tanks and some in cavitation tunnels in uniform axial flow conditions. The data from these tests are most useful for design purposes, in particular in the initial stage when various parameters have to be varied. This would usually be rather tedious by theoretical methods. It should be noted that only data obtained from experiments with sufficiently large models and not too low water speeds (Reynolds numbers $>3 \times 10^5$) can now be regarded as suitable. Earlier propeller test data (from Froude, Taylor, Schaffran and others) were often too much affected by laminer flow effects. Table A contains a number of published propeller series which can be recommended for most applications.

Some more series may be found in the literature. Most work has been done on subcavitating propellers. The only systematically tested and published series of supercavitating fixed pitch propellers is that of Newton and Rader (Vosper Cavitation Tunnel). Results of controllable pitch SC propellers have been reported by Pehrsson (ref. 21).

The governing factors for the determination of the screw geometry are the loading of the propeller, the rate of advance (ratio of advance speed and rotational velocity) and the cavitation number. Special design charts—most of them for subcavitating conditions ($\sigma = \sigma_{ATM}$)—are often prepared by conversion of the above mentioned $K_T - K_Q - J$ diagrams, which allow a quicker assessment of the propeller dimensions. Some of the more frequently used loading and advance coefficients may be mentioned here:

(*a*) non-dimensional thrust loading coefficient

$$C_T = {}^{(786)} \frac{T}{\frac{\rho}{2} V_A{}^2 \frac{D^2 \pi}{4}} = \frac{K_T}{J^2} \cdot \frac{8}{\pi}, \qquad (23)$$

Fig. 114   Race boat model tested at Westland Aircraft Ltd.

(a) Craft fitted with Appendages

(b) Craft with Appendages removed

Table A   Propeller Series

Series	Test Condition	Type of Section	Number of Blades	Blade Area Ratio	Reference
Wageningen B Series (NSMB, Troost)	non-cavitating	aerofoil/segmental	2, 3, 4, 5, 6, 7	0·3, 0·38; 0·35 to 0·80; 0·40 to 1·0; 0·45 to 1·05; 0·5 to 0·8; 0·55 to 0·85	4, 5, 15
Gawn Series	non-cavitating	segmental	3	0·2 to 1·10	16
Yazaki, AU-Series	non-cavitating	aerofoil/segmental	4, 5, 6, 7	0·4, 0·55; 0·5, 0·65; 0·55, 0·7; 0·65	17
SSPA Series (Lindgren—Bjärne)	non-cavitating	aerofoil/segmental	3, 4, 5, 6	0·45; 0·47 to 0·60; 0·60; 0·60	18
Gawn—Burrill Series	non-cavitating and cavitating (cavitation tunnel)	segmental	3	0·5 to 1·10	8
SSPA MA-Series (Lindgren)	non-cavitating and cavitating (towing tank and cavitation tunnel)	segmental	3, 5	0·75 to 1·20	19
Newton—Rader Series	supercavitating (cavitation tunnel)	SC type	3	0·475 0·71 0·85	20

power loading coefficient

$$C_P = {}^{(114\cdot47)}\frac{P_D}{\frac{\rho}{2}V_A{}^3\frac{D^2\pi}{4}} = \frac{K_Q}{J^3}\cdot16, \qquad (24)$$

advance coefficient

$$J = {}^{(101\cdot3)}\frac{V_A}{nD}. \qquad (25)$$

The factors in brackets ( ) apply only if the following dimensions are used:

speed in advance	V_A in knots
number of revolutions	n in rpm.
diameter	D in ft
propeller thrust	T in tons
delivered horsepower at propeller (DHP)	P_D in hp
density of medium	$\rho = 1\cdot99$ lb sec²/ft⁴ for seawater = $1\cdot94$ lb sec²/ft⁴ for fresh water

(*b*)   not dimensionless (quasi—non-dimensional)
thrust loading coefficient

$$B_u = \frac{n}{V_A{}^2}\sqrt{T} = 13\cdot36\sqrt{\frac{K_T}{J^4}}, \qquad (26)$$

power loading coefficient

$$B_P = \frac{n}{V_A{}^2}\sqrt{\frac{P_D}{V_A}} = 33\cdot48\sqrt{\frac{K_Q}{J^5}}, \qquad (27)$$

velocity coefficient

$$\delta = \frac{nD}{V_A} = \frac{1}{J}101\cdot3. \qquad (28)$$

The Taylor design coefficients B_u and B_P and δ are obtained with V_A in knots, n in rpm, D in ft, T in lbs, P_D in hp.

The overriding effect of the propeller loading on the efficiency has already been discussed (Fig. 97). Fortunately fast craft have, in most cases, lightly loaded propellers because of their lower drag/velocity² values (leading to low thrust loading coefficients C_T) and therefore normally reach high efficiencies. However, cavitation often becomes a more delicate problem, which can, up to approx. 30 to 35 knots, usually be dealt with by choosing a larger blade area ratio. From about 40 knots upwards super-cavitating propellers will be advantageous for small or medium sized craft because no cavitation-free propeller can be designed (see also Fig. 119). If the

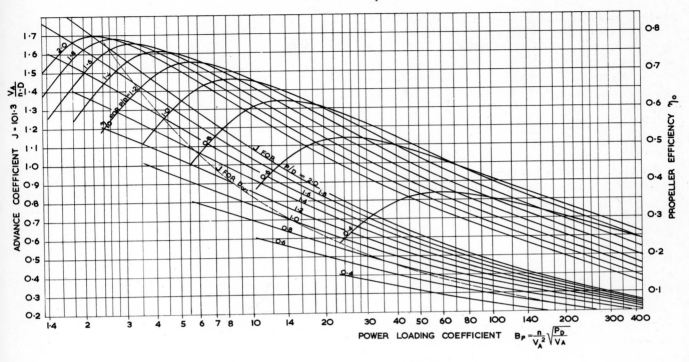

Fig. 115 $B\rho - J$ *diagram for Gawn propeller series 3 − 0·65* (P_D *in hp,* V_A *in knots,* η *in rpm,* D *in ft*).

propeller immersion can be increased considerably, as, for instance, on larger navy craft (frigates, destroyers, etc.), the suitable speed for a subcavitating type will be higher, say 40 knots, due to the higher cavitation number.

There may be four possible combinations of design data for an "optimum" propeller, either for a given shaft speed (D_{opt}-propeller):

(a) P_D, V_A, n,   (b) T, V_A, n,

or for a given diameter (n_{opt}-propeller):

(c) P_D, V_A, D,   (d) T, V_A, D.

If both n and D are given, only a "non-optimum" propeller can be selected.

In Fig. 115 a $B_P - J$ design chart prepared for Gawn propellers with blade area ratio $A_D/A_O = 0·65$ (ref. 15) is shown as an example which may be used if the power is known (case (a) and (c) or if a "non-optimum" propeller has to be designed). This presentation is similar to that of Fig. 97, but based on a power coefficient. It is a modified vision of a series of non-dimensional design charts (ref. 23), converted for English units and seawater.

For case (a) B_P can be calculated according to equation 27; P/D and J can be read off for maximum propeller efficiency, or easier by the use of "J for D_{opt}" line. The diameter can then be obtained

from $D_{opt} = 101·3\dfrac{V_A}{nJ}$. For case (c) the procedure of case (a) has to be repeated for some assumed n and the optimum combination of n and P/D may be selected. For given n and D the speed V_A may be assumed (or varied). P/D and η_o can be read off for the calculated B_P and J. D_{opt} and η_{opt} for case (a) and (c) can also be determined from Fig. 116.

The propeller thrust $T = \eta_o\eta_R 2\pi nQ/V_A$ and the thrust required curve (equ. 22) may be plotted against V to determine the craft speed, P/D and D by intersection; Q is the torque available on the propeller.

8. *General Aspects of Propeller Design*

For a new design several aspects have to be examined. The designer will usually have to decide upon diameter, shaft speed, propeller type, pitch, number of blades, blade area ratio etc. If different engines or gear ratios are available (or the latter can be decided upon), it is important to determine the most suitable shaft speed at an early stage of the project. The propeller diameter will depend on this decision and it must be acceptable from several points of view: space available, draught, shaft inclination, etc. The choice may be between a relatively fast running small propeller and a slow running screw of large diameter. The lower efficiency of the first one may be outweighed by the fact that, besides the lighter engine/gearbox arrangement, the appendages could be kept smaller, i.e. diameter, length and inclination of shaft, shaft brackets, and would consequently have lower drag. One may also have to decide between a standard (series) propeller and a theoretically designed propeller, or between a subcavitating and a supercavitating type. The SC propeller would allow a higher rpm and hence smaller propeller and appendage dimensions; but it would, of course, be a more sophisticated design. The possibility of this application may be judged from Fig. 119. A basically subcavitating type with some cavitation may be chosen. The effect of cavitation on the performance of a conventional propeller is indicated by the experimental results of the Gawn-Burrill series (Fig. 103 and ref. 8).

The main aspects regarding the propeller parameters may be briefly summarized as follows:

(a) Propeller Diameter and Shaft Speed

The optimum diameter of a propeller can be estimated roughly from Burtner's formula (ref. 23), based on the 4 bladed Wageningen B–Series:

$$D = 50 \frac{P_D^{0 \cdot 2}}{n^{0 \cdot 6}} \quad \text{(D in ft, } P_D \text{ in hp, n in rpm)} \quad (29)$$

For the 3 bladed Gawn series (ref. 16) and the 3 bladed supercavitating Newton-Rader series (ref.

20) a graph has been prepared for the optimum J as a function of B_P (Fig. 116)*. If P_D, n and V_A are known, J_{opt} can be read off for the calculated B_P and the optimum diameter be determined from $D = 101 \cdot 3 \frac{V_A}{nJ}$. If both the shaft speed n and the diameter D can be chosen, the procedure described may be repeated for some assumed n and the optimum combination of n and D can be found.

In the case of a diameter restriction or for given n and D more complex design diagrams, such as shown in Fig. 115 and given in other papers (Table A), have to be used. Somewhat better efficiencies may then be obtained with a higher number of blades. The optimum diameter decreases slightly with increase in number of blades.

(b) Pitch Ratio

The pitch of a propeller is determined by the propeller loading C_T or B_P and the advance ratio J—once the propeller type has been decided upon. Highly loaded propellers—for high power/low speed craft, tug boats, trawlers, auxiliary propulsion, etc.—will have low pitch ratios (may be $P/D = 0 \cdot 6$ to $0 \cdot 9$), associated with low efficiencies. Fast craft or lightly loaded propellers—for high speed/low displacement craft—require higher pitch ratios (often between

* For SC propellers only those η and J values have been plotted which are acceptable from the cavitation point of view (somewhat below η_{opt}).

Fig. 116 B_P−J diagram for optimum 3 bladed propellers (B_P in hp, V_A in knots, η in rpm, D in ft).

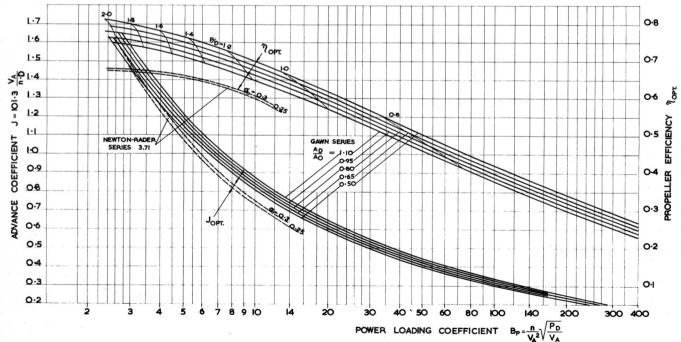

1·2 and 1·6, or even up to 2·0). For propellers with various duties or working conditions, such as free running and towing or thrusting in empty and fully loaded condition (tankers), a compromise pitch or a controllable pitch propeller might be suggested. A reduction of the pitch at the tip or near the root in the order of 10 to 20% may be useful if tip or root cavitation has to be delayed. (The "effective" pitch of such a propeller will then be somewhat lower). Within certain limits a deviation in pitch (or diameter) can be compensated by a slight change of diameter (or pitch) in such a way that the sum of pitch and diameter remains the same $(D + P = const.)$. This rule is useful, in particular if existing propellers are to be used.

(c)   Number of Blades
The number of blades usually varies between 2 and 5. The choice is mainly influenced by vibration considerations, but efficiency, cavitation and manufacturing problems are also involved. An increase in number of blades (say 3 to 5) reduces the blade loading and the propeller induced forces (pressures) on the hull (blade-frequency vibrations) for a given tip clearance. Resonance problems and/or the number of cylinders may influence the choice. With more conventional stern configurations even numbers of blades may lead to larger fluctuations of thrust and torque than odd numbers because two blades pass simultaneously the wake peaks of the stern (see also ref. 24). If the diameter is restricted, better efficiencies may be obtained with a higher number of blades. The effect of the number of blades on cavitation is normally regarded as a second order one, although in fact a somewhat increased area ratio is required for more blades. Higher numbers of blades are sometimes preferred to avoid wide blades (high blade area ratios). 3 or 4 bladed propellers are adopted in most cases. Fast running and supercavitating propellers usually have 3 blades. 2 bladed propellers are often used in sailing ships (low resistance in "sailing" position).

(d)   Blade Area Ratio
The blade area ratio A_D/A_0 or A_E/A_0 respectively, which may be between 0·35 and 1·10 (sometimes higher), is determined for the subcavitating propeller type by the limits within which the required lift or thrust can be developed without or with some acceptable amount of cavitation. This again will depend to some extent on the section shape or propeller type. The determination of the required area has already been discussed in Section 4. Other aspects may be stopping ability and blade strength; if good

stopping capabilities are required a larger blade area ratio (>0·5) may be desirable. The smaller area is preferable from the efficiency point of view, but is more liable to cavitation.

For subcavitating propellers the area ratio may be below 0·50 for low duty screws (low speed and power) and greater than 0·6 to 0·7 for high duties (high speed and power).

(e)   Section Shape
In most cases the profile data of the published propeller series can be used for the design. Alterations, such as lifting of the leading edges at the inner sections or increasing of nose radii, are often applied, but they should be made with care. Some types of sections are shown in Fig. 117.
(a) conventional aerofoil section, *(b)* segmental (or circular back) section, *(c)* NACA 16 section, cambered, *(d)* supercavitating TMB-Tulin section, *(e)* supercavitating Newton-Rader section. Modifications are sometimes required after first trials. Face cavitation may be reduced by lifting the leading edges. "Cupping" (bending down of the trailing edges) may be applied to increase the effective pitch

Fig. 117   Propeller section S.

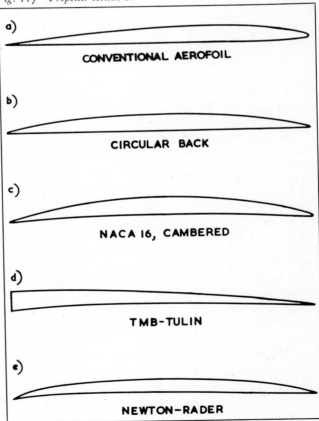

a)   CONVENTIONAL AEROFOIL

b)   CIRCULAR BACK

c)   NACA 16, CAMBERED

d)   TMB-TULIN

e)   NEWTON-RADER

(pitch correction by increased camber)*. Holes drilled through the root sections may reduce or eliminate root cavitation erosion. Special modifications at the trailing edges of the outer sections may be required to avoid propeller "singing".

Aerofoil section *a* was mainly used for reasons of efficiency, whereas the segmental section *b* has better cavitation characteristics because of its flatter pressure distribution. However, for modern designs calculated by the circulation theory mainly cambered "constant pressure" sections such as NACA 16, NACA 66 or elliptic-parabolic sections are employed both for efficiency and cavitation reasons. The lift is produced by camber rather than by incidence in order to achieve shock free entrance with "even" pressure distribution. Most of the systematic propeller series are based on more conventional aerofoil or flat face segmental sections.

(f) Blade Thickness, Strength, Material

The blade thickness is mainly determined by strength considerations. The virtual thickness at the propeller axis t_0/D (Fig. 95) usually varies between 0·045 and 0·06. The blade thickness should normally be kept to a minimum, an increase above the strength requirements is in most cases detrimental from the efficiency and cavitation point of view. For first strength calculations the following formula according to Taylor (ref. 3/25) may be used:

$$t_0 = \sqrt[3]{\frac{420 P_D C}{Z n S_P}} \qquad (30)$$

t_0 ...virtual thickness at the propeller axis (in.)
P_D...delivered horsepower at the propeller (hp)
n ...propeller shaft speed (rpm)
S_P ...maximum permissible stress (lb/in²)
C ...coefficient according to the following table:

P/D	0·6	0·7	0·8	0·9	1·0	1·1	1·2	1·3
C	1700	1450	1280	1140	1035	950	880	840

The permissible stress will depend on the blade material, on the service conditions etc. Values as given in Table B are suggested for normal design practice.

The higher figures may be applicable if the maximum power is only used for a small percentage of the running time or in other exceptional cases. Race boat propellers may require rather thicker sections than those calculated in this way because of the high

---

* It may be noted that marked improvements at hump speed and in acceleration performance due to "cupping" have frequently been reported.

Table B Propeller design stresses

Material	For commercial ships (lb/in.²)	For navy ships, fast boats, etc. (lb/in.²)
cast iron	3500–4000	
manganese bronze	7000–7700	
nickel-aluminium bronze (NAB)	8800–9600	15000

stresses occurring when breaking through the surface and re-entering the water ("propriding", boat "jumping"). Special stainless steel (very suitable for high speed propellers) is similar to NAB. From the strength point of view both nickel aluminium bronze and stainless steel have proved reasonably satisfactory for fully cavitating propellers. However, titaniums alloys appear to be even better for high speed propellers because of their favourable fatigue characteristics in sea water, but are extremely expensive. The cavitation erosion resistance (low weight loss) is relatively high for stainless steel and nickel-aluminium bronze, but lower for manganese bronze, cast iron, etc.

(g) Blade Outline, Rake and Clearance

The shape of the blade outline has little effect on the efficiency, but skew may reduce vibration because wake peaks are not passed simultaneously by all sections. It has also advantages in weed infested waters. Unusually large chord lengths at the middle of the blades may be found on special high duty propellers, if the loading at tip and blade root is reduced to minimize cavitation and noise. The effect of blade rake (0° to 10°, max. 15°) on the performance characteristics is negligible. The main reason for rake is to provide an acceptable clearance between screw and ship structure or appendages (normally about 0·15D); but additional root stresses due to centrifugal forces have to be taken into account. The clearance between the propeller tip and the more flat parts of the hull may depend on the propeller loading and the number of blades; it should normally be about 0·15D to 0·20D. The lowest point of the propeller circle should be somewhat above the keel line, whenever possible.

(h) Number of Propellers

For most small craft the number of propellers is dictated by engineering requirements. If no diameter restrictions are imposed a (conventional) single screw ship would show the best performance, because more energy can be regained behind the ship by a C.L. propeller operating in a zone of higher (frictional) wake. However, this is usually less important for fast craft with low wake fractions. If the propeller diameter is restricted, better efficiencies may be achieved with twin or multi-screw arrangements because of the reduced loading per propeller (see also Figs. 97, 115 and 116). Cavitation is often another reason to distribute the power on more propellers.

9. *Special Aspects of Supercavitating Propellers, Ventilation Problems and Propeller Arrangements*

Supercavitation or fully developed cavitation is a state where the back of a section is completely in the cavity and has practically no contact with the water. The cavitation bubbles collapse behind the section and cannot cause any erosion. This feature is utilized in the design of so-called supercavitating (SC) propellers (ref. 20, 21, 26/29). They operate successfully in speed ranges where conventional screws would be subject to cavitation erosion and show poor efficiencies.

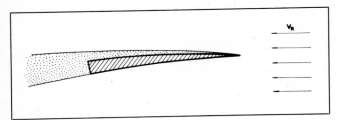

Fig. 118   Supercavitating section.

Because the back contributes little (or nothing) to the lift it can be shaped for maximum strength as long as the thickness is kept within the cavity. This often leads to a wedge type section. The lift in fully cavitating flow is ideally $\frac{1}{4}$ of that for fully wetted flow. The frictional drag of the upper side is eliminated, but so-called cavity drag has to be accounted for (ref. 26). For maximum efficiencies supercavitating sections have to be cambered and require a thin leading edge. The trailing edge is either blunt (for instance Tulin or DTMB sections), or thin if good performance at low speeds is important (Newton-Rader and KaMeWa sections, ref. 20, 21). As a guide for the application of this propeller type Fig. 119 (based on ref. 27, see also 7, 29 and 30) may be used. It shows the theoretically most suitable ranges for supercavitating and non-cavitating screws. As indicated, efficient SC propellers (Newton-Rader type) have been designed for higher cavitation numbers and used successfully

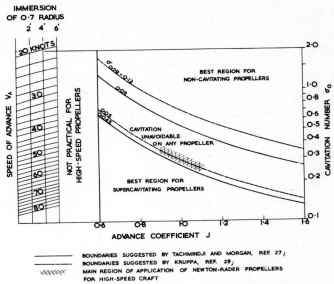

Fig. 119   Region of practical application of supercavitating propellers.

in Vosper gas turbine driven Fast Patrol Boats, race boats, etc. (propeller efficiency usually in the order of 65%). The application of SC propellers can be extended if the load is increased (increase of rpm, reduction of D). The loss is efficiency at the lower J may be outweighed by the lightweight construction (see also Section 8).

The main advantages of this propeller type are apart from its necessity at high speeds:

(1) smaller propeller diameter due to higher shaft speeds,
(2) reduction in size and weight of the appendages, smaller shaft angle,
(3) erosion-free operation at high speeds,
(4) lower vibratory propeller forces from variations of angle of incidence or speed (shaft inclination, ship's wake),
(5) possibility of direct drive (elimination of gear box) or the use of a lighter high revving engine.

The design point should be chosen in the fully cavitating range, which is for the Newton-Rader type always at J values to the left of the K_T and K_Q hump (Fig. 120)*.

Extensive running at medium speeds in the partially cavitating range is not advisable because erosion may occur, although from practical experience this is not very noticeable. Damaged leading edges, causing a strip-like cavitation erosion, are often

---

* The hump of the propeller curves is partly due to model scale effects and less pronounced for full scale propellers.

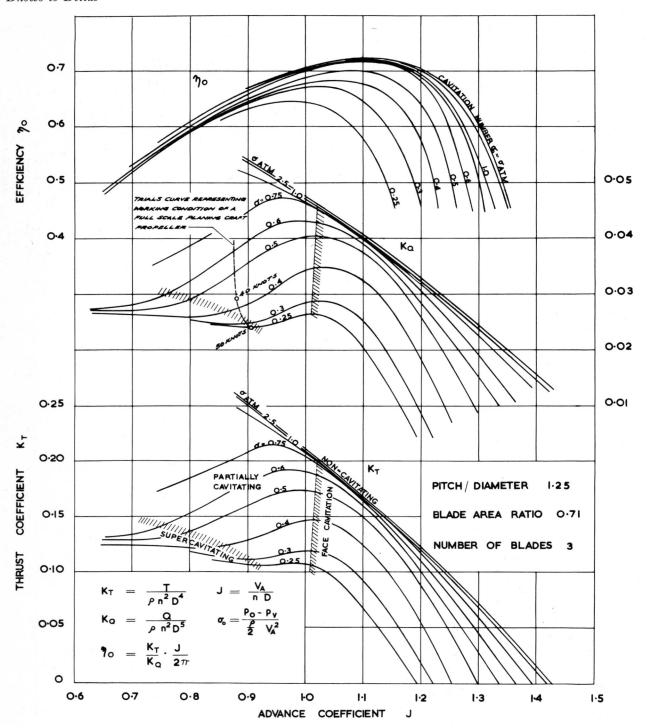

Fig. 120 $K_T - K_Q - J$ *diagram for SC propeller of Newton Rader type.*

more serious. Regular inspections of these edges could be advisable. Blades too thin near the leading edges are susceptible to fatigue failures.

Ventilation problems may arise from surface piercing struts or shafts in front of the propeller, resulting in loss of performance, propeller-induced vibrations or propeller racing. This may be supressed

(1) by arranging the screw under the hull (Fig. 121a).
(2) by deeper screw (or appendage) immersion,
(3) by an anti-ventilation plate ("cavitation plate") (Fig. 121b), or a "fence" to stop the air entering into the separated flow region behind struts, etc. at high speed, or
(4) in the case of a twin screw craft, by arranging the propellers closer to the craft centre line to achieve better submergence, particularly in turns.

On supercavitating propellers ventilation of the cavity flow is likely to occur if the propeller tip is close to the free surface (ref. 34). The characteristics of a subcavitating propeller can be similarly affected (thrust and torque decrease or propeller racing, even without ventilation), if tip submergence is less than about 0·25D, depending on the propeller load (see also ref. 31). Systematic investigations of this kind

Fig. 121 Propeller arrangements (a) on inclined shaft, (b) Z-drive, (c) semi-submerged.

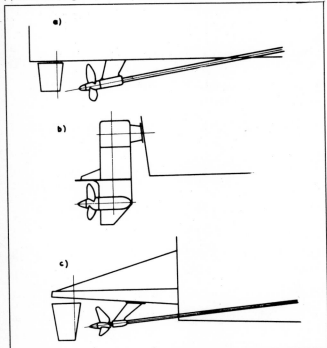

Fig. 122 (a) Model of supercavitating propeller (Newton-Rader type) (b) "Surface" propeller (Ph. Rolla, Lugano).

can be made by model tests in a so-called "free-surface" cavitation tunnel.

Some typical propeller arrangements are shown in Fig. 121: (a) an inboard drive, (b) an outboard drive and (c) a semi-submerged propeller. The inboard drive is the most common one. For smaller craft and also for race boats outboard drives are becoming more popular. They offer certain advantages for very fast craft such as the possibility of adjusting the angle (and the height) to optimize trim and immersion (shaft speed) for different running conditions, the locating of the weight (LCG) further aft and a simpler installation (ref. 32). The gear losses in the Z-drive and the additional drag of the underwater gear housing may be outweighed by the elimination of the propeller shaft and normal V-drive.

A special propeller type, very successful for race boats and other high speed craft, is the semi-submerged SC propeller ("surface" propeller, ref. 33, 34). Shaft and bracket drag, often a high percentage of the total resistance of fast boats, is eliminated, as the propeller is only submerged to the hub. The efficiency is very similar to that of a fully submerged propeller.

The thrust is approximately proportional to the immersed area; cavitation erosion is unlikely. However, problems may arise from vibratory loads and fatigue; but these can possibly be overcome by the use of thicker sections. As stated by Hadler and Hecker (ref. 33), a wedge type section should be employed; aerofoil sections appear to be less suitable for this kind of operation.

Dhows to Deltas

In order to achieve quasi-supercavitating conditions at lower speeds attempts have been made to ventilate the propeller through air ducts in the blades (ventilated propellers). So far no practical applications are reported to the authors' knowledge. By arranging the exhaust gas pipe in the propeller race similar effects may be observed; shaft speed and propeller slip may increase.

Successful controllable pitch SC propellers have been developed by KMW, Sweden (ref. 21). This propeller type can offer significant advantages for craft with a rather pronounced resistance hump (hydrofoil craft, hovercraft and planing craft) (Fig. 112). It may be impossible to overcome this hump with a fixed pitch propeller, or else only poor performance may be achieved in low speed conditions because of the high design pitch.

10. *Waterjet Propulsion*
Waterjet propulsion (ref. 35 to 40), although still in the development stage for high speed applications, can offer many advantages for hovercraft, hydrofoil, planing craft, etc., such as smaller draught, reduced underwater noise (or air noise if compared with air screw propulsion), excellent manoeuvrability, the elimination of long drive shafts (drag reduction) and of the liability to propeller damage, etc. This may

Fig. 123 Waterjet systems.

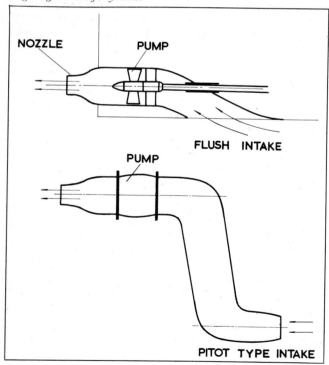

often outweigh hydrodynamic disadvantages. Many commercial waterjet systems have poor propulsive efficiencies due to high internal losses. However, well designed waterjets for high speed craft may be competitive with SC propellers above 40 to 50 knots, taking draught, appendage drag reduction, propeller and engineering problems into account. On the other hand, many data claimed in publications seem to be rather optimistic. The application of waterjets for highly sophisticated race boats does not appear to be advisable at present.

For an optimum solution the pump should be specially designed for a particular waterjet application in order to match flow rate, head, cavitation, weight and efficiency requirements.

The type of pump has to be decided upon, either axial flow, mixed flow or centrifugal pump (also single or multistage and single or multipath). The choice is mainly dependent on the specific speed ($n_s = nQ^{\frac{1}{2}}/H^{\frac{3}{4}}$) Because of the high head requirements centrifugal or mixed flow pumps are usually suggested for fast craft, but multistage axial flow pumps can offer alternative solutions. Single stage axial flow pumps are more suitable for low head and high mass flow applications (lower speeds).

The rate of flow Q is determined by the thrust required and the chosen jet velocity V_J (Fig. 124). Neglecting wake ($w = 0$, $V_A = V$), the thrust is (as in equ. (2)):
$$T = m\Delta V = \rho Q(V_J - V); \qquad (31)$$
and the flow will be:
$$Q = \frac{T}{\rho(V_J - V)} = \frac{T}{\rho V(\frac{V_J}{V} - 1)}, \qquad (32)$$

with Q...rate of flow (ft³/sec),
   V_J...jet velocity (ft/sec),
$$\rho = 1\cdot99 \ (1\cdot94) \ \frac{lb \ sec^2}{ft^4} \ \text{density of seawater (fresh water).}$$

The pump power required is:
$$P_p = \frac{\rho g Q H}{\eta_p},$$
with η_p ... pump efficiency,
   $g = 32\cdot2\frac{ft}{sec^2}$ acceleration due to gravity.

The total pump head H is determined by the difference between the jet and the free-stream velocity head $\frac{V_J^2}{2g} - \frac{V}{2g}$ as well as by the system losses, such as: intake loss $h_1 = \zeta_1 V^2/2g$, diffuser loss $h_2 = \zeta_2 V^2/2g$, duct loss $h_3 = \zeta_3 V^2/2g$, discharge loss $h_4 = \zeta_4 V_J^2/2g$ and elevation loss $h_5 = \Delta h$; ζ are non-dimensional loss coefficients. Therefore, the total pump head has to be:

$$H = h_1 + h_2 + h_3 + h_4 + h_5 + \frac{V_J^2}{2g} - \frac{V^2}{2g} \quad (34)$$

$$= \frac{V^2}{2g}\left(\zeta_1 + \zeta_2 + \zeta_3 + \zeta_4\left(\frac{V_J}{V}\right)^2 + \left(\frac{V_J}{V}\right)^2 - 1\right) + \Delta h.$$

The intake, usually either Pitot (ram) or flush type, requires special attention. It is often the cause of poor system efficiencies. Flow separation, velocity distribution and cavitation are serious problems. A diffuser may be necessary to reduce the velocity at the pump entry (conversion of kinetic into potential energy) in order to avoid pump cavitation. For high speed applications, the discharge above water level (elevation loss Δh) has little effect on the efficiency.

The ideal jet efficiency or Froude efficiency (identical with equ. 6) is

$$\eta_i = \frac{2V}{V + V_J} = \frac{1}{1 + \frac{1}{2}\frac{\Delta V}{V}}. \quad (35)$$

However, in reality head losses and pump efficiency have to be taken into account and a so-called thrust efficiency, as used mainly for waterjet problems, can then be defined:

$$\eta_T = \eta_J \eta_P. \quad (36)$$

η_J is the jet efficiency (Fig. 124), dependent on the total loss coefficient (ref. 29)

$$\zeta = \zeta_1 + \zeta_2 + \zeta_3 + \zeta_4\left(\frac{V_J}{V}\right)^2 + 2g\frac{\Delta h}{V^2}, \quad (37)$$

and the velocity ratio V_J/V; η_P is the pump efficiency, usually between 0·80 and 0·90. The optimum jet velocity can be determined for maximum jet efficiency, V_J/V normally between 1·6 and 2·2.

In actual cases the total loss coefficient ζ varies in the range of 0·25 to 0·50 for well designed systems and 0·50 to 1·0 for poorly designed systems (ref. 40). A slightly higher V_J/V than the optimum may be chosen, thus reducing the weight of the waterjet unit, including that of the entrained water.

It should be noted that this thrust efficiency, often wrongly quoted as waterjet propulsive efficiency, does not take hull interaction effects (thrust deduction, wake) and additional intake drag into account and cannot usually be directly compared with propulsive efficiencies as defined for normal ship propulsion.

The pump revolutions n (rpm) should be chosen as high as possible in order to obtain a small and light pump and duct system. However, this is limited by cavitation, and therefore pumps with high suction performance (suction specific speeds) are to be selected. For craft with pronounced resistance humps (hydrofoil craft, hovercraft, etc.) the most critical condition, from the cavitation point of view, occurs in the off-design condition at hump speed, where—because of the low dynamic head—only low pressures above the vapour point are available on the suction side of the pump (low net positive suction head (npsh)), but at the same time high thrust has to be produced. Also, an intake designed for high speeds may act as a restriction device at high intake velocity ratios V_i/V (low craft speed); a multi-geometry intake may be required. Furthermore, intake ventilation problems may have to be examined.

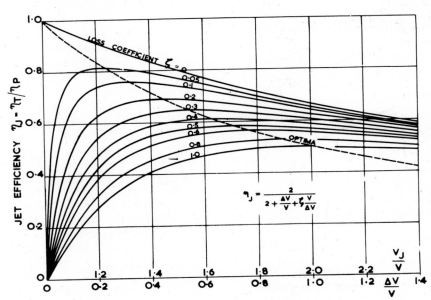

Fig. 124 Jet efficiency.

References

1. Todd, F. H. Resistance and Propulsion. Principles of Naval Architecture, New York, 1967.
2. Lerbs, H. W. Moderately Loaded Propellers with a Finite Number of Blades and an Arbitrary Distribution of Circulation. Trans. SNAME 60, 1952.
3. Eckardt, M. K. and Morgan, W. B. A Propeller Design Method. Trans. SNAME 63, 1955.
4. Van Manen, J. D. Fundamentals of Ship Resistance and Propulsion, Part B, Propulsion. Int. Shipb. Progr. 1957.
5. Van Lammeren, W. P. A., Troost, L. and Koning, J. G. Resistance, Propulsion and Steering of Ships. Haarlem, Holland, 1948.
6. O'Brien, T. P. The Design of Marine Screw Propellers. London, 1962.
7. Kruppa, C. The Design of Screw Propellers. Chapter XX in Ref. 13.
8. Gawn, R. W. L. and Burrill, L. C. Effect of Cavitation on the Performance of a Series of 16 in. Model Propellers. Trans. INA 99, 1957.
9. Barnaby, K. Basic Naval Architecture. London, 1967.
10. Hadler, J. B. The Prediction of Power Performance on Planing Craft. Trans. SNAME, 1966.
11. Gutsche, F. Untersuchung von Schiffsschrauben in schraeger Anstroemung (Investigation on Ship Propellers in Oblique Flow). Schiffbauforschung 3, 1964.
12. Du Cane, P. Contribution to Ref. 10.
13. Du Cane, P. High-Speed Small Craft. London, 1964.
14. De Groot, D. Resistance and Propulsion of Motor-Boats. Int. Shipb. Progr. 2, 1955.
15. Troost, L. Open Water Test Series with Modern Propeller Forms. Trans. NECI, 1950–51.
16. Gawn, R. W. L. Effect of Pitch and Blade Width on Propeller Performance. Trans. INA, 1953.
17. Yazaki, A. Design Diagrams of Modern Four, Five, Six and Seven-Bladed Propellers Developed in Japan. 4th. Symposium on Naval Hydrodynamics, Office of Naval Research, Washington, D.C., 1962.
18. Lindgren, A. and Bjärne, E. The SSPA Standard Propeller Family Open Water Characteristics. Publ. Swed. State Shipb. Experim. Tank, No. 60, 1967.
19. Lindgren, A. Model Tests with a Family of Three and Five-Bladed Propellers. Publ. Swed. State Shipb. Experim. Tank No. 47, 1961.
20. Newton, R. N. and Rader, H. P. Performance Data of Propellers for High Speed Craft. Trans. RINA 103, 1961.
21. Pehrsson, L. Controllable Pitch Propellers. Chapter XXII in Ref. 13.
22. Gutsche, F. and Suhrbier, K. Entwurfsdiagramme fuer 3-fluegelige Propeller nach Versuchen von Gawn 1952. (Design Charts for 3-Bladed Propellers According to Gawn's Experiments 1952.) Schiffbautechnik 7, 1957.
23. Burtner, E. A Relationship for Preliminary Propeller Diameter. Journ. Americ. Soc. Nav. Eng. 65 1953.
24. Van Manen, J. D. The Choice of the Propeller. Marine Technology (SNAME), April, 1966.
25. Taylor, D. W. Speed and Power of Ships, Washington, 1943.
26. Tulin, M. P. Supercavitating Propellers—History, Operating Characteristics, Mechanism of Operation. 4th Symposium on Naval Hydrodynamics, Office of Naval Research, Washington, D.C. 1962.
27. Tachmindji, A. J. and Morgan, W. B. The Design and Estimated Performance of a Series of Supercavitating Propellers, 2nd. Symposium on Naval Hydrodynamics, Office of Naval Research, Washington, D.C., 1958.
28. Venning, E. and Habermann, W. L. Supercavitating Propeller Performance. Trans. SNAME 70, 1962.
29. Kruppa, C. High Speed Propellers, Hydrodynamics and Design. University of Michigan, Oct. 1967.
30. Du Cane, P. Contribution to Ref. 27.
31. Gutsche, F. Einfluss der Tauchung auf Schub und Wirkungsgrad von Schiffspropellern (Effect of Immersion on Thrust and Efficiency of Ship Propellers). Schiffbauforschung 6, 1967.
32. Teale, J. Outboards Offshore. Motor Boat and Yachting, 13 Dec. 1968.
33. Hadler, J. B. and Hecker, R. Performance of Partially Submerged Propellers. 7th ONR Symposium on Naval Hydrodynamics, Rome, 1968.
34. Lindenmuth, W. T. and Barr, R. A. Study of the Performance of a Partially Submerged Propeller. Hydronautics Techn. Rep. 760–61, July 1967.
35. Gasiunas, A. and Lewis, W. P. Hydraulic Jet Propulsion: A Theoretical and Experimental Investigation into the Propulsion of Seacraft by Water Jets. Trans. Inst. Mech. Eng., 1963.
36. Johnson, V. E. Waterjet Propulsion for High-Speed Hydrofoil Craft. 1st. AIAA Annual Meeting, Washington, D.C., 1964.
37. Brandau, J. H. Aspects of Performance Evaluation of Waterjet Propulsion Systems and a Critical Review of the State-of-the-Art. AIAA/SNAME, Advance Vehicles Marine Meeting, Norfolk, Virginia, 1967.
38. Traksel, J. and Beck, W. E. Waterjet Propulsion for Marine Vehicles. AIAA/USN Marine Systems and ASW Conference, San Diego, California, 1965.
39. Kruppa, C., Brandt, H. and Oestergaard, C. Wasserstrahlantriebe fuer Hochgeschwindigkeitsfahrzeuge (Waterjet Propulsion for High-Speed Craft). Jb. STG 62, 1968.
40. Kim, H. Ch. Hydrodynamic Aspects of Internal Pump Jet Propulsion. Marine Technology (SNAME), Jan. 1966.

"Surfury Specification"

Delta 36 Offshore Racing Powerboat

(Part one—hull)
Designed by: RENATO LEVI

General

This specification is to cover the construction and out-fitting of the Delta 36 Offshore Racing Powerboat, which is to be built in accordance with the drawings supplied by the Architect.

The vessel to be constructed in an enclosed shed, so as to offer complete protection from the weather during the entire construction.

Since there are several design features in this competition craft which are a departure from normal practice, it is essential that the drawings and the actual vessel under construction be kept strictly confidential.

The craft to be insured by the builder against fire and usual boat builders risks.

Prior to commencing construction, full scale lofting to be carried out in accordance with the lines drawing and table of offsets supplied.

In view of the type of construction involved, the hull to be built upon a wooden male mould and each layer of planking when laminating to be stapled on with very closely spaced tacking strips, independently so as to ensure thorough adhesion between each layer of planking. The same process to apply to the cabin top and front which is a one piece laminated structure.

Workmanship to be of the highest boat building practice throughout following detailed drawings supplied. Internal joinery work to be carefully executed and to contribute to the structural strength of the hull.

All timber to be carefully selected, thoroughly seasoned material having a humidity content not exceeding 15%. Timber to be carefully selected, free of knots and other defects. Two main types of timber to be used throughout the construction which are first grade cedar and Sitka spruce as shown on the drawings.

All plywood to conform to BSS 1088 or equivalent specification. All wood adhesive to be of the best quality resorcinol formaldehyde resin such as Aerodux and where glass reinforced plastic work is involved, epoxy resins to be used such as Araldite, excluding the lining of tanks, where polyester resins may be used. Glass reinforcement to consist of two layers of 2 oz. glass mat or an equivalent scheme to be approved by the Architect.

All lamination work, bonding of timber and glass reinforced plastic work to be done under permissible limits of temperature for which heating arrangements must be made whilst this work is in process, as required.

This specification is to cover the complete construction of the vessel and the builder to be responsible for the vessel until after completion of satisfactory trials.

The specification and drawings to cover this vessel are to include any minor items of equipment, fittings or woodwork that are necessary for the proper completion of this powerboat in the spirit of the contract.

The builders are to carry out any adjustments to gear and fittings which may be found necessary after trials and to be responsible for the vessel until the Owner takes delivery.

Note: It is of the utmost importance that the builders do not, under any circumstance, work into the construction any additional material or alter the materials mentioned in the specification without prior approval from the designer.

The success of the design is very closely related to maintaining the weight originally estimated.

Since this powerboat is intended for serious offshore racing and the design incorporates many experimental features, it is understood that the yard will, after preliminary trials have been undertaken and should it be necessary, carry out modifications to the hull structure, etc., as required, for which a separate estimate will be submitted to the Owner for approval prior to undertaking such modifications.

Leading Dimensions

Length overall	36'
Maximum beam	10' 6½"
Draught (hull)	1' 11"
Deadrise aft plane	25°
Light weight	3·1 Tons
Loaded weight	4·57 Tons (excluding ballast)
Maximum speed	50 Knots.

Description

The hull form of this craft is designed for fast offshore

racing. It is a rounded chine hull with a heavily raked bow and deep deadrise carried to the transom. Longitudinal risers are incorporated so as to increase dynamic lift and reduce wetted surface.

Construction

The Hull Shell: to be a cold moulded structure consisting of four thicknesses of cedar laminates of $\frac{1}{4}$" thick on the bottom and top sides placed diagonally. The planking to be continuous from keel rabbet to sheer.

Main Internal Hull Framing: to consist of four hollow longitudinal girders, two per side on the bottom. These longitudinals are placed parallel to the keel and are bedded down onto the hull with a 2 oz. Mat impregnated with epoxy resin.

The outer two girders are the tank longitudinals which are placed with their outboard edges 2' 8" from the centre line of the boat.

The inner two girders are the engine bearer longitudinals which are placed with their inboard edge 1' from the centre line of the boat. See drawing no. 881/9 for fixing details, scantlings and method by which tank fronts and internal joinery work form part of these bearers.

Keel: Cedar 1" sided parallel throughout moulded to suit lines.

Hog: Cedar laminated in four $\frac{3}{8}$" laminates 4" sided × $1\frac{1}{2}$" parallel throughout.

Longitudinal risers: To be placed externally on bottom of hull as shown on the drawing. Spruce and triangular in section $3\frac{1}{2}$" sided aft and a depth perpendicular to planking of $1\frac{1}{2}$" throughout. Where the deadrise in the bows increases, the siding to be reduced so as to keep the bottom faces horizontal and a constant depth of $1\frac{1}{2}$" on their outboard edges. Risers to be tapered at their extremities except where they extend to the transom where they are cut flush with the transom. Risers are bonded to the hull without fastening; particular care to be taken to ensure that the inner feather edges of the risers are well bonded onto the planking.

Chine Rubber: Spruce $2\frac{1}{2}$" × 2" shaped as shown on the detail drawing. Tapered at the bows and cut flush at the transom. To be bonded to the hull shell with the same method as the risers.

Transom: Plywood 18 mm thick laminated with two 9 mm 5 ply.

Transom Framing: Cedar laminated $2\frac{1}{2}$" × 1" with four cedar upright members in way of longitudinal 3" × 1" and 1" thick playwood filler over hog in way of propeller strut flange.

Bulkheads: 12 mm 5 ply.

Bulkhead frames: Spruce $2\frac{1}{2}$" × 1".

Main deck beams: Those from bulkhead 3 to stem laminated spruce 3" × $\frac{3}{4}$" dovetailed into gunwales.

Half beams: Spruce $2\frac{1}{2}$" × $\frac{3}{4}$" dovetailed into gunwales and carlins. Half beams to be laminated.

Gunwales: Spruce $3\frac{1}{2}$" × 1" with lower inboard corners chamfered 45°. Aft ends secured with laminated knees to transom.

Carlins: Spruce $3\frac{1}{2}$" × 1". Extending from bulkhead 3 to transom secured to bulkhead and transom with solid cedar triangular knees as shown.

Covering boards: Cedar $3\frac{1}{2}$" × $\frac{3}{4}$" with outboard and inboard edge radiused as shown.

Deck: $\frac{1}{4}$" 5-Ply glued to beams covering boards and carlins. All deck panel joints with feather edge scarfs at least 1 in 10.

King plank: Cedar 8" × $\frac{1}{2}$" bonded over ply deck and extending from bulkhead 3 to stem. Upper corners well chamfered.

Cabin top and front: Cedar laminated in one piece with four diagonal veneers to give a finished total thickness of $\frac{5}{8}$". Glued and screwed to cabin sides, corner bars, bulkhead beams and triangular fashion piece on fore deck.

Cabin sides and cockpit coamings: 12 mm 5 ply extending from bulkhead 3 to transom. In way of cockpit, coamings to be lined on inside with 6 mm 5 ply to form a hollow box section. See drawing no. 881/8.

Corner Bar: Spruce 3" × $\frac{3}{4}$" in way of cabin. Laminated in the forward portion. In way of coaming reduced to $2\frac{1}{2}$" × $\frac{1}{2}$".

Fuel Tanks: To have a total capacity of approximately 400 gallons in four tanks. To be of 9 mm 5 ply lined with glass reinforced plastics as shown on drawing no. 881/9. Tank diaphragms, inspection doors and cover only to be secured with glass mat fillets and epoxy resin. Light alloy inspection doors to be provided over each compartment of the four tanks. Tank fittings such as fillers and breathers to be secured to inspection doors. See part two: mechanical specification. Each tank to be tested with a four foot head of water for 24 hours to ensure complete water tightness.

Water Ballast Tanks: To have a total capacity of 120 gallons in two side by side longitudinal tanks. To be of 9 mm 5 ply lined with glass reinforced plastics and to be constructed in the same way as the fuel tanks, with diaphragms and cover, water inlet and breather fittings, secured with glass mat fillets and epoxy resin. Upon completion tanks to be tested in the same way as the fuel tanks.

In operation these tanks to be filled by two retractable water intakes, one for each tank. See drawing no. 881/11. The water intakes to be situated aft in the cockpit and to be piped up to the tanks by means of best quality neoprene or plastic tubing. Each tank to be fitted with 1" I.D. breathers placed as far forward on the tank covers as possible and led out on the fore deck by means of skin fittings suitably placed so that the crew can see when the tanks are full.

Fresh water tank: To have a capacity of two gallons. To be of 16 gauge light alloy and to be situated in the galley locker. Tank to be filled by means of a filler cap on galley top and to have air vent on cap. Tank to be piped to galley sink and toilet wash basin by means of $\frac{1}{2}''$ plastic or similar pipe. Tap to be of light alloy and of the plunger type.

Aft Cockpit Floor: To consist of four hinged hatches one forward and aft narrow fixed floors and a central bridge deck between the forward two and aft two hatches. The centre section of the bridge deck to be removable. Hatches to be provided with easily removable pin hinges, and an inspection window of $\frac{3}{8}''$ perspex to be fitted on each hatch. For construction details of cockpit floor see drawing no. 881/5.

Cabin Sole: To be of 9 mm 5 ply supported on 9 mm 5 ply web floors positioned as shown on drawing no. 904/4. Four light alloy flush sockets to be provided on the floor for dining table legs. Soles of galley and toilet also to be 9 mm 5 ply supported on spruce members $1\frac{1}{2}'' \times \frac{3}{4}''$.

Galley and toilet furniture: To be of 6 mm 5 ply fronts and tops with internal spruce members $1\frac{1}{2}'' \times \frac{3}{4}''$. Toilet to be fully enclosed with a 9 mm 5 ply partition. Access door to be provided on inside with folding light alloy tubular legs $1''$ O.D. $\times \frac{1}{8}''$ and easily removable drop nose pin hinges so that this door may be used as dining table.

Berths: Front and top of berths to be 9 mm 5 ply. The front to be scarfed (at least 1 in 10) to inboard side of cabin longitudinals and to have openings in them as shown on drawing no. 904/4. The tops to be well secured to the fronts and bulkheads with internal corner members of spruce $2'' \times \frac{3}{4}''$ and to the planking with triangular shaped spruce members having a depth of at least $2''$. Note these berths form a structural part of the hull. Berths to be provided with $1''$ foam mattresses and covered with a suitable light weight material.

Console: to be made following drawing no. 881/8. To bridge the aft cockpit from coaming to coaming in the position shown. To be built of 9 mm 5 ply with spruce internal corner members. The console to be fixed to the coamings by means of light alloy fixing plates so as to permit this to be hinged open when engines require to be removed. All control cables, wires, etc., to pass under the starboard side of the console. The coamings are reinforced in this area by means of 9 mm 5 ply L shaped knees which are secured under the side decks and over the tanks.

Miscellaneous

Toilet: to be of light alloy HYDRA or equivalent make with separate inlet and outlet fittings with sea cocks.

Bilge Pump: To be located on fixed portion of aft cockpit floor. To have its section pipe as near the transom as possible. To be of the Henderson Diaphragm type or equivalent.

Bilge Drain: Limber holes to be provided on either side of the hog for the whole length of the craft up to the ballast tanks. Bilge water to drain out through two neoprene or equivalent reed valves fitted on the transom.

Cabin access ladder: To be removable of light alloy tubing $1''$ O.D. $\times \frac{1}{8}''$.

Cooker: To be a single burner light alloy alcohol stove secured on the galley top.

Galley Stowage: To be provided for crockery, cutlery, glasses, for a crew of three under the side deck and the locker to be for dry food stowage.

Finishing

Craft to be finished as follows:

1 Protective and sealing coat of resorcinol resin on bottom to 6'' above level water line (resorcinol resin to be diluted with alcohol to facilitate application).

2 Coats of primer to entire craft externally and internally followed by filler as required and thoroughly rubbed down.

3 Finishing coats of synthetic enamel to outside of hull.

   2 Coats of synthetic enamel inside hull and cabin.

   2 Coats of anti slip paint on deck and cockpit floor and cabin soles.

Note: Particular care to be taken on the external finish of the craft.

   Colour scheme to be approved by the client.

Deck Fittings

To be of sea water resisting light alloy unless otherwise stated and to include the following:

   1 9'' Bow cleat
   2 5'' Bow fairleads
   2 8'' Stern cleats
   4 3'' Fender cleats
   1 $2' \times 1\frac{1}{4}''$ O.D. $\times \frac{1}{8}''$ Bow pulpit
   1 $2' \times 1\frac{1}{4}''$ O.D. $\times \frac{1}{8}''$ Stanchions
   2 Ballast tank breathers
   1 Set navigation lights
   1 $6'6'' \times 1\frac{1}{4}''$ O.D. $\times \frac{1}{8}''$ Mast (to serve also as boat hook) with sockets.
   1 $1\frac{1}{4}''$ O.D. $\times \frac{1}{8}''$ Stern pulpit
   1 Horn (light weight)
   2 S.S. fuel filler caps
   2 9'' diameter $\times \frac{1}{4}''$ Perspex deck lights.

Safety Equipment

To be supplied following the requirements laid down by "BRADS" and such equipment to be provided with proper stowage arrangements.

Note: As there have been several changes for the compulsory equipment required the most up-to-date issue of "BRADS" to be followed.

ADDENDUM
to Specification of Delta 36 Offshore Racing Powerboat

General

This addendum to the specification indicates all the changes which have been made to the original specification. These changes have necessitated redoing and editing all the drawings.

In order to avoid any misunderstanding, all previous drawings issued are to be returned to the owner and the new drawings, which are related to this addendum, can be distinguished by the /1 at the end of all the drawing numbers, for example, the profile and deck plan of the modified drawing is no. 881/6/1.

The builder is also requested to place an identification mark against the items in the original specification which have been modified or corrected in this addendum, in order to avoid any possibility of misinterpretation.

Main Modifications to Hull

Sheer: The sheer aft of bulkhead n. 1 is cut away in a fair curve as shown in the lines drawing to the height of the top of the fuel tanks, thus doing away with this portion of the freeboard, the side decks, beams and carlins. The tank tops therefore are now the side decks in the aft portion of the craft.

Gunwales: Since the upper gunwales terminate on the fuel tank tops aft of the bulkhead n. 1, a further gunwale of spruce of the same dimensions as the main gunwales, to be placed inside the fuel tanks extending from the transom through bulkhead n. 1, terminating on bulkhead n. 2.

Cabin Top: This is to be a one piece laminated unit built in four diagonally placed veneers of cedar of equal thickness to produce a total finished thickness of $\frac{1}{2}''$. This one piece cabin top terminates aft at bulkhead n. 1.

Cockpit Coamings: The cockpit coamings are to be of 3 mm ply secured to laminated spruce stanchions as shown in the drawing. The forward portion of the coaming to be scarfed on to the cabin top. The coaming extends across the transom of the cockpit. The coaming sides are to be well secured to the tank tops so as to produce a watertight joint. To run along the top of the coamings a light alloy tubular handrail of $1\frac{1}{4}''$ O.D. $\times \frac{1}{8}''$ strengthened in way of console as shown in the drawing.

Planking: The planking thickness to be reduced throughout from $1''$ to $\frac{7}{8}''$. This to be constructed with four diagonal veneers of cedar of equal thickness, continuous from keel to gunwale.

Bulkheads: Bulkhead n. 1 to be 12 mm plywood, all other bulkheads to be 9 mm plywood.

Keel and Hog: To be of first grade spruce instead of cedar.

Longitudinals: Engine bearer longitudinals to be reduced to $2\frac{1}{2}''$ in width and to be placed with their inboard edges $12\frac{1}{2}''$ from the centre line of the boat. These longitudinals aft of bulkhead 1 to be solid throughout, built up with 9 mm plywood sides. Since the engines will be inclined approximately $5°$ to port, corresponding to approximately $\frac{1}{2}''$ on the depth of the light alloy engine beds, wedges to be glued on to the longitudinals along the entire length of the engine beds. A further support to be provided to the underside of the metal engine beds in the form of $\frac{1}{2}''$ hard wood stringer to be bonded to the inside of the engine bearer longitudinals.

Tank longitudinals to be reduced to $2\frac{1}{2}''$ in width and to have their outboard edges $2'8''$ from the centre line of the boat.

Engine Bearer Webs: Two webs to be positioned as shown in the construction drawing. These webs to be of 9 mm plywood with spruce framing.

Bunks: The bunk fronts in the main cabin to be scarfed to the outboard sides of the engine bearer longitudinals instead of the inboard sides, reducing the bunk widths by a corresponding amount.

Ballast Tank: The capacity of the water ballast tanks to be reduced from 160 gallons to 100 gallons in two tanks of 50 gallons each.

Toilet: Toilet to be modified as shown in accommodation drawing. Sink to be eliminated and the HYDRA W.C. to be substituted with a MINI Toilet which is to be provided with a flush screw on plug to the outlet.

Forward Engine Hatch: To be modified as shown on the drawing so that hatches open fore and aft.

Inspection Windows on Engine Hatches: These to be enlarged as shown on the drawing and to be reinforced on their underside with spruce members.

Fresh Water: The light alloy tank to be substituted with a plastic container which will be supplied by the owner. This container has a capacity of 3 gallons and is of the following approximate dimensions: $10'' \times 6'' \times 18''$.

Propeller Strut Reinforcement: A packing of two layers of $\frac{1}{2}''$ plywood to be bonded onto the inside of the transom between engine bearer longitudinals to the required height to provide adequate reinforcement for the attachment of the propeller strut.

Cleats: The two stern cleats to be substituted by one $8''$ stern cleat placed centrally on the fixed portion of the aft cockpit near the transom.

Cabin Ventilation: A perspex "Sudbury Sky Vent" or similar ventilator to be fitted to cabin top in the position shown.

Stanchions: Bow pulpit to be eliminated and the following stanchions to be provided:

1 $18'' \times 1\frac{1}{4}''$ O.D. $+ \frac{1}{8}''$ stanchion
2 $24'' \times 1\frac{1}{4}''$ O.D. $\times \frac{1}{8}''$ stanchions
2 $6'' \times 1''$ O.D. $\times \frac{1}{8}''$ stanchions.

Specification of Delta 36 Offshore Racing Powerboat

(Part two—mechanical and electrical)

(1) General

This specification is to cover the installation of the propulsive machinery and all the mechanical and electrical work detailed in this specification. The contractor is to ensure that this work is correctly executed and is responsible for the proper functioning of all the equipment installed. It is understood that this specification and related drawings include any minor items of equipment and fittings that are necessary for the completion of work detailed here.

The contractor is to carry out any adjustments to gear and fittings which may be found necessary after trials and to be responsible for the vessel until the Owner takes delivery after completion of satisfactory trials.

Note: It is of the utmost importance that the contractor does not, under any circumstance, work into the construction any additional material or alter the materials mentioned in the specification without prior approval from the Owner or designer.

(2) Tandem Engine Unit

This unit consists of two 400 HP Daytona petrol engines driving on to the upper shaft of a spiral bevel geared V drive. The aft engine is fitted with an ahead-neutral-astern gear box. The forward engine has a simple IN-OUT gear box. The two engines and V drive are mounted on two 7 foot cast aluminium channels, having an approximate depth of 6". The engines will have approximately $\frac{3}{8}$" adjustment up or down and sideways.

The V drive has the same limits of movement. Flexible gear couplings between the engines and the V drive will permit a misalignment of approximately 1°. Lining up instructions for the two engines and gear box on the aluminium channels, the shaft log gland bearing and the propeller strut bearing, will be supplied and are to be meticulously followed. In conjunction with these lining up instructions, it is to be borne in mind that the entire unit, i.e. tandem engines and V drive on the aluminium engines beds, are to be inclined between $4\frac{1}{2}$° to 5° to port so as to offset the propeller (centre of hub) to starboard 2" off the centre line of the boat.

The tandem engine unit will be supplied complete with the following equipment:

(a) 1 $\frac{1}{4}$" cooling water inlet on the propeller strut with a 1" sea strainer and adequate rubber hose to connect the cooling water inlet to the 2 engines and V drive.

(b) A complete self-contained lubricating system for the engines and V drive.

(c) An independent fuel system for each engine comprising fuel filter and mechanical fuel pump. In addition the two engines will be supplied with three electrical fuel pumps which are to be connected in parallel with the mechanical fuel pumps. See diagram of fuel system in the specification (Fig. 1).

(d) Electric senders for: oil pressure and temperature, water temperature, fuel pressure and V drive, oil temperature, a large terminal block will be supplied to which the above units will be wired together with voltage regulators, ignition and starter circuits.

(e) 4" high riser exhaust mixers will be fitted to the engines.

(f) Two Jones MU3-G tachometers and drives.

(g) A ceramic stuffing box seal which is to be incorporated to a cast bronze shaft log by means of a rubber hose.

(h) A one unit transom mounted propeller strut and rudder (Daytona Marine Zip Strut), complete with cavitation plate sprocket and short chain to match.

(i) Four $2\frac{1}{2}$" rubber exhaust flaps.

(j) Three different propellers.

(3) Tandem Engine Unit Installation

(a) *Alignment and fixing of unit:* The tandem engine unit to be installed between the fore and aft engine bearer longitudinals. The tandem unit to be aligned horizontally along the length of the boat and to be inclined as described earlier between $4\frac{1}{2}$° to 5° to port so as to offset the propeller (centre of hub) to starboard 2" off the centre line of the boat. Between the engine bed light alloy channels and the engine bearer longitudinals, wedges to be placed as shown in the drawing and a further support of hard wood to be provided to the underside of the metal engine beds as described in the addendum to specification, part one, and following the detailed drawings provided. The engine beds to be bolted to the engine bearer longitudinals with $\frac{3}{8}$" steel bolts placed at approximately 1' apart. These engine fixing bolts to be provided with large washers and locknuts or checknuts. The alignment of the engines themselves and the V drive in relation to the engine beds is to be carried out following detailed instructions supplied by Daytona Marine.

(b) *Shaft line:* The propeller shaft to be $1\frac{1}{2}$" diameter monel. The inboard end of the propeller shaft to be coupled by means of half coupling to the V drive output flange. This half coupling to be fitted to the shaft by means of a standard taper ($\frac{3}{4}$" per foot) and standard steel key with nut and checknut. The propeller shaft to pass through a shaft log, containing a ceramic seal on the inboard end and a fibre water lubricated bearing on the outboard end. The ceramic seal to be secured to the shaft log by means of a strong rubber hose and two jubilee clips on the ceramic seal and shaft log spigots.

The aft end of the shaft to be supported by means of a water lubricated fibre bearing contained in the transom mounted propeller strut. The propeller to be fitted to the shaft by means of a standard taper ($\frac{3}{4}''$ per foot) and standard bronze key washer and nut with two locking grub screws of Monel or stainless steel. Since three different propellers will be fitted, during the course of trials, each propeller to be supplied with key (which should be marked) and propeller washer of required thickness to suit the different lengths of bolts.

(c)   Exhaust system: The exhaust pipes to consist of 3″ O.D. aluminium tubing (6061T6) $\frac{1}{16}''$ wall thickness. These pipes to be secured to the high riser exhaust mixers with 3″ I.D. heavy rubber hose and two jubilee clips on the pipes as well as the high riser spigots. The fore exhaust pipes to be led out through the transom. The forward engine exhaust pipes to pass on the outside of the exhaust pipes to the aft engine. The aft end of the exhaust pipes to be secured to the outlet transom flange by means of 3″ I.D. heavy rubber hose and two jubilee clips on the pipes and on the spigots of the transom outlet flanges. The exhaust pipes, whilst being led out, to be gently sloped downwards towards the stern and the exhaust pipes outlets not to be placed below the water line. The forward engine exhaust pipes, because of their considerable length, to be supported with light alloy brackets in two places where convenient. The flange fittings for the exhaust outlet through the transom to be made up of the same material as the exhaust pipes. The flanges to be $\frac{1}{8}''$ thick and to have a width of $1\frac{1}{4}''$ approximately, all round the pipes, which should extend approximately 3″ outside the transom and have rubber flaps (provided with the engine) fitted to the ends.

(d)   Engine, V Drive and stuffing box cooling systems: The engine cooling water is taken from a spigot in the propeller strut to a $1\frac{1}{4}''$ copper pipe via a short length of rubber hose secured by means of jubilee clips. This copper pipe to be carefully led and held so as to clear the steering gear. Then to a seacock and salt water strainer (supplied with the engine). The water supply then to be split so that one branch to be led to the lower cooling pump on the rear engine and the other branch to the V drive, oil cooler and lower pump on the front engine. All $1\frac{1}{4}''$ diameter rubber pipes to be of top quality hard walled hose.

Note: A pressure gauge should be fitted in the cooling supply near the sea strainer for early trials to ensure that sufficient water pressure exists for adequate cooling.

The stuffing box and the forward bearing cooling water to be supplied by means of a $\frac{1}{4}''$ diameter copper pipe which is to protrude through the skin and to form a small scoop on the outside. This pipe to be firmly secured to the inside of the hull by means of a flange and then to be connected to the stuffing box with a $\frac{3}{8}''$ I.D. flexible rubber hose which is to be clipped at both ends.

(e)   Fuel System: All pipes to be aeroquip with aeroquip terminals and unions. The outlet of each tank to be placed at the bottom and aft on all tanks. The outlet fitting from the tanks to be specially prepared with large bearing surface and to be through bolted to the tank with fibre glass washers impregnated with epoxy resin. These flanged skin fittings to be secured prior to closing up the tanks. These fittings to be threaded to receive the fuel cocks. As near as possible to the outlet of each tank, a filter to be inserted in the fuel lines. The three tanks are then to be interconnected as shown in the diagram with $\frac{3}{4}$ inch aeroquip pipe.

One pipe to lead up from the interconnection tank pipe to the fuel pump gallery where three electric Stuart Warner pumps supply fuel to the two engines through $\frac{3}{8}''$ aeroquip pipes. On the intake side of the fuel gallery, two $\frac{3}{8}''$ aeroquip pipes to be connected to the mechanical pumps fitted to the engines. The filling of the four tanks to be done through filler caps fitted on the inspection doors of the tanks. Similarly, the air vent pipe is to be connected to an angle fitting located on the inspection doors. These air vents to be laid up the side of the coaming and bent over to form a goose neck at the top. These vent pipes to be of 16 gauge $4\frac{1}{2}''$ I.D. pipe. The portion of these vent pipes which run along the side deck to be covered with a half round moulding of cedar to protect them. Along the coaming, the pipes to be clipped as required.

(f)   Instruments: All instruments to be electrical, except the tachometers, and to be supplied with the engine, including the respective sending units on the engines themselves. These instruments include the following:

2 Tachometers
2 Boost Gauges
2 Water Temperature Gauges
2 Oil Pressure Gauges
2 Ammeters
1 V Drive Oil Temperature Gauge.

All the wiring and cables connected with these, to be loomed and to be passed through the starboard side of the console and down through a hole in the fixed portion of the cockpit floor into the engine compartment and fixed to their respective terminals.

(g)   Controls: The throttle and gear box controls are to be Morse. The throttle controls are to be a twin lever unit firmly secured in the position shown on the console drawing and to be provided with a fabricated light alloy arm rest which should be shaped to suit the owner's requirements and should be well padded. The gear box controls, namely the aft engine ahead-neutral-astern and the forward engine IN-OUT gear box controls, to be two single lever controls placed conveniently on the port side under the console. The control cables to be led as in the case of the instrument wiring through the engine compartment from the starboard side of the console. Morse terminal units to be adopted to secure control cables to gear box levers and adequate supports to be

provided for these cables in a convenient place on the engines.

(*h*) *Ventilation:* The central circular aperture on bulkhead n. 1 will provide air to the engine compartment. In addition to this normal ventilation, and in order to remove fuel fumes from the engine compartment, two 3″ diameter 12 volt suction blowers to be placed on either side of bulkhead n. 1 so that the outlet is situated in the toilet and gallery compartments and piped up with light ventilation tubing to an outlet through the bulkhead on either side into the cockpit.

(*i*) *Electrics:* Two heavy duty 12 volt automotive type light weight batteries to be approved by the owner and to be positioned on either side of the V drive in light weight ply glass fibre lined battery boxes firmly secured to the engine bearer and tank longitudinals. Batteries to be firmly clamped down to battery boxes and to be so connected so as to permit the use of these batteries independently or in parallel. Battery cables to be of adequate capacity and to be of best quality. As already advised, large terminal blocks will be supplied. The wiring from engine starters and generators or alternators through voltage regulators to terminal blocks, will be included with the engine unit. Apart from the wiring required from terminal blocks to console for the instrumentation, there will be the following additional circuits, each one of which to be protected by fuses placed in the console.

The switches, as shown in the console drawing, to be recessed so as to protect them from rain and spray and to be provided with a rubber cover. To include the following:

  2 Starter switches
  2 Ignition switches
  3 Fuel pump switches
  1 Bilge pump switch
  2 Ballast tank pump switches
  1 Switch for all navigation lights which are to include side, steaming and stern lights.
  1 Twin Trimatic Tab switch.

In addition, a lighting circuit to be provided through the accommodation of the craft and to include the following ceiling lights with integral switches:

  1 in w.c. compartment
  1 in toilet compartment
  2 in main cabin
  1 in forward cabin.

A circuit to be provided also for one electric plug point in the engine compartment and one electric plug point in the accommodation. One inspection light with protective grille and 20 feet of wandering lead to be supplied.

(*j*) *Other installation particulars:*
(1) All hoses adopted to be of best quality hard walled or flexible, as required, reinforced material.
(2) All hose connection spigots to have annular grooves or collars so as to prevent hoses from sliding off.

(3) All jubilee clips and wiring clips to be of Monel or 18/8 quality stainless steel.
(4) All pipes, wires and cables to be adequately clipped where necessary, to avoid possibility of chafing.
(5) It is suggested, in order to produce a neat installation and to ensure water tightness where leads from the console enter the engine compartment, that these be led through a 2″ light hose extending from the starboard underside of the console to the point of entry into the engine compartment on the bridge deck. This hose to be secured to the console and bridge by means of light alloy spigotted flanges and clips.
(6) All nuts to be provided with locknuts or locking wire or to be of the Simmonds type, where possible.
(7) Where possible, in order to keep weight down, seawater resisting light alloy should be employed for fittings, pipes, brackets, etc., in lieu of brass or steel.

(*4*) *Steering*
A Morse steering wheel to be located as shown in the console drawing. Twin Morse racks to operate the rudder tiller by means of Morse cables led into the engine compartment in the same way as the other control cables, leads and wires.

The steering wheel to be well padded and to have a quick action friction device for temporarily locking of wheel, which feature is included with this type of Morse equipment, rack assemblies to be firmly mounted to console with plywood doublers where necessary.

(*5*) *Bennett Transom Flaps*
A pair of heavy duty TRIMATIC trim tabs, type 24165 with 12 volt electric motors adequate wires and switches, will be provided by the Owner. These flaps will be supplied complete with fixing screws. They are to be mounted on the transom in the position shown on the drawing and installed and wired with switches on the console following carefully the instructions supplied by Bennett Marine. Since the transom of this power boat is heavily radiused, it will be necessary to cut the outboard edges of the flaps so that these are parallel to the centre line of the boat.

(*6*) *Bilge System*
Limber holes to be provided throughout the length of the craft and to be at least 1½″ diameter. A 1¼″ Morse or equivalent electric bilge pump to be placed aft with outlet rubber hose and skin fitting through the transom. In addition to these pumps, two non return reed valves of the Tempo No. 900 or equivalent type to be fitted through the transom at the lowest part possible on either side of the hog so as to ensure complete drainage of the boat when under way.

(7) Ballast Tank Piping

The two ballast tanks to be filled and emptied by means of two retractable skin fittings Dr. n. 881/11/1, which are to be situated under the cockpit floor to port and starboard and piped forward to the respective ballast tanks with rubber hose and jubilee clips.

In order to fill the ballast tanks when the craft is at rest, two 1″ Jabsco electric or equivalent water pumps, one for each tank, to be inserted into the piping leading to the tanks by means of two two-way cocks. The switches of these pumps to be placed on the steering column.

(8) Fire Extinguisher System

A Graviner or similar automatic and remotely controlled fire extinguisher system to be installed in the engine compartment. Confirmation on this equipment to be obtained from the Owner.

Particular care to be taken with the installation of the cylinder which should be well secured and the weight to be kept off the planking.

Fig. 125 Surfury *fuel system.*

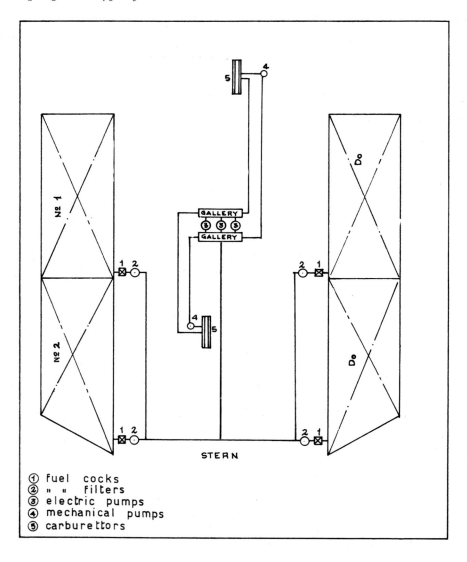

STERN

① fuel cocks
② „ „ filters
③ electric pumps
④ mechanical pumps
⑤ carburettors

INDEX